ADVANCE PRAISE

"Debbie has been a path-breaker, and this wonderful book is, like Debbie, path-breaking. It offers a fresh look—and usefully compiles the thinking and research—about topics central to our profession, like the billable hour and better approaches to charging for legal services, building legal skills and work/life balance. It is also full of good judgment and advice, especially about careers. I unhesitatingly recommend it—to law students, lawyers and leaders in the profession."

Brackett B. Denniston, Senior Vice President & General Counsel General Electric Co.

"*Law & Reorder* is a compelling call for the entire profession to come to terms with the evolution of the law firm model while embracing alternative designs to capture value and retain talent. Debbie offers real life guidance to lawyers on how they can thrive in today's changing environment. At the same time, she inspires employers to recognize the issues of work/life balance facing lawyers, and particularly women, while providing immensely valuable advice in creating an environment of flexibility and productivity. This book gets to the heart of the legal profession and how it must be reordered for future success."

Carol Ann Petren, Executive Vice President & General Counsel, CIGNA Corporation

"In the wake of the recession, traditional workplace models are giving way to innovative practices that satisfy the forward-thinking lawyer and serve the modern client. In *Law & Reorder*, Debbie convincingly makes the business case for embracing these new, flexible workplace models and gives us a play book on how to successfully integrate them into our profession."

Stephen P. Younger, President, New York State Bar Association; Partner, Patterson Belknap Webb & Tyler LLP

"Study after study shows that flexibility in the workplace correlates with sustained attorney retention. Kudos to Debbie for writing such a compelling case for the use of flexible schedules in the legal industry."

Jeffrey Gearhart, Executive Vice President, General Counsel, & Corporate Secretary, Wal-Mart Stores, Inc.

"*Law & Reorder* is nothing short of groundbreaking. This beautifully written and comprehensive volume is a blueprint for redesigning the legal workplace and workforce to meet the needs of lawyers, employers, and clients. It is certain to become the go-to guide for anyone seeking to maximize high standards, client service, profitability and personal satisfaction in today's quickly changing legal marketplace."

Marci Alboher, former columnist, The New York Times*;*
Vice President, Civic Ventures

"Figuring out how to best deploy and retain top lawyers is one of the top issues of the day—for both in-house departments and outside firms. Debbie is not only the top authority on deploying and retaining top lawyers: she is our most passionate and visionary leader. *Law & Reorder* is a must read for every legal manager in our profession."

Susan Hackett, Senior Vice President & General Counsel,
Association of Corporate Counsel

"Dinosaurs running law firms and legal departments had best read *Law & Reorder*, and quickly. Debbie expertly surveys the creative alternatives to traditional law firm billing, hiring and retention policies that will eventually put some firms—and the legal departments that use them—at a competitive advantage. Managing partners and general counsel also need to heed Debbie's advice to lawyers seeking to change the traditional view of a life well lived in the law, for sooner or later you will certainly hear it from your own employees."

Randal S. Milch, Executive Vice President & General Counsel,
Verizon Communications Inc.

"We've heard that the billable hour model no longer works, but what's the alternative? In this thorough and compelling look at the challenges facing the legal profession, Debbie offers fresh ideas about how to make firms more profitable and hospitable, including for women. It all starts with leadership support and openness. *Law & Reorder* is a must read for the forward-thinking leaders in law."

Carol Evans, President, Working Mother Media

"In *Law & Reorder*, Debbie surveys varying experiences of law firms responding to the changing legal environment and presents a comprehensive view of the successes and challenges faced by those firms. Such depth and detail on these issues has not previously been available in one spot. That, coupled with the positive and practical solutions Debbie offers, makes this book a valuable tool for any firm considering changes to such things as firm structure, compensation, billing arrangements and client relationships. *Law & Reorder* is a unique 'hornbook' for law firm management in the 21st century."

Ralph Baxter, Chairman & CEO, Orrick, Herrington & Sutcliffe LLP

"I've always thought of change as an acquired taste, even when the ingredients for change are obvious. You cannot read this insightful, compelling work without developing a strong appetite for sustainable change and a recipe for long overdue action."

Michele Coleman Mayes, Senior Vice President & General Counsel, Allstate Insurance Company

"For lawyers—just as for everyone else—work is crucial to happiness, and happiness is crucial to work. *Law & Reorder* is packed with practical, creative ideas for anyone striving to make the demanding lives of lawyers more satisfying, productive and profitable—all at the same time."

Gretchen Rubin, The Happiness Project; Former law clerk, Justice Sandra Day O'Connor

"As we all get more sophisticated about managing and measuring legal work, law's traditional emphasis on effort will give way to a focus on results that drive value. In this 'New Normal,' happy and well-supported lawyers will be able to deliver superior value, regardless of whether they are working 20 or 80 hours a week. *Law & Reorder* has provided an invaluable roadmap for law firm leaders and clients to implement the tools and context they will need to improve value."

Paul Lippe, CEO, Legal OnRamp

"Debbie asks tough questions and provides smart answers. *Law & Reorder* is a must read for lawyers and their employers seeking to redesign career paths to better align work and life."

Sylvia Ann Hewlett, President, Center for Work-Life Policy; Author, most recently, Top Talent: Keeping Performance Up When Business Is Down *(Harvard Business Press)*

"*Law & Reorder* is a must read! This timely book unveils the key challenges facing the legal profession today and provides answers about how to creatively solve them. Debbie takes a holistic approach of redesigning the legal workplace by aligning the economic interests of legal employers with the skills, interests and needs of lawyers and law students. *Law & Reorder* is a unique guide to effecting change, combining practicality with ingenuity."

Laurel G. Bellows, Principal, The Bellows Law Group, P.C.

"*Law & Reorder* is an indispensable resource for legal employers who seek a win-win, mutually rewarding, and genuinely productive relationship with their lawyers. It is delightfully written and well-researched. Presenting a compelling case for action, *Law & Reorder* suggests creative solutions to the work/life balance issues facing lawyers and their firms today."

Joan G. Wexler, President, Brooklyn Law School

"Debbie has presented a most thought-provoking read. She effectively weaves together personal experience and anecdotes, well-collected and organized research, and careful reflection on changes in the legal profession and in society that will impact the profession—even if traditional forces hope that won't be so. Change is here, and a lot more change is coming. I recommend *Law & Reorder* for those who want to thrive through change rather than be left behind by it."

Michael E. Nannes, Chairman, Dickstein Shapiro LLP

"If you are a lawyer or thinking about a career in the law, *Law & Reorder* is THE book for you. It includes wonderful stories and insightful analyses of new models of legal practice that enable firms to attract, develop and retain talent and that enable lawyers to have a good fit between their work and personal lives. You won't have to look any further than this book for great examples of work-life initiatives that work."

Ellen Galinsky, President, Families and Work Institute

"Women have made up nearly half of entering associate classes for 25 years, yet they comprise only 16 percent of partners in large law firms. Stemming this exodus is one of the greatest challenges facing law firms today. Combining meticulous research with insights developed over years spent in the trenches, Debbie offers the reader proven strategies that will lead to improvements in the development, promotion, and retention of attorneys—women and men. *Law & Reorder* is a must-read for law firm leaders."

Walfrido Martinez, Managing Partner, Hunton & Williams LLP

"*Law & Reorder* is an uncommonly sophisticated analysis of the complex relationship between trends in law firm practice and the opportunities and challenges of fashioning a satisfying legal career. The book is firmly grounded in an appreciation of the financial, organizational, and cultural dimensions of modern law firms, even as it creatively explores ways in which current realities may be amenable to change. Debbie has made a major contribution to the important debate about how we might ensure that lawyers in the 21st century can lead lives as both productive professionals and integrated and balanced human beings."

Milton Regan, Jr., Professor of Law and Co-Director, Center for the Study of the Legal Profession, Georgetown University Law Center

"Debbie's book is unique in addressing work/life issues from the standpoint of both management and individual lawyers. She shows how both the organization and the individual benefit when the organization embraces a broad range of individual choices, and she provides actionable advice on how to achieve balance in the midst of a sea-change in the legal industry. While all lawyers struggle with work/life integration, Debbie recognizes that the struggle is particularly difficult for women in their child-raising years. As a managing partner and a mother, I applaud this important work."

Marianne D. Short, Managing Partner, Dorsey & Whitney LLP

"*Law & Reorder* is a must-read for anyone who wants a clear-eyed view of the future of the legal profession. By confronting challenges with problem-solving ideas, *Law & Reorder* teaches us how to shape our strategy to fit the future. Like a good novel, this book stays with you. Its thoughtful analysis and creative suggestions for the future will change for the better how we think and what we do."

JoAnne A. Epps, Dean, Temple University Beasley School of Law

"This excellent book provides a much-needed compass for law firms, lawyers and law students to help them find their way in an ever-changing legal profession. Debbie is on top of the trends that are profoundly changing the practice of law, and her keen insights and practical strategies will prove invaluable in helping firms and lawyers to adapt and succeed. *Law & Reorder* comprehensively addresses the many unique challenges that continue to confront women lawyers, and it sets forth a number of concrete ideas and suggestions as to how law firms can help their women lawyers advance and, equally important, maintain a work/life balance. Debbie makes a compelling case that innovative and flexible law firm policies are a 'win-win' for both law firms and their lawyers."

Roberta D. Liebenberg, Chair, American Bar Association Commission on Women in the Profession; Senior Partner, Fine, Kaplan and Black, R.P.C.

"Empowering and clarifying—*Law & Reorder* is a real manual for navigating the disorienting change that's seizing this industry."

Mark Harris, CEO & Founder, Axiom

"It's easy to forget that terms like 'book of business' and 'billable hours' are foreign to most first-year law students, and the path to partnership in a law firm remains mysterious even to many junior associates. *Law & Reorder* serves as a guidebook for the uninitiated. The thorough review of current and best practices, common pitfalls, and opportunities for change will be an invaluable reference guide first as a woman chooses a firm, then as she joins as a summer clerk and new lawyer, next as she navigates retention and advancement—maybe with a growing family—and then as she attains positions of influence. Sit *Law & Reorder* on the shelf with your other treatises—it will be just as relevant and serve you well."

Jessie Kornberg, Executive Director, Ms. JD

"This is a well-researched book that keenly analyzes the profession not only as it currently is but, aspirationally, as the profession could be—with increased flexibility, client service, productivity, and career satisfaction. *Law & Reorder* also provides a helpful, hands-on guide to 'blueprinting' women lawyers for success, with practical guidance by way of cheat sheets and checklists."

Dorian S. Denburg, President, National Association of Women Lawyers

LAW & REORDER

Legal Industry Solutions for Restructure, Retention, Promotion & Work/Life Balance

LAW & REORDER

Legal Industry Solutions for Restructure, Retention, Promotion & Work/Life Balance

AMERICAN BAR ASSOCIATION
Defending Liberty
Pursuing Justice

Cover design by ABA Publishing.

Printed in the United States of America

14 13 12 11   5 4 3 2

Library of Congress Cataloging-in-Publication
Data is on file with the Library of Congress.

Law & Reorder: Legal Industry Solutions for Restructure, Retention, Promotion & Work/
Life Balance
Deborah Epstein Henry
ISBN: 978–1–61632–072–0

To my parents, Sylvia and Stanley Epstein, for your love and encouragement to have it all.

To my husband, Gordon Henry, for your love and partnership in life.

To my sons, Oliver, Spencer and Theodore Henry, for all that you are and will be.

CONTENTS

WHY I WROTE THIS BOOK

My husband and I have three sons—Oliver (14), Spencer (12), and Theodore (9). When Spence was five years old, he was desperate to get a dog. He loves animals and he was constantly negotiating with me to get a dog. I'm very straightforward with our kids, and I told Spence: "With three boys and Dad and I both working, I can't do it. It'll push me over the edge." Spence responded: "I know, Mom. We've had this talk before. But I've got an idea." "Okay, Spence, what is it?" I said, thinking, Here's my future lawyer talking. Spence replied: "We could trade in Theo for the dog."

Why do I tell this story? In my mind, it illustrates the key to effecting change in the legal profession.

1. *Lawyers seeking change must be creative and artful negotiators. We are trained to be zealous advocates but we seldom remember to advocate for ourselves.*
2. *To make change stick, it must be a win-win situation in which all sides compromise and benefit. In our house, we've had several fish (but no dog)—and Theo remains a resident member of the family.*

Growing up in the New York suburbs, I always felt women could "have it all." My parents, Sylvia and Stanley Epstein, raised me to believe that boys were my equal (although my dad did emphasize "Don't throw a ball like a girl"). At Yale, where I went to college, I competed with men in the classroom and lived across the hall from them in the dorms. It was not until years later that I considered the difference that being a woman might mean in my career.

In most professional settings, I have found it an advantage to be a woman. This has usually been because the expectations were, for some reason, lower. Or because some of my male adversaries—for example, at other law firms—felt uncomfortable competing against me as a woman. I was often one of the few women in the room or one of the youngest, which also helped me stand out. I only started to think about work/life balance issues seriously when I got to Brooklyn Law School and began to ponder the impact my intended career would have on my plans to have a family.

After my second year in law school, I married Gordon Henry. I graduated from law school at the top of my class in 1994 and clerked for the Honorable Jacob Mishler in the Eastern District of New York for two years. Gordon, who is six years older than me, was ready to have kids right away. I told him I needed to be working at least a year before having kids. So at 27, I became pregnant with our first child. I was terrified to tell Judge Mishler that I was pregnant. But, when I did, his response was simple: "Mazel Tov."

During my pregnancy, law firm lawyers would walk into the Judge's chambers and ask me to direct them to the law clerk, thinking that a young pregnant woman must be the Judge's secretary, not an educated professional. Prior to the clerkship, I was a summer associate at a large New York City firm and I had an offer to return to work full-time beginning in the fall. But I had planned to look around and interview further. Although it was an unscientific method of choosing, I started by eliminating from consideration the firms whose lawyers had assumed I was the Judge's secretary because I was pregnant.

Fourteen months into my clerkship, our first son, Oliver, was born. Judge Mishler told me, "Take all the time you need." So following a three-month maternity leave, I returned to work full-time. Having a child a year out of law school was against conventional wisdom, but it was the right choice for us. The truth is, professionally, it's never a good time to have kids. But while it would have been more prudent to get a few more years of practice under my belt before becoming a mother, Gordon and I both felt we were ready to start a family.

After finishing up my clerkship, I joined New York firm Patterson Belknap Webb & Tyler LLP as a full-time litigation associate. Less than a year into my career there, Gordon accepted a job in Philadelphia and we decided to move. It was 1997, I was pregnant with Spence, and it was a hot job market for lawyers looking to make lateral moves. In my job search, I disclosed to prospective employers that I was looking to work reduced hours[1] and I ultimately got seven reduced-hour offers. Philadelphia firms were eager to hire a displaced New York–trained associate. I negotiated going into Philadelphia firm Schnader Harrison Segal & Lewis LLP pregnant and "part-time"—I was quite a package.

By 1999, I was a commercial litigator and a mother-of-two working a 75 percent schedule on the partnership track, albeit a delayed one. Despite the support from many colleagues, I felt isolated and preoccupied with the challenge of being a lawyer and playing an integral role in my kids' lives. When I spoke to other professional mothers about these issues, they were equally concerned. At work, we felt we were being judged by some as "uncommitted." Outside the office, we often felt excluded from the stay-at-home-mom circles. I occasionally had lunch with three other female reduced-hour litigators at my firm and I found it helpful. We would talk about our strategies, successes, and challenges. I decided I wanted to do more with these occasional colleague lunches. I shared the notion with a former colleague and friend, Tracey Diamond. She loved the idea and offered to help and give feedback as I got it off the ground.

In 1999, I e-mailed six women lawyers who were working reduced hours. The e-mail announced that I was starting a brown-bag lunch group for lawyers interested in work/life balance issues. I encouraged recipients to forward the invitation to anyone they thought might be interested. I proposed running monthly programs where we would discuss a designated work/life balance topic and having different firms across Philadelphia host the programs. Lawyers who were less likely to attend when a program was down the street would be more inclined to do so if it were down the hall. I hoped that having different venues would also give attendees greater ownership and interest in the issues as they brought them to their own places of employment.

Within days of the e-mail invite, 150 lawyers e-mailed me back in response. Still a fresh New York transplant, I remember thinking that I didn't even know there were this many lawyers in Philadelphia. Thrilled at the response, I knew I had struck a nerve. After running that first brown-bag lunch program in July 1999, I felt that this little support group would be much more.

Soon to be incorporated as Flex-Time Lawyers LLC, the organization became a network where lawyers could derive support and career guidance as well as find clients, jobs, board placements, and even nannies. But it also became a vehicle for change. Until then, working flexible or reduced hours or even indicating an interest in a life outside of your legal job was virtually taboo. Suddenly there was a forum to compare notes about challenges and successes, about which employers were receptive to creating progressive work/life policies, and about how these policies were being implemented.

Case in point: One member, Lisa Carney Eldridge, was a senior associate at a Philadelphia law firm whose partnership policy would not allow her to be considered for promotion to partner, given her reduced-hour schedule. So I held a program with the topic "Part-Time Partnership" and attendees came from the large Philadelphia firms armed with written policies, ad hoc procedures, and anecdotes to share. Lisa took the information, drafted a reduced-hour partnership policy and informed her colleagues about competitors who were elevating their reduced-time associates to partner. Her draft policy was adopted—and she became the first reduced-hour lawyer in her firm to be elevated to partner.

Initially, it was exciting just to find and speak with like-minded lawyers facing the same challenges as I was. But it soon became clear that to effect change, we would need to show employers why changing was in their interest.

> My mission became clear: competition as an instrument of change. Make work/life balance and women's issues a basis of competition among legal employers, like salary or pro bono work. Historically, when a top law firm raised its first-year salary and that salary was published in a city's legal publication, within a week that firm's top ten competitors matched the raise. I believed the same principle would work for work/life balance and women's issues. Given that law firms are so similarly structured and therefore easily comparable, the ability to create competition for female legal talent existed as long as there was a forum to share information and make it public.

That's where the press came in. In January 2000, *The Legal Intelligencer*, Pennsylvania's daily legal publication, ran a feature on Flex-Time Lawyers LLC. I then solicited press from 50 top news organizations. National Public Radio decided to showcase a Flex-Time Lawyers LLC program and broadcast excerpts of interviews with me, my members, and the Chairman of my law firm on *Morning Edition*. The response was viral. I had hoped getting press would help to dispel misconceptions about the motivations of lawyers seeking work/life balance. It did much more. Within months, my inbox was inundated with "Dear Debbie" e-mails from lawyers all over the country. I now had not just 150 Philadelphia names in my address book, but a growing national listserve and dialogue among (today, about 10,000) lawyers.

In 2002, I thought it was time to start a New York chapter of Flex-Time Lawyers LLC. I remember thinking that if I could just get a prestigious firm to host the first event, I could be on my way. So I called Scott Musoff, my former co-clerk, who was an associate at Skadden, Arps, Slate, Meagher & Flom LLP and asked if he would reserve a conference room for a small gathering of women lawyers. When Scott started fielding inquiries from the *New York Law Journal* and more than 100 lawyers showed up to that first New York program, I knew we could succeed in New York.

In New York, there was noticeably more work to be done. The pressure to bill hours was so intense that an open discussion of work/life balance was viewed as career threatening. Firm lawyers who attended that first program were afraid to put their last name on the sign-in sheet. Many who had secured reduced-hour arrangements had done so clandestinely, and had never been public about their arrangements. I remember my own concern that Scott's hosting and support for my event would in some way tarnish his reputation and interfere with his partnership consideration (thankfully, it did not).

Once the New York chapter was launched, the audience expanded. I was no longer just preaching to the choir. New York law firms purchased corporate memberships, in addition to individual lawyer memberships, and started sending management, diversity, and professional development representatives. Corporations with legal staffs started signing up and sending attendees, and government and not-for-profit attorneys attended too. And competition took hold. Soon all of the top New York firms offered to host and even provide lunch at the events.

A dialogue ensued between those seeking balance and employers interested in discovering whether work/life policies could benefit the bottom line. Also, the range of topics covered at the programs expanded to include the retention and promotion of women and new models of legal practice.

As the New York chapter became established, so did my consulting practice. I stopped practicing law. Although I remained affiliated with my Philadelphia law firm for another five years, I started writing more, consulting to employers on their work/life and women's initiatives and their models of legal practice, and speaking nationally to legal employers. I also started giving talks at law schools, conferences, bar associations, and other venues about work/life balance, strategies for the retention and promotion of women attorneys, and new models of legal practice. The ideas I've shared in response to the thousands of "Dear Debbie" e-mails, the hundreds of programs where I've spoken, and the countless queries from lawyers, law firm management, corporate general counsels, and law students are what compelled me to write this book.

What began as a small grassroots movement of stigmatized working moms back in 1999 is now a universal cry for change in the legal profession. The old excuse that the low representation of women at the top was just a "pipeline" issue is no longer accepted and there is general recognition that specific challenges to women need to be addressed to ensure women's success. Additionally, work/life balance issues have become a strong priority for men. Although work/life balance policies are still used more by working moms, "Generation Y" has been vociferous in articulating its desire for both men and women to achieve balance. Even Baby Boomers are changing the work/life picture and bringing flexibility into a phased retirement process. Technology has played an important role, giving lawyers more flexibility and challenging legal employers to reconsider how and where work gets done. Add to this the recession, increased client pressure to lower rates in order to deliver more value, outsourcing, and the threat to the traditional billable-hour structure, and the need for change has become clear.

I see today an unprecedented opportunity to empower not just women lawyers, but all lawyers, to take charge of their careers, to improve the control they have over their lives, and to change how and where work gets done. I also believe that the time is ripe for employers to revamp their traditional models or invent new ones. I invite you to join me on a journey to redesign the legal workplace, to realign the interests of lawyers, clients, and legal employers, and to embrace a more hospitable, productive, and profitable environment for all.

NOTES

1. The term "reduced hours" is being used throughout this book rather than "part-time" which is a misnomer. Reduced-hour law firm lawyers typically work about 40 hours a week and that does not include the increased hours that pile up when litigation is heating up or a deal is closing. Reduced-hour lawyers work a reduced number of hours or days in the office or a reduced percentage of required billable hours if they are law firm lawyers, typically 60–80% of the target billable hours of full-time lawyers.

ACKNOWLEDGMENTS

My husband, Gordon Henry, has been encouraging me to write this book for years. As a former professional writer, he knew the value of putting one's thoughts down on paper. When Gordon took the time to edit this book not once but twice, I was overwhelmed with not just his talent but also his generosity. When people you love take time to help you in a way that they can truly contribute, it is touching and brings you closer than you thought possible. When Gordon edited this book, he became a part of my work as he never has before. Since a large focus of my work has always been about work/life balance, it was the perfect metaphor that he should become integral to this project as he is in my life. I will always be overcome by the time, love, and support Gordon has shown for this work and for me.

Claudia Trupp has been one of my closest friends since I was eleven. A gifted and successful New York criminal defense attorney, Claudia is also the author of an inspiring and beautifully written memoir, *Hard Time & Nursery Rhymes: A Mother's Tales of Law and Disorder*. Writing a book is a lonely process. When Claudia offered to do a hard copy edit of the first draft of this book (in handwriting that I remember from our seventh grade notes about boys), it was a regular reminder that I was not alone. I also enjoyed the scrawls about first-degree robberies or time incarcerated that I would occasionally find among her comments. I am so touched by Claudia's dedication and friendship and I will always be grateful for the insights, candor, and wisdom that she brought to this book.

I am grateful to my family for their generous contributions to this book and to my life. My mother, Sylvia Epstein, showed me, by example, that a woman can successfully raise three kids and have a fulfilling career. When I was two, she went back to school for her Ph.D at night and over time, developed a thriving psychology practice. All the while, she attended my sporting events and drove me to violin lessons and to Hebrew school. I didn't always love the crock pot meals but I deeply appreciate the role model she has been for me to make it all work. My father, Stanley Epstein, was the first feminist I have ever known and he has inspired me to advocate for women. In training me for mini-marathons or being my tennis partner against all the other father-son teams, or advocating for changes to policies discriminating against women as discussed in Chapter 10, my dad has shown me that girls deserve all that boys do and that the "world is your oyster."

My sister, Susie Rubin, Founder of The Copy Machine and copywriter extraordinaire, came up with the clever title, *Law & Reorder*. She took other mundane phrases and headings in the book and made them snappier too. Susie also provided me with daily counsel, encouraging me to work through the many ups and downs of book writing, as she has otherwise done my whole life. I'm convinced that my brother, Joel Epstein, was secretly trained in the newspaper clipping service business. He and my mom rival *Google Alert* in their abilities to flag for me every article that I should read and every person that I should contact. I'm grateful for Joel's tireless efforts to connect me to others and provide opportunities for me to grow.

My boys, Oliver (14), Spencer (12), and Theodore (9) are the true inspiration for my work. Not until Oliver was born in 1995 did I develop the compelling need to redesign my work and life. The various stages of development that the boys have been through are the motivation for me to continually re-balance my work and life. So many professional women over the years have told me that they have remained in the workforce to be a role model for their daughters. I find it is equally important to serve as that role model for my boys. Ollie—his intensity and kindness;

Spence—his intuition and humor; and Theo—his drive and spirit, are what inspire me to be the best that I can be at home and work.

I also want to acknowledge my in-laws, Sondra and Edward Henry. Sonny and Ed have been regular fixtures at my Flex-Time Lawyers LLC events in New York and I always learn from Sonny's e-mail re-caps about what has changed in the profession since she graduated Columbia Law School in 1953, one of just eight women to do so that year. Sonny was the first paid member to my organization (even though, of course, her admittance would always be free)—a symbolic and fitting gesture of the support my in-laws have always shown me for which I am eternally grateful.

Twelve years ago, I met Elaine Christopher who became a surrogate grandmother to the kids and a surrogate mother to Gordon and me. We have been charmed by Elaine's South Philly warmth, humor, wisdom in how to raise three boys (having done so herself), talent for making homemade "gravy," and so much more. Renee Newell has been my loyal and talented assistant and I credit her for making my life more manageable on a daily basis. A detail maven, Renee is a joy to work with both in terms of her manner and efficiency, and I am appreciative of all that Renee does—big and small—every day. Lisa Small has been a wonderful assistant as well. I am grateful for the projects that she takes on and the administration she handles at my events. Laura Nazginov, a hard-working law student, was an invaluable assistant for the book. She read each chapter, pointed out shortcomings, followed up on missing information, and checked citations. Laura's agreeable nature, enthusiasm, and strong work ethic are what make her a pleasure to work with on any project. I am also thankful to the talented actors who have administered my Flex-Time Lawyers LLC events over the years with grace and professionalism. These include: Sarah Connelly, Laura Covelli, Le-Anne Garland, Ahmon Williams, and Angela Williams.

I have been privileged to have mentors who have made a significant difference throughout my life. I am so grateful to each of them for taking an interest in me and encouraging me to pursue both my professional and personal dreams. They include: Marie "Waggie" Wagner, for her German pancakes and lullabies and care in helping to raise me; Rashid Silvera, for inspiring my love of learning at Scarsdale High School and beyond; Peter Salovey, for helping me see the creative side of law at Yale University and for his continuing interest in my development; Carol Ziegler, for always having tissues on her desk and opening doors for me from Brooklyn Law School; and David Smith, for teaching me how to litigate and showing ongoing support even when I chose no longer to do so.

I am grateful to the American Bar Association for publishing this book. In particular, I want to acknowledge my editor, Timothy Brandhorst, and Neal Cox, who has handled promotion on my behalf. Tim and Neal have been tireless in participating in brainstorming sessions with me to enhance the resonance and profile of this book. Tim has been a true advocate on my behalf and served as an ally in the lonely editorial process. He has also given me valuable insights about the book's tone and flow and shown leadership and creativity in everything from the book's design, content, and promotion. Neal has shown great enthusiasm since the inception and has been flexible and insightful in how to promote this book. I am enormously appreciative to both Tim and Neal for the dedication they have shown to this project. I am also grateful to Annie Beck for overseeing the meticulous copyedit process to ensure a professional final product.

Rachel Somers has been my daily confidant since I moved to Philadelphia from New York thirteen years ago. Rachel's friendship, humor, love, and support are a gift that I feel privileged to have. Rachel, her husband, Barry Siegel, and their kids are what have made Philadelphia a second home for us. I am fortunate to have many other friends and professional contacts who have lent a generous hand and been instrumental to my professional development, the growth of Flex-Time Lawyers LLC, and the publication of this book, including: Marci Alboher, for her ongoing advice and inspiration and help with networking and technology; Garry Berger, for his legal counsel and ingenuity in running a law firm; Dorene Blythe, for her helpful information about corporate childcare; Carrie Cohen and the New York City Bar Committee on Women in the Profession for their partnership in The Cheat Sheet; Elizabeth Daniels, for her partnership in Balanomics™ and her spirit of collaboration; Darragh Davis, for her partnership in Balanomics™ and her wisdom about in-house lawyering; Tracey Diamond, for her support in launching Flex-Time Lawyers LLC and being an ongoing advisor; Lisa Carney Eldridge, for being a loyal member since the inception; Carol Evans, for her partnership in the Best Law Firms for Women initiative; Cynthia Frank of Cynthia Frank Design, for her generous and talented insights in design; Donna Gerson, for her book writing advice and collaborative spirit; Patricia Gillette, for her candor, generosity, and willingness to be an invaluable sounding board; Sylvia Ann Hewlett, for including me in a transformative experience as an advisor to the Hidden Brain Drain Task Force; Sara Holtz, for her openness and wisdom in running a consulting practice; Lisa Horowitz, for her inclusiveness and willingness to debate and share concepts; Arnie Kanter, for being a role model and encouraging me to start a consulting practice; Sue Kendall, for her thoughtful insights about book selling; Stanley Komaroff, for being the lawyer of the "family" and always taking an interest in my career; Jonathan Kops, for his talent in website development and management; Roberta Liebenberg, for her enthusiasm for my work and generosity in opening doors; Andrew Margolis, for his networking efforts on my behalf; Nancy Margolis, for her humor and support beginning with the first Flex-Time Lawyers LLC meeting; Michael Melcher, for his generous introduction to his editor and publisher; Susan Michini, for her clever prose and giving of her time; Honorable Jacob Mishler, for his humor and the opportunities he gave to me; Scott Musoff, for his willingness to take a stand and support me; Marjorie Ochroch, for her helpful legal and business advice; Tammy Palazzo, for her vision and willingness to take a chance on me; Lynn Rosner Rauch, for her support and availability as an ongoing resource; Lauren Stiller Rikleen, for her generous insights about book publishing; Caryn Karmatz Rudy, for her wisdom about the many mysteries of the book industry; Thomas Sager, for his public support and enthusiasm for my work; Laura Saklad, for her creative thoughts about changes in large law firms; Honorable Norma Shapiro, for providing much needed mentoring to women in the legal profession; Peggy Shiller, for her interest in my work and thoughtfulness in making introductions; Rupa Singh, for her partnership in Balanomics™ and her valuable editorial insights and collaboration; Peter Sloan, for sharing the creativity of his work and welcoming my interpretation of it; Alison Stein, for the intelligence and passion she brings to the next generation of lawyering; Brande Stellings, for her colleagueship and valuable intuition; Anne Weisberg, for her inspirational work and help in advancing mine; and, Scott Westfahl, for sharing his enormous contribution to professional development.

Additionally, I want to recognize other women lawyer leaders with whom I have had the privilege to collaborate and whose work I admire (some of which is cited to in this book), including: Ida Abbott, Cynthia

Thomas Calvert, Linda Bray Chanow, Holly English, Amy Gewirtz, Jessie Kornberg, Lisa Linsky, Karen Lockwood, Vernā Myers, Dr. Ellen Ostrow, Dr. Arin Reeves, Veta Richardson, Stephanie Scharf, Lauren Wachtler, and Joan Williams.

The birth of Flex-Time Lawyers LLC took place during my stint as a commercial litigator at Schnader Harrison Segal & Lewis LLP. I am very thankful to my former Schnader colleagues who showed support and enthusiasm for my work. Back in 1999, most people were not talking about work/life balance and my Schnader colleagues were progressive and willing to provide a platform for me to start a dialogue on these and many other issues. In particular, I want to acknowledge the following Schnader colleagues who demonstrated support and interest in my work: Robert Collings, Diana Donaldson, Julia Fineman, Jennifer DuFault James, Margaret Kalalian, Ronald Karam, Wilbur Kipnes, Stacy Levitan, Maryann Mackey, Eleanor McCourt, Reena Meltzer, James Meyer, Deena Jo Schneider, Kaethe Schumacher, Carl Solano, Samuel Silver, David Smith, Dennis Suplee, Ralph Wellington, Nancy Winkelman, and Margaret Woodruff.

Last, and certainly not least, I am deeply indebted to the members of Flex-Time Lawyers LLC and the authors of the "Dear Debbie" e-mails. They have generously shared their stories and insights and given me the forum to explore these important issues and exchange ideas. I am also thankful to the New York and Philadelphia law firms that have graciously hosted my events and fed my members since our first program back in July 1999.

There are many others who I have met along the way for whom I am also thankful. If I have been remiss in not naming you personally, my apologies. I am truly grateful for all who have made this journey possible.

FOREWORD BY THOMAS L. SAGER, SENIOR VICE PRESIDENT AND GENERAL COUNSEL, DUPONT

The last several years have created a surreal environment for many professions. The legal community has not been spared from this tumult. Three years ago, we experienced, in most instances, the highs of generating value for our clients and significant income for many in our profession. The client, in turn, was willing to pay for the services rendered; and, while not always seen as a job well done or a journey worth taking, the outcome met any number of pre-determined success criteria. Overall, the status quo was more than acceptable, although the legal industry itself was fairly rigid and predictable.

Then came the Lehman weekend and life, as we once knew it in the profession, came to a screeching halt. For general counsel and managing partners, the "New Reality" was upon us. Our collective performance was viewed through a far more penetrating lens, defined as much by the cost of the service delivered as by the result obtained.

The immediate challenge for all of us was to develop new and creative business models and ways of working seamlessly, collaboratively, and resourcefully with our fellow professionals both from outside and from within. It placed tremendous pressure upon relationships that had withstood, up until then, many years of traditional, substantive lawyering. As a result of this new economic order, some relationships flourished and others withered as hard decisions required changes in the way we do business that were both transformational and sustainable.

Today, the environment remains every bit as challenging and the client now realizes that the legal industry is *not* immune to the pressures of the overall business environment. The rules of engagement are clear: we must be more proactive, disciplined, creative, and client focused.

Our profession is now at a crossroads where we need to re-define how we bring value to clients and, at the same time, do so resourcefully. Many of us feel ill-equipped to address these challenges given our historic, regimented, and hierarchical ways of delivering service. While we are no longer in a survival mode, circumstances continue to test the bounds of our ingenuity and client-driven efforts.

The changes our legal industry must continue to undergo are profound and permanent. There is no turning back. To effectuate the response needed to enable our corporate legal departments, law firms, lawyers, and law students to succeed in this new environment requires an entirely new level of trust, transparency, and engagement. The creative solutions required will of necessity force a far deeper understanding of the workplace, its pace and flow, and how best to motivate and inspire the current and future talent pool that is more willing than ever to actively participate but strives for work/life balance and new ways to work.

This book is an incredible roadmap for those who, like myself, want to be part of a revolution that seizes the opportunity that the recent economic crisis has presented. *Law & Reorder* gives us the knowledge and tools that we need to transform the legal profession so that our clients see us both as visionaries and as trusted partners meeting the challenges of today's dynamic global marketplace.

Thomas L. Sager

INTRODUCTION: THE KEY TO UNDERSTANDING THIS BOOK

A *reorder* of the legal profession requires fundamental changes to how legal employers are structured and how lawyers practice law. Hence the focus of this book.

The theme that runs through this book is *making the exception the rule*.

The legal profession was founded on a traditional, hierarchical model. As I demonstrate in this book, over the years, the model has eroded and alternative ways to practice law have evolved. Yet these alternatives are still viewed as ancillary and most employers cling to the way things have always been done.

The profession must move beyond the single traditional model for legal practice and embrace the exceptions to the rule—the array of successful new models that are being developed: 1. by legal employers to design their businesses; and, 2. by lawyers to design their career paths. This is necessary (and inevitable) because clients and, increasingly, lawyers themselves demand it. Clients demand it because they want reasonable and predictable fee structures that do not require them to subsidize the training of new associates and the constant recruiting of replacements. Lawyers demand it because they seek multiple paths to success and a greater degree of work/life balance than conventional venues have offered. Add to this global competition that is altering the availability and price of legal talent and services, and technology that is radically changing the ability of lawyers to communicate, gain efficiencies, and access information, and the status quo no longer serves the lawyers or clients for whom it was designed.

To improve profitability for employers, reasonableness and predictability of fees for clients, and productivity and satisfaction for lawyers, the profession needs a re-alignment. A makeover. There is a yearning for change.

Part I of this book is directed to legal employers and why and how they should restructure. Although some advice in Part I is specific to law firms, most of it applies generally to firms, companies, government agencies, and not-for-profits that employ lawyers. Part I starts with an exploration of the changes facing the legal industry, including the threat to the billable hour, the rise of new models of practice, the morphing of large law firms, and new talent management strategies. The focus then shifts to designing a woman- and work/life-friendly employer and why it is in an employer's financial interest to do so. Part I concludes with strategies to make flexible and reduced hours work, manipulate the billable hour to meet employer and lawyer needs, and use reduced hours and other alternatives to increase profitability in a recession.

Part II of this book is directed to lawyers and law students and provides advice on how to develop the skills needed to thrive in today's legal environment. The emphasis is on lawyers and law students being their own entrepreneurs. They must demonstrate creativity and initiative to chart their own course rather than wait for senior lawyers to show them the way. Part II starts with advice to lawyers and law students on productivity, work/life balance and transition issues. The emphasis is on maximizing productivity and satisfaction, negotiating parental leave, making flexible and reduced hours work, and developing effective time management skills. There is also advice to lawyers who are in transition or who are seeking to re-enter the profession. The focus then shifts to issues specific to women. These concluding chapters provide advice on planning future success to become a leader, be mentored, be promoted, be fairly compensated, use effective networking and business development skills, and manage the gender and generational issues women lawyers may face.

You may ask: why break out this book into Parts I and II? Why not just have Parts I and II be two separate books? Here's why.

Many legal management books directed to legal employer representatives do not address the lawyer issues. They do not address the challenges and solutions for individual lawyers, including issues specific to women and those seeking work/life balance. I have deliberately included the discussion of issues impacting women and work/life balance in Part I of this book, which is directed to legal employers. I have also deliberately included, in Part II, the specific challenges facing individual lawyers and law students. The challenges facing lawyers and law students and the subjects involving women and work/life balance are essential for employers to read and understand in building a future profession that is profitable and productive. Women constitute half of the legal talent pool and work/life balance is a predominant concern of most lawyers, especially those entering the profession. In restructuring the workplace, management, general counsel and employer representatives must understand the concerns and issues raised in Part II of this book because the management of today's talent pool must be integral to any employer's strategic plan.

Similarly, many legal "how to" books dispense advice to lawyers but ignore the management perspective and the economic challenges facing legal employers. However, a lawyer cannot thrive in today's legal environment without understanding the economic and managerial issues his or her employer is facing. Thus, Part I of this book is required reading for lawyers and law students to understand how the profession in which they seek to practice is changing and what demands are being placed on legal employers to create a new workplace. As lawyers and law students learn and apply the skills taught in Part II, they need to understand how the steps they take will resonate in today's legal environment as explored in Part I.

In each chapter of the book, I start with a personal story to illustrate the chapter's message. I do this to symbolically demonstrate how I have integrated my work and home lives and how the two blend. My home life regularly informs my professional life and vice versa. I encourage you to similarly look at how your home experiences can improve your thinking with regard to your profession or business and how your work experiences can clarify your role and purpose outside the office.

While this book is geared towards legal employers, lawyers, and law students, I have found in my work that the issues prevail for all professionals. The ideas and strategies provided in this book can and should be applied to individuals and employers across industry.

Making the exception the rule means reaching a point in the legal profession where "alternative" models become the new norm. And where the number of lawyers pursuing "alternative" career paths becomes so great that "alternative" becomes the new mainstream.

The future of the profession will be bright if lawyers, clients and employers break from their tradition of looking backward to guide the future—if they stop relying on precedent for ingenuity. The key to the future lies in embracing *reorder.*

PART I

STRUCTURAL SOLUTIONS FOR LEGAL EMPLOYERS

CHAPTER 1
CHANGE IS GOOD

I organized a basketball party for our middle son Spencer's sixth birthday at the local YMCA. On the Wednesday before the party, I got a call from the Y with an apology that the party would have to be postponed. John from the Y simply told me that something "bigger" had come up and we could either have the party that Friday (in two days) or the following Friday. Because that Friday was Spence's actual birthday, I called around to see if I could muster enough friends to have the party in two days and was able to work it out. So we switched the party date.

When we arrived at the Y on Friday night, we learned why the rescheduling was necessary. President George W. Bush was coming to speak at the Y on Monday and they needed to close the Y early for a security sweep. After the party, we opened presents and relayed the story to the kids. Upon learning the reason for the party date switch, Oliver, our eight-year-old, replied: "Why didn't the President just change his schedule around or come to Spence's party?" It seemed that the local paper, the Philadelphia Daily News, *agreed with Oliver's assessment. It ran a blurb the next day about Spence's party being bumped for the President's visit and the article was entitled "Party Pooper."*

The ability to look at a set of circumstances differently, with a fresh set of eyes (as Oliver did), is what often gives people the vision to recreate an old concept and make change.

Change Comes to the Legal Profession

Aspiring to become an attorney has long been viewed as a worthy goal. The role of lawyer has been seen as bestowing prestige and power on those who entered the bar. Yet the legal profession today is, by all accounts, facing unprecedented change. The need for change is partly the result of years of resistance to new developments but also partly the result of significant shifts in the larger economy as well as in the lifestyle habits of lawyers.

If the profession proves to be insightful in examining itself and embracing the need to reinvent, it will, I believe, enjoy continued success. However, if the need for change is resisted or fumbled, the profession will find its foundations threatened and its role increasingly questioned. This chapter begins with a discussion of the issues that are at the core of the changes facing the industry. In subsequent chapters, I discuss the alternatives to the current model and provide advice to employer representatives—law firm managers and corporate counsel—on how they can successfully navigate the new environment to enable their employers and lawyers to thrive and prosper.

Why the Billable Hour No Longer Works

The severe global economic downturn that began in 2008 has forced many law firms to rethink the billable-hour model. The flaws in the billable hour are not new. In fact, the American Bar Association (ABA) launched the Law Practice Management Section Task Force on Alternative Billing Methods in 1989 and issued a report in 2002, analyzing the billable hour's challenges, merits, and alternatives.[1] The severe economic meltdown that was ushered in with the fall of Lehman Brothers in September 2008, and the unprecedented difficulties that have since been faced by large American blue-chip clients, shed new light on the billable hour's many problems.

The billable hour became widespread in the 1950s as lawyers feared they were losing economic ground to doctors and other professionals.[2] In 1965, the ABA found that American lawyers billed between 1,200 and 1,600 hours annually.[3] As years went by, lawyers' billing rates—and the hours billed—escalated. But it was not until competition intensified and the economy fluctuated that many lawyers found they could not easily increase their rates. Consequently, they did the only other thing they could do to increase revenues. They increased the number of billable hours expected of each attorney. At the large law firms, by 2007 the billable hours expectation was hovering between 2,000 and 2,200,[4] while billing 2,500 to 3,000 hours was not unusual.[5] As one lawyer put it, "the profession's obsession with billable hours is like 'drinking water from a fire hose,' and the result is that many lawyers are starting to drown."[6] Meanwhile, by 2007, top lawyers began reaching the $1,000 per hour billing mark.[7]

In addition to the increasing number of billable hours and the rise in rates, other billable-hour problems were mounting. There was "widespread consensus among practitioners, judges, recruiters and academics that hourly billing leads to punishing work schedules, unhappy lawyers, ill-served clients, over-lawyered cases, perverse incentives and outright fraud."[8]

> One of the biggest problems with the billable hour is that it created a conflict of interest between clients and lawyers, penalizing productivity and efficiency while leaving clients with unpredictable fees.

The billable hour also created a temptation to pad hours, reduce associate training, minimize pro bono work, and decrease the kind of traditional collegial firm events that might detract from the number of hours that could be billed.[9] Further, the billable hour was seen to discourage case planning and communication between clients and outside counsel.[10] Clients were unwilling to pay for law firm lawyers to strategize and confer, and law firm lawyers did not want to take time to do so if that time would get written off from their bills.

Even in a stronger economy, such as that which the United States enjoyed between 2002 and 2007, billable hours were seen as problematic because they contributed to high attrition within firms. According to a 2005 report of the National Association for Law Placement Foundation that tracked law firm associate retention from 2002 to 2004, 78 percent of female and male associates left their firms within five years.[11] Such attrition did not come cheaply. By conservative estimates, law firms were spending $200,000 to $500,000 to replace a second-year associate.[12] While law firms claimed to rely on the attrition model and an "up or out" approach, they still wanted to be able to influence and select which associates would leave.

Further, when billable hours increased, lawyers expressed dissatisfaction with their work/life balance. This was recognized as an important factor in why lawyers left law firms.[13] In a 2007 MIT study, lack of work/life balance was the number-one reason why women left law firms while remaining in the workforce and among the top three reasons why men left.[14] Indeed, the sheer number of hours expected became a drain on the profession.

Additionally, technology, especially the ubiquitous Internet-enabled BlackBerrys, gave lawyers the gift of flexibility but the curse of around-the-clock availability. Technology enabled large firms to compete in global markets and time zones, but caused never-before-seen work/life challenges for lawyers. Lawyers found they had difficulty delineating the boundary between work and home because their clients, partners, and managers expected immediate responsiveness and accessibility.[15] More than 60 percent of female and 40 percent of male lawyers who left law firm practice cited difficulty integrating work with family and personal life.[16]

Why the Billable Hour Is So Entrenched

So what is the future of the billable hour and its attendant evils? The billable-hour model is dying—but slowly. Why? The answer is that the billable-hour billing method is easy to explain, easy to calculate, and, most importantly, it has been profitable for law firms. Billable hours attach a price to a service that many argue is hard to value, and the concept fits within the profession's characteristic risk aversion.[17] The billable hour also minimizes transaction costs for both sides because hourly billing is a standard that allows law departments to easily compare costs.[18] Additionally, while the model has been called into question, many firms have been afraid to make dramatic changes during the recent economic crisis. They want to cling to what is familiar even when what is familiar no longer works.

The Economic Downturn—Furthering the Push to Eliminate Billable Hours

As the economy worsened between 2008 and 2010, law firms found they were generally unable to increase revenues by billing more hours or raising billing rates. The challenges law firms faced caused them to further rethink their business models and contemplate alternative models, which are discussed in Chapters 2 through 4. In a November 2008 Altman Weil study, 115 general counsel surveyed said that their number-one target for spending cuts was outside counsel fees.[19] Nearly three-quarters of respondents said they were implementing 2009 budget cuts of between 6 percent and 35 percent that included a significant focus on reducing outside counsel fees.[20] General counsel cited outside counsel fees and their lack of predictability as their two biggest worries.[21] In 2009, 65 percent of general counsel surveyed said they were going to bring more work in-house.[22]

In response to these concerns, in the first quarter of 2009, the demand for legal services dropped by more than 8 percent compared to the first quarter of 2008.[23] Attorney productivity, measured by billable hours per lawyer, dropped 11.5 percent compared to the first quarter of 2008.[24] As a result of the decreasing demand for legal services, firms laid off attorneys across the country. Indeed, about 5,000 lawyers were reportedly laid off in 2009, from a total of 138 firms.[25] In turn, billing rate growth slowed. Over each of the four years prior to 2009, law firms raised their billable-hour rates by an average of about 7 percent a year.[26] During the first quarter of 2009, billable-hour rate growth was up by a little less than 3 percent compared to the year before.[27]

Clients Demanding Change

In addition to decreased hours and slower billable rate growth, the threat to the billable hour has been heightened by clients showing less loyalty and demanding more value.[28] An initiative launched by the Association of Corporate Counsel (ACC) in 2008 called The Value Challenge embodies the changes facing firms. The Value Challenge's mission is, among other things, "to reconnect value and costs for legal services," "drive change in the performance of value-based legal services," and "enhance awareness and communicate success stories in achieving value and alignment."[29] To facilitate ACC Value Challenge changes, ACC has held forums around the country where law firm leaders and general counsel have convened to brainstorm about ways to bring more value to clients.

Law Firm Talent: Further Undermining the Stability of the Existing Model

Beyond the market, client, and law firm structural considerations, talent issues have impacted the billable hour's relevancy. For female talent, the billable hour has not been a friend. Though women have comprised 40 to 50 percent of law school graduating classes for 25 years,[30] they account for less than 16 percent of law firm equity partners nationally.[31] Female lawyers of color represent just 11 percent of law firm associates and 1.4 percent of law firm equity partners.[32] According to the Center for Work-Life Policy, 31 percent of women lawyers take a leave of more than six months at some point in their careers.[33] Thus, the numbers reflect that many women leave and long hours are an important factor in why women lawyers leave law firms.[34]

For female lawyers hoping to remain in the profession, the billable hour has interfered with promotion rates. One reason: many law firm partners equate long hours with economic value and invariably look askance at lawyers who wish to reduce their hours. The majority (72.5 percent) of lawyers working reduced hours are women[35] and 40 percent of women law firm lawyers with children work reduced hours at some point in their tenure at a firm.[36] These reduced hour lawyers are less likely to make partner than their male counterparts who work traditional schedules because their billable hours are almost invariably less impressive.[37]

For female lawyers working reduced hours, however, there is an interesting wrinkle in the billable-hour issue. Some women view the billable hour as their ally because they can generate the same hours—and revenue—if they are working from home as they can sitting at their desk in their office. The billable hour also serves as proof that these lawyers are working hard and living up to their end of the bargain.[38] Given the flexibility that the billable hour affords, one might think the need for "face time" at the office would decrease.[39] However, this has not been the case. Stigma and culture have prevented firms from transcending their traditional ways, and the billable hour has remained an impediment.

Beyond female lawyers, others are demanding a change in the billable-hour system. The 80 million "millennials" from Generation Y—Americans born between 1980 and 2000—do not want to make the same lifestyle sacrifices that their Traditionalist[40] and Baby Boomer parents and grandparents made.[41] Millennials see work as one of multiple priorities. They value things other than income and status as primary in life, and they are willing to make trade-offs consistent with their values.[42] They are confident, impatient, eager to live life now, pro-education, goal-oriented, socially conscious, highly tolerant, plugged into technology, parallel thinkers, and family-centric.[43] Similarly, the 46 million Generation X members born between 1965 and 1980 are less inclined to conform to existing models. They are typically self-reliant, prone to rule-morphing, comfortable accessing a wide variety of information, and place loyalty to friends above loyalty to institutions.[44]

The members of Gen X and Gen Y have demonstrated repeatedly that they want to and plan to work differently. For example, in April 2007, two male Stanford Law School students sent 100 letters to the nation's top law firms, requesting that firms either switch to billing systems that charged clients per transaction, not per hour, or expect lower billable hours of associates, with improved work/life balance in exchange for lower salaries.[45] As one proponent, Craig Holt Segall, put it, "The way firms work now does not serve their clients, the community or the associates."[46]

Even as the economy weakened, the Millennials showed their dissatisfaction with hourly billing. In a 2008 A Better Balance survey of New York University School of Law students, eight out of ten students said they were willing to earn less in exchange for flexible or reduced hours.[47] Indeed, both male and female students surveyed stated that work/life balance was their biggest concern, with 72 percent of male students and 76 percent of female students saying that they were "very" or "extremely" worried about successfully integrating a career and family life.[48]

The younger generations are not the only ones clamoring for a more reasonable life and a different way to practice. Change is also occurring at the retirement stage, and law firm policy changes are facilitating the shift. Among the American Lawyer's AmLaw 200 firms (America's 200 top-grossing firms, according to *The American Lawyer*) in 2007, 64 percent had mandatory retirement ages of 65 to 70 while 36 percent of firms had no limits on age.[49] In August 2007, the ABA adopted the New York State Bar Association recommendation that firms end mandatory retirement.[50] Baby Boomers make up 70 percent of law firm partners,[51] and many are seeking to phase into retirement over five to ten years, rather than retire outright like their Traditionalist predecessors.[52] This was a trend that was already afoot before the economic downturn[53] but it has continued as Baby Boomers have seen their 401(k) plans and other savings reduced.[54]

Some senior partners are interested in phasing into retirement by working flexible or reduced hours.[55] They may seek more specialist, niche, or advisory roles at their firms.[56] These senior partners may be more available to mentor junior lawyers, train junior partners in leadership skills, and transition their clients gradually. Having revered senior partners work flexible and reduced hours may de-stigmatize these schedules traditionally held by working mothers. At Wilmer Cutler Pickering Hale and Dorr LLP, for example, the firm introduced the title of Senior Partner for older partners who want to work reduced hours.[57]

The delayed departure of Baby Boomers from the workforce will present challenges for succession planning at law firms and it may impede junior partners' ability to take over the reins.[58] It may also impact lateral hiring because prospective hires will evaluate their opportunities for growth as well as their long-term future. Flexible, individualized retirement packages and individual pay packages with financial incentives may smooth the process and facilitate senior partners' willingness to transition their clients. However, when Baby Boomers eventually retire, there remains a concern that there will not be enough Gen X lawyers to fill their shoes. There are 76 million Baby Boomers born between 1946 and 1964 and only 46 million Gen Xers[59] and the research projects that by 2018, "we will have more jobs than people to fill them."[60] Thus, the needs and demands of Gen Y will continue to be critical to building a future in the profession.

Disaggregation and Globalization of Work

The disaggregation and unbundling of legal work is another trend that is changing the legal profession's business model. Clients are segmenting out the work they have. Rather than have a large law firm handle all the litigation for a significant matter, for example, a client might hire one firm to handle the discovery phase of a case and another to handle the oral argument and trial work. Some clients are saving costs by reducing the number of outside firms they use in exchange for obtaining bulk discounts. These clients are also improving their efficiency by reducing the amount of time their in-house lawyers spend managing outside counsel.

The unbundling of work is due to an increased recognition that some of the work that has been handled by high-priced lawyers either need not be done by lawyers at all or can be broken out and done by other lawyers. Clients have become more savvy about recognizing that certain work is more routine and can be performed by less experienced or less impressively credentialed lawyers at a lower rate.

There is increased competition and a globalization of work with more work moving east.[61] As discussed in Chapter 2, some of the work is going offshore to less expensive places such as India. Harvard Law School Professor David B. Wilkins also reports an increased blending or "disintegration" of work such as law, accounting, and business where knowledge is becoming multi- and interdisciplinary.[62]

Intersection of Commoditization and Technology

Author and consultant Richard Susskind, in his book *The End of Lawyers?*, predicts that commoditization and technology will dictate the future of legal services.[63] He sees a pull of legal work towards commoditization, which is being enabled by existing and new technologies.[64] As Susskind puts it, "the market is increasingly unlikely to tolerate expensive lawyers for tasks (guiding, advising, drafting, researching, problem-solving, and more) that can equally or better be discharged by less expert people, supported by sophisticated systems and processes."[65]

Susskind anticipates that some lawyers will be replaced by technology while others who use technology to enhance their practice will thrive.[66] Susskind also believes that there will always be a place for certain sophisticated, highly customized legal work but that the demand for this type of work will decrease.[67] "The big issue is where does that leave the 'middle class' of lawyers (defined either as by ability or by seniority) if the top parts of the practice are being innovative and valued and the bottom parts of the practice are being commoditized by technology and outsourcing."[68]

Clients are also increasingly using technology to save on legal fees. Clients are benefiting from the Internet as an open source. As a result, clients' increased access to legal information will encroach on what attorneys will be paid to do.[69] Law firm lawyers will no longer be able to compete if they are proprietary about information that can be readily accessible.[70] Further, clients are collaborating and using technology to access legal content for which they previously paid. One example of clients joining forces and using technology effectively is Legal OnRamp, a collaboration system for in-house counsel and invited outside lawyers and third-party service providers to share content and technology resources.[71]

In sum, the legal industry is facing numerous challenges. The time for change is under way. The legal profession as we have known it will no longer exist and will undergo significant change in the next ten years. In the next chapter, we will explore the innovators who are facilitating the transition to the next stage of legal practice.

Notes

1. *See generally* Am. Bar Ass'n, ABA Commission on Billable Hours Report 2001–2002 (2002), *available at* http://www.abanet.org/careercounsel/billable/toolkit/bhcomplete.pdf [hereinafter ABA Commission Report].

2. Adam Liptak, *Stop the Clock? Critics Call the Billable Hour a Legal Fiction*, N.Y. Times, Oct. 29, 2002, *available at* http://www.nytimes.com/2002/10/29/business/businessspecial/29LIPT.html.

3. *Id.*

4. Scott Turow, *The Billable Hour Must Die*, A.B.A.J., Aug. 2007, *available at* http://www.abajournal.com/magazine/article/the_billable_hour_must_die/; Liptak, *supra* note 2.

5. Liptak, *supra* note 2.

6. ABA Commission Report, *supra* note 1, at vii.

7. Nathan Koppel, *Lawyers Gear Up Grand New Fees*, Wall St. J., Aug. 22, 2007, *available at* http://online.wsj.com/article/SB118775188828405048.html?mod=googlenews_wsj.

8. Liptak, *supra* note 2.

9. ABA Commission Report, *supra* note 1, at 5–7.

10. *Id.* at 5–6.

11. Paula A. Patton & Cynthia L. Spanhel, Nat'l Ass'n for Law Placement, Toward Effective Management of Associate Mobility. A Status Report on Attrition, 21, tbl.6 (2005).

12. Joan Williams & Cynthia Thomas Calvert, *Balanced Hours: Effective Part-Time Policies for Washington Law Firms*, *in* The Project for Attorney Retention Final Report 7 (2d ed. 2001), *available at* http://www.pardc.org/Publications/BalancedHours2nd.pdf.

13. Mona Harrington & Helen Hsi, *Women Lawyers and Obstacles to Leadership*, *in* A Report of MIT Workplace Center Surveys on Comparative Career Decisions and Attrition Rates of Women and Men in Massachusetts Law Firms 12–13 (2007), *available at* http://web.mit.edu/workplacecenter/docs/law-report_4-07.pdf.

14. *Id.*

15. *See, e.g.*, Lauren Stiller Rikleen, Ending the Gauntlet: Removing Barriers to Women's Success in the Law 248–49 (2006); *see also* Maggie Jackson, What's Happening to Home? 21–38 (2002).

16. Harrington & Hsi, *supra* note 13, at 13, chart 2(a) and (b).

17. ABA Commission Report, *supra* note 1, at 7–11.

18. *Id.*

19. Emily Heller, *General Counsel Pressuring Firms Amid Recession*, Nat'l L.J., Apr. 6, 2009, *available at* http://www.law.com/jsp/cc/PubArticleCC.jsp?id=1202429666843.

20. *Id.*

21. *Id.*

22. Leslie A. Gordon, *Economic Pressure May Force Permanent Shift in Corporate Legal Costs*, GC Cal. Mag., Apr. 16, 2009, *available at* http://www.law.com/jsp/cc/PubArticleCC.jsp?id=1202429931212.

23. Karen Sloan, *Law Business Index Reports Ugly First-Quarter Results*, Nat'l L.J., May 11, 2009, *available at* http://www.law.northwestern.edu/career/markettrends/2009/pr8urou5ri7s.pdf (citing Hildebrandt International Peer Monitor Index, released May 11, 2009).

24. *Id.*

25. Drew Combs, *THE AM LAW 100: How Badly Did Am Law Firms Really Fare Last Year?*, AmLaw Daily, Jan. 26, 2010, *available at* http://amlawdaily.typepad.com/amlawdaily/2010/01/amlaw2009.html (citing Law Shucks blog).

26. Sloan, *supra* note 23.

27. *Id.*

28. Heller, *supra* note 19.

29. Association of Corporate Counsel Value Challenge, http://www.acc.com/valuechallenge/about/index.cfm.

30. Am. Bar Ass'n, First Year and Total J.D. Enrollment by Gender for 1947–2008, *available at* www.abanet.org/legaled/statistics/charts/stats%20-%206.pdf.

31. Stephanie A. Scharf et al., Nat'l Ass'n of Women Lawyers, Report of the Fourth Annual National Survey on Retention and Promotion of Women in Law Firms 2 (2009), *available at* http://www.nawl.org/Assets/Documents/2009+Survey.pdf.

32. Nat'l Ass'n of Women Lawyers, Report of the Third Annual National Survey on Retention and Promotion of Women in Law Firms 2–3 (2008), *available at* http://www.nawl.org/Assets/Documents/2008%2bSurvey.pdf.

33. Sylvia Ann Hewlett et al., Off-Ramps and On-Ramps Revisited at 8 (2010).

34. Harrington & Hsi, *supra* note 13, at 12–13.

35. Nat'l Ass'n for Law Placement, Most Lawyers Working Part-time Are Women—Overall Number of Lawyers Working Part-time Remains Small (2009), *available at* http://www.nalp.org/parttimesched2009.

36. Harrington & Hsi, *supra* note 13, at 32.

37. *Id.* at 29–30.

38. Deborah Epstein Henry, *Facing the FACTS: Introducing Work/Life Choices for All Firm Lawyers Within the Billable Hour Model*, Diversity & the Bar, Nov./Dec. 2007, *available at* http://www.flextimelawyers.com/pdf/art10.pdf.

39. *See generally* Deborah Epstein Henry, *What's to Love about the Billable Hour? The Benefits of Law Firm Flexibility*, The Balance Beam, 2008–2009, *available at* http://www.flextimelawyers.com/pdf/newsletter_09.pdf.

40. BSG Concours, Engaging Today's Young Employees (Preliminary Report) 5–14, 46 (2007). There are 59 million Traditionalists born between 1928 and 1945 who are characterized as being comfortable with hierarchy, loyal to institutions, and respectful of authority, and seen as rule makers and conformists, motivated by financial rewards and security. *Id.* at 46.

41. *Id.* at 46. There are 76 million Baby Boomers born between 1946 and 1964, characterized as antiauthoritarian, idealistic, motivated to change the world, and competitive. *Id.*

42. *Id.* at 5–14, 46.

43. *Id.*

44. *Id.* at 5, 46.

45. John Roemer, *Students Prod Big Firms to Change*, S.F. Daily J., Apr. 10, 2007.

46. *Id.*

47. Nancy Rankin et al., *Seeking a Just Balance*, A Better Balance 3 (June 2008), *available at* http://abetterbalance.org/cms/index.php?option=com_docman&task=cat_view&gid=33&Itemid=99999999.

48. *Id.* at 6.

49. Elizabeth Goldberg, *Law Firms Face Gray Area as Boomers Age*, The American Lawyer, Dec. 10, 2007, *available at* http://www.law.com/jsp/article.jsp?id=1197021878240.

50. *Id.*

51. *Id* (citing Hildebrandt International).

52. Barbara Rose, *Not Done Yet? If 65 Is the New 50, How Will Baby Boomers Remake Retirement?*, A.B.A.J., Apr. 1, 2010, *available at* http://www.abajournal.com/magazine/article/not_done_yet/; Goldberg, *supra* note 49.

53. Goldberg, *supra* note 49.

54. Shannon Henson, *Delayed Partner Retirement Has Its Costs for Firms*, Law360, June 25, 2009, *available at* http://www.flextimelawyers.com/news/news72.pdf.

55. Goldberg, *supra* note 49.

56. *Id.*

57. Zach Lowe, *Wilmer Freezes Salaries, Breaks Lockstep*, AmLaw Daily, Dec. 15, 2009, *available at* http://amlawdaily.typepad.com/amlawdaily/2009/12/salaries.html.

58. Goldberg, *supra* note 49.

59. *See* Concours, *supra* note 40, at 5–14, 46.

60. Barry Bluestone and Mark Melnik, *After the Recovery: Help Needed. The Coming Labor Shortage and How People in Encore Careers Can Help Solve It*, Civic Ventures 2010, *available at* http://www.encore.org/files/research/JobsBluestonePaper3-5-10.pdf.

61. Ron Friedmann, Prism Legal Consulting, Inc., David Wilkins on Mega Trends for Legal Profession, Session Report, Georgetown Law Conference (Mar. 23, 2010), *available at* http://www.prismlegal.com/wordpress/index.php?p=1049.

62. *Id.*

63. *See generally* Richard Susskind, *The End of Lawyers?* (2008).

64. *Id.* at 28.

65. *Id.* at 2.

66. *Id.* at 27–39.

67. *Id.* at 39.

68. Jason Mendelson, Law Firm 2.5—Richard Susskind—The End of Lawyers, Mendelson's Musings, Mar. 28, 2009, *available at* http://www.jasonmendelson.com/wp/archives/2009/03/law-firm-25-richard-susskind-the-end-of-lawyers.php.

69. Susan Beck, *Innovation Agenda (Part Two): Are You Betting Against the Web?*, AmLaw Daily, Dec. 30, 2008, *available at* http://amlawdaily.typepad.com/amlawdaily/2008/12/innovation-agenda-part-2-are-you-betting-against-the-web.html.

70. *Id.*

71. Legal OnRamp, http://legalonramp.com/.

CHAPTER 2

THE RISE OF NEW MODELS OF LEGAL PRACTICE

When my middle son, Spencer, was six, an acquaintance asked him how old he was. An innocent enough question. He responded with this: "Age is not important unless you're cheese." He got this adage from a folk art museum sign he saw hanging at my parents' house. I think that acquaintance is still scratching her head about Spence's remark.

The legal profession is founded on the concept of "precedent"—looking back at age-old cases to help decide the future. But the economic downturn that began in 2008 has shaken things up and accelerated the need for the profession to innovate. In a Georgetown University Law Center conference entitled "Law Firm Evolution: Brave New World or Business as Usual?," Mark Harris, founder of a new model law firm called Axiom, remarked that it is difficult to look to lawyers to innovate when they are trained to look backward, at precedent, in order to interpret the future.

As the legal profession is faced with challenges to reinvent itself, it cannot exclusively seek wisdom in age-old concepts. Instead it should focus on responding to the demands of the market—including those of clients and the talent pool—and looking to other industries and countries for fresh ideas and new practices.

Alternatives to the traditional legal model have been unfolding for some time now. Some of these alternatives are new ways to practice law that will be covered in this chapter while others will be covered in the next chapter, "The Large Law Firm of the Future." The question remains whether these alternatives to the traditional model will continue to develop at exponential rates and whether there will be multiple future models to legal practice.

Axiom and Other New Law Firm Models

In 2000, Mark Harris founded Axiom. The impetus was simple: both parties to the exchange of legal services—the clients and the lawyers—were unhappy. Clients felt they were overpaying for services that were not always the quality they expected. Attorneys felt overworked and were dissatisfied with their treatment. So Harris decided to "take the traditional [law firm] and put it in a wind tunnel . . . and strip away all the pieces that create drag and waste."[1] Rather than operate under the large law firm leveraged pyramid of three to four high-priced associates to every one partner, Axiom removed most of the costs associated with large firms including young lawyer training, office space rentals, and leverage-based finances.[2]

Axiom clients are in-house legal departments, not law firms. The Axiom model relies on contracting directly with corporate clients on a retainer basis, usually for a fixed fee.[3] Occasionally, when circumstances dictate, an hourly rate is used, but in such situations, the more the client buys, the more the hourly rate is reduced. Typical assignments involve an Axiom lawyer being staffed on a client matter for 11 months. Axiom lawyers are W2 employees with benefits and 401(k) plans, but when they are not staffed on a matter (when they are "on the beach"), they are not paid.[4] However, benefits continue when salary shuts off. Axiom does not hire first-year lawyers; typically it hires lawyers with four to five years experience following law school.

By removing traditional cost structures, Axiom freed itself to charge clients half the fees or less.[5] It removed overhead costs by having its lawyers work at the client site or at a subsidized home office. Axiom also proved that high-level talent was willing to accept a position with some income security risk in exchange for more control and flexibility in the work they do.

Axiom recognized that internal legal departments were getting bigger and were holding on to the more interesting work while sending specialized matters to large firms.[6] Its goal has been to provide extra help for the work that legal departments keep. Additionally, Axiom advises in-house departments on how to reduce their legal budget. It was ahead of the curve in recognizing that legal work is being disaggregated. That is, such work is being broken out into smaller pieces with different parties handling different pieces of the work. Disaggregated work often requires more case management, and Axiom handles case management for its clients.[7] Seeing its role as servicing the in-house client and making its needs a priority, Axiom advises in-house legal departments on reducing their legal expenses by unbundling, outsourcing onshore and offshore, and creating processes to more efficiently handle routine work. Rather than being threatened about shrinking legal service needs, Axiom provides advice to in-house departments as part of its client service.

In addition to Axiom, a multitude of new-model firms and variations have cropped up—Advent Lawyers; FSB FisherBroyles; GCA Law Partners LLP; GenCounsel, LLC; Gerber Growth, LLC; Outside GC LLC; Paragon Legal Group, P.C.; Phillips & Reiter PLLC; and The General Counsel, Ltd., among others. Many of them mirror the Axiom model of supplementing work directly for in-house legal departments. Some also serve as part-time general counsel for companies that cannot justify hiring someone full-time.[8]

Mae O'Malley started Paragon Legal Group, P.C. in Silicon Valley in 2006 to provide working-mother attorneys well-paid, interesting work with flexible schedules.[9] Specializing in technology licensing and corporate transactions, Paragon lawyers work with law firms and in-house legal teams on a project basis when, for example, an in-house attorney is on maternity or medical leave or a company needs overflow support.[10] Paragon lawyers do not work overtime, and they can take as much time off as they like between assignments.[11] As of late 2009, Paragon had 30 attorneys working between 10 and 50 hours a week and another 30 lawyers on call for niche projects. The top earners earned as much as $270,000 per year. Paragon does not provide benefits, but the lawyers receive professional liability insurance through the firm.[12] Since its founding, O'Malley has recognized that more attorneys—not just parents—are seeing the appeal of project-based work.[13]

Advent Lawyers is another variation of the Axiom model that does not bill by the hour. The firm, established in Sydney, Australia, in 2008, operates on a secondment-based model. Secondments are where lawyers are "borrowed" from their employer and work on temporary assignment for another organization. At Advent Lawyers, for example, lawyers work directly at client premises on a project-by-project or fixed-fee basis.[14]

The success of the Axiom-type model is intuitive. It has not only been effective in reducing client costs but also in responding to client needs. In 2009, while about two-thirds of general counsel said they were going to bring more work in-house, nearly one-third also said they were planning to cut lawyers and other law department staff.[15] This combination of more work and less in-house staff is the perfect opportunity for Axiom-type outside counsel to handle spillover work of in-house legal departments.

Additionally, the Axiom-type model has been responsive to the needs of many individual lawyers who seek more flexibility and predictability in how, where, and when they work. The model is a good fit for Gen Y, a generation that is generally more willing to take risks and less willing to work within the confines of traditional law firms.[16] The model also has been particularly appealing to working mothers.

Lawyers working for these new-model firms are happier, because of the flexibility they garner and because of the opportunity to work on-site, at the client.[17] Attorneys also see the appeal of project-based work—not only because it gives them flexible hours but because of the exposure to a larger variety of clients.[18] There are risks for the attorneys too. The work is not always consistent and the attorneys' career path may look more disjointed. However, in the recent economic downturn, these risks seem less specific to new-model law firms. Indeed, the traditional law firm path has become much less certain and therefore the new-model law firms will likely continue to gain popularity. These new options, however, do not exist for most junior lawyers. The nontraditional firms are still looking to traditional firms and other established employers to train their lawyers. Once those lawyers are trained, the new-model firms offer what they believe is something better.

Virtual Law Firms

Virtual law firms have been gaining momentum over the past 10 to 15 years. At its core, a "virtual firm is a flattening of the traditional model through tools of technology and a philosophy of sharing, rather than joining by hierarchy and physical space."[19] For many of the virtual firms, the formula is simple: hire partner-level lawyers with established clients, cut their large law firm rates in half, and let the lawyers keep almost all of what they bill.[20] Some virtual firms hire experienced but not partner-level lawyers. Also, some virtual firms expect all of the lawyers to develop business while others relegate business development to a select few.

There are numerous virtual firms that have evolved. Some of the ones in the United States include Berger Legal; Chase Sensale Law Group; Delta Law Group; Natoli-Lapin; Vantage Counsel; Virtual Law Partners; and XDL Group. Virtual firms are also catching on in the United Kingdom, including Excello Law; Halebury; Keystone Law; and Woolley & Co. While all of these firms are virtual, they vary in their offerings.

At one virtual firm, Virtual Law Partners (VLP), founded in 2008, partners with 10 to 15 years of experience work remotely and communicate through video chat and e-mail.[21] They bill $275 to $400 per hour and use a centralized infrastructure for billing, information technology, marketing, and recruiting.[22] Clients pay about one-third the cost of large firms. VLP attorneys do not have billing requirements but they are not paid if they don't work.[23] A significant incentive for VLP attorneys is that they earn 65 percent of what they bill and collect. Additionally, attorneys who manage their projects get 85 percent of their collected billables and an additional 20 percent of each working attorney's collected billings on a project.[24] The remaining 15 percent goes to firm overhead. Lawyers split the cost of malpractice insurance.[25] This revenue allocation is in stark contrast to the traditional law firm model where 33 percent of collections go to overhead, 33 percent go to partner profits, and 33 percent go to the working attorneys.[26] VLP went through some rocky times in late 2009 when its cofounder and visionary, Craig Johnson, died and another cofounder left six weeks later. But the firm has revived, and as of April 2010 was thriving with 38 virtual lawyers.[27]

Berger Legal, another virtual firm, handles traditional outside counsel work as well as overflow work from in-house legal departments. It also acts as outside general counsel for smaller businesses and "seconds" (lends) its lawyers to clients on a full-time or reduced hour basis. These seconded lawyers work on specific projects or cover staffing gaps such as those resulting from maternity or medical leaves.[28]

Rimon Law Group distinguishes itself as a virtual law firm with a "satisfaction-based billing" program where a client can elect to pay up to 20 percent more or less of the firm's normal rates, depending on the client's level of satisfaction.[29] The firm uses project management software where all communications, tasks, files, documents, and deadlines are stored in a location to increase collaboration and efficiency. Rimon has also partnered with Virtual Paralegal Services, Inc. (VPS), enabling Rimon to delegate certain tasks to deliver more effective legal services.[30]

At Chase Sensale Law Group, lawyers are connected by voice-over-IP phones, and the firm has an online database of more than 20,000 files.[31] This database is a cost-saving measure, as it avoids the overhead of warehouse storage while offering flexibility in how work gets done.[32]

Along with some of the larger virtual law firm models, there are numerous smaller virtual practices that focus on individuals and entrepreneurs. At these smaller shops, e-lawyering provides legal services online including non-contested divorces, wills, limited liability company formations, bankruptcy filings and real estate leases and closings.[33] Richard Granat, head of the American Bar Association's e-lawyering task force, predicts that this is the wave of the future. "As the generation that has grown up on Facebook and MySpace matures and has legal problems, they [will] all want to deal with lawyers online,"[34] Granat said.

The benefits of virtual lawyering are numerous. For clients, they are able to have services provided by top-notch lawyers at significantly reduced prices—sometimes a third to a half of the rates. They benefit from the more flexible infrastructure of virtual law firms that often allows them to structure alternative fee arrangements more freely.[35] For individual lawyers, there is the opportunity to work more autonomously and potentially earn more while gaining significantly more freedom and flexibility. Lawyers working from home also avoid wasted time commuting or chatting at the water cooler. Lawyers enjoy having no billable-hour requirements since there is no need to cover associate or staff salaries or expensive office space. Many of the lawyers are also proud to be part of a green business with a small carbon footprint. The virtual firm lifestyle appeals to many working parents and those who seek more control and flexibility in their lives to pursue interests outside the law. Since everyone at virtual firms is working from home, there is no stigma attached to doing it.[36]

There are also challenges facing virtual firms. A significant one is building a brand. Many of the virtual firms are deliberate in hiring senior attorneys with impressive credentials and prestigious schools as a way to help enhance their credibility and image. Another challenge of a virtual firm is to facilitate camaraderie and make people feel connected, as if they are part of a common experience and community. Virtual firms try to achieve this by fostering attorney collaboration—so it's not just a group of attorneys who share e-mail addresses and a law firm name. Virtual firms also use technology including teleconferencing and Skype video and have regular get-togethers in person with and without family members. At VLP, for example, lawyers hold parties and retreats at vacation homes. VLP also encourages its lawyers to participate in business groups to have more of a presence in the community.

A key question for virtual law firms is whether they will be able to compete to handle large matters or whether a greater infrastructure is necessary for the type of work typically performed by larger firms. Some clients are skeptical of a virtual firm's ability to compete for large, sophisticated matters. "I think a certain domain will remain exclusive to the big firms, such as complex litigation, or big corporate deals," says Tim Reis, the general counsel of EMS Technologies, Inc.[37] I disagree. I think it will depend on effective project management and collaboration. A virtual firm should be able to compete for the large and complex matters with proper management and collaboration with other boutique firms and by outsourcing some of the lower-level work.

Firms Abandoning the Billable Hour

Some law firms are basing their marketing campaigns on abandoning the billable hour. These campaigns are a way for firms to distinguish themselves and lure away clients who crave predictability in their legal budgets as well as high-quality work. These forward-thinking firms tend to innovate on not just the billable-hour issue—they often bring other new ideas to the table. One example is Summit Law Group, founded in 1997. At Summit, all lawyers and staff members have an equity stake in the business and all have the same size offices.[38] All lawyers at the firm are partners and reduced-hour partners are allowed as well.[39] Lawyers and staff are paid based on individual and firm performance (rather than seniority). Financial information, including quarterly budgets and cash flow statistics, is distributed firmwide.[40] The firm's compensation team asks each lawyer to submit a pay proposal for himself or herself and for each lawyer at the firm based on the circulated financial information.[41] Clients are encouraged to adjust a proposed fee upward or downward through the firm's value-adjustment billing, depending on their level of satisfaction.[42]

Another example is Valorem Law Group, formed in January 2008 by refugees from traditional firms. The vast majority of Valorem's fees are based on alternative fee arrangements. They use project and case management tools to maximize efficiency. Like Summit, they have a "Value Adjustment Line" in their bills, allowing the client to adjust the agreed-upon fee to reflect the client's satisfaction in the service. They also offer holdbacks where a certain agreed-upon portion of the fee is held until the end of the matter or another predetermined benchmark is reached, when the holdback is paid or refunded.[43] Jeffrey Carr, Vice President and General Counsel, FMC Technologies, Inc., sits on Valorem's Advisory Board and is a leader in supporting these types of satisfaction fees. He advocates under his Alliance Counsel Engagement System (ACES) that law firms should be paid 80 percent of their invoice and the remaining 20 percent should be placed in an "at-risk bucket" for potential payment with bonuses based on performance.[44]

Another example of a firm distinguishing itself on an alternative fee platform is Shepherd Law Group, P.C. It offers what it calls "upfront pricing"—like a general contractor doing home renovations—so clients know the cost of the work before it is done.[45] If the scope of a job changes, the firm will send the client a change order, setting out the new scope and the associated price change.

Smithline Jha LLP, a firm focused exclusively on technology transactions, markets a specific type of alternative fee. It offers monthly fixed-fee subscription pricing that covers all of the services provided to a client during the month. This fee includes negotiating all of a client's technology transaction deals, creating and updating forms, providing deal and legal counseling, implementing a deal flow process, and attending company meetings and training sessions.[46] The fee is mutually agreed upon in advance and the client's commitment is month-to-month. The first month of service is exploratory. The firm provides its services and learns about the client's business. At the end of the month, there is another meeting to mutually agree upon a monthly rate going forward, which will continue until either party requests an adjustment.[47]

There are numerous other firms that are based on the alternative fee, rather than the billable hour, model. Natoli-Lapin LLC offers flat fees targeting entrepreneurs, artists, and other new business owners. The firm's lawyers work virtually, keeping overhead low with 80 percent of the firm's revenue as profit.[48] Bartlit Beck Herman Palenchar & Scott LLP conducts highly sophisticated litigation under an alternative fee model.[49] The Rosen law firm, a large divorce firm in North Carolina, provides predictability to its clients by billing on a flat fee basis.[50] Family law firm Chinn and Associates, PLLC in Mississippi operates on the alternative fee model, which it calls "value pricing,"[51] and Raymond & Bennett LLC, a Connecticut firm specializing in business and personal injury litigation, uses alternative fees through what it calls "Real-Value."[52] A more extensive discussion of the benefits and challenges of alternative fees will be explored in the next chapter.

Hybrid Firms

Blended Professional Services Firms

Some firms are marketing themselves to appeal to the client seeking both legal and business advice. One example is Resources Global Professionals, providing consulting in fields including accounting, law, finance, information technology, human resources, and other specialties.[53] Resources has a large infrastructure to manage administration, recruitment, and clients. Originally part of Deloitte, Resources has $736 million in revenue and 3,200 people on assignment internationally.[54] For its legal work, it may send large teams into companies for projects such as Sarbanes-Oxley changes or acquisition integration.[55] Resources allows clients to expand and contract professional teams according to their needs, without additionally hiring full-time staff.[56] Associates have flexibility because they are paid by the hour instead of earning a salary and they can choose their projects, take off long periods of time, or work fewer days a week.[57]

At Exemplar Companies, Inc., the firm is also bridging different professional realms—selling legal service and business advice. Exemplar calls this approach "convergence" and describes it as "the unique combination of professional services across the disciplines of Law and Business to achieve superior results, add more value, craft more comprehensive solutions, and solve complex problems more effectively."[58] Exemplar has also abandoned the billable hour and adopted a satisfaction guarantee. If clients feel dissatisfied with the service, Exemplar will negotiate its price with the client.[59]

Publishing Law Firm

Practical Law Company (PLC) helps attorneys navigate transactional law by providing Web-based tools to lay out the deal-making process and improve efficiency.[60] It does this by offering subscription-based online resources including document templates, model clauses, practice notes, deal checklists, how-to guides, new law updates, and a searchable database of deals and securities findings.[61] Subscribers are both in-house and law firm lawyers who access the online training resources on a fixed-fee basis, depending on the number of users. "We're a sort of hybrid between a law firm and a legal publisher; it's a unique model," says Chris Millerchip, who cofounded PLC in 1990 in Great Britain with Robert Dow and opened a New York City office in 2008.[62] Most of the lawyers PLC employs write content for the Web pages.[63] The biggest benefit of the service is facilitating efficiency among practicing lawyers, which Millerchip argues will increase profitability, especially with alternative fees becoming more popular.[64]

Small Firm Alternatives to Practice

Alternative Hour Firms

With client needs front and center, some law firms are seeing opportunities in marketing to clients for work at certain times of the day. For example, E. James Perullo founded Bay State Legal Services as an after-hours law firm that meets with its clients between 6 and 10 p.m. Monday through Friday, and otherwise by appointment.[65] The firm's target clients are small business owners and working-class clients, and these clients cannot easily leave work to meet with a lawyer in the middle of the day. Perullo and the other attorneys have a variety of jobs during the day, including managing their own legal practices or practicing for other firms.[66] Bay State is able to lease the office space only during the evening hours, which gives them affordable space in a prime location. Lawyers affiliated with the firm keep 60 percent of the fees from cases assigned to them after expenses and 90 percent from cases they originate when they serve as primary counsel.[67] Another firm, Scott Sagria, is open Saturdays to appeal to clients. The firm offers payment plans instead of up-front retainers.[68] Currently, small law firms are the largest and fastest-growing sector of the legal community.[69] We can expect to continue to see creative structures developed to appeal to small firm clients.

Flex-Time Firms

The Law Offices of Joanne R. Sternlieb developed out of founder Sternlieb's desire to practice trusts and estates law while gaining more control over her life. In 2002, Sternlieb started her own firm. She now has four lawyers and two assistants who work from their homes, on their own schedules. Each is an independent contractor who works a flexible schedule with no set hours, no billable-hour requirements, no guaranteed hours, and no guaranteed pay.[70] When Sternlieb gets a new matter, she contacts the lawyers on her roster to see who is fitting and available to handle the work. If all four of her lawyers decline the opportunity or are not suitable, then she handles the work herself. Sternlieb pays her associates and charges her clients on a preset project basis except for an hourly rate she charges for estate administration.[71]

Women-Owned Firms

Litigation and transaction boutique Schoeman, Updike & Kaufman LLP is an example of a woman-owned law firm certified by the Women's Business Enterprise National Council (WBENC) and the National Association of Minority and Women-Owned Law Firms (NAMWOLF). Other women-owned firms may fall into the categories outlined above as well as more conventional structures. Schoeman, Updike is among the largest of the women-owned firms, with about 30 lawyers. It distinguishes itself by emphasizing alternative fee arrangements and welcoming flex-time lawyers, including those interested in project-based work.[72] The flex-time attorneys have no billable-hour requirements and their pay is adjusted based on hours worked, among other factors. The firm recognizes the value of flex-time attorneys and how they can enhance the practice and complement the work of lawyers with a traditional schedule.

Legal Process Outsourcing (LPO)

Legal Process Outsourcing (LPO) is the process of sending work offshore to a lower-cost jurisdiction. It is becoming increasingly acceptable to law firms and in-house legal departments for legal work to be disaggregated and unbundled, which is what is enabling the LPO process. The types of work that are being parsed out include document review; litigation preparation; deposition summaries; legal research and writing; patent prosecution; contract management; compliance services; and drafting of memoranda, trial and appellate-level pleadings, and briefs. LPO providers are most often hired by law firms that conduct legal outsourcing on behalf of clients or pharmaceutical, technology, and manufacturing company law departments that hire LPOs directly.[73]

It is debatable whether a discussion of LPOs belongs in a chapter about new models of legal practice. Most legal outsourcers contend that they are not practicing law. Many say there is nothing inherent in the outsourcing tasks that require an attorney to do them.[74] Additionally, legal outsourcers typically handle just part of a legal representation, so some would argue that they are not technically a new model of legal practice. That being said, I still believe LPOs belong in this chapter because they have created their own category in law practice.

Global revenues generated by legal outsourcing are already significant, at about $250 million in 2009, and they are projected to grow to $4 billion by 2015.[75] The legal outsourcing sector employed about 10,000 lawyers in 2009, and is expected to expand to 79,000 by 2015.[76] A majority of the work comes from the United States, the United Kingdom, and Canada. In early 2009, India enacted the Limited Liability Partnership Act, which permits foreign law firms to establish an office in India. Although foreign lawyers will still not be able to practice in India, many view the Act as an opening of the Indian legal market with further growth opportunities.[77]

LPOs employ newly graduated lawyers or those from legal firms with experience across different sectors.[78] India is the top destination for outsourcing. There are also LPOs in the Philippines, Israel, and South Africa.[79] Additionally, the LPOs recruit U.S. lawyers to train and supervise their workforces.[80]

The savings in using lawyers in India are considerable. For example, the lawyers in India charge $25 per hour, compared to $150 to $300 per hour billed by paralegals and associates doing the same work at American law firms.[81] With 80,000 English-speaking law graduates annually, India has a ripe talent pool to do the work.[82] Some of the leading LPO companies founded in the last ten years include American Discovery;

Clutch Group; CPA Global (founded earlier but focusing on outsourcing more recently); Exactus Corporation; Integreon, Inc.; Intellextra; LawScribe, Inc.; LegalEase Solutions LLC; Lexadigm Solutions LLC; Manthan Legal; Mindcrest, Inc.; Pangea3 LLC; SDD Global Solutions Pvt. Ltd.; Stratify Inc.; and Tusker Group. Some of these LPOs also provide outsourcing in industries other than law, including finance, accounting, corporate strategic management, foreign direct investment, secretarial services, software, and Web development.

LPOs offer a variety of billing arrangements. Billable hours are still popular with project-based work including legal research, due diligence, and e-discovery.[83] Another model offered in LPOs is the full-time equivalent (FTE), where clients effectively have an LPO employee serve as an additional in-house member for a period of time.[84] Unit pricing is used at times where a client is billed per document or per case, rather than by time.[85] Flat fees and flat fees with a cap are also popular.[86] The two key factors influencing pricing for the LPO providers are efficiency and the willingness of clients to commit to longer and larger projects, allowing for greater efficiencies.[87] The longer and larger projects bring the greater discounts to clients.

The biggest benefit to employers of using LPOs is economic. LPO providers are cutting their clients' legal bills in half—or smaller.[88] The other significant employer benefit is efficiency. Work can be done on a 24-hour basis, with the outsourced laborers working while lawyers in the United States are asleep.[89] Another benefit is that law firms and law departments can have teams of lawyers available to do work without needing to keep associates on the payroll.[90] Additionally, employees in offshore companies in India and the Philippines are often more educated and dedicated than temporary employees in the United States.[91]

A bonus to individual lawyers in the U.S. who work for outsourcing providers is lifestyle. At Clutch Group, for example, the firm has lawyers in India but the founder reports that the U.S. lawyers work 40 to 50 hours a week rather than the more typical escalating hours of law firm lawyers.[92] The nature of the work, however, is typically less challenging, so that will diminish the appeal for some lawyers. On a broader scale, LPOs may improve work/life balance by helping to eliminate the face-time debate. If lawyers prove to be competent delivering work product from another part of the globe, it's hard to justify not allowing someone to have more flexible hours to work from home 30 miles away.

The most commonly voiced concerns against LPOs are work quality and data security/confidentiality.[93] To improve work quality, extensive training has been put into place at the LPO providers. Additionally, U.S. lawyers are sent to most of the LPO providers to manage the process as it has customarily been performed in the United States.[94] As for the issue of data security and confidentiality, these offshore providers have extensive security measures to ensure no breach of the highly sensitive matters handled.[95] For example, document reviewers often work directly on their clients' servers through a secure Internet connection, or work on computers with inoperable USB ports and no Internet access.[96] There are also concerns raised about the difficulty of avoiding conflicts of interest when vendors serve clients with inconsistent interests, or the lack of recourse if an Indian lawyer violates an ethical rule.[97] These concerns, and others, will continue to arise with increased outsourcing. However, given the economic savings and efficiencies gleaned from outsourcing, LPOs will undoubtedly become more practiced at overcoming these challenges.

THE JUNIOR LAWYER FALLOUT

One significant concern stemming from these new models to legal practice is the fallout for the junior lawyer. Where will junior lawyers in the United States get trained? In the virtual and other new law firm models, only mid- to senior-level lawyers are being hired. There is an expectation that junior lawyers will be trained elsewhere. At present, it is unclear where those venues will be. Due to LPOs, a lot of the entry-level work given to junior associates will be outsourced to India and elsewhere. Also, clients are pushing back and questioning why they should bear the expense of training new lawyers. These questions raise uncertainty for graduating law students and the legal profession pipeline. They will be addressed more fully in Chapter 4.

NOTES

1. Heather Smith, *A New Breed of Legal Services Provider Tries to Fill the Gap Between Law Firms and Temp Agencies*, CORPORATE COUNSEL, Aug. 2004, *available at* http://www.axiomlegal.com/flash_content/content/news/01CorporateCounselB.pdf.

2. Jill Schachner Chanen, *Have Law, Will Travel*, A.B.A.J., Dec.1, 2007, *available at* http://www.abajournal.com/magazine/article/have_law_will_travel/.

3. Leigh Jones, *The Rise of the New Model Firm*, NAT'L L.J., May 21, 2007, *available at* http://www.axiomlaw.com/html_content/nlj/NLJ-Axiom.pdf.

4. *Id.*

5. Chanen, *supra* note 2.

6. Jones, *supra* note 3.

7. *Id.*

8. *Id.*

9. Chanen, *supra* note 2.

10. Sue Pierce, *Life of a Legal Mom*, STAN. MAG., Sept./Oct. 2008, *available at* http://www.stanfordalumni.org/news/magazine/2008/sepoct/classnotes/omalley.html.

11. *Id.*

12. Rachel M. Zahorsky, *Mae O'Malley: Mogul Mom*, A.B.A.J. LEGAL REBELS, Sept. 9, 2009, *available at* http://www.legalrebels.com/profiles/mae_omalley_mogul_mom.

13. Pierce, *supra* note 10.

14. *Advent Lawyers Launches Melbourne Office*, LAW. WEEKLY, Sept. 23, 2009, *available at* http://www.lawyersweekly.com.au/blogs/top_stories/archive/2009/09/23/advent-lawyers-launches-melbourne-office.aspx.

15. Leslie A. Gordon, *Economic Pressure May Force Permanent Shift in Corporate Legal Costs*, GC CAL. MAG., Apr. 16, 2009, *available at* http://www.law.com/jsp/cc/PubArticleCC.jsp?id=1202429931212.

16. Jones, *supra* note 3.

17. Chanen, *supra* note 2.

18. Pierce, *supra* note 10.

19. Katrina Dewey, *What Makes a Firm Virtual?* LAWDRAGON, INC., July 16, 2008, *available at* http://www.lawdragon.com/index.php/newdragon/fullstory/what_makes_a_firm_virtual/.

20. Francesca Heintz, *Does the Future Belong to Virtual Law Firms?*, AM. LAW., Aug. 3, 2009, *available at* http://www.law.com/jsp/lawtechnologynews/PubArticleLTN.jsp?id=1202432696190.

21. *Id.*

22. *Id.*

23. Eric Young, *Virtual Firm Is Enjoying Real Growth*, S.F. Bus. Times, July 16, 2009, *available at* http://sanfrancisco.bizjournals.com/sanfrancisco/blog/2009/07/virtual_firm_is_enjoying_real_growth.html?t=printable.

24. Stephanie Francis Ward, *Virtually Practicing*, A.B.A.J., June 1, 2009, *available at* http://www.abajournal.com/magazine/article/virtually_practicing/.

25. *Id.*

26. *Id. See also* Katrina Dewey, *Time for the Virtual Revolution*, Lawdragon, Inc., July 16, 2008, *available at* http://www.lawdragon.com/index.php/newdragon/fullstory/time_for_the_virtual_revolution/.

27. Brian Baxter, *Its Leader Gone, Virtual Law Partners Soldiers On*, AmLaw Daily, Apr. 15, 2010, *available at* http://amlawdaily.typepad.com/amlawdaily/2010/04/virtual-law-firm-soldiers-on.html.

28. http://www.bergerlegal.com/.

29. http://www.rimonlaw.com/.

30. http://www.rimonlaw.com/.

31. Michael H. Samuels, *Law Firms Boost Their Image and Client Base by Going Social*, Long Island Bus. News, July 9, 2009, *available at* http://libn.com/blog/2009/07/09/law-firms-boost-their-image-and-client-base-by-going-social/.

32. *Id.*

33. *Id.*

34. *Id.*

35. Erin Coe, *Virtual Law Firms May Rise Out of Tougher Economy*, Law360, Nov. 3, 2008, *available at* http://www.law360.com/articles/75201.

36. Ward, *supra* note 24.

37. Heintz, *supra* note 20.

38. Ralph H. Palumbo, Summit Law Group, Creating the Law Firm of the Future 2001, *available at* http://www.summitlaw.com/PalumboArticle.pdf.

39. Steven T. Taylor, *Running Ahead of the Pack: Trailblazers in the Law Firm World*, Law Prac. Mag., Apr./May 2009, *available at* http://www.abanet.org/lpm/magazine/articles/v35/is3/pg30.shtml.

40. Zahorsky, *supra* note 12.

41. *Id.*

42. Palumbo, *supra* note 38.

43. http://www.valoremlaw.com/.

44. Value Practice: Alternative Billing by Paying for Performance: Focus on FMC Technologies' ACES (Alliance Counsel Engagement System) Program, Interview with Jeffrey Carr Sept. 2008, *available at* http://www.acc.com/advocacy/valuechallenge/toolkit/upload/Value-Practice-FMC-Alternative-Billing.pdf.

45. http://www.shepherdlawgroup.com/.

46. http://www.smithlinejha.com/.

47. *Id.*

48. Karen Sloan, *New Firm Uses Fixed Fees to Tempt Entrepreneurial Clients*, Nat'l L.J., June 22, 2009, *available at* http://www.law.com/jsp/nlj/PubArticleNLJ.jsp?id=1202431666707&hbxlogin=1.

49. http://www.bartlit-beck.com/about-success.html.

50. Lisa Belkin, *Who's Cuddly Now? Law Firms*, N.Y. Times, Jan. 24, 2008, *available at* http://www.nytimes.com/2008/01/24/fashion/24WORK.html.

51. http://www.chinnandassociates.com/value.html.

52. http://www.raymond-bennett.com/CM/Custom/Alternate-Fees.asp.

53. Alison Maitland, *Take the Law into Your Own Hands*, Fin. Times, Nov. 27, 2007, *available at* http://www.axiomlegal.com/financialtimes/financial%20times.pdf.

54. *Id.*

55. *Id.*

56. http://www.resourcesglobal.com/.

57. Maitland, *supra* note 53.

58. http://www.exemplarcompanies.com/site/innovations/convergence/topic/1.

59. Taylor, *supra* note 39.

60. Ross Todd, *The Innovation Agenda: Practical Law Company Sets Up Shop in New York*, AmLaw Daily, Jan. 20, 2009, *available at* http://amlawdaily.typepad.com/amlawdaily/2009/01/plc.html.

61. Gina Passarella, *BigLaw Behemoth Behind the Times, GCs Say*, Legal Intelligencer, June 8, 2009; Todd, *supra* note 60.

62. Steven T. Taylor, *Tomorrow: A Sneak Preview. For These Firms, the Future is Now*, Law Prac. Mgmt., Jan./Feb. 2010, *available at* http://www.abanet.org/lpm/magazine/articles/v36/is1/pg38.shtml.

63. *Id.*

64. *Id.*

65. Sheri Qualters, *Keep Your Day Job, Then Clock in Nightly at the Firm*, Nat'l L.J., Apr. 10, 2008, *available at* http://www.law.com/jsp/law/sfb/lawArticleFriendlySFB.jsp?id=900005561277.

66. *Id.*

67. *Id.*

68. Debra Cassens Weiss, *BigLaw Lawyers Jump to Small Firms, Law's Fastest Growing Sector*, A.B.A.J., Feb. 16, 2010, *available at* http://www.abajournal.com/news/article/biglaw_lawyers_jump_to_small_law_firms_legal_practices_fastest_growing_sect/.

69. *Id.*

70. Aleksandra Todorova, *In the Trenches: Building a Better Law Firm*, SmartMoney, Sept. 29, 2005, *available at* http://www.jsestateplanning.com/smartmoney_9_29_05.php.

71. *Id.*

72. Jerry Crimmins, *Woman-Owned Firm Comes In*, Chi. Daily L. Bull., Mar. 8, 2007.

73. David A. Steiger, *The Rise of Global Legal Sourcing*, Bus. L. Today, Nov./Dec. 2009, *available at* http://www.abanet.org/buslaw/blt/2009-11-12/steiger.shtml; Keith Ecker, *The Offshore Option*, Inside Couns., Jan. 2009, at 45, *available at* http://www.insidecounsel.com/Issues/2009/January-2009/Pages/The-Offshore-Option.aspx?k=the+offshore+option.

74. Steiger, *supra* note 73.

75. Pranav Nambiar, *Slump Brings More Work for LPOs*" DNA, May 8, 2009, *available at* http://www.dnaindia.com/money/report_slump-brings-more-work-for-lpos_1253940.

76. *Id.*

77. Martin Desmarais, *Coming Through in the Clutch*, IndUS Business Journal, May 7, 2009, *available at* http://www.indusbusinessjournal.com/ME2/Audiences/dirmod.asp?sid=&nm=&type=Publishing&mod=Publications%3A%3AArticle&mid=8F3A7027421841978F18BE895F87F791&AudID=6EF55B05AA694954939FA7B6FB605DAB&tier=4&id=8E53C442A6D64F7BA437413B0942B49D.

78. Nambiar, *supra* note 75.

79. Stephen Seckler, *Legal Process Outsourcing: New Threat or New Opportunity*, Complete Law., Apr. 29, 2009, *available at* http://www

.thecompletelawyer.com/law-practice-management/legal-process-outsourcing-new-threat-or-new-opportunity-4518.html.

80. Lynne Marek, *India Beckons to U.S. Lawyers*, NAT'L L.J., July 14, 2009, *available at* http://www.law.com/jsp/law/international/LawArticleIntl.jsp?id=1202432216040.

81. V. Dion Haynes, *Recession Sends Lawyers Home*, WASH. POST, Mar. 9, 2009, *available at* http://www.washingtonpost.com/wp-dyn/content/article/2009/03/08/AR2009030801549_pf.html.

82. Nambiar, *supra* note 75.

83. Lesley Sutherland, *Fitting the Bill*, INDIA BUS. L.J., June 2009, *available at* http://www.indilaw.com/pdfs/LPO%20billing%20rates%20demystified.pdf.

84. *Id.*

85. *Id.*

86. *Id.*

87. *Id.*

88. Desmarais, *supra* note 77.

89. *Id.*

90. Seckler, *supra* note 79.

91. Ecker, *supra* note 73.

92. Desmarais, *supra* note 77.

93. Marek, *supra* note 80.

94. *Id.*

95. Ecker, *supra* note 73.

96. Mike Dolan & John Thickett, *The Tipping Point: Offshore Document Review and the "New" Legal Industry*, LEGAL MGMT., Aug. 2009, *available at* http://www.alanet.org/publications/issue/aug09/LM-Aug09-BigIdeas.pdf.

97. Seckler, *supra* note 79.

CHAPTER 3
THE LARGE LAW FIRM OF THE FUTURE

When my oldest son, Oliver, turned six, I decided to coach his soccer team. My first year, there were 24 coaches in the division. I was the only mom—the rest were all dads. At the preseason coaches' meeting, I was introduced to the two other dads who would be my co-coaches for Ollie's team. The two knew each other and seemed chummy. We discussed how we would run practices and we went over some of the rules and logistics for games. As we were wrapping things up, one of the coaches turned to me and said: "You know, you should really consider coaching your daughter's team. You'd really enjoy it." The other coach chimed in: "Oh yeah, I coach my daughter in basketball and it's a lot of fun."

I found it surprising that at the start of the season, my two co-coaches were urging me to coach elsewhere, and specifically in a girls' league. I also found it interesting that they were presuming I had a daughter to coach, which I did not. I was put off by what I interpreted to be their effort to convey to me that I didn't belong. I responded: "I don't have a daughter. I have three sons, which is why I'm at the coach's meeting for the boys."

As I experienced throughout the season, my two co-coaches were the kind of guys who wanted things to stay the same. They were threatened by someone new entering the playing field. They were not unlike some of the large law firms who are resisting inevitable change. But the reality is that large law firms are facing a choice. They can innovate and embrace the changing times or watch from the sidelines as the next generation reinvents the rules.

Many law firms, including the largest firms, are bracing for permanent changes in staffing and non-hourly billing arrangements.[1] According to the "BTI Premium Practices Forecast 2010: Survey of Corporate Legal Spending" study, spending by general counsel on outside counsel fees dropped 10.8 percent, from an average of $20.8 million in 2008 to $18.5 million in 2009. Another 4.3 percent drop in spending to $17.7 million is expected in 2010.[2] These cuts in spending, among other challenges, are an impetus to change to the traditional law firm model that will be explored below.

Alternative Fees

In April 2009, William Henderson, Professor at the Indiana University Maurer School of Law, and a leading Australian risk manager, Anthony Kearns, convened a group of thought leader lawyers in a role-playing game called FutureFirm. They tried to devise a strategy for a hypothetical law firm to survive another decade.[3] The lawyers at FutureFirm agreed that future firms would need to offer alternative fee arrangements to share risk with their clients.[4]

The concept of alternative fees is not new. It has been around for decades and discussed at length. Indeed, the American Bar Association (ABA) launched the Law Practice Management Section Task Force on Alternative Billing Methods in 1989. The Task Force's work culminated in the 2001–2002 ABA report on billable hours, which discussed a range of alternative fee options.[5] There is greater urgency to heed these recommendations today. While clients are pushing harder, many large law firms are still uncomfortable moving away from billable hours and incurring more risk.[6] They are concerned about the new level of budgeting, planning, and projecting of lawyer and staff time required to manage alternative fee arrangements.

Although many large law firms fear alternative fees, they no longer have a choice. In a November 2008 Altman Weil survey of 115 general counsel, less than 10 percent reported that legal expenses were paid via alternative fees.[7] In contrast, more than 50 percent of general counsel said they would require alternative fee arrangements when working with outside counsel in 2009.[8] Law firms will need to be receptive to these general counsel demands or lose business. The 2008 Altman Weil survey showed 53 percent of general counsel plan to move current work or send new work to lower-priced outside counsel.[9] The outlook for 2010 is similarly focused on alternative fees. According to a Hildebrandt survey of 200 in-house legal departments, 55 percent have used or plan to use alternative fee arrangements with their outside law firms in 2010.[10]

The push for alternative fees has gained momentum from the Value Challenge, an initiative of the Association of Corporate Counsel, which has held forums around the country and facilitated the sharing of resources, alternative fee models, and best practices regarding alternative fee arrangements.[11] Some large law firms have been receptive to adopting alternative fees. Some recognize that alternative fees provide opportunities to increase a client's commitment to a law firm and increase the amount of work a firm does for a client. For example, Varian Medical Systems Inc. is reducing the number of firms it uses and increasing the amount of work it gives to outside firms that are using alternative fees.[12]

Back in 2007, certain firms began reporting their alternative fee usage. Morgan, Lewis & Bockius LLP reported that 40 percent of its work was generated from alternative fees, Fenwick & West LLP reported 10 to 25 percent, and Howrey LLP reported 10 percent.[13] In 2009, K&L Gates LLP estimated that about 40 percent of its revenue was from outside the billable hour[14] while Crowell & Moring LLP estimated 30 percent[15] and Orrick, Herrington & Sutcliffe LLP (Orrick) reported about 25 percent.[16]

With so much discussion of alternative fees, it is important to identify the more popular arrangements and understand what they entail. What follows below is a summary of the pros and cons of popular alternative fee arrangements. For a more extensive discussion of alternative fees, an excellent source is the "Fee Arrangements" chapter in *Successful Partnering Between Inside and Outside Counsel.*[17] A firm that adopts any of these alternatives, at least initially, should continue to track hours, realization, utilization, and collection. This is important as a means to compare profitability and revenue generation.[18]

Fixed or Flat Fees/Unit Pricing. With fixed or flat fees, there is usually one set fee for a whole matter. Unit pricing sets one fee for each stage of a transaction or proceeding. These approaches are well received by clients because it gives them predictability and removes the problem of receiving astronomical legal bills that have no association with results or value.[19] For law firms, fixed or flat fees reward efficiency and minimize delays in payments and declining realization rates.[20] Fixed or flat fees work well with simple transactions like real estate closings, wills, employee contracts, or corporate filings. The risk is that they create incentives for firms to take shortcuts or not assign their talented lawyers to the work.[21]

Fixed and flat fees are more difficult to manage when time and workload is less predictable—for example, in litigation, buy-sell transactions, or bankruptcies.[22] However, it can be done. In a litigation, for example, a fixed monthly fee can be determined based on factors including the number of parties in the suit, the number of depositions required, the location of the people to be deposed, and the judge's likelihood of holding an expedited schedule.[23] Both law firms and corporations have extensive information on the past costs of different types of matters, and this can be a starting point for determining a fixed fee. Also, if a client has repeatedly worked with a law firm, they have a pattern of dealing that should reduce the risk.

Unit pricing, where the fixed fee is broken down based on the various stages of the representation, often makes more sense for complex and high-risk matters.[24] Particularly with unit pricing, it is important to define the scope of the transaction or proceeding clearly.[25] Also, because certain matters are unpredictable, it is often appropriate to periodically review the pricing structure to ensure that it is fair.[26]

Fixed fees can be more profitable for law firms. One example of an unusually large flat fee arrangement is the deal between Orrick and Levi Strauss & Co. for Orrick to handle nearly all of Levi's legal work worldwide for an annual fee, paid in monthly increments.[27]

Success, Bonus, or Incentive Fees. Success, bonus, or incentive fees are structured by determining a standard fee and then, prior to engagement, agreeing to reward fees commensurate with varying levels of success. For example, success may be defined as resolving a case within a specified period, settling a case under a certain amount of money, or reaching a determined favorable resolution at trial. As with unit pricing, it is important to clearly define the success targets.[28] A success fee ensures that law firm lawyers don't cut corners. It usually aligns lawyers' incentives with the clients'.[29] However, the client and law firm interests do not always line up, because resolutions of matters are not always tied to performance. For example, an opponent's willingness to settle a case may have little to do with a law firm's performance[30] but it may have a significant impact on a firm's reward.

Holdbacks. A holdback is when a percentage of an engagement or monthly fee is withheld until the end of a matter or a predetermined time when a goal has been reached. "For example, the monthly payment in a litigation could be 80 percent of the fixed fee. If a satisfactory settlement (defined at the outset) is reached, then the firm receives the withheld 20 percent. If the matter goes to trial with a positive result, the firm receives 125 percent of the fixed fee. If neither a good settlement nor a good trial outcome occurs, then the firm receives the original 80 percent of the fixed fee."[31] Some refer to holdbacks as success fees.

Retainers. With a retainer, a law firm provides certain services for an agreed-upon fee on a monthly basis or another specified period of time.[32] Retainers provide predictability but their fairness depends on how accurate the law firm and client are in estimating the volume of work.[33] Retainers are most popular when there is a large volume of relatively small matters.[34] As with fixed fees, it may be appropriate to agree in advance to regularly review retainers, either monthly or quarterly, to ensure the fairness of the fee.

Contingent Fees. Contingent fees require a lawyer and client to agree on a goal to be achieved to trigger a payment and the consequences of achieving that goal. If the goal is not achieved, the client does not pay for the legal services rendered. Contingent fees are most commonly used with litigation plaintiffs where the lawyer's fee is typically one-third or one-fourth of a settlement or judgment they obtain.[35] Contingent fees are a form of "value billing" where the lawyer's fee is directly linked to the value received by the client.[36] There are negative contingent fees, too. For example, if a monetary claim is made against a client and a law firm is able to resolve it for less than the claim, the law firm receives a percentage of the savings.[37]

Alternative Fee Variations of the Billable Hour

There are variations on the billable-hour model that some consider to be alternative fee arrangements. Some firms and clients that struggle with designing creative alternative fees fall back on variations of the billable hour.[38]

Discounted Hourly Rates. Some clients negotiate a discount on hourly rates, often for commodity work. Law firms often accede to this for significant clients with leverage.[39] There are risks associated with this arrangement on both sides. For law firms, the clients get accustomed to the discounts and when firms try to revert back to charging regular rates, it is often interpreted as a price increase.[40] The risk to the client is that their work will no longer be prioritized and lower-caliber lawyers will be staffed on their matters.[41] Also, discounting does not limit the numbers of hours billed and it does not improve efficiency.[42] In fact, it might encourage the opposite.

Volume Discounts. Volume discounts occur when clients commit to a certain amount of work if the work is performed at a discounted hourly rate. Thus, a firm agrees to charge a lower percentage of its standard hourly rates when its billable hours reach a negotiated threshold or series of thresholds.[43] For example, a firm may agree to a 5 percent discount of its fees when the bills reach $500,000 and a 10 percent discount when the bills reach $1 million. Clients face the same risk here as with discounted hourly rates.

Blended Rates. For blended rates, one hourly rate is negotiated for all the time spent by different timekeepers on a project. Blended rates have been more popular in the litigation context.[44] While the benefit is potentially more efficient staffing, the detriment is an incentive to inflate hours or produce lower quality of work by delegating to less senior or less capable lawyers or paralegals.[45]

Frozen Rates. Frozen rates are adopted when a law firm agrees not to raise its rates by more than an agreed-upon percentage for the length of a matter or during a certain period of time.[46]

Per Diem Rates. Some clients prefer a daily rate, rather than an hourly rate, for certain lawyer time. For example, some clients may negotiate a per diem rate for trial time, travel time, or time spent on matters that consume lawyers' entire day, such as a lengthy mediation or transactional negotiation.[47]

Fee Cap. A fee cap places a limit on the maximum number of hours that will be billed for a matter or task. Law firms incur the loss if the maximum number of hours is exceeded.[48] Meanwhile the client risk, as with blended or discounted rates, is that they may receive lower-quality work and unwittingly provide an incentive to the firm to delegate their work to less senior or less capable lawyers.[49]

Hybrid. A hybrid is a combination of alternative fee arrangements and demonstrates the flexibility that can be exercised—for example, a flat fee plus an hourly fee or an hourly fee plus a contingency.[50] Or, another hybrid might be a fixed fee plus a negative contingent fee.[51]

There are some common elements among the alternative fee arrangements described above. In most, law firms share the risk with clients, and the law firm and client interests are aligned. Some firms fear shared risks but this can be mitigated by quarterly, or even monthly, assessments. Most alternative fee arrangements (that are not variations of the billable hour) focus on efficiency and results and present the opportunity for firms and clients to return to relationships founded on trust and fairness.

Alternative Fee Opportunities for Women and Work/Life Balance

Alternative fees also present significant opportunities for women and those working flexible and reduced hours. Women have been largely unsuccessful competing over time. Since 40 percent of women law firm lawyers with children work reduced hours in any one year,[52] these women will be hard pressed to ever achieve the same level of success when the measure of value is simply hours worked. However, with alternative fees, if the measure of value becomes quality of work, efficiency, and results, then women have the opportunity to level the playing field.

Additionally, firms that support flexible and reduced hours stand to benefit from the transition to alternative fees. The link between flexibility and increased productivity has been clearly demonstrated in other industries and should prove to be the same in law. For example, in 2005, the BOLD Initiative, a workplace diversity advocacy organization, found that ten large employers reaped sizeable economic gains after implementing workplace flexibility programs.[53] The BOLD Initiative arranged pilot projects for companies including the Chubb Corporation; Gannett Company, Inc.; Johnson & Johnson Services, Inc.; PepsiCo Inc.; Macy's Northwest; and Prudential Financial, Inc., among others. The pilot projects yielded compelling findings. Programs such as telecommuting, flex-time, and compressed workweeks resulted in decreased overtime, fewer unscheduled absences, increased productivity, and more efficient work processes. Each employer increased productivity by 5–10 percent.[54] Thus, lawyers working flexible and reduced hours will likely be even more profitable to firms adopting alternative fees.

Changes in Legal Staffing

Use of Temporary Attorneys

Another change to the large law firm model is the disaggregation and unbundling of legal services. As discussed in Chapter 2, much of the work previously performed by junior associates will be outsourced to India and elsewhere.[55] Some firms have resisted the pressure to work with Legal Process Outsourcing (LPO) firms while others have embraced them.

In London, large firms are now considering using temporary attorneys. Leading London firms convened in late 2009 to discuss bringing in contract lawyers to do discrete projects through a service called ItsMyLaw.[56] Under this service, firms hire a prescreened pool of temporary lawyers, similar to a virtual law firm, for particular deals or cases.[57] London firm Berwin Leighton Paisner (BLP) is using a fixed pool of temporary attorneys through a service it created internally called Lawyers on Demand, aimed at clients for an in-house "secondment."[58] Through Lawyers on Demand, a pool of 28 freelance lawyers (only one of whom is a BLP alumna) are vetted and supported by the firm and work with the firm's clients on a contract basis.[59] At a discount, these lawyers handle the more routine work that in-house legal departments do not want to handle internally.[60] BLP benefits by generating revenue from Lawyers on Demand and by retaining existing clients and attracting new ones.[61]

An extension of this model that some large firms may consider is one created by a Canadian energy law boutique, Thackray Burgess, which has 29 partners and no associates.[62] Instead, the firm employs 20 independent contractors called "consultants" who are paid by the hour and choose the number of hours per year they want to work.[63] These consultants pay the firm a fee to cover their overhead costs and a percentage of the hourly rate they charge to clients. They keep the rest themselves.[64]

Other large law firms are contemplating the use of temporary lawyers by turning to their alumni networks. Allen & Overy LLP, for example, has been using alumni on an ad hoc basis but is considering creating a central pool of lawyers to assist on certain projects.[65] The notion of using alumni as a talent pool is not new. In 2006, *The National*

Law Journal reported an increasing trend among law firms to tap their alumni networks as a rich pool of proven talent.[66] Firms have also specifically targeted lawyer mothers who left their firms to become full-time caregivers who may be ready to return or work on a project basis.[67]

Employers that are not already rethinking their staffing model should do so. The use of temporary attorneys is a smart alternative for firms that are less certain of their staffing needs. Creating or turning to a team of pre-vetted attorneys is preferable to ensure quality control.

Shrinking Associate Classes and Increasing Use of Staff and Non-Partnership Attorneys

Due to the disaggregation and unbundling of legal services, among other factors, other staffing needs at large law firms are changing. In an *American Lawyer* survey of the top 200 law firm leaders, 72 percent said they expect their 2010 first-year associate class to be smaller.[68] This is because the traditional "leveraged associate" staffing model used by large law firms, which typically relies on a billing ratio of at least three associates for every partner, is being challenged.[69] The unleveraged model used by many smaller and midsize firms has associate/partner ratios that are more typically one-to-one, with partners more engaged in daily work matters.[70]

With shrinking associate classes, another staffing trend emerging is the increased role of staff attorneys or two tiers of associates, with one a partnership track and one not. These staff or non-partnership attorneys do more routine work for less pay and at lower rates, and they are not on a firm's partnership track.[71] McDermott Will & Emery LLP is one firm that is expanding the staff attorney role because of quality control concerns about outsourcing in the United States or India.[72] Firms also plan to have larger pools of non-lawyer professionals who work at a reduced cost and increase efficiency for the client.[73]

Some firms are developing other creative solutions to combat the trend toward shifting work to LPOs or midsize and regional firms.[74] At Orrick, for example, the firm has created an "insourcing" model in an office in West Virginia, where real estate and hourly labor are less expensive than in urban centers. As of mid-2009, Orrick's West Virginia office housed 175 employees and had plans to increase its staff of non-attorney professionals including project managers, document reviewers, compliance specialists, due diligence specialists, document assemblers, and legal researchers.[75] The firm also announced plans to expand the number of attorneys doing routine legal work who can be paid and billed at lower rates.[76] In April 2010, Wilmer Cutler Pickering Hale and Dorr LLP (Wilmer) announced plans to move its business operations, including finance, human resources, information technology, document review, operations, and practice management to Dayton, Ohio.[77] Other firms are likely to follow.

Levels/Tiers of Associates

Another change to the large law firm staffing model is to create levels or tiers of associates. In 2000, Dickstein Shapiro LLP was the first firm to publicly establish levels[78] and in 2001, Blackwell Sanders Peper Martin LLP (now Husch Blackwell LLP) created four associate levels and built the foundation for the level system in law firms by later memorializing its system in a book.[79] Other firms have followed suit after Orrick and Howrey publicly changed their ways. The level system replaces lock-step associate promotion with typically three or four tiers of associates within its partner track.[80] At Orrick, associates will advance through the stages of associate, managing associate, and senior associate at their own pace, and compensation will be based on merit.[81] In addition to the staff attorneys in West Virginia (called "career attorneys"),[82] Orrick has created a "custom track" for lawyers who have outstanding skills but who do not aspire to partnership or who seek a less traditional path.[83]

Firms that provide levels or tiers of associates have more flexibility in channeling motivation, promotion, and compensation and in identifying and investing in "partner potential" associates at hiring.[84] They also have more staffing alternatives so that savings and efficiencies can be passed on to clients.[85] At Howrey, for example, the firm hires about 20 partner-track associates who undergo intensive training.[86] The firm also hires a second tier of non-partner-track lawyers, called "specialty lawyers," who handle lower-level assignments and work fewer hours.[87] The level system will be more fully discussed in Chapter 4.

Temporary, Staff, and Non-Partnership Track Attorney Work: The Impact on Women

The increased need for temporary, staff, and non-partnership track attorney work presents both risks and opportunities for women attorneys. Nearly one-third of women lawyers leave law firm practice[88] and many become full-time caregivers because of, among other reasons, the difficulties in managing a career with erratic hours and demands. But with an increased temporary, staff, and non-partnership attorney presence, these women may be more inclined to stay. As I wrote back in 2007, "Some lawyers are willing to make sacrifices in their quality of work in exchange for more control over their schedules. Firms, in turn, often have certain work that is more predictable, but perhaps less high profile or exciting."[89] This is what I call Fixed Hours work, which is more fully explored in Chapter 9. "This work has historically been assigned to contract attorneys. It is not always available, and therefore may be offered on a temporary basis."[90]

If talented lawyers announce their plans to leave because of practice demands, temporary, staff, and non-partnership attorney positions should be offered as an alternative. Additionally, employers should recognize that if they can hire at-home mothers to do temporary work on an hourly basis, they will benefit. These lawyers will be more engaged in the work because of the lifestyle it offers them for the period of time that their kids are young. In turn, employers will benefit from having a stable pool of reliable workers rather than transitory lawyers looking toward their next move.

With the increased role of staff and non-partnership attorneys, there is a significant risk that more women will be "mommy tracked" and fewer will pursue the challenging alternative. The risk stems from the fact that generally, two groups of attorneys pursue the staff and non-partnership attorney path. One group of these attorneys is not as well credentialed or otherwise would not be hired for or cannot manage the higher paid, partnership track work. The other group of attorneys who pursue these roles are high-caliber lawyers who are seeking the less challenging work because it is more predictable and consistent with their lifestyle needs. This second group of lawyers is often women who work flexible or reduced hours in the staff or non-partnership attorney role.

The bottom line is that many women have left the workforce entirely or have left law firms. If we provide women with another opportunity to remain engaged in the profession, these alternative positions should better serve them in the long run as long as certain cautionary measures are taken. In other words, it is better that women continue practicing law in a less challenging capacity than leave the profession entirely—as long as the overall representation of women in the profession increases, including the representation of women at the top.

There are critical safeguards law firms should implement to minimize the risk that the increased role of staff and non-partnership attorneys will be detrimental to women. These include the following:

1. *Track All Levels of Female Representation*: The representation rates of women at all levels of seniority needs to be tracked annually. The objective is to increase representation of women at the equity partner level and overall. In other words, the increased role of staff and non-partnership attorneys will only be beneficial if it results in more women staying in the profession overall *and* more women being represented at the highest level.
2. *Create an On-Ramp for Talented Attorneys to Return to Partnership Track*: Law firms need to recognize that some lawyers seek staff or non-partnership track work only temporarily during a certain life stage. Those staff or non-partnership attorneys capable of doing the more sophisticated, higher-paid work (often with irregular hours) should be given the opportunity to resume doing so if the business needs exist.[91] At some firms, it may be appropriate to separately label the non-partnership attorneys who are capable of doing the more sophisticated, higher-paid work but who have sought the less challenging and predictable work for lifestyle reasons. These high-caliber lawyers can be called "Fixed hour attorneys" rather than staff attorneys. The term "Fixed" suggests the predictability that this high-caliber talent is seeking and also separates this group of attorneys from those who do not have the capacity to do partnership-level work. If firms separately label these two groups of non-partnership track attorneys, attention must be paid not to degrade those attorneys who are in the permanent staff attorney role.
3. *Educate to Inform and Avoid Stereotyping*: Firm lawyers need to be educated about the different career paths that are available to them, what each path entails, and what are the risks and tradeoffs of electing the different career paths. Law firms must be vigilant that women are not being disproportionately steered into the staff and non-partnership attorney positions. Firms must also guard against assumptions that all women or all mothers belong in these positions. The message must be clear that many women with and without children will seek the highly challenging and higher-paid work that is often accompanied by more irregular hours. Additionally, the option for high-level talent to pursue staff or non-partnership attorney work should be available to men and women for reasons in addition to parenting.

Compensation

Over the past 10 to 15 years, there has been a growing pay gap between large law firms and the rest of the profession. Starting pay used to be distributed similar to a bell curve but it transitioned into a "double-peaked" distribution in 2000, as large firms gradually increased starting salaries while lower salaries remained relatively the same.[92] From 1997 to 2007, median starting salary at the largest law firms doubled from $80,000 to $160,000, plus bonus.[93] A survey of starting associate salaries for 2008 law graduates showed a clustering of salaries in the $40,000 to $65,000 range and then a dramatic spike at $160,000 for large law firms, with relatively few attorneys falling in between these two ranges.[94]

Rising compensation appears to be disappearing as a result of the recession, like other bygone practices. The factors that are driving the decline in associate compensation include clients' resistance to rate hikes, a decreased demand for legal services, and an increase in contract lawyers, LPOs, and virtual law firms.[95] As Venable managing partner Karl Racine put it: "With associate salaries, there is no doubt there is a correction taking place."[96] According to a 2009 *American Lawyer* survey of the top 200 law firms, 40 percent of the firms had reduced associate starting pay and another 44 percent were considering cuts for 2010.[97] While some Wall Street firms have not reduced salary by the typical $15,000 to $30,000, their associates still felt the impact in their bonuses, which in 2009 were about 25 percent of what they were in 2007.[98] Regardless of whether firms abandon lockstep compensation, it seems that compensation among most associates in the United States will decline. It remains to be seen, however, whether UK firms will follow the United States' downward compensation trend. Linklaters, a firm considered a trendsetter for the London market, announced in March 2010 that it is keeping its lockstep compensation and avoiding pay freezes for its associates.[99]

As of February 2010, almost 30 Am Law 200 firms (America's 200 top grossing firms, according to a law firm ranking by *The American Lawyer*) abandoned lockstep in favor of a merit-based system.[100] The new structure being established by nearly all of the firms has three tiers, with bonuses, raises, and promotions tied to annual evaluations.[101]

Two firms that have been public about their new pay structures are Orrick and Howrey. Salaries for Orrick's first tier, called "associates," start at $160,000 for its larger city offices including New York, Los Angeles,

San Francisco, Orange County, and Washington, D.C., with $145,000 as the base for the Pacific Northwest and Sacramento.[102] In the larger markets, $185,000 is the base salary for the second tier, called "managing associates," with $170,000 for the smaller markets.[103] For the third tier, called "senior associates," the base salary is $235,000 in the larger markets and $215,000 in the smaller ones.[104] Bonuses will be determined by the competitive market rate, with top associates at each tier earning bonuses from 5 to 15 percent,[105] with a likely cap at $250,000.[106] For those seeking Orrick's non-partnership track new associate role, the salaries start at $80,000.[107] At Howrey, the Firm has put two different pay structures in place for its partner-track and non-partner-track associates. The partner-track associates who undergo extensive training in their first year start at $125,000.[108] The non-partner track "specialty lawyers" who handle lower-level assignments and work fewer hours start at $80,000.[109]

In terms of future compensation for associates, the picture is not entirely bleak. Top associate talent may earn more than associates do today.[110] Many think the issue is not that all associates are overpaid, just that many are.[111] Wilmer, for example, moved from lockstep to a level system and plans to pay top performers at each level more than they made under the former lockstep system.[112]

If compensation declines for most associates, there will likely be other accompanying trends. Perhaps the long hours will go by the wayside with the high compensation.[113] It also may result in fewer graduating law students taking top law firm jobs as a means to repay their law school debt. These lawyers entering the profession may have the opportunity to choose work that is more closely aligned to their interests[114] or pursue midsize or regional firms where the pay gap with large law firms may be shrinking.

Changes in Recruiting

As large law firms change staffing, the recruiting process will become another ripe area for a market correction. Recruiting changes have been discussed widely since the economic downturn began in 2008 and even before. The recruiting problems start with the unrealistic premise that a legal employer should be able to accurately predict its hiring needs two years before a lawyer's start date. The problems are compounded by the fact that the leveraged associate pyramid model at law firms relies on the attrition of most of the associates hired.

The result is that law firms plan to shrink the number of law students hired to fill summer and first-year associate classes. A handful of firms took a stark approach and canceled on-campus interviewing in the fall of 2009 and their 2010 summer associate programs.[115] Most other firms shrunk the sizes of their summer associate classes, hoping they could reduce attrition by being more effective at screening applicants.[116] William Henderson anticipates this rigorous screening will take the shape of "behavioral interviews, psychometric tests, and parsing of résumés in search of non-academic indicators associated, at statistically significant levels, with long-term success within particular law firms."[117] The goal at many firms now is to cut the incoming class in half and expect a higher percentage of the class to be promoted to partner, rather than expecting only a 10 to 15 percent promotion rate.[118] Executing on this goal will prove challenging if firms do not significantly change their talent management system, as more fully explored in Chapter 4.

Contemplating Outside Investors

One more change that could revolutionize the future of large law firms is to bring outside investors into law firms. This change is already under way in England and Australia, and regulations may change in the United States to allow it. "Focusing on share price rather than individual productivity measured by hourly output and profits per partner could lead outside investors to make greater investments in law firms. The result might be very different service delivery, billing and compensation systems, minimizing individual performance and maximizing team, practice and firm performance."[119]

Ultimate Challenge Facing Large Law Firms: Determining Value

With all of the challenges facing large law firms, one theme is consistent throughout: the challenge of measuring value. This challenge resonates in three ways.

1. Measuring the value of a case or matter is a challenge that makes alternative fee arrangements hard to effect. Firms and clients need measures to assess the value of a representation. Neither side wants to incur more than its fair share of risk.

2. Measuring the value and profitability of a law firm is another challenge. Firms are looking for new metrics and may move away from profits per equity partner as a defining measure to assess performance.[120] It is uncertain whether firms will develop varying metrics to measure profitability or if a new standard for all firms will evolve. If the measure moves away from profits per equity partner, then it is likely that the partnership structure itself will change. With all of the structural shifts being discussed regarding large law firms, there is an unusual silence about the future of law firm partners. Partner roles will inevitably need to evolve given all of the expected changes with law firm associates.
3. Measuring the value of associates for promotion purposes is a third challenge as firms move away from lockstep promotion and compensation. This is made more difficult by the use of blended methods. For example, if 30 percent of a firm's revenue is earned from alternative fees and the rest from billable hours, does that confuse the evaluation process? How much should billable hours be considered in evaluating associates, if at all? As firms transition from lockstep to competency-based evaluations, this concern may diminish. However, the challenge of assessing a lawyer's value based on a measure other than time will remain. This last issue will be explored in the next chapter.

One thing is clear: as large law firms face the obstacles of today, they should look closely at the new models emerging around them. These new-model firms have been built on the inefficiencies and imperfections of traditional law firms and the failures of the billable-hour model. In turn, traditional firms can improve their productivity and profitability through close examination and lessons learned from their alternatives.

Notes

1. Ross Todd, *Law Leaders: Crunch Won't Cause Legal Revolution*, LegalWeek, May 13, 2009, *available at* http://www.legalweek.com/legal-week/news/1171379/law-leaders-crunch-won-cause-legal-revolution.

2. Sheri Qualters, *Outside Counsel Spending Projected to Drop by 4.3 Percent Next Year*, NAT'L L.J., Oct. 9, 2009, *available at* http://www.law.com/jsp/article.jsp?id=1202434410545.

3. Aric Press, *Legal Professionals Role-Play the Future of Big Law*, AM. LAW., Apr. 21, 2009, *available at* http://www.law.com/jsp/article.jsp?id=1202430052156.

4. *Id.*

5. AM. BAR ASS'N, ABA COMMISSION ON BILLABLE HOURS REPORT 2001–2002 (2002), *available at* http://www.abanet.org/careercounsel/billable/toolkit/bhcomplete.pdf [hereinafter ABA COMMISSION REPORT].

6. Eric Young, *More Bay Area Firms Adopt Creative Legal Fees*, S.F. BUS. TIMES, Jan. 1–7, 2010, *available at* http://sanfrancisco.bizjournals.com/sanfrancisco/stories/2010/01/04/story10.html.

7. Emily Heller, *Squeeze Play*, GC CAL. MAG., June 12, 2009, *available at* http://www.virtuallawpartners.com/pdf/Squeeze_Play.pdf.

8. Leslie A. Gordon, *Economic Pressure May Force Permanent Shift in Corporate Legal Costs*, GC CAL. MAG., Apr. 16, 2009, *available at* http://www.law.com/jsp/cc/PubArticleCC.jsp?id=1202429931212.

9. *Id.*

10. Young, *supra* note 6.

11. http://www.acc.com/valuechallenge/.

12. Young, *supra* note 6.

13. Zusha Elinson, *Are Big Firms Warming Up to Alternative Fee Deals?*, RECORDER, July 11, 2007, *available at* http://www.law.com/jsp/article.jsp?id=1184058401567.

14. D.M. Levine, *Where Do We Go from Here?*, AMLAW DAILY, Dec. 4, 2009, *available at* http://amlawdaily.typepad.com/amlawdaily/2009/12/where-do-we-go-from-here.html.

15. Amanda Royal, *Alternative Is the New Mainstream*, RECORDER, Nov. 23, 2009, *available at* http://reaction.orrick.com/reaction/MorningReport/NewsAlert/2009/Leviarticle.pdf.

16. Young, *supra* note 6.

17. Richard J. Rawson, et al., *Fee Arrangements*, *in* Successful Partnering Between Inside and Outside Counsel, 8-1–8-77 (Robert L. Haig ed., 2000).

18. Alan G. Badey, *The Alternative Billing Debate Continues*, N.Y.L.J. (2009).

19. Ben W. Heineman Jr. & William F. Lee, *Two Veteran Lawyers Say Now Is the Time for Fixed Fees*, Corp. Couns., Aug. 24, 2009, *available at* http://www.law.com/jsp/cc/PubArticleFriendlyCC.jsp?id=1202433261281.

20. *Id.*

21. David Gialanella, *Taming the Billable Beast*, A.B.A.J., Feb. 1, 2008, *available at* http://www.abajournal.com/magazine/article/taming_the_billable_beast/.

22. Badey, *supra* note 18.

23. Jeanne Graham, *Alternative Billing Increasingly Important for Texas Firms, Survey Shows*, Tex. Law., July 1, 2009, *available at* http://www.law.com/jsp/law/sfb/lawArticleSFB.jsp?id=1202431903623.

24. Heineman & Lee, *supra* note 19.

25. Badey, *supra* note 18.

26. Evan R. Chesler, *Kill the Billable Hour*, Forbes, Jan. 2009, *available at* http://www.forbes.com/forbes/2009/0112/026.html.

27. Debra Cassens Weiss, *Levi's Is Paying Orrick a Flat Fee to Handle All But Its IP Work*, A.B.A.J., Nov. 23, 2009, *available at* http://www.abajournal.com/news/article/levis_is_paying_orrick_a_flat_fee_to_handle_all_but_its_ip_work/.

28. Badey, *supra* note 18.

29. Chesler, *supra* note 26.

30. Rawson, et al., *supra* note 17, at 8-24.

31. Heineman & Lee, *supra* note 19.

32. Rawson, et al., *supra* note 17, at 8-17. A retainer, as described here, is the same as the subscription pricing described in the prior chapter. Note that the term "retainer" can also be used to refer to an up-front payment made by a client to assure payment (rather than as an alternative fee arrangement). *Id.*

33. *Id.*

34. *Id.*

35. ABA Commission Report, *supra* note 5, at 18.

36. Rawson, et al., *supra* note 17, at 8-18.

37. Graham, *supra* note 23.

38. Rachel M. Zahorsky, *Majority Say Law Practice Is Undergoing a Sweeping Evolution, Survey Says*, A.B.A.J., Mar. 26, 2010, *available at* http://www.abajournal.com/news/article/majority_say_law_practice_is_undergoing_a_sweeping_evolution_survey_says/.

39. ABA Commission Report, *supra* note 5, at 17.
40. Badey, *supra* note 18.
41. *Id.*
42. ABA Commission Report, *supra* note 5, at 17.
43. Rawson, et al., *supra* note 17, at 8-15.
44. ABA Commission Report, *supra* note 5, at 17.
45. Rawson, et al., *supra* note 17, at 8-14.
46. *Id.* at 8-15–8-16.
47. *Id.* at 8-16.
48. *Id.* at 8-14.
49. *Id.*
50. ABA Commission Report, *supra* note 5, at 18.
51. Graham, *supra* note 23.
52. Mona Harrington & Helen Hsi, *Women Lawyers and Obstacles to Leadership*, *in* A Report of MIT Workplace Center Surveys on Comparative Career Decisions and Attrition Rates of Women and Men in Massachusetts Law Firms 32 (2007), *available at* http://web.mit.edu/workplacecenter/docs/law-report_4-07.pdf.
53. Leah Carlson, *Flexibility Proves Profitable for Large Firms*, Emp. Benefit News, Sept. 15, 2005, *available at* http://www.allbusiness.com/labor-employment/working-hours-patterns-flextime/8008526-1.html.
54. *Id.* The Chubb Corporation also experienced a 50 percent reduction in unscheduled absences and a 40 percent decrease in overtime hours per employee at a claims service center. *Id.*
55. David Lat & Elie Mystal, *The New Biglaw Business Model, According to O'Melveny & Myers*, Above the Law, Sept. 16, 2009, *available at* http://abovethelaw.com/2009/09/the-new-biglaw-business-model-according-to-omelveny-myers/.
56. Claire Ruckin, *Leading City Firms in Talks to Bring in Teams of Contract Lawyers*, Legal Week, Oct. 29, 2009, *available at* http://www.legalweek.com/legal-week/news/1560094/leading-city-firms-talks-bring-teams.
57. *Id.*
58. Neil Rose, *How Virtual Lawyers Are Weathering the Recession*, Times (London), July 30, 2009, *available at* http://business.timesonline.co.uk/tol/business/law/article6731082.ece.
59. *Id.*
60. *Id.*

61. *Id.*

62. Jordan Furlong, *The Disappearing Associate*, LAW21.CA, Feb. 13, 2009, *available at* http://www.law21.ca/2009/02/13/the-disappearing-associate/.

63. *Id.*

64. *Id.*

65. Ruckin, *supra* note 56.

66. Leigh Jones, *A Promising Talent Pool: Alumni*, NAT'L L.J., Oct. 16, 2006.

67. *Id.*

68. Debra Cassens Weiss, *40% of Firms Cut Starting Associate Pay, While 44% Consider 2010 Cut*, A.B.A.J., Dec. 1, 2009, *available at* http://www.abajournal.com/news/article/40_of_firms_cut_starting_pay_for_associates_while_44_consider_2010_cut/.

69. David A. Scherl, *Leverage and Rates*, N.Y.L.J., 2009, *available at* http://www.morrisoncohen.com/downloads/NYJL%20Report%20Mid%20Size%20Firms.pdf; *see also* Dan Slater, *At Law Firms, Reconsidering the Model for Associates' Pay*, THE NEW YORK TIMES, Apr. 1, 2010, *available at* http://www.nytimes.com/2010/04/01/business/01LEGAL.html; Debra Cassens Weiss, "*O'Melveny Aims to Become Fixed-Fee Leader, Leaked Plan Says*," A.B.A.J., Sept. 17, 2009, *available at* http://www.abajournal.com/news/article/omelveny_aims_to_become_fixed-fee_leader_leaked_plan_says/.

70. Scherl, *supra* note 69.

71. Amanda Royal, *Orrick Breaks Lockstep in Response to Clients' Cost Concerns*, RECORDER, July 2, 2009, *available at* http://www.law.com/jsp/article.jsp?id=1202431956146&rss=newswire; Lynne Marek, *DLA Piper Plans to Keep Reducing Associate Classes, Discard Lockstep System*, NAT'L L.J., June 25, 2009, *available at* http://www.law.com/jsp/article.jsp?id=1202431748925.

72. Royal, *supra* note 71.

73. Marek, *supra* note 71.

74. Zach Lowe, *This Isn't the End of Big Law Firm Associates*, AMLAW DAILY, Mar. 10, 2010, *available at* http://amlawdaily.typepad.com/amlawdaily/2010/03/clobiglawassociates.html. The idea of using lawyers outside of New York, Washington, D.C., and other big cities is gaining momentum. *Id.*

75. Jill Redhage, *Orrick Shakes Up Big-Firm Staffing Model*, Daily J., July 2, 2009.

76. *Id.*

77. Debra Cassens Weiss, *WilmerHale Plans Business Center in Ohio*, A.B.A.J., Apr. 27, 2010, *available at* http://www.abajournal.com/news/article/wilmerhale_plans_business_center_in_ohio/.

78. *Dickstein Shapiro Morin & Oshinsky LLP Reinvents Associate Development and Compensation System*, in Dickstein Shapiro Morin & Oshinsky LLP News Release, Apr. 3, 2000.

79. Peter B. Sloan, From Classes to Competencies, Lockstep to Levels (2007 ed.).

80. Royal, *supra* note 71.

81. Redhage, *supra* note 75.

82. Royal, *supra* note 71.

83. *Id.*

84. Dan Slater, *At Law Firms, Reconsidering the Model for Associates' Pay*, N.Y. Times, Apr. 1, 2010, *available at* http://www.nytimes.com/2010/04/01/business/01LEGAL.html.

85. Royal, *supra* note 71.

86. Slater, *supra* note 84.

87. *Id.*

88. Harrington & Hsi, *supra* note 52, at 8.

89. Deborah Epstein Henry, *Facing the FACTS: Introducing Work/Life Choices for All Firm Lawyers Within the Billable Hour Model*, Diversity & the Bar, Nov./Dec., 2007, *available at* http://www.flextimelawyers.com/pdf/art10.pdf.

90. *Id.*

91. *Id.*

92. Karen Sloan, *Study Shows Sharp Disparities in Law Associate Compensation*, Nat'l L.J., June 29, 2009, *available at* http://www.law.com/jsp/nlj/PubArticleNLJ.jsp?id=1202431876322&Study_shows_sharp_disparities_in_law_associate_compensation.

93. Slater, *supra* note 84.

94. Sloan, *supra* note 92 (citing National Association for Law Placement survey).

95. Debra Cassens Weiss, *Associate Pay May Need to Return to 1998 Levels, Consultant Says*, A.B.A.J., Nov. 5, 2009, *available at* http://www

.abajournal.com/news/article/associate_pay_may_need_to_return_to_1998_levels_consultant_says/.

96. Weiss, *supra* note 68 (citing *The American Lawyer*); *see also* Julie Triedman, *Associate Pay Cuts Here to Stay, Say Firms, Analysts*, AmLaw Daily, Dec. 10, 2009, *available at* http://amlawdaily.typepad.com/amlawdaily/2009/12/associate-compensation-cuts-not-temporary-say-firms-analysts.html (quoting Steven Davis, chairman of Dewey & LeBoeuf, saying: "'In the medium term, we're seeing, and will continue to see, a paradigm shift' in associate compensation.")

97. Weiss, *supra* note 68.

98. Triedman, *supra* note 96.

99. Zach Lowe, *Linklaters Back to Full Lockstep*, AmLaw Daily, Mar. 31, 2010, *available at* http://amlawdaily.typepad.com/amlawdaily/2010/03/linklaters-lockstep.html.

100. Julie Triedman, *Are Merit-Based Pay Switchovers Simply Hidden Salary Cuts?*, Am. Law., Feb. 18, 2010, *available at* http://www.law.com/jsp/article.jsp?id=1202443769098.

101. *Id.*

102. Sarah Randag, *Orrick Reveals New Associate Pay Structure*, A.B.A.J., Dec. 3, 2009, *available at* http://www.abajournal.com/news/article/orrick_reveals_new_associate_pay_structure/.

103. *Id.*

104. *Id.*

105. *Id.*

106. Triedman, *supra* note 100.

107. *Id.*

108. Slater, *supra* note 84.

109. *Id.*

110. *Id.*

111. *Id.*

112. Zach Lowe, *Wilmer Freezes Salaries, Breaks Lockstep*, AmLaw Daily, Dec. 15, 2009, *available at* http://amlawdaily.typepad.com/amlawdaily/2009/12/salaries.html.

113. Adam Cohen, *With the Downturn, It's Time to Rethink the Legal Profession*, N.Y. Times, Apr. 1, 2009, *available at* http://www.nytimes.com/2009/04/02/opinion/02thu4.html.

114. *Id.*

115. See, e.g., Rachel Breitman, *Morgan Lewis Cuts 2010 Summer Program*, NAT'L L.J., July 20, 2009, *available at* http://www.law.com/jsp/nlj/PubArticleNLJ.jsp?id=1202432352838; Debra Cassens Weiss, *Triple Bad News for Law Students: Three Firms Ax Summer Associate Programs*, A.B.A.J., July 20, 2009, *available at* http://www.abajournal.com/news/article/triple_bad_news_for_law_students_three_firms_ax_summer_associate_programs.

116. Lisa Smith, *Report from Law Firm Leaders Forum—Change Is the Name of the Game*, Hildebrandt blog, Mar. 12, 2010, *available at* http://www.hildebrandt.com/blog/archive/2010/03/12/change-is-the-name-of-the-game.aspx; *see also* Jeff Jeffrey, *Howrey Introduces Apprenticeship Program for Associates*, NAT'L L.J., June 22, 2009, *available at* http://www.law.com/jsp/nlj/PubArticleNLJ.jsp?id=1202431654426&rss=nlj242&hbxlogin=1.

117. William D. Henderson, *The Class of 2009: Recession or Restructuring?*, NALP BULLETIN, July 2010, at 22, *available at* http://www.nalp.org/uploads/NALPJuly2010_Henderson.pdf.

118. Smith, *supra* note 116.

119. Joel Henning, *A Broken Business Model, Will It Take a Revolution to Change the Way Law Firms Operate?*, NAT'L L.J., Aug. 17, 2009, *available at* http://www.law.com/jsp/nlj/PubArticleNLJ.jsp?id=1202433025155.

120. Smith, *supra* note 116.

CHAPTER 4

REDESIGNING LAWYERS' CAREER PATHS

In March 2010, I was moderating a Flex-Time Lawyers LLC program and one of the panelists was discussing his firm's new core competency system. A competency (or level) system is one where associates advance through levels of progression by achieving certain defined competencies at each level, rather than receiving annual lockstep promotions based on the passage of time. The panelist's core competency program was similar to the one developed in 2001 by Blackwell Sanders Peper Martin LLP (now Husch Blackwell LLP and referred to herein as Blackwell).[1] *In Blackwell's program, the firm evaluates associates for promotion and future partnership consideration based on four areas of competency: professional competencies, work ethic, interpersonal skills, and client relations.*[2]

Something funny struck me as I listened to the panel discussion and read Peter Sloan's book about Blackwell's system. The core competencies outlined were similar to those that I had been reviewing on my youngest son Theodore's third-grade report card. At Blackwell, the associates were required to graduate through four levels of competencies before being considered for partnership. The third graders were also evaluated on four levels of success in meeting the competency expectations of the school district. The kids' areas of competency to master were work habits and social skills, and the measurement system included four levels: meets expectations all the time, meets expectations most of the time, meets expectations some of the time, and does not meet expectations at this time. Look how similar the competency requirements are for these two groups:

CORE COMPETENCIES	
LAWYERS[3]	**THIRD GRADERS**[4]
PROFESSIONAL COMPETENCIES:	**WORK HABITS:**
Written Communication	Turns in neat, legible work
Oral Communication	Listens attentively
Research and Analytical Ability	Asks for help when necessary
Creativity and Flexibility	Accepts suggestions and learns from mistakes
Judgment	Contributes relevant information to class discussion
Professional Ethics	Follows directions
	Checks own work for accuracy
Crisis Management	Organizes work space and materials
	Shows responsibility for personal belongings
WORK ETHIC:	
Efficiency and Effectiveness	Uses time efficiently
Timeliness	Comes to class prepared
	Completes homework assignments
Initiative, Ambition, Drive	Works independently
	Shows consistent effort
INTERPERSONAL SKILLS:	**SOCIAL SKILLS:**
Teamwork and Cooperation Within the Firm	Works cooperatively with others
	Practices verbal self-control
	Practices physical self-control
Tact and Diplomacy	Participates appropriately
Delegation and Supervision	Respects the rights and opinions of others
	Accepts rules and limits

CLIENT RELATIONS:	
Client Relations	Displays a positive attitude
Client Management	Shows self-confidence
Business Development Activities	

As I identified the parallels between developing lawyers and developing elementary school students, I recognized the true value of the core competency system. It creates a standardized framework to allow associates to identify the skills they need to advance and it gives partners the tools to effectively evaluate and compare associates' progression. Theo's third-grade report card, in the same way, gives my husband Gordon and me, as well as Theo himself, the opportunity to evaluate his skills and identify the areas where he can grow. It also gives Theo's teacher a basis to fairly evaluate him against other students.

The parallel between child and adult development is not new. The best example is the life lessons from Robert Fulghum's book All I Really Need to Know I Learned in Kindergarten.[5] *In this chapter, as we explore the different ways that law firms are training their future talent, keep in mind the importance of both nurturing lawyers and fairly assessing their development as we do our children. Just as children develop differently, so too do lawyers.*

Particularly in light of the recession beginning in 2008, law firms and law schools are rethinking the management of law student and associate talent. Many firms are rolling out core competency merit-based systems and tossing aside the lockstep compensation and promotion systems. Some firms have revamped their associate training model and invested in increased training and reduced salaries for first- and second-year associates. Additionally, law schools are reconsidering their curriculum in terms of what needs to change to meet the demands of today's practice. Through this chapter, we will consider whether changes to talent management processes will improve the development of law students and associates. We will also look at how to properly align employer demands with the strengths of the talent pool.

In realigning employer and talent demands, it is critical to remember that improved talent management is only part of the bigger changes discussed in Chapter 3 that must occur within the law firm infrastructure. As Patricia Gillette, partner at Orrick, Herrington & Sutcliffe

LLP and founder of the Opt-In Project, aptly put it: "The mistake most law firms make as they try to implement structural changes that involve alternative billing arrangements, measuring by core competencies, and merit based compensation is that these issues are interdependent. There is a domino effect. Thus, if you change one aspect of the structure, you must change the others. Without this holistic approach, the structural changes cannot be effective."[6]

Core Competency Programs

Increasingly, law firms are moving away from lockstep compensation and evaluation systems toward merit-based systems of competencies and levels. In a July 2009 survey of The Am Law 100 (America's 100 top-grossing firms, according to a ranking of law firms by *The American Lawyer*) by the Law Firm Group at Citi Private Bank, almost half of the top 50 firms said they planned to switch to a performance-based or merit-based system.[7] In a lockstep system, bonuses and billable rates are largely dictated by the number of hours logged by the associate and the number of years out of law school. Instead, by focusing on skills and experience gained at each level of progression, comprehensive level systems would create core competencies and performance expectations.

Most firms creating level systems are dividing associates into three or four levels.[8] The groupings and numbers of competencies vary by firm but the concept is the same. For example, Blackwell's framework evaluates associates at four levels of competency to determine if they are partner eligible. The firm identified 16 core competency areas that apply across all areas of practice.[9] For each of the 16 competencies, the firm outlined definitions and articulated specific expectations of an associate at each of the four levels.[10] Also, each department and practice area developed a skills list, tied to the four levels outlining practice area expectations.[11]

Training, Evaluations, and Promotions

The ultimate goal of a level system is to revamp associate evaluations, training, advancement, compensation, and billing rates.[12] Developing an effective level system is time consuming. It requires partner support and buy-in and is not a system that staff can implement singlehandedly. Ideally, a core competency model is better than a lockstep system. "[I]t requires the firm to be clear about its expectations for its lawyers, to provide them with feedback on their progress and to link their compensation to their contributions . . . ."[13]

In implementing a core competency system, most firms conduct evaluations once or twice a year. To ensure fairness, law firms must distribute work assignments equitably, and effectively evaluate and measure associate performance.[14]

> When faced with the issue of assigning work fairly, the focus should not only be on giving equal opportunities to associates so they can attain the requisite competencies. A fair assignment system should also give associates equal access to working with influential partners and clients. Without equal access to assignments and influential lawyers, there will not be equal access to promotions.

Perception is a critical component in an effective core competency program. Core competencies cannot be perceived by associates as a cover for reducing compensation, increasing hours, and getting rid of associates, even if these events may occur.[15] For a level system to be effective, lawyers must believe that they have been evaluated fairly. Their pay and seniority depend upon it.[16] With lockstep, pay is predictable. But with a merit system, firms are veering from predictability in pay and, therefore, compensation decisions must be clearly justified.

Firms adopting core competencies must train associates to achieve each level of competency. Training should be linked to the outlined competencies.[17] At some firms, business skills training, including management, is part of the curriculum. At Reed Smith LLP, for example, the firm plans to have associates take business courses and learn about the quantitative and accounting side of business at the junior level; matter management, client development, and strategic aspects of business would be stressed at the senior level.[18]

Other firms are bringing in outside consultants to train attorneys in project management[19] and they are reporting that project management is improving the bottom line.[20] Project management includes "legal work breakdown and process mapping; start-up and initiation; defining project scope and requirements; project activity planning and resource allocation; project tracking, control and review; and after action review and assessment."[21] Project management also includes developing communication protocols and feedback loops to ensure effective communication with the client.[22]

Compensation

Most firms adopting a levels system create compensation bands at each level that often vary in a firm's different city offices. At Blackwell, compensation was set on a trajectory from entry level toward the new partner base and the firm created the most meaningful pay increases between each level.[23] For Blackwell associates who spend more than one year at a given level, there may be compensation increases within levels, too, although these are not uniform.[24] At some firms, there is one established base pay at each level with no pay increases within a level, even if a lawyer is not promoted to the next level. At some firms like Wilmer Cutler Pickering Hale and Dorr LLP, pay will vary considerably within tiers based on individual bonuses, and a larger percentage of each lawyer's compensation will be based on an annual performance bonus.[25]

What law firms have not decided yet is how billable hours will be factored into an evaluation based on competencies. Under a true core competency evaluation system, compensation should not be billable hour dependent. Competencies and successes achieved, rather than hours logged, should determine compensation. In reality, firms are still using billable hours as part of associates' assessments. However, particularly if firms move away from billable hours and toward alternative fees, there is no basis to consider hours worked as part of the evaluation and compensation process.

For firms that transition to a core competency system, it remains to be seen whether clusters of firms at each prestige level will match starting salaries with their peer firms. For the time being, firms with new core competencies will likely stick with the copycat model and measure up with competitors, at least at the entry level. Recent indications reflect that continued trend.

Billing Rates

The largest impetus for firms to transition to a core competency system is client pressure. Clients who have pushed back on billing rates feel reassured to see associate billing rates matching their level and contribution.[26] Blackwell is one example where the firm determined that billing rates would be directly tied to an associate's level status.[27] The firm adopted four tiers of associate billing rates linked to levels and a fifth tier for new attorneys who were hired prior to receiving their license.[28] Some firms have more than one billing rate per level while other firms, like Blackwell, have only one billing rate per level. A clear benefit to linking billing rates, associate level, and compensation is that incentives become aligned between the associate and the firm. If a firm invests in its associates and facilitates their promotion, the firm generates more revenue by being able to charge higher rates for its associates at higher levels.[29]

Elimination of Bias

Effective core competency systems must be managed by someone who can ensure the synchronicity of the recruiting, training, evaluation, promotion, compensation, and billing processes.[30] It may be appropriate at some firms for this "point person" to be a partner or a professional development person. The key is that it is part, if not all, of the point person's job responsibilities to manage the core competency process.

Merit-based systems must be unbiased so that women, people of color, and reduced-hour lawyers are not negatively impacted. The evaluation system should not be—or be perceived as being—discriminatory. Under the lockstep promotion model, 28 percent of white women and 14 percent of women of color, but less than 3 percent of white men, reported being denied promotion opportunities due to gender.[31]

Establishing a bias-free core competency system requires an outlining of competencies clearly and specifically.[32] As developed in the American Bar Association Commission on Women in the Profession report, *Fair Measure*, the system should have a standardized performance evaluation form that outlines performance criteria, includes a rating scale to compare attorneys' performance to the criteria, and provides a narrative space for comments on behavior and performance.[33] *Fair Measure* emphasizes that attorneys performing evaluations should be trained in the evaluation process and, before the evaluations are shared, an independent reviewer should review the evaluations to look for trends across the firm, practice groups, or supervising attorneys and identify and eliminate any bias in the evaluations.[34] Tracking the retention and promotion trends of all lawyers, paying particular attention to the progress of women, people of color, and reduced-hour lawyers, is also important.[35] Specifically tracking the progression of women, people of color, and reduced-hour lawyers, as compared to their promotion rates under the prior lockstep system, will shed light on whether the merit system will have a less discriminatory effect.

Impact on Women

One of the significant problems with lockstep promotion and compensation has been the underutilization of women lawyers. Under the core competency system, these concerns remain. Some believe the lockstep system was an objective way to ensure that base level pay for associates was fair, while the core competency system will rely on subjective factors outside of an associate's control, including what matters you are staffed on or with which lawyers you work. But there are also real opportunities for women to thrive. A well-structured merit system delineates the competencies and criteria under which associates will be evaluated at each level. It gives associates a road map of what they must achieve to graduate to the next level and provides supervisory lawyers the guidelines necessary to evaluate and compare associate skills and development. A well-designed competency system should also have a clear method for doling out assignments fairly. If these steps are put into place, it should minimize the risk of women associates not gaining equal access to staffing and promotion.

All lawyers stand to benefit from the clear articulation of expectations and benchmarks created in a core competency system. Women and people of color, in particular, have the opportunity to thrive under the new system. Under the lockstep system, women and people of color have often been excluded from networks and mentoring[36] that would have facilitated their promotion. While core competency systems cannot replace the value of mentors and networks in supporting junior lawyers and familiarizing them with the unwritten rules of practice, women and people of color still stand to benefit from the clarity of the criteria to advance.

Additionally, detailed core competencies that are properly implemented may reduce the subjectivity often associated with attorney evaluations. With benchmarks and criteria outlined, there is more accountability for evaluating attorneys. That should create more objectivity in the evaluation process.

Women also stand to benefit from some of the criteria identified in core competency systems because they encompass areas where many women naturally flourish, including interpersonal skills, teamwork, cooperation, tact, diplomacy, delegation, and supervision.[37] At Blackwell, women thrived under the core competency model. The firm had about the same number of female and male associates and more than half of the associates with the highest evaluation results and rates of promotion were women.[38] Additionally, attrition dropped after the model was implemented in January 2001. In 2002, attrition was 26 percent; five years later, in 2006, attrition was 11 percent (roughly half the national rate).[39] This bodes well for all lawyers but in particular women and people of color, as they have been the groups with higher attrition rates.

Impact on Reduced-Hour Lawyers

Core competency programs have been recognized for their flexibility. Lawyers can advance at their own rate, in line with their own skill.[40] In the lockstep system, reduced-hour lawyers face the stigma of being put in a separate category and marginalized. If firms allow reduced-hour lawyers to excel at their own rate in the core competency system, that should minimize the stigma, even if these lawyers advance at a slower pace.

However, with the flexibility and opportunities come identifiable risks for lawyers seeking work/life balance who want to remain on partnership track in a core competency program. These include:

Compensation: In some core competency systems, lawyers within each level have the same base pay. If an associate is working a 60 percent schedule at a firm that does not award pay raises within a level, then that reduced-hour associate would not be awarded a pay raise if he or she stays at the same level during any one year. At other firms, lawyers may receive incremental pay raises within each level if they show improved competency but not enough to move to the next level. If associates within a level are eligible for pay raises, a reduced-hour lawyer should be similarly eligible. Lawyers working reduced hours may stay within a level for a longer period of time than their full-time counterparts who are working more hours.

The objective for reduced-hour lawyer compensation is fairness, not preferential treatment. If competencies and successes achieved, rather than billable hours, determine compensation, then a pro rata adjustment need not be made for reduced-hour lawyers for compensation purposes. Instead, those lawyers should be evaluated based on the competencies they have achieved, just as full-time lawyers would be considered. The same would hold true for bonus eligibility. At firms where billable hours are still being used to determine compensation, then a pro rata adjustment should be made for reduced-hour lawyers. If full-time lawyers work in excess of their hours and, at years' end, they are paid a bonus or they are paid for the actual hours they bill, then reduced-hour lawyers should similarly be paid a bonus or for the additional hours they bill. If full-time lawyers are paid for origination credit and/or on an ongoing basis for new clients, then reduced-hour lawyers should also be paid for origination credit and/or on an ongoing basis with no discount applied. Whichever system a firm adopts, the key is that reduced-hour lawyers are compensated based on the same system as full-time lawyers. For additional issues impacting reduced-hour lawyer compensation, see Chapter 8.

Accountability: Successful core competency programs have a "point person" charged with overseeing the program's success. As part of the point person's responsibilities, he or she should ensure that the associates working reduced hours are:

1. Given equivalent assignments and opportunities to meet their competencies;
2. Staffed on high-profile matters with influential partners and clients; and
3. Not being overtaxed with more than their fair share of work.

Contribution: If reduced-hour lawyers are staffed on high-profile matters, compensated commensurate with their contributions, and eligible for promotion within the core competency system, they should also be contributing to their firms in non-client work. This may involve doing business development, article writing, recruiting, or getting involved in other initiatives to help the firm's visibility and development. This non-client work contribution should be proportionate to the reduced-hours schedule that the lawyer works.

Nonbillable contribution is important for reduced-hour lawyers' professional development and to demonstrate that reduced-hour lawyers are still members of the team, thereby enhancing camaraderie and diminishing colleague resentment.

Misconstruing Work/Life Balance as Lack of Aspiration:

> The key issue that has not been addressed at law firms in a core competency system is how to manage top-credentialed lawyers who seek work/life balance *and* highly challenging work that leads to partnership promotion. There is a fundamental misunderstanding among many employers that lawyers who seek work/life balance are automatically willing to settle for less challenging work that would remove them from the promotion track. That's not so. Many lawyers seeking reduced hours still want to be partner eligible and do sophisticated work, but just less of it. These lawyers recognize that it may take longer for them to advance but they want to be on track to do so.

The greatest risk in a core competency system for lawyers seeking work/life balance is that they will be presumed not to want high-quality work and not be partner eligible. Employers often mistakenly think that lawyers working reduced hours are willing to forgo challenging work and the opportunity to advance in exchange for predictability and control. Not necessarily. There are typically two separate categories of reduced-hour lawyers:

1. Those desiring to move off the partner track on a temporary or permanent basis in exchange for less challenging work and more predictability and control; and
2. Those desiring the opportunity to make partner and perform challenging work, just at a reduced pace that allows them to spend more time with their families or pursue other commitments or interests.

The risk in confusing these two groups is acute given the increased role that staff and non-partnership attorneys will play in the future of the profession. (For a further discussion of the risks and opportunities that staff and non-partnership attorney roles present for women and reduced hour lawyers, see Chapter 3). A common misunderstanding is to presume that every lawyer seeking reduced hours is also seeking a staff or non-partnership attorney role. With women making up 72.5 percent of the lawyers working reduced hours,[41] the concern is that all women will be sidelined and "mommy tracked" into staff and non-partnership attorney roles and will not be partner eligible in the core competency system.

> Many lawyers seeking work/life balance are willing to work long hours when necessary and be accessible and responsive to client and colleague needs in order to remain on partnership track. These lawyers seek reduced hours but recognize the need to forgo predictability because the highly challenging work is often accompanied by erratic hours. These reduced-hour lawyers are accountable for their matters 100 percent of the time but are staffed on proportionately fewer matters. They do not expect to punch the clock. Instead, they hope that in being staffed on fewer matters, they will have fewer crises. Also, they do not expect weekly predictability in their work, but they do hope to glean more flexibility and by year's end work the reduced percentage target that they had negotiated with their employers.

Some argue that lawyers seeking fewer hours should not be eligible for sophisticated work. However, as will be discussed in Chapter 8, as long as reduced-hour lawyers are performing at a high level, being responsive to clients and colleagues, and meeting the competency requirements, there is no basis to deny their eligibility for advancement. Some firms place highly talented reduced-hour lawyers on an alternate track where they are still performing high-level work but they are not partner eligible until they return to the mainstream track. This policy does not make sense unless, once again, these lawyers are no longer doing high-profile work and have assumed a staff or non-partnership attorney role. If a lawyer is working at a slower pace but is still delivering sophisticated top-notch work and meeting the demands of colleagues and clients, then the lawyer's work should be evaluated within the core competency system.

Additionally, with the move to alternative fee arrangements, reduced-hour lawyers who pursue and commit to challenging work should be partner eligible. Under alternative fee arrangements, lawyers should be evaluated according to their results and efficiency, not hours. If a reduced-hour lawyer achieves competencies and favorable results in less time, that lawyer should be further rewarded with advancement rather than penalized.

Progression and Promotion: Firms implementing competency systems generally expect that associates will progress through the levels every two to three years. Thus, under the core competency system, there is still risk of stigma when colleagues see that some associates are progressing through levels more quickly than those associates voluntarily electing to work at a slower pace. From the outside, associates working reduced hours may be indistinguishable from associates who do not excel through the levels because of lack of skill or talent. It is therefore essential that associates working reduced hours be evaluated fairly and be eligible to progress through the levels, assuming they meet the requisite competencies at each level. Even given the stigma risk, it is still preferable to mainstream the reduced-hour lawyers and keep them in the core competency system and not create a separate track for their progression. Thus, associates seeking reduced hours should be evaluated within the same core competency system, with the recognition that progression may be at a slower rate.

At Deloitte, Cathleen Benko and Anne Weisberg introduced a model for how careers are built called Mass Career Customization (MCC) that serves as a helpful example for why reduced-hour lawyers should remain on the mainstream track.[42] Under MCC, each employee (including each partner) works with his or her manager to customize his or her career path by selecting options along four "career dimensions": pace, workload, location/schedule and role.[43] There are many laudable characteristics of the MCC model, including:

- Each person has an MCC profile—it is not an exception or accommodation for some.[44] This recognizes that every person has to fit work into life and life into work and that this "career-life fit" changes over time, so that it is important to at least annually evaluate his or her pace, workload, location/schedule, and role.
- Each person has the option to "dial up" or "dial down" along the MCC dimensions depending on his or her personal demands

and the demands of the firm that year.[45] Deceleration along the pace dimension does not permanently take a person off the track to partner, although it might slow down the person's career progression.

- MCC is incorporated into the performance management process so that it is integrated into goal setting.[46] It is part of the full picture of how the person will work and develop his or her skills.

Deloitte's approach of having everyone in the MCC system, which gives everyone permission to talk about "career-life fit" as part of their career conversations, is a model to be emulated. Tailoring special paths for lawyers seeking work/life balance *and* advancement will perpetuate the stigma traditionally attached to flexible and reduced-hour arrangements. It will also lead to automatic and erroneous conclusions that all lawyers seeking work/life balance are also willing to forgo partnership consideration.

Apprenticeship and Training

Associate training is another area where firms are rethinking how to manage their talent. One recommendation of the 2001–2002 ABA Billable Hours report was that firms vary billable hour minimums by experience, by not requiring, for example, billable minimums for first- and second-year associates.[47] This ABA recommendation was reinvigorated in 2007 by the Opt-In Project report that recommended that law firms consider having no billable hour requirement and lower salaries for an associate's first two years, allowing more time for training and skill development.[48] Beginning in 2007, many firms began to rethink their training of associates, and a handful of firms have taken it a step further and implemented apprenticeship models.

An apprenticeship model provides structured training to incoming associates and increased exposure to senior lawyers from whom they can learn. The model is also typically accompanied by reduced billable hour targets and reduced salaries. Clients are the most significant impetus for implementing apprenticeship models. Many have refused to pay for a new lawyer's learning curve.[49] For firms setting up an apprentice model, it is advisable to establish a person who can oversee the lawyers and ensure that their training goals and workloads are being met.[50]

In August 2007, Ford & Harrison LLP announced that it was abandoning billable hour minimums for its first-years and not charging clients for contributions by first years.[51] The first-years were to be paid $115,000 and the acknowledged reason was to relieve clients from the burden of paying for new associate training.[52] In October 2007, Dallas-based Strasburger & Price LLP reduced first-year billable hour requirements from 1,920 to 1,600 to allow more time for associate training.[53] These first-years were to be paid $120,000 with a $10,000 bar stipend, and very few, if any, of their hours would actually be billed to clients.[54] Specifically, the firm outlined new requirements for its first-years to spend 550 hours shadowing senior attorney mentors, participating in training sessions, and working on pro bono projects.[55]

In 2009, other firms followed the apprenticeship trend with variations. Frost Brown Todd LLC adopted an apprenticeship model where first-years would have a 1,000 billable hour requirement with less pay at $80,000, and an expectation of spending their remaining hours learning on the job.[56] Frost Brown has also arranged with clients that first-years could work some days inside legal departments so they could learn the clients' business.[57] In 2009, Howrey LLP also introduced its apprenticeship model where associates spend the first two years as apprentices and spend the majority of their time attending training seminars and working on pro bono projects to gain experience.[58] The first-years are expected to bill 700 hours; in the second year, associates will continue to take classes but also be "seconded" to clients' offices while billing 1,000 hours at a reduced rate of $150 to $200 an hour.[59] Secondments of law firm lawyers, in which they work for clients at the client's site, help junior lawyers more readily learn the needs of clients, and also strengthen a firm's bond to its clients. The Howrey apprentices may also work in federal appellate judges' chambers.[60] First-years are paid $100,000 with an additional $25,000 to mostly help pay off loans; second-years are paid $125,000 with an additional $25,000 bonus if they successfully complete the program.[61]

In May 2009, Drinker Biddle & Reath LLP announced that it was joining the ranks of firms adopting apprenticeships. The pressure, once again, came from clients, but Drinker's six-month apprenticeship program also allowed the firm to reduce salaries and avoid deferring start dates of associates, as so many other firms had done in the economic downturn.[62] So, in September 2009, Drinker welcomed its 37 new associates and paid them $105,000 (rather than $145,000). These associates shadowed partners and engaged in training, rather than focusing on billable hours.[63]

Some firms are even rolling out apprenticeship programs for their summer associates. Day Pitney LLP announced that in 2010, it would adopt a summer apprenticeship program for its two largest offices.[64] Law students were to shadow Day Pitney lawyers, work with teams handling client matters, participate in coaching sessions, attend training workshops, and participate in diversity and community service activities.[65] The training was scheduled to include a focus on billing practices, the importance of prioritizing the client, and other economic realities of law firm practice.[66]

There are a lot of bonuses to apprenticeship programs. Law firms earn tremendous goodwill from clients who no longer have to pay for new associate training.[67] Firms also save money by cutting salaries.[68] Law firms adopting apprenticeships believe that their enhanced training programs will distinguish them in terms of recruiting.[69] According to a February 2007 straw poll conducted by the *ABA Journal*, about 84 percent of associates said they would prefer a more manageable billable-hour requirement, even if it means smaller paychecks.[70] Adopters of apprenticeship programs are also hopeful that by investing in their associates, they will build loyalty in them.[71] Indeed, some junior associates are thrilled to be gaining access to influential partners and exciting work, without the pressure to bill, at such a junior level.[72]

There are also some risks and challenges with apprentice programs. The training can be costly and the loss of billable hours can result in an economic hit for the firm.[73] At Howrey, for example, Managing Partner and CEO Robert Ruyak estimated that the apprenticeship program would cost between $3–4 million to implement when calculating unbilled hours and training costs.[74] Ruyak, however, anticipated the firm turning a profit faster once associates are trained and ready to handle client matters.[75] He also explained that this is money the firm would have otherwise spent—just that it would ordinarily have spent the money over seven years, rather than two.[76]

Some believe that law students will not be drawn to firms' apprenticeship programs and instead will be enticed by bigger money at other firms. If a firm with the apprenticeship model is offering $80,000 to $100,000 while another firm is offering $160,000, many top students may be lured to the higher-paying firm.[77] Also, more prestige may be associated with the higher-paying firms. Some contend that existing training programs at many firms are good and are not convinced that sitting in a classroom will give young lawyers the training they need.[78] There may be a risk in too much observing—some believe learning to practice law actually requires practicing, and associates won't really learn until they have to do the work themselves. There is also concern about whether lawyers will simply take their training and run. These junior lawyers may benefit from the training and reduced pressure to bill and then, being very marketable, choose to leave.

Changes to Law Schools and Law Student Paths

When we consider all of the changes facing the legal profession, we must also consider the impact on legal education. Many argue that law schools must reform their curriculum. With law jobs more scarce and clients no longer willing to pay for law firm associate training, law schools should be more pressed to implement changes such as those recommended by the Carnegie Foundation for the Advancement of Teaching report.[79] The Carnegie report concluded that law schools are not proficient enough in helping students develop professional competence and identity.[80] It called for a changed curriculum that integrates traditional analytical courses with practical training that prepares students for practice.[81] Questions remain, however, whether law schools are prepared to accept a new role of training law students, whether they are best suited to provide the training, and, if they are, what the best format is for doing so.[82]

In terms of specific curriculum changes, some believe law schools should better prepare students to operate in a business environment by teaching law students effective communication, business management skills, and a foundation in financial principles.[83] Some think law students should learn strategic thinking and organizational management skills more often taught in business schools.[84] Some also believe that the process of working in teams done in business schools will benefit students. Still others believe that law schools may need to include in their coursework classes that prepare students for the non-legal careers that lawyers have always sought, including business, government, journalism, and others.[85] With all of these suggested changes, though, some fear that if legal education becomes too focused on practicality, it will stifle creative thinking.[86]

There has also been discussion of whether there should be multiple models of future law schools.[87] Perhaps certain schools could have specialties to distinguish themselves and train different types of lawyers.[88] Also, some schools may focus on experiential learning.[89] Tuition is another significant factor that will impact law school structure. From 1990 to 2003, the cost of private law schools rose at almost three times the rate of consumer prices.[90] As of 2009, the average law school student graduated with more than $80,000 in debt.[91] Such debt already prohibits many students from pursuing government or public interest jobs.[92] In the future, law schools will need to moderate their tuition and costs.[93]

Some law schools have been innovators in anticipating the need to change legal education. David Van Zandt, Dean of Northwestern University School of Law, is one law school pioneer. In addition to unveiling an accelerated JD program in two years with a full semester of experiential learning in the third year,[94] Northwestern Law launched a plan to teach a "core set of competencies—in communication, strategic understanding, basic quantitative skills, cross-cultural work, project management and leadership . . . ."[95] In the core competency of communication, Northwestern law students not only learn to write excellent briefs and present persuasive appellate arguments but also to communicate complex legal ideas clearly to non-lawyers.[96] The core competency of quantitative skills is being honed by Northwestern law students through a course focused on accounting, finance, and statistics, while more specialized courses are offered to focus on business strategy, organization, and decision-making.[97]

Other law school innovators have focused on experiential learning and a greater understanding of today's legal market. In 2006, Stanford Law School changed its second- and third-year curriculum from semesters to quarters so that students could take classes in other disciplines or take classes with other graduate programs and work on problem solving.[98] Stanford also created a clinical rotation where students could spend a quarter working in a clinic, similar to a medical school rotation.[99] At Harvard Law School, first-years in 2010 were required to take a three-week problem-solving course where they analyzed an issue, worked in teams, and presented their solution to lawyers in Boston. Georgetown University Law Center has a Center for the Study of the Legal Profession focused on the trends and developments of modern practice.[100] One of the Center's codirectors, Milton Regan, teaches a class focused on the opportunities, risks, and trade-offs of working in large law firms.[101]

Another area that law schools should consider adding to the curriculum is addressing and advising on how to overcome the challenges that many women face that impede their success as lawyers. In 2006, Flex-Time Lawyers LLC and the New York City Bar's Committee on Women in the Profession released *The Cheat Sheet*, a guide for women law students for selecting, creating, and ensuring a woman-friendly employer.[102] Since *The Cheat Sheet*'s release, I have advocated to train women law students on the specific challenges women face as they enter the profession. These specific challenges, identified in *The Cheat Sheet*, include five areas: mentoring; promotion; leadership; flexibility; and business development/networking. In March 2008, I developed a workshop at Yale Law School entitled "Women Law Students' 'Blueprint' for Success at Law Firms." The focus was on what I call "blueprinting"—training women law students on the above five identified challenges, the areas that have traditionally caused the careers of women lawyers to stall. The "blueprinting" goal is to enable women law students and junior women lawyers to design blueprints—plans for their success—by training them at the law school and junior associate levels.

Blueprinting programs are the flip side of the popular reentry programs designed to retool women professionals to get back to work after leaving their professions, primarily for child rearing. By blueprinting as women enter their legal careers, we can ensure that more women will not need to leave their careers midstream. Law schools should incorporate blueprinting programs into their curriculum and train students on the subjects of mentoring, promotion, leadership, flexibility, and networking.[103] A complete framework for blueprinting programs is outlined in Chapter 16. Effective blueprints will empower women to navigate the hidden ingredients to success, to plan for the challenges they will face, and to gain the awareness and skills to succeed.

A wonderful example of a law school preparing its women law students to succeed is the work of Paula Monopoli, Founding Director of the Women Leadership & Equality Program of the University of

Maryland School of Law.[104] Paula leads a women and leadership seminar, workshops, and experiential opportunities for women law students to develop insights and skills in exercising leadership. Linda Bray Chanow of The Center for Women in Law of the University of Texas School of Law has also developed an inspiring leadership program for women. The Center's "Leadership Boot Camp" focuses on communication, networking, and self promotion for women law students and women lawyers at different stages of their development.[105]

As the law school curriculum is changing, the student body may also need to change. It may be more fitting for entering law students to have two or more years of work experience, like those traditionally entering business schools. Back in 1998, Northwestern Law began requiring that its students have significant work experience prior to law school, and applicants were interviewed to assess maturity and interpersonal skills.[106] If students enter law school with more practical experience, they may be able to apply their learning more readily.

Law schools should not only be focused on educating and training their law students but also on training their alumni. Specifically, they should train their "lawyers in transition" (lawyers who have been laid off or are voluntarily seeking a career change) and "reentry" lawyers (lawyers who have left the profession for one or more years, mostly to become full-time caregivers).[107] Law schools should consider developing reentry programs designed to get these lawyers back to work, like the ones designed at American University Washington College of Law, Pace University School of Law, and University of California Hastings College of the Law.

It is in a law school's financial and reputational interest to have its alumni employed. Law schools could be doing much more to get their reentry and lawyers in transition back to work. Law schools should train their alumni to maximize their opportunities to return to work by advising them how to use their leave time productively; address the specific challenges they and their prospective employers face; choose the right work venue; use flexibility as an asset; network and interview effectively; and ensure a smooth transition back to work. Law schools should designate a knowledgeable representative for reentry and lawyers in transition and actively engage in programming to foster a successful return. Law schools should also develop creative ways to use their alumni networks to facilitate introductions and networking. Additionally, law schools should consider creating special interview opportunities for reentry and lawyers in transition and developing relationships with legal employers to either entice them to interview these lawyers on campus or to review these résumés in a special alumni pool. A further discussion of the issues impacting reentry and lawyers in transition is explored in Chapter 15.

A new focus at law schools should reflect an understanding that the traditional path to practicing law is no longer the norm, and the market demands that law school curriculums respond to the changed profession. The challenge for law schools is to educate and train their law students and alumni for adaptability and practicality, in addition to critical thinking.

Remaining Challenge: Who Will Train Law Students and Incoming Lawyers?

With all of the changes confronting the legal profession, law students and new lawyers face the risk of becoming casualties of the shifting climate. Under the new law firm models, experienced, well-trained lawyers, rather than entry-level ones, are the sought-after talent. Under the new large law firm models, associate classes are shrinking. Lawyers who do join the large law firms will find clients no longer willing to pay for their training. Outside of firms that have adopted the apprenticeship model, it remains a mystery where junior lawyers will get trained.

The lack of training of junior lawyers will not only negatively impact graduating law students and law firms. It also does not bode well for in-house legal departments who get the benefit of hiring well-trained lawyers from law firms. As Michael Reilly, assistant general counsel at FMC Corporation, put it: "[T]he legal industry is 'jeopardizing our own farm system.'"[108] Virtual law firms and other new-model firms will also suffer, as they typically pluck senior talent that has been groomed by traditional law firms.

The best two training options under the new law firm models are either through apprenticeship programs or secondments, where law firm associates work for a limited term in client offices at a discount.[109] If other legal employers elect to no longer train incoming lawyers, the question remains whether law schools will change their curriculum enough to train law students practically, as well as analytically, to practice law.

Notes

1. Peter B. Sloan, From Classes to Competencies, Lockstep to Levels (2007 ed.).

2. *Id.* at 20.

3. *Id.* at 20, fig.1.

4. Lower Merion School District, Report to Parents/Guardians Third Grade (the order of the Work Habits and Social Skills taken from the report card have been rearranged for proper comparison).

5. Robert Fulghum, All I Really Need to Know I Learned in Kindergarten (1988).

6. E-mail from Patricia Gillette to Deborah Epstein Henry (July 27, 2010) (on file with author).

7. Dan DiPietro et al., *The Shifting Associate Paradigm*, Am. Law., Nov. 17, 2009, *available at* http://amlawdaily.typepad.com/amlawdaily/2009/11/the-shifting-associate-paradigm.html.

8. Amanda Royal, *Reed Smith the Latest Big Firm to Drop Associate Lockstep*, Recorder, Oct. 28, 2009, *available at* http://www.law.com/jsp/article.jsp?id=1202434987961.

9. Sloan, *supra* note 1, at 20.

10. *Id.* at 20–22.

11. *Id.* at 22–23.

12. *Id.* at 12.

13. Jill Redhage, *Orrick Shakes Up Big-Firm Staffing Model*, Daily J., July 2, 2009 (interviewing Ralph Baxter, Chairman and CEO, Orrick).

14. Larry Richard, *From Lockstep to "Levels,"* N.Y.L.J., October 19, 2009; *see also* Scott A. Westfahl, Nat'l Ass'n for Law Placement, You Get What You Measure: Lawyer Development Frameworks & Effective Performance Evaluations (2008) (extensive resource on identifying competencies and implementing performance evaluations to measure associate development).

15. Kristen B. Frasch, *Holding Associates Accountable*, Human Resource Executive Online, Nov. 25, 2009, *available at* http://www.hreonline.com/HRE/story.jsp?storyId=295525600 (citing Littler Mendelson P.C. partner Garry Mathiason).

16. Richard, *supra* note 14.

17. DiPietro et al., *supra* note 7.

18. Royal, *supra* note 8.

19. *See, e.g.*, Gina Passarella, *Dechert Puts Its Attorneys Through Project Management Training*, Legal Intelligencer, Apr. 2, 2010, *available at* http://www.law.com/jsp/law/LawArticleFriendly.jsp?id=1202447368069.

20. DiPietro et al., *supra* note 7.

21. Pamela H. Woldow & Douglas B. Richardson, Altman Weil, Inc., Legal Project Management: A Trend at the Tipping Point 3 (2010).

22. *Id.*

23. Sloan, *supra* note 1, at 15.

24. *Id.* at 16.

25. Zach Lowe, *Wilmer Freezes Salaries, Breaks Lockstep*, AmLaw Daily, Dec. 15, 2009, *available at* http://amlawdaily.typepad.com/amlawdaily/2009/12/salaries.html.

26. Amanda Royal, *Bingham McCutchen to Adopt "Merit Lockstep" System*, Legal Intelligencer, Oct. 6, 2009, *available at* http://www.law.com/jsp/article.jsp?id=1202434318710.

27. Sloan, *supra* note 1, at 16.

28. *Id.*

29. *Id.*

30. *Id.* at 15.

31. Am. Bar Ass'n Comm'n on Women in the Profession, Visible Invisibility 9 (2006), *available at* http://www.abanet.org/women/VisibleInvisibility-ExecSummary.pdf.

32. Joan C. Williams & Consuela A. Pinto, Am. Bar Ass'n Comm'n on Women in the Profession, Fair Measure 25–26 (2008).

33. *Id.* at 26–28.

34. *Id.* at 29–30.

35. Ida Abbott, *Ins and Outs of Lockstep*, Management Solutions, Fall 2009, at 27, *available at* http://www.idaabbott.com/news/news27.html.

36. Ida O. Abbott, Nat'l Ass'n for Law Placement, The Lawyer's Guide to Mentoring 51 (2000).

37. Sloan, *supra* note 1, at 20.

38. *Id.* at 40.

39. *Id.* at 42.

40. Redhage, *supra* note 13; Sloan, *supra* note 1, at 38.

41. Nat'l Ass'n for Law Placement, Most Lawyers Working Part-time Are Women—Overall Number of Lawyers Working Part-time Remains Small, Dec. 17, 2009, *availabe at* http://www.nalp.org/parttimesched2009.

42. Cathleen Benko & Anne Weisberg, Mass Career Customization (2007).

43. *Id.* at 82–88.

44. *Id.* at 86.

45. *Id.* at 91–92.

46. *Id.* at 98–102.

47. Am. Bar Ass'n, ABA Commission on Billable Hours Report 2001–2002, at 44 (2002), *available at* http://www.abanet.org/careercounsel/billable/toolkit/bhcomplete.pdf.

48. Patricia K. Gillette et al., Heller Ehrman LLP, *Opt-In Project Report*, at Observation 1, May 31, 2007, *available at* http://amlawdaily.typepad.com/files/opt-inprojectreport5_22_07_v4cs.pdf.

49. David Gialanella, *Taming the Billable Beast*, A.B.A.J., Feb. 1, 2008, *available at* http://www.abajournal.com/magazine/article/taming_the_billable_beast/.

50. Jeff Jeffrey, *Law Firm Apprentice Programs Add Extra Step for New Associates*, Nat'l L.J., June 30, 2009, *available at* http://www.law.com/jsp/article.jsp?id=1202431845167&Law_Firm_Apprentice_Programs_Add_Extra_Step_for_New_Associates.

51. Gialanella, *supra* note 49; Leigh Jones, *Midsize Law Firms Go for Big Changes*, Nat'l L.J., Oct. 23, 2007, *available at* http://www.law.com/jsp/article.jsp?id=1193043814292.

52. Jeffrey, *supra* note 50; Jones, *supra* note 51.

53. Jones, *supra* note 51.

54. Jeffrey, *supra* note 50.

55. Jones, *supra* note 51.

56. Molly McDonough, *Frost Brown Todd Launches Apprentice Program*, A.B.A.J., June 12, 2009, *available at* http://www.abajournal.com/news/article/frost_brown_todd_launches_apprentice_program/.

57. Steven T. Taylor, *Tomorrow: A Sneak Preview. For These Firms, the Future Is Now*, Law Prac. Mag., Jan./Feb. 2010, at 40, *available at* http://www.axiomlaw.com/Docs/ABA%20Law%20Practice%20Magazine.pdf.

58. Jeff Jeffrey, *Howrey Introduces Apprenticeship Program for Associates*, Nat'l L.J., June 22, 2009, *available at* http://www.law.com/jsp/nlj/PubArticleNLJ.jsp?id=1202431654426&Howrey_introduces_apprenticeship_program_for_associates&hbxlogin=1.

59. Jeffrey, *supra* note 50; Jeffrey, *supra* note 58.

60. Jeffrey, *supra* note 58.

61. *Id.*

62. Jeffrey, *supra* note 50.

63. Jeff Blumenthal, *Law Firm Drinker Biddle Slashes Starting Salaries, Sets New Training Regimen*, Phila. Bus. J., May 11, 2009, *available at* http://www.bizjournals.com/philadelphia/stories/2009/05/11/daily14.html.

64. Debra Cassens Weiss, *Day Pitney to Transform Summer Associates into Apprentices*, A.B.A.J., Aug. 6, 2009, *available at* http://www.abajournal.com/news/article/day_pitney_to_transform_summer_associates_into_apprentices/.

65. *Id.*

66. *Id.*

67. Jeffrey, *supra* note 50; Jeffrey, *supra* note 58.

68. Jeffrey, *supra* note 50.

69. Gialanella, *supra* note 49.

70. *Id.*

71. Jeffrey, *supra* note 50.

72. Gialanella, *supra* note 49.

73. Jeffrey, *supra* note 50.

74. Jeffrey, *supra* note 58.

75. *Id.*

76. *Id.*

77. Jeffrey, *supra* note 50.

78. *Id.*

79. Adam Cohen, *With the Downturn, It's Time to Rethink the Legal Profession*, N.Y. Times, Apr. 1, 2009, *available at* http://www.nytimes.com/2009/04/02/opinion/02thu4.html.

80. Karen Sloan, *Consensus: Law Schools Aren't Changing Fast Enough*, Nat'l L.J., Apr. 9, 2010, *available at* http://www.law.com/jsp/nlj/PubArticleNLJ.jsp?id=1202447864826.

81. *Id.*

82. Joanne A. Epps, *A Tipping Point for Law Schools?*, NAT'L L.J., July 20, 2009, *available at* http://www.law.com/jsp/nlj/PubArticleNLJ.jsp?id=1202432335929.

83. Irene Plagianos, *And Now for Something Completely Different: The Future of Legal Education*, AMLAW DAILY, Apr. 11, 2010, *available at* http://amlawdaily.typepad.com/amlawdaily/2010/04/futureoflegaled.html; Sloan, *supra* note 80.

84. Epps, *supra* note 82.

85. Cohen, *supra* note 79.

86. Plagianos, *supra* note 83.

87. Jocelyn Allison, *Tight Job Market Could Drive Legal Ed Reform*, LAW360, Feb. 2, 2010, *available at* http://www.law360.com/articles/128906.

88. Plagianos, *supra* note 83.

89. *Id.*

90. Cohen, *supra* note 79.

91. *Id.*

92. *Id.*

93. Allison, *supra* note 87.

94. *Id.*

95. David Van Zandt & Michelle Greene, *Stress Core Competencies*, NAT. L.J., July 7, 2008, *available at* http://www.law.com/jsp/nlj/PubArticleNLJ.jsp?id=1202422732240&slreturn=1&hbxlogin=1.

96. *Id.*

97. *Id.*

98. Allison, *supra* note 87.

99. *Id.*

100. http://www.law.georgetown.edu/LegalProfession/.

101. http://www.law.georgetown.edu/curriculum/tab_courses.cfm?Status=Course&Detail=1419.

102. FLEX-TIME LAWYERS LLC & THE NEW YORK CITY BAR, COMMITTEE ON WOMEN IN THE PROFESSION, *The Cheat Sheet*, Sept. 2006, *available at* http://www.flextimelawyers.com/pdf/art3.pdf.

103. Deborah Epstein Henry, *"Blueprint" for Success: A Career-Changing Tool for Women Lawyers*, THE YOUNG LAWYER, A NEWSLETTER OF THE AMERICAN BAR ASSOCIATION YOUNG LAWYERS DIVISION, Feb./Mar. 2009, *available at* http://www.flextimelawyers.com/pdf/art14.pdf.

104. http://www.law.umaryland.edu/faculty/profiles/faculty.html ?facultynum=083.

105. *See* http://www.utexas.edu/law/academics/centers/cwl/.

106. Van Zandt & Greene, *supra* note 95.

107. Deborah Epstein Henry, *Comeback Lawyers: A Look at Why Re-Entry Is a Hot Work/Life Balance Topic*, DIVERSITY & THE BAR, Jan./Feb. 2007, *available at* http://www.flextimelawyers.com/pdf/art11.pdf.

108. Zach Lowe, *This Isn't the End of Big Law Firm Associates*, AMLAW DAILY, Mar. 10, 2010, *available at* http://amlawdaily.typepad.com/amlawdaily/2010/03/clobiglawassociates.html.

109. *Id.*

CHAPTER 5
DESIGNING A WOMAN-FRIENDLY EMPLOYER

Our oldest son, Oliver, played travel soccer for years. When our middle son, Spencer, was six years old, he started eyeing Ollie's soccer uniform longingly. I was in a store and happened to see the same Nike shorts that matched Ollie's uniform, but for Spence they were too big. I succumbed to the pressure and bought them anyway.

A few days later, my parents were visiting and Spence came downstairs with the Nike shorts inside out with the white mesh showing. Spence had cut up the exterior in an effort to make them fit, and the result was a ridiculous jagged look. I was really upset and I told my mother that I was concerned that Spence lacked good judgment.

My parents returned to New York and a short time later, I got a call from one of their friends, Stanley Komaroff, a former managing partner of a top New York City law firm. He recounted how, when he was a kid, he cut his cub scout uniform to shreds in an attempt to shorten the pants. He told me that my reaction to Spence's scissor episode was the wrong one. He thought Spence's actions reflected ingenuity and creativity. Spence was—Stanley promised—someone who will grow to be an innovator and creator.

We need to show that same ingenuity integrating women into legal workplaces. The law firm infrastructure, for example, evolved when women were significantly underrepresented in the profession. In turn, few women rose to the higher ranks, and those privileged few who did had little say about how the law firm would function. Years later, women have entered the profession in greater numbers. Yet the existing model still does not suit many women. To put it simply—the shorts don't fit. It is now up to each of us to show ingenuity and creativity to design an environment where women can thrive as well as men.

Why Design a Woman-Friendly Employer?

A threshold issue in designing a woman-friendly employer is: Why is it necessary? Is this about preferential treatment? The statistics demonstrate that the answer is no. Women have made up 40 to 50 percent of law school graduating classes for 25 years[1] yet they are still only 16 percent of law firm equity partners.[2] Female lawyers of color represent just 11 percent of law firm associates and 1.4 percent of law firm equity partners.[3] Among the Fortune 500 companies in 2010, only 94 had women as their top legal officers, with 82 white/Caucasian (non-Hispanic), 7 African American, 3 Hispanic, and 2 Asian Pacific American.[4] With women making up nearly half of law school graduating classes for 25 years, this is more than a pipeline problem. It is a problem that impedes the success of the profession. Half of the talent pool is being underutilized or not being used at all.

This chapter provides national benchmarks and explores what more needs to be done to make the workplace environment hospitable for women lawyers to succeed. Where possible, legal employers should benchmark themselves against any available national data to assess how they measure up. While many of the statistics and examples in this chapter are from law firms, the principles carry through in other legal venues too.

How to Design a Woman-Friendly Employer

Creating a woman-friendly environment starts with leadership support and openness. This requires legal employers to be open about their efforts to support women lawyers internally to their fellow lawyers and externally to clients, competitors, law schools, the media, and beyond.

In designing a woman-friendly employer, there are five key areas to focus on:

- Workforce Profile
- Family-Friendly Benefits and Policies
- Flexibility
- Leadership, Compensation, and Advancement of Women
- Development and Retention of Women

These five areas are the bases used to evaluate a woman-friendly law firm in a national survey conducted by Working Mother Media and Flex-Time Lawyers LLC entitled Best Law Firms for Women. These areas are also based on *The Cheat Sheet*, a guide to selecting, creating, and ensuring a woman-friendly employer released by the New York City Bar, Committee on Women in the Profession and Flex-Time Lawyers LLC, that will be explored in Chapter 16. The work/life issues covered in the Best Law Firms for Women survey address issues impacting both women and men. The survey then addresses other challenges specific to women.

Within the five subject areas identified above, the Best Law Firms for Women survey addresses topics including:

- Female representation at all levels of the law firm
- Parental leave
- Childcare
- Flex-time
- Reduced hours
- Reentry
- Billable hours
- Vacation
- Compensation
- Partnership and advancement
- Presence and leadership on committees and in departments
- Mentoring
- Business development and networking
- Women's initiatives
- Training
- Diversity
- Accountability

In the first three consecutive years of the Working Mother & Flex-Time Lawyers Best Law Firms for Women initiative, law firms with 50 or more lawyers were invited to register to participate in a free survey with several hundred questions. Surveys were scored based on an algorithm that gave different weight to specific survey sections and questions. Each year, 50 Best Law Firms for Women were selected. These were the top-scoring firms generated in response to the applied algorithm.[5] After each survey year, we published a summary of the aggregate statistics on work/life balance and women trends identified from the winning firms.[6] These summary findings of the 50 winning firms are generally based on large national law firms. For example, the average number of lawyers at the 50 winning firms in 2009 was 548.[7]

In designing a woman-friendly employer, the Best Law Firms for Women survey is a guideline for employers to use. The aggregate statistics of the 50 winning firms that are noted throughout this chapter are valuable benchmarks that law firms can use to assess how they measure up. The ultimate objective of the survey and list of winning firms is to start a dialogue, measure where we are, provide firms with information to change, and create competition among firms to raise the bar of what makes a best law firm for women.

> In the Best Law Firms for Women survey, every time a policy question is posed, it is followed by either a representation or a usage rate question. This is because asking about employer policies is not enough. The real assessment of whether an environment is women-friendly is based on two factors—high representation and high usage rates.
>
> - Representation reflects whether women are represented at all levels of seniority and leadership within a place of employment.
> - Usage rates reflect whether lawyers are availing themselves of the work/life policies without stigma.

Workforce Profile

Representation

Workforce profile looks at the representation of women at all levels of seniority. This is an important starting point because it is critical that employers have strong female representation at every level. According to a challenge set by the National Association of Women Lawyers (NAWL), by 2015 women should constitute 30 percent of all equity partners, 30 percent of all chief legal officers, and 30 percent of all tenured law faculties.[8]

In the Best Law Firms for Women survey, we looked at representation of women across the seniority levels. Among the 50 winning firms in 2009, women represented 47 percent of associates and 40 percent of counsel, which included all lawyers who are not associates or partners, including but not limited to staff attorneys, senior attorneys, counsel, of counsel, senior counsel, and special counsel. Among the 2009 partners, women represented 28 percent of non-equity partners and 20 percent of equity partners.[9] The representation of female equity partners, in particular, is critical in assessing a woman-friendly law firm. The equity partnership title is held by the most powerful and most highly compensated lawyers at a firm.

It is also important to assess whether the responsibilities of women equity partners are compatible with motherhood. In the Best Law Firms for Women initiative, each year we have compared the representation of equity partners who are fathers and mothers. We should see parity in these numbers. In 2009, 72 percent of the female equity partners at the 50 winning firms were mothers and 83 percent of the male equity partners at the 50 winning firms were fathers.[10] Firms that evaluate their representation of mothers and fathers at each level of seniority are taking an important step to determine whether their environments are hospitable to being both a lawyer and a mother.

But these measurements cannot be the sole criteria to evaluate whether women are thriving. Many women lawyers do not want or aspire to be equity partners. They often do not want to devote the time to the extra business development or assume the additional leadership roles that are required of an equity partner. Thus, it is important also to evaluate representation of women at the lower levels at law firms.

Recruitment and Attrition

Legal employers should also track their recruitment and attrition rates to determine whether their environments are ones that women intend not only to join but to stay. Recruitment of Caucasian women has not been a recent challenge in the profession.[11] However, recruitment continues to be a problematic for lawyers of color of both genders, who have accounted for only 10 to 20 percent of law school graduating classes for

25 years.[12] To assess recruiting trends, employers should look at their own recruiting numbers of men versus women at each of the seniority levels over a five-year period. Once an employer has a baseline for its recruitment trends, it should look at its attrition rates.

Attrition of women is an issue that plagues employers. Designing a woman-friendly workplace requires that employers evaluate the numbers of women leaving and their reasons for doing so. As with recruiting, to assess attrition trends, employers should look at their own attrition numbers of men versus women at each of the seniority levels over a five-year period. If an employer has a mandatory retirement policy, this should be factored into the analysis.

To understand attrition rates, it is important for employers to keep track of their alumni to determine where their lawyers go. A 2007 MIT study found, for example, that of the women law firm lawyers who left, 37 percent joined in-house legal departments, 9 percent went to the government, 8 percent joined nonprofits, 24 percent worked as non-lawyers, and 22 percent reported being unemployed.[13] The preferred new workplaces of former employees often shed light on what inherent workplace problems exist and what would have made the work environment more hospitable.

When women leave the profession entirely, employers need to obtain honest feedback about why they leave. Exit interviews performed by independent evaluators more accurately trace the real reasons behind departures. Many employers automatically assume that when mothers leave the workforce, it is solely because of work/life balance issues. While work/life balance is an important factor in why women leave, there are other compelling factors that drive women out the door. In a 2010 study entitled *Off-Ramps and On-Ramps Revisited*, the Center for Work-Life Policy found five major factors why women left law:

- 72 percent said they wanted or needed to spend more time with their children;
- 40 percent said their spouses'/partners' income was sufficient for their family to live on one income;
- 34 percent said their career was not satisfying or enjoyable;
- 31 percent said they wanted or needed to spend more time with their parents or other family members; and
- 14 percent said they felt stalled in their career.[14]

The reasons why women leave should be the script for employers to follow to design a more hospitable and challenging work environment. These issues are more fully explored below and in Chapters 7 and 15.

Family-Friendly Benefits and Policies

In this chapter, I outline some of the parameters and statistics relating to family-friendly benefits and policies. Then, in Chapter 7, I describe more fully how to create a work/life-friendly employer.

Parental Leave

Designing a woman-friendly employer includes providing strong parental leave and support policies for both men and women. In 2009, the 50 Best Law Firms for Women, on average, offered 14 weeks of paid maternity leave, 6 weeks of paid paternity leave, and 11 weeks of paid adoption leave.[15] These offerings were more generous than in 2007 when we first started tracking this data.[16] Law firm parental leave policies are often more generous than in other industries. In addition, many law firms allow lawyers to add paid and unused vacation time to their leave, as well as extend it with unpaid leave time.

> With parental leave, as with other work/life policies, an employer should assess not only the offerings of its policies but the usage rates. High usage rates are typically indicia of the viability of an employer's policies.

Parental leave usage rates at law firms are typically high, although they decrease with lawyer seniority. Among the 50 Best Law Firms for Women in 2009, on average, associate mothers took 18 weeks, counsel and non-equity partner mothers took 11 weeks, and equity partner mothers took 9 weeks.[17] The gap in usage among female equity partners may be attributable to the fact that many equity partners are concerned about relinquishing their role as a primary contact to clients for fear they will lose their valued relationships. It also may partially be explained by the lack of written maternity leave policies for equity partners at many firms. Among the 50 Best Law Firms for Women in 2009, 48 percent did not have policies related to maternity leave for equity partners or they approached leave on an ad hoc basis.[18]

The fact that only about half of the winning firms have written and standardized parental leave policies for equity partners means that many female partners are reinventing the wheel each time they have a baby and they are not benefiting from the previous wisdom of other women partners. It also treats pregnancy as an exception, requiring permission and special treatment, rather than a process anticipated and provided for as a matter of course. This silence or ad hoc treatment may result in female equity partners being more apprehensive about taking maternity leave. They may have anxiety about the amount of leave that is appropriate or feel that the non-standardized treatment of leave reflects a lack of support. Another problem with not being clear about leave policies at the equity partner level is that it may cause more junior lawyers to opt out for fear that the environment is inhospitable and not one where they could envision their future. Although I have spoken to a handful of women who say they like the silence because it has enabled them to potentially negotiate a better leave, the overwhelming numbers of women I have counseled agree that any potential benefit is significantly outweighed by the value of having a written policy. Therefore, I encourage firms to provide written parental leave policies for equity partners, entitling them to at least as much leave as associates.

It is also instructive to look at parental leave policies and usage rates relating to men. High usage rates of work/life policies among men help de-stigmatize usage by women. Among the Best Law Firms for Women in 2009, 92 percent of the 50 winning firms offered paid paternity leave to lawyer fathers with at least one year of service.[19] These lawyer fathers took an average of three and a half weeks of leave.[20] It is heartening to see that men are increasingly availing themselves of work/life benefits. However, parental leave benefits are temporary and, therefore, the stigma is minimized and male usage is more acceptable. The same ease in usage is not reflected in men's use of reduced-hour schedules on a regular basis.

Phase Back

Parental leave policies are an important means for employers to support working parents. What is equally important is for employers to support working parents as they transition back to work and once their children are beyond the newborn stage. A trend among employers is to have a written phase-back policy, giving women the automatic option to work reduced hours for up to one year when transitioning back from maternity leave. This policy is helpful because parental leave is a critical transition point, and easing a lawyer's successful return will enhance the likelihood of the lawyer staying and thriving in the workforce. Among the 50 Best Law Firms for Women, 58 percent had a written phase-back policy in 2009.[21]

Childcare

Employers can provide additional support by having on-site or near-site full-time childcare facilities, emergency backup corporate childcare, and at-home emergency backup care. Of the 50 Best Law Firms for Women in 2009, 28 percent offered on-site or near-site full-time childcare[22] and another 6 percent purchased childcare center slots for everyday usage in centers unaffiliated with the firm.[23] Meanwhile, 76 percent offered emergency backup corporate childcare.[24] The emergency backup provides support when, for example, a lawyer's nanny is sick or unavailable to come to work or the lawyer's regular day care is closed and the well child can be brought to a childcare facility. Additionally, 52 percent of the 50 Best Law Firms for Women in 2009 offered the steadily growing benefit of at-home emergency backup childcare.[25] This benefit helps parents on evenings, nights, or weekends or when their children are sick and the children cannot be brought to a center and the parents do not have regular coverage at home. With work/life coverage, one must also be mindful of the double-edged sword. Coverage should not become so great that the end result is that lawyers are always working.

Reentry

It is also important for employers to support lawyers' transitions into and out of the profession. According to the Center for Work-Life Policy, 31 percent of women lawyers take a leave from practice of more than six months at some point in their careers.[26] With nearly one-third of women lawyers on a nonlinear career trajectory, these paths should no longer be viewed as unconventional. Legal employers need to design their environments to be receptive to welcoming back those who have left in order to enable more women to be integrated and promoted in the profession.

The notion of reentry, where women lawyers leave the profession typically for one year or more to become full-time caregivers but remain interested in reentering the profession, is gaining more traction. Among the 50 Best Law Firms for Women in 2009, 34 percent had a written policy to keep in touch with and train women who left the firm for family obligations and whose return the firm wanted to encourage.[27]

Another 54 percent of the 50 winning firms in 2009 (up from 16 percent of the 50 winning firms in 2007) hosted or sponsored programs to keep in touch with, identify, and hire reentry lawyer mothers.[28]

In 2006, in response to an increasingly tight market for trained legal talent, law firms nationally were focusing more on recruiting from their alumni talent pool, including reentry female attorneys.[29] These law firms took steps to enhance their alumni relations programs to effectively recruit back their talent.[30] As the market strengthens again, I anticipate that reentry will be a growing focus. Firms will develop written policies and programs, recognizing reentry lawyers as a valuable trained yet untapped talent stream.

Retirement

Retirement is another transition point where employers should provide more support. As discussed in Chapter 1, Baby Boomers make up 70 percent of law firm partners and many of them are interested in phasing into retirement over five to ten years rather than retiring outright.[31] This trend, which had already taken hold, has perpetuated during the recent economic downturn. As lawyers' personal equity dropped because of the declines in the stock and housing markets, they plan to stay longer before retiring, perhaps at a flexible or reduced-hour pace. Among the 50 Best Law Firms for Women in 2009, 72 percent have phased retirement programs to assist lawyers who are transitioning into retirement and want to work flexible or reduced hours.[32]

Flexibility

In this chapter, I outline some of the parameters and statistics relating to flexible and reduced hours. Then, in Chapter 8, I describe more fully how to make flexible and reduced-hours work, and in Chapter 9, I explain additional flexible work arrangements.

> A woman-friendly employer must have viable work/life policies in place. It is also critical that employers make their work/life policies available to men. If we can move work/life balance away from being a "mommy" issue, the stigma will be minimized and historically low usage rates will improve.

In developing a supportive work/life environment, written policies are an important starting point. Also, it is important that an employer have different types of flexible and reduced hour policies to meet the needs of different practice areas, individuals, and work arrangements.

Flexible and Reduced Hour Arrangements

At a minimum, employers should offer a range of the following flexible and reduced hour arrangements:

1. **Full-time flex-time**: This arrangement involves regularly working one or more days outside the office, or compressed or shortened days in the office, or unconventional hours while billing a firm's full billable hour requirement or assuming a full workload. Full-time flex-time lawyers may telecommute part or all of the time each week but do not work reduced hours or job share. Full-time flex-time does not pertain to lawyers who work a full workweek at the office and do spillover work at home or those who occasionally work outside the office without advance and regular approval.
2. **Core hours:** This arrangement is the same as full-time flex-time but the hourly or work commitment may be lower and less than full-time.
3. **Reduced hours:** This arrangement involves spending a reduced number of hours or days in the office per week, month, or year, resulting in a reduced number of hours or days worked. In the law firm context, reduced hours most often means 60 to 80 percent of the required billable hours of the firm but some firm lawyers work above or below these percentages. A reduced-hours arrangement includes job shares and annualized hours.
4. **Job shares:** This arrangement usually involves two lawyers sharing a job, each typically working a 60 percent schedule and stepping into each other's shoes midweek so that one takes over the work flow of the other. Job shares can include other variations. For example, what I call a "seasonal job share" with semi-retired lawyers is where one lawyer works six months of the year and the other lawyer works the other six months.
5. **Annualized hours:** This arrangement involves lawyers working on a transaction-by-transaction basis, often with long and erratic hours, and then either taking a longer reprieve between deals,

or working seasonally, or stopping work at a certain point if they have met their yearly, hourly, or project commitment. The goal is for the lawyers to take breaks in between being staffed on more cases or deals and to meet an agreed-upon reduced-hours target at the end of the year.

6. **Telecommuting:** This arrangement involves lawyers working part of the time or exclusively from home or another location with a full workload or a reduced one. Some telecommute certain days or hours or every day.
7. **Fixed Hours:** This arrangement involves lawyers working a full workload or a reduced one. Fixed hours' work is less challenging work that is sought by high-caliber lawyers in exchange for more predictability and control over their schedules. Given the nature of the work, fixed-hour lawyers are not partner eligible. They are also paid less given that the work is less challenging and more predictable and that clients are billed less for the end product. Some highly talented lawyers pursue this work temporarily or during a certain life stage. It is important that those high-caliber lawyers who wish to resume the more challenging, higher-paid, partner eligible work should be able to do so if the business needs exist.
8. **Contracting/Consulting:** This arrangement involves independent contractors who work for one or multiple employers on a reduced-hours basis. These lawyers typically work hourly, and they do not receive benefits and are not employees

Reduced-Hour Usage

Among the 2009 Best Law Firms for Women, 96 percent of the 50 winning firms had written policies for reduced-hour lawyers and 8 percent of the lawyers from these firms worked reduced hours.[33] Among the 96 percent offering reduced hours, all of these firms allowed reduced hours for reasons in addition to childcare.[34] The Best Law Firms for Women usage rates are higher than the national usage rates but still relatively low. According to the National Association of Law Placement, Inc. (NALP) 2009 study, only 5.9 percent of law firm lawyers worked reduced hours and reduced hours were offered in 98 percent of the 1,475 law offices nationally surveyed.[35] Of the 5.9 percent of law firm lawyers working reduced hours, 3.5 percent were partners, 5.0 percent were associates, and 20.7 percent were "other" lawyers including, for example, counsel and staff attorneys.[36] Additionally, 72.5 percent of those working reduced hours in the NALP survey were women.[37]

The meager usage rates in the NALP study reveal that lawyers are not generally availing themselves of reduced-hour schedules despite the almost universal availability of this benefit. The low usage rates become even more apparent when comparing law to other industries. According to the Bureau of Labor Statistics, approximately 14 percent of those employed in professional specialties, e.g., engineers, physicians, and architects, worked reduced hours compared to the mere 5.9 percent usage rate of law firm lawyers.[38]

Significantly increased usage rates would demonstrate that reduced-hour arrangements are accepted without stigma. Some employers have historically put childcare references into policies in an effort to steer usage to only women or to only parenting reasons. Taking out childcare references in work/life policies and having male leaders use these policies will help de-stigmatize them and increase usage for men and women for reasons in addition to parenting.

Reduced-Hour Promotion

The promotion rate among reduced-hour lawyers is another area on which legal employers need to focus. As discussed in Chapter 8, when reduced-hour lawyers are doing high-level work and meeting the criteria for advancement, they too should be eligible for promotion. Among the Best Law Firms for Women that have a two-tier partnership track, on average three lawyers per firm were promoted from associate or counsel to non-equity partner while working reduced hours over the course of five years, from 2004 to 2008.[39] For equity partnership, 96 percent of the 50 Best Law Firms for Women in 2009 allowed reduced-hour lawyers to be eligible for consideration.[40] At these firms, on average, two lawyers per firm were promoted from associate, counsel, or non-equity partner (where applicable) to equity partner while working reduced hours over the course of five years, from 2004 to 2008.[41] Until there are higher promotion rates at the partner level, the stigma associated with work/life policies will prevail.

Full-Time Flex-Time

In addition to reduced-hours policies, employers should have full-time flex-time policies. Among the 2009 Best Law Firms for Women, 42 percent of the 50 firms had written full-time flex-time policies and 11 percent of the lawyers from these firms worked full-time flex-time.[42] I anticipate full-time flex-time will become more popular and firms will allow their lawyers to regularly telecommute more and work less conventional hours.[43] Twenty years ago, most firms did not have written reduced-hours policies and it resulted in secrecy, favoritism, and ad hoc treatment. As the need became more public, many firms produced written policies, as evidenced by the Best Law Firms for Women statistics. I anticipate the same will be true with full-time flex-time policies. Through full-time flex-time, legal employers can offer greater flexibility and satisfaction among lawyers without impacting the bottom line.

Some employers are resistant to embracing full-time flex-time because they fear an opening of the floodgates—that affording broad-based flexibility will negatively impact training and mentoring and threaten the corporate culture. However, given the technological opportunities for all lawyers to work flexibly, the demands of Generation Y lawyers entering the profession, and the interests of Baby Boomers to gradually phase into retirement, full-time flex-time is an issue that is not going away. Particularly in the law firm context, firms that can harness and capitalize on the flexibility of the billable hour will be at a competitive advantage.

The ability to afford lawyers more flexibility in where and how they work without impacting the bottom line is an opportunity that firms should not pass up. As discussed in Chapter 8, the way to ensure that lawyers who use these policies thrive is to impose parameters around the work arrangements and provide training and programming to help breathe life into the policies.

Other Flexible Work Arrangements

In addition to reduced hours and full-time flex-time, women-friendly employers should also offer other viable flexible work arrangements. Among the 50 Best Law Firms for Women in 2009, 62 percent offered full-time telecommuting, 6 percent offered job shares, and 46 percent offered annualized hours.[44] However, usage rates were low. Among the 2009 Best Law Firms for Women, only 1 percent of the 50 winning firms had lawyers who full-time telecommuted, none worked a job share,[45] and 5 percent worked annualized hours.[46] Each of these arrangements is described more fully in Chapters 8 and 9. They are mentioned here as part of the full range of flexible work arrangements that a woman-friendly employer should offer to ensure that different individual and practice area needs are met.

Leadership, Compensation, and Advancement of Women

Leadership

To design a woman-friendly firm, it is critical to focus on the advancement of women, and specifically their leadership, promotion, and compensation. A few highlights of the 2009 Best Law Firms for Women findings reflect how much more work is required in these areas. As an initial and immediate goal, employers should ensure that women are represented in leadership roles in an organization at least as much as they are represented at the highest levels of an organization. For example, at the 50 Best Law Firms for Women in 2009, women constituted 20 percent of equity partners[47] and therefore, as a minimum starting point, women should compose at least that same representation in the different leadership roles in a firm.

Examples of key leadership roles at firms include being the chairperson or managing partner, or chairing practice groups, departments, or committees. Among the 2009 Best Law Firms for Women, 14 percent had female managing partners and 10 percent had female chairpersons.[48] Of those who chaired, cochaired, or vice-chaired the firms' departments or practice groups, 18 percent were women.[49] Additionally, 28 percent of those who chaired, cochaired, or vice-chaired the firms' committees were women.[50] However, this included leadership of all the committees at a firm—ranging from those of great importance to those that are not recognized as such.

Leadership at law firms should also be assessed by looking at representation on the most influential committees at a firm. Among the 2009 Best Law Firms for Women, female representation on the most influential firm committees was as follows: 17 percent of the management or executive committee; 20 percent of the compensation or finance committee addressing issues of equity partner compensation; and 23 percent of the firm's committee deciding equity partner promotion.[51]

The national averages for women leaders are lower than those of the 2009 Best Law Firms for Women. According to NAWL, the average firm's highest governing committee was 15 percent women and about 14 percent of the nation's largest law firms had no women at all on their governing committees.[52] The most glaring leadership vacuum is at the most visible and prominent position. The national average of female managing partners was only about 6 percent.[53]

Aiming for women's leadership representation to match the current female equity partner representation is only a minimum starting point. If women assume 16 to 20 percent of the leadership roles, it will not give them the voice they need to change the way institutions operate. A better target is the 30 percent representation target set by NAWL.[54] Women need to achieve both representation and leadership at the 30 percent level in order to effectuate change and thrive.

Employers should seek out and groom women for leadership opportunities so that they are equally comfortable assuming and performing in such roles. At a recent Flex-Time Lawyers LLC program on leadership, one female managing partner said that she saw leadership as an opportunity to provide service and give back. This depiction of leadership may help engage more women to assume such roles. Some women are less inclined to assume leadership roles because they are concerned that they already manage a disproportionate share of mentoring and leadership roles, given the dearth of women in positions of power. To entice more talented women and men into such roles, employers should consider financial incentives, such as awarding bonuses to lawyers based on their assuming such roles.

By placing qualified women onto influential committees at law firms, the change could be dramatic. Such leadership may bring fast results. In the 2010 study *New Millennium, Same Glass Ceiling? The Impact of Law Firm Compensation Systems on Women* (the *New Millennium, Same Glass Ceiling?* study), the Project for Attorney Retention and the Minority Corporate Counsel Association, with the assistance of the American Bar Association Commission on Women in the Profession (ABA Commission on Women), found that executive committees have the most influence on compensation, followed by compensation committees.[55] By increasing female representation to 30 percent on the three most powerful committees at law firms, women would immediately have more of a voice on firm governance, pay, and promotion, and in turn could strongly influence firm policies as well as women's presence and power.

Promotion

Promotion is another area where employers need to pay close attention in designing a woman-friendly environment. When assessing an employer's promotion trends for women, it is important to review a five-year period, because one or two years may be outliers and not representative of a trend. In the 2009 Best Law Firms for Women initiative, we looked at promotion rates over the five-year period from 2004 to 2008 and found that among one-tier equity partner–track firms, 29 percent of the newly admitted equity partners over five years were women.[56] Among two-tier track firms, 28 percent of the newly admitted equity partners and 32 percent of the newly admitted non-equity partners over five years were women.[57] With the national average of female equity partners at 16 percent[58] and the Best Law Firms for Women average of female equity partners at 20 percent, it is heartening to see that the five-year promotion trend is higher. Yet it is necessary to continue tracking these statistics to see that the progression reaches equity.

Some of the impediments to women's promotion stem from not understanding what is underlying women's stalled progress. As Brande Stellings, Vice President of Catalyst's Advisory Services, Professional Services Practice aptly explained: "Work-life challenges are an important issue, but not THE issue. So often when we ask people within firms the question, 'why not more women partners,' we hear about work-life choices made by women. But often, when we talk to women partners, many have found a way to organize their lives in a way to make work and life fit, but they still find challenges related to gender. For these senior women, gender stereotypes and bias are often a bigger problem than work-life issues."[59]

One area where these biases and stereotypes regularly arise is in providing lawyers with feedback about their work. In the *Visible Invisibility: Women of Color in Law Firms* study issued by the ABA Commission on Women in 2006, for example, many women of color felt they received "soft evaluations" that impeded their opportunity to correct problems and gain experiences that could lead to promotions.[60] Some felt their accomplishments were ignored or not as highly rewarded or that their mistakes were exaggerated.[61] As a result, 20 percent of women of color (compared to only 1 percent of white men) felt they were denied promotion opportunities.[62]

Feedback must be constructive and promotion expectations and criteria need to be transparent so that lawyers know what is required to get to the next level. Additionally, a fair assignment system is critical so that women are staffed on matters that will get them the experience they need to be eligible for promotion. They also need access to influential senior lawyers in order to gain the backing, exposure, and experience to be promoted. The representation statistics reflect that paying additional attention to women is not about getting women preferential access. Instead, the focus on women is about giving them the support they need to obtain equal representation.

Compensation

Employers must ensure that women are being fairly and equitably compensated. According to the 2010 *New Millennium, Same Glass Ceiling?* study, key factors in determining law firm partner compensation are origination of client work, revenue collected, and a partner's own billable hours.[63] Among the nearly 700 female partner survey respondents, there was a lot of dissatisfaction in the compensation determinations. For example, 80 percent of the female equity partner respondents said they had been denied their "fair share" of origination credit; about one-third of female equity partner respondents said they were uncomfortable appealing their firms' compensation decisions; and a staggering one-fourth of white equity partner respondents and about one-third of minority partner respondents said they were subjected to intimidation, threats, or bullying when they expressed their disagreement.[64] These statistics reflect significant dissatisfaction and discomfort among women with the compensation system that demonstrates the need to revamp it.

When assessing the fairness of compensation, employers must look at how many women are above and below the mean profits per equity partner, paying close attention to how many women are in the bottom quartile of profits per equity partner. They should also assess the average compensation differential among male and female full-time equity partners. In the 2009 NAWL survey, women equity partners earned about $66,000 less than their male counterparts at the 200 largest law firms.[65] This disparity is less than prior years, which may be explained by the decrease in average compensation in firms in 2009, which therefore narrowed the gender gap as well.[66] According to a recent U.S. Census Bureau report, the median income of women lawyers is only 78 percent of their male counterparts, with the largest gap at the equity partner level.[67]

The *New Millennium, Same Glass Ceiling?* study outlines important best practices and recommendations to gradually create a fair and effective compensation system, including:

1. Improving transparency
2. Benchmarking
3. Improving diversity on compensation committees and introduce other checks on bias and in-group favoritism
4. Re-examining the billable hours threshold
5. Redesigning origination credit
6. Ensuring a diverse committee handles disputes over reward allocation, particularly origination credit
7. Taking pro-active steps to check the hidden bias that will otherwise surely emerge in the context of compensation systems
8. Developing a process that does not penalize women for self-advocacy
9. Conforming to standard business practice by linking compensation to individuals' contributions to the long-term viability of the firm
10. Designing a compensation system that does not penalize part-time partners [68]

Some of these best practices will be addressed more fully in the *Training and Business Development* section that follows. For a discussion about compensation of reduced-hour lawyers, see Chapters 4 and 8. For the remaining issues, see the *New Millennium, Same Glass Ceiling?* study for concrete recommendations to implement these best practices effectively.

Development and Retention of Women

Training and Business Development

National statistics reflect that law firms need to more effectively support women's efforts in business development. In the 2009 NAWL survey, there were no women among the top ten rainmakers at 46 percent of the 200 largest law firms surveyed.[69] Another 32 percent of the firms had only one woman among the top ten rainmakers; some 15 percent had two women among the top ten rainmakers; and the remaining 6 percent had three or four women rainmakers in their top ten.[70] The dearth of women in the rainmaker role negatively impacts women's compensation, power, and equity partner representation at law firms.

Women's low representation in the rainmaker ranks must be improved by transparency and standardization. In the *New Millennium, Same Glass Ceiling?* study, only 60 percent of equity partners, 30 percent of income partners, and 34 percent of minority partners said they were "clear" or "extremely clear" about how their firms' compensation systems worked.[71] These numbers demonstrate the need for a standardized process that fairly and explicitly articulates how business credit, origination, and inheritance is awarded. With business credit, origination, and inheritance directly impacting compensation, power, and influence at law firms, there is no justifiable basis to continue to keep the process vague. Specifically, there must be transparency about: how decisions are made about who attends pitches; whether attorneys who attend pitches will work and be awarded credit on the new matters that result from the pitches they attend; whether and how credit is shared for expansion of work or otherwise; how matters are inherited; how to become a billing or relationship partner; how origination credit is awarded and for how long; how the executive and compensation committees impact the award of credit; and how self-advocacy impacts the award of credit. Clients can help to bring transparency by applying pressure and specifying that certain law firm lawyers get credit for the business generated.[72]

In addition to creating transparency, it is important that firms create an infrastructure for lawyers to share credit for business. Rather than just award credit for origination, firms should also award credit to those who service the clients and expand the business. "This teamwork approach not only incentivizes everyone to pitch in and help grow the client's business, it also strengthens the client's ties with a larger base of firm partners. An added benefit of such a team approach is that in this increasingly mobile legal market, the departure of a single partner may not necessarily result in the loss of that partner's clients."[73]

Employers also need to develop and seek out effective training for women. Employers should provide management, leadership, and networking/business development training for their women lawyers internally, externally, or both. Most women face specific challenges with respect to leadership, networking, and self promotion. Training in these issues will help develop women lawyers and make them become more valuable lawyers. In Chapter 16, I provide guidelines for training and in Chapter 17, I provide specific business development and networking tips for women lawyers. Ideally, training should be ongoing rather than a one-time experience. Among our 2009 Best Law Firms for Women, 80 percent offered management or leadership training targeted for women lawyers.[74]

In addition to paying for training, employers should reimburse their lawyers for participation in networking organizations and trade associations. Employers should also consider an online women's network to facilitate further connections. Law firms should have a budget specifically targeted for women's business development training and initiatives.

Firm-hosted women's initiatives should include specifically tailored events with clients of the firm. Many women's initiatives at firms have spearheaded events in creative ways by hosting art openings, auctions, cooking classes, golf clinics, self-defense workshops, spa outings, book readings, wine tastings, and the like. Among the 2009 Best Law Firms for Women, 64 percent had budgets targeted for women business development training and initiatives and 90 percent offered networking events for women lawyers and the firms' women clients.[75] By aligning a venue more closely to the interests of women lawyers for these events, it will help with engagement and participation.

Mentoring

Mentoring programs are also critical for employers committed to developing their women lawyers. Mentoring can take shape in a variety of ways. Some employers have a formal mentoring program, with a program coordinator, linking a mentor and mentee and providing a framework for the relationship. Like any attempt at matchmaking, the process of matching mentors and mentees is an imperfect one. Ideally, mentees should provide input into the type of mentor they are seeking and all participants should be willing and interested. There are different types of mentors. Some help navigate the less obvious aspects of the workplace and convey internal politics. Others help develop a mentee's career, and still others advocate, vouch for, and provide opportunities for a mentee. To be successful, the relationship needs to be mutual and the mentee needs to engage the mentor and give something back.

Some employers have had greater success with mentoring circles than one-on-one mentoring. A mentoring circle is typically composed of five to ten lawyers at varying levels of seniority who meet regularly in a group. These group sessions provide more opportunities for different people to connect. The arrangement also helps with continuity, because an individual is not as subject to the whims of one person's erratic schedule and the core group of people interested in participating usually can meet with regularity. Mentoring circles work well when there is a designated facilitator who may vary meeting to meeting.

Some law firm clients have expressed their frustration with getting mentoring circles off the ground. One common problem is that the junior and senior women do not effectively mix and conversation does not flow. In this case, I recommend a break from the process. Some of the junior and senior women should pair off and schedule a few coffee dates one-on-one. Then the group can resume meeting about six months later. When they do, I recommend a seating chart that would thoughtfully mix the junior and senior women and seat people next to those who might have a natural connection. A different seating chart may be helpful for the next meeting and those that follow until conversation begins to naturally flow. It may also be appropriate to pose a topic for each meeting or a few discussion questions to frame the discussion.

Some law firms have adopted the successful model of targeted mentoring like Ernst & Young's "Career Watch," where mid- to senior-level associates identified as high-potential women are matched with senior leaders to help guide their career development.[76] For each participant, there is a plan that identifies strengths and weaknesses and the skills and qualities they need to develop to get to the next level. The goal is to ensure that these women get both the necessary experience and the necessary exposure to advance to their highest promotional opportunity. Among the 2009 Best Law Firms for Women, 76 percent offered mentoring circles for women and 72 percent offered mentoring targeting senior women associates or newly admitted partners.[77]

Diversity and Accountability

Affinity Groups

A woman-friendly employer needs to be supportive of diversity, a term that should be defined as broadly as possible to include lawyers from different racial and ethnic groups, female lawyers, lawyers who are lesbian, gay, bisexual, and transgender (LGBT), lawyers with disabilities, lawyers seeking work/life balance, etc. The diversity focus should be on inclusiveness. An example along these lines is the Minority Corporate Counsel Association's recognition of the important role of white men in diversity.[78] One such visionary is Thomas Sager, Senior Vice President and General Counsel of DuPont Co., who has been a leading advocate for increased diversity in the legal profession. After all, if the end result of diversity is that white men are alienated, then there has not been progress. Yet, in being inclusive, it is equally important not to diminish the varied challenges that different disadvantaged groups have faced. For example, the experiences and issues facing African American women are quite distinct from those that Asian men may confront and they should be addressed differently.

The challenges facing women of color are particularly acute. As outlined in Catalyst's 2009 *Women of Color in U.S. Law Firms* study, there are a number of effective steps that can be taken to improve the status of women of color, including one-on-one meetings and strategic informal sessions with leaders, pairing women of color with influential partners or sponsors, ensuring that formal mentors receive training in mentoring across differences, and monitoring and tracking career development of women of color.[79] Creating better communication and understanding through mentoring programs allows mentors and mentees to build trust by sharing their differing views and experiences and helps to educate each participant on issues of diversity.[80]

More generally, employers can support diversity through affinity groups. Employers provide a venue and opportunity for similarly situated individuals to meet regularly (usually monthly or quarterly) to speak freely about the specific challenges they face, provide a forum to discuss professional concerns, and build a sense of community within an organization. Among the 2009 Best Law Firms for Women, 86 percent had affinity groups for women, 80 percent had affinity groups for lawyers of color, and 66 percent had affinity groups for LGBT lawyers.[81] Additionally, among the 2009 Best Law Firms for Women, 90 percent had an active women's initiative and 54 percent had a work/life task force or committee.[82]

Some firms use the term "women's initiative" interchangeably with the notion of an affinity group for women. Other firms may have a women's initiative that focuses on women's programming, training, and events and a women's affinity group where women convene to more informally discuss issues facing them. The key for women's initiatives is that they have real budgets to effectuate their programming, training, and events and pursue their mission to improve the status of women in the profession. Some firms have a work/life task force or committee as part of the women's initiative. I recommend that the two be separated. Although women have largely been the voice for work/life issues, a work/life task force should be gender neutral and focus on the full range of work/life issues—not just parenting.

Accountability

Accountability is an important part of diversity, as it holds an employer responsible for its actions with regard to hiring, retaining, and promoting diverse lawyers. Employers can take steps to ensure that diverse lawyers are getting the same opportunities and exposure. Some areas where diverse lawyers have historically not gained equal access include opportunities to assume leadership roles or exposure to influential partners and assignments. Other areas where more accountability is necessary are in determining how client pitches are staffed, how clients are inherited when senior lawyers retire, and how credit is attributed when new matters are originated or sustaining.

In the *Visible Invisibility: Women of Color in Law Firms* study, the findings reveal the specific challenges facing women of color. Nearly two-thirds of women of color surveyed (versus 4 percent of white men) reported being excluded from informal and formal networking opportunities, marginalized and peripheral to professional networks within their firms.[83] Additionally, 67 percent of women of color wanted better or more mentoring by senior attorneys and partners whereas only 32 percent of white men expressed a similar need.[84] Also, for women of color, 44 percent reported being denied desirable assignments (while only 2 percent of white men reported the same) and 43 percent of women of color reporting having limited access to client development opportunities (while only 3 percent of white men reported the same).[85] Instituting fair and objective performance evaluations is a critical accountability issue. Nearly one-third of women of color felt they received unfair performance evaluations while only 1 percent of white men reported the same experience.[86]

To create more accountability, employers should tie performance evaluations or bonuses to benchmarks that lawyers seek. Employers should also implement training around diversity issues. For example, antiharassment, antidiscrimination, and diversity sensitivity training are important to provide. Employers should solicit information anonymously by conducting lawyer opinion surveys to assess the work culture. Challenges and successes and a plan to address those challenges should be tracked and reported.

In sum, the current law firm model needs to be rethought to enable women to succeed. The benchmarks and statistics reveal the gaps. Chapters 7 and 8 go into depth about designing a work/life friendly environment while Part II of the book outlines what steps lawyers themselves can take to improve their status. When women are provided with the identified support, training, and opportunities, they will be able to achieve greater success and earn their equal place in the profession.

Notes

1. Am. Bar Ass'n, First Year and Total J.D. Enrollment by Gender for 1947–2008, (2009), *available at* www.abanet.org/legaled/statistics/charts/stats%20-%206.pdf [hereinafter Am. Bar Ass'n, Enrollment Study].

2. Stephanie A. Scharf et al., Nat'l Ass'n of Women Lawyers, Report of the Fourth Annual National Survey on Retention and Promotion of Women in Law Firms 7 (2009), *available at* http://www.nawl.org/Assets/Documents/2009+Survey.pdf.

3. Stephanie A. Scharf et al., Nat'l Ass'n of Women Lawyers, Report of the Third Annual National Survey on Retention and Promotion of Women in Law Firms 2–3 (2008), *available at* http://www.nawl.org/Assets/Documents/2008%2bSurvey.pdf.

4. *MCCA's 2010 Survey of Fortune 500 Women General Counsel*, Diversity & the Bar, 23, Jul./Aug. 2010, *available at* http://www.mcca.com/index.cfm?fuseaction=page.viewPage&pageID=2107. While 94 remains a low number for the total women to serve as top legal officers of Fortune 500 companies, it is a welcome increase from the total of 85 women who were top legal officers in 2009. *MCCA's 2009 Survey of Fortune 500 Women General Counsel*, Diversity & the Bar, Jul./Aug. 2009, *available at* http://www.mcca.com/index.cfm?fuseaction=page.viewPage&pageID=1931.

5. For more information about the survey methodology and the reasons behind the Best Law Firms for Women initiative, *see* Deborah

Epstein Henry, *Why a Best Law Firms for Women List?*, THE BALANCE BEAM, 2006–2007, *available at* http://www.flextimelawyers.com/pdf/newsletter_07.pdf and http://www.flextimelawyers.com/best.asp.

6. When reporting the aggregate statistics of the winning firms, not all 50 firms answered all questions. Additionally, some of the statistics reported in this book are from unpublished findings of the 2009 survey and will be noted as such.

7. Working Mother Media & Flex-Time Lawyers LLC, 2009 Best Law Firms for Women Survey, unpublished aggregate statistics of the 50 winning firms [hereinafter Unpublished aggregate statistics].

8. NAT'L ASS'N OF WOMEN LAWYERS, NAWL NEWS, Jul./Aug. 2006, *available at* http://www.nawl.org/Assets/Documents/NAWL_News_July-August_2006.pdf [hereinafter NAT'L ASS'N OF WOMEN LAWYERS].

9. WORKING MOTHER MEDIA & FLEX-TIME LAWYERS LLC, EXECUTIVE SUMMARY: HIGHLIGHTS OF WORK/LIFE AND WOMEN TRENDS FROM THE 2009 BEST LAW FIRMS FOR WOMEN SURVEY, *available at* http://www.flextimelawyers.com/best/press20.pdf [hereinafter EXECUTIVE SUMMARY].

10. Unpublished aggregate statistics, *supra* note 7.

11. Women have comprised 40 to 50 percent of law school graduating classes for 25 years. AM. BAR ASS'N, ENROLLMENT STUDY, *supra* note 1.

12. AM. BAR ASS'N, FIRST YEAR J.D. AND TOTAL J.D. MINORITY ENROLLMENT FOR 1971–2007 (2008), *available at* www.abanet.org/legaled/statistics/charts/stats%20-%208.pdf.

13. Mona Harrington & Helen Hsi, *Women Lawyers and Obstacles to Leadership*, *in* A REPORT OF MIT WORKPLACE CENTER SURVEYS ON COMPARATIVE CAREER DECISIONS AND ATTRITION RATES OF WOMEN AND MEN IN MASSACHUSETTS LAW FIRMS 10 (2007), *available at* http://web.mit.edu/workplacecenter/docs/law-report_4-07.pdf.

14. SYLVIA ANN HEWLETT ET AL., CTR. FOR WORK-LIFE POLICY, OFF-RAMPS AND ON-RAMPS REVISITED 65, Fig. A.2 (2010).

15. EXECUTIVE SUMMARY, *supra* note 9.

16. Among the 50 winning firms in 2007, there was 12 weeks of paid maternity leave, 5 weeks of paid paternity leave, and 8 weeks of paid adoptive leave. EXECUTIVE SUMMARY, *supra* note 9 (comparing trends of years 2007, 2008, and 2009).

17. Unpublished aggregate statistics, *supra* note 7.
18. *Id.*
19. *Id.*
20. *Id.*
21. *Id.*
22. Executive Summary, *supra* note 9.
23. Unpublished aggregate statistics, *supra* note 7.
24. Executive Summary, *supra* note 9.
25. *Id.* In 2007, only 36 percent of the 50 winning firms provided this benefit. *Id.*
26. Hewlett, *supra* note 14, at 8.
27. Unpublished aggregate statistics, *supra* note 7.
28. Executive Summary, *supra* note 9.
29. Leigh Jones, *A Promising Talent Pool: Alumni*, Nat'l L.J., Oct. 16, 2006.
30. *Id.*
31. Elizabeth Goldberg, *Law Firms Face Gray Area as Boomers Age*, Am. Law., Dec. 10, 2007, *available at* http://www.law.com/jsp/article.jsp?id=1197021878240 (citing Hildebrandt International).
32. Executive Summary, *supra* note 9.
33. *Id.*
34. Unpublished aggregate statistics, *supra* note 7.
35. Nat'l Ass'n for Law Placement, Most Lawyers Working Part-time Are Women—Overall Number of Lawyers Working Part-time Remains Small (2009), *available at* http://www.nalp.org/parttimesched2009. In the NALP study, the terminology used is "part-time" rather than "reduced hours," which is the term being used interchangeably in this book.
36. *Id.* "Counsel" in the 2009 Best Law Firms for Women survey is synonymous with "other" lawyers in the NALP study.
37. *Id.*
38. *Id.* (citing a 2008 Bureau of Labor Statistics summary).
39. Unpublished aggregate statistics, *supra* note 7.
40. *Id.*
41. *Id.*
42. Executive Summary, *supra* note 9.
43. *See* Deborah Epstein Henry, *Facing the FACTS: Introducing Work/Life Choices to All Firm Lawyers Within the Billable Hour Model*,

DIVERSITY & THE BAR, Nov./Dec. 2007, *available at* http://www.flextimelawyers.com/pdf/art10.pdf.

44. EXECUTIVE SUMMARY, *supra* note 9.

45. *Id.*

46. Unpublished aggregate statistics, *supra* note 7.

47. EXECUTIVE SUMMARY, *supra* note 9.

48. *Id.*

49. Unpublished aggregate statistics, *supra* note 7.

50. *Id.*

51. EXECUTIVE SUMMARY, *supra* note 9.

52. SCHARF ET AL., *supra* note 2, at 2.

53. *Id.*

54. NAT'L ASS'N OF WOMEN LAWYERS, *supra* note 8.

55. JOAN C. WILLIAMS & VETA T. RICHARDSON, THE PROJECT FOR ATTORNEY RETENTION & MINORITY CORPORATE COUNSEL ASSOCIATION, NEW MILLENNIUM, SAME GLASS CEILING? THE IMPACT OF LAW FIRM COMPENSATION SYSTEMS ON WOMEN 12 (2010), *available at* http://www.pardc.org/Publications/SameGlassCeiling.pdf [hereinafter NEW MILLENNIUM, SAME GLASS CEILING? STUDY].

56. EXECUTIVE SUMMARY, *supra* note 9.

57. *Id.*

58. SCHARF ET AL., *supra* note 2, at 2.

59. E-mail from Brande Stellings to Deborah Epstein Henry (July 30, 2010) (on file with author).

60. AM. BAR ASS'N COMM'N ON WOMEN IN THE PROFESSION, VISIBLE INVISIBILITY 10 (2006), *available at* http://www.abanet.org/women/VisibleInvisibility-ExecSummary.pdf [hereinafter AM. BAR ASS'N, WOMEN IN THE PROFESSION STUDY].

61. *Id.*

62. *Id.*

63. NEW MILLENNIUM, SAME GLASS CEILING? STUDY, *supra* note 55, at 26, tbl. 4.

64. *Id.* at 33–35, 40.

65. SCHARF ET AL., *supra* note 2, at 3.

66. *Id.*

67. Roberta D. Liebenberg & Julia M. Rafferty, *Give Credit Where Credit Is Due*, LEGAL INTELLIGENCER, Apr. 20, 2010, *available at* http://

www.stradley.com/articles.php?action=view&id=548 (citing U.S. Census Bureau).

68. New Millennium, Same Glass Ceiling? Study, *supra* note 55, at 55–63.

69. Scharf et al., *supra* note 2, at 3. These statistics are in the context of NAWL's law firm sample with a median of 22 female equity partners and a median of 120 male equity partners.

70. *Id.* at 9.

71. New Millennium, Same Glass Ceiling? Study, *supra* note 55, at 22.

72. Gina Passarella, *Women GCs Must Speak Up to Effect Change, Study Says*, Legal Intelligencer, Apr. 29, 2010, *available at* http://www.law.com/jsp/article.jsp?id=1202454529463&Women_GCs_Must_Speak_Up_to_Effect_Change_Study_Says.

73. Liebenberg & Rafferty, *supra* note 67.

74. Executive Summary, *supra* note 9.

75. *Id.*

76. *Working Mother 100 Best Companies 2009*, Working Mother, Apr. 28, 2010, *available at* http://74.125.47.132/search?q=cache:JIsWKSTzC0sJ:www.workingmother.com/BestCompanies/work-life-balance/2009/08/ernst-young+%22Ernst+%26+Young%22+and+%22Career+Watch%22&cd=8&hl=en&ct=clnk&gl=us.

77. Executive Summary, *supra* note 9.

78. Dr. Arin N. Reeves & Stephen Pickett, *White Men and Diversity. A Closer Look. The Call to Action*, Diversity & the Bar, Sept./Oct. 2008, *available at* http://www.mcca.com/index.cfm?fuseaction=page.viewpage&pageid=1799.

79. Deepali Bagati, Catalyst, Women of Color in U.S. Law Firms (Women of Color in Professional Services Series) 48–49 (2009), *available at* http://www.catalyst.org/file/304/woc_law-report.pdf.

80. Ida O. Abbott, *Mentoring Across Differences. Mentoring Programs for Minority Lawyers: A Word to the Wise*, Minority Corporate Counsel Association, Jan./Feb. 2006, *available at* http://www.mcca.com/index.cfm?fuseaction=page.viewpage&pageid=926.

81. Executive Summary, *supra* note 9; for more information about LGBT issues, see Lisa A. Linsky, *Out and About: LGBT Legal* at www.huffingtonpost.com.

82. Unpublished aggregate statistics, *supra* note 7.

83. Am. Bar Ass'n, Women in the Profession Study, *supra* note 60.

84. *Id.*

85. *Id.*

86. *Id.*

CHAPTER 6

WHY WORK/LIFE WORKS: THE BUSINESS CASE

When our middle son, Spencer, was four years old, his preschool teachers would post a "Question of the Day" and each child would provide an answer. I loved the exercise because it was a great way to capture what was on the kids' minds. One spring morning when I brought Spence to school, I saw that the question was "What does your mother do?" The school's demographic was mostly dual career households, so this was a fitting question. I was excited because I had talked to Spence about being a lawyer and Flex-Time Lawyers LLC and I was curious how he would respond. When I arrived back at school to pick him up, each kid's name was written on the board with his or her mother's job listed afterward. Spence's name was toward the bottom, so I read through each name, listing doctors, lawyers, teachers, etc. Next to Spence's name, it simply said: "My mom makes my lunch."

I remember being not only surprised but disappointed by this response. But my sister, Susie, reassured me: it's a good thing that Spence only sees me in relation to what I do for him. At age four, his response reflected that I was meeting his needs. As with children, employers need to know that their needs are being met, especially when it comes to economics.

Flexible and reduced-hour schedules have historically caused a lot of anxiety and ambivalence among legal employers. Many legal employers are concerned about being supportive of reduced-hour schedules for fear of opening the floodgates—everyone will want to work reduced hours, or so it would seem. But the statistics do not support this concern. According to the National Association for Law Placement, Inc. (NALP) and as discussed in Chapter 5, reduced-hour schedules were available in 98 percent of the 1,475 offices surveyed in 2009.[1] Yet only 5.9 percent of lawyers nationally worked reduced hours.[2] Of those lawyers working reduced hours, 3.5 percent were partners, 5.0 percent were associates, and 20.7 percent were counsel, of counsel, senior attorneys, and staff attorneys.[3] Also, 72.5 percent of those working reduced hours were women.[4] These low usage rates for reduced hours reflect that some lawyers will never want to work reduced hours, some lawyers cannot afford to take the pay reduction that comes with working reduced hours, and many who work reduced hours do so only on a temporary basis.[5]

For those concerned about opening the floodgates, it is useful to look at the statistics for the last 15 years. In 1994, when NALP first started tracking reduced-hour schedules, such schedules were available in 86.4 percent of the 995 offices surveyed, yet only 2.4 percent of lawyers nationally worked reduced hours.[6] Of these lawyers working reduced hours, 1.2 percent were partners and 4.0 percent were associates.[7] This small percentage and the slow incremental usage over the past 15 years demonstrate that the fear of too many attorneys opting for such arrangements is unfounded.

Because employers often cite economic concerns as a reason to reject reduced-hour schedules, here I will focus on the business case for supporting reduced-hour schedules.[8] While Chapter 10 will address these economic issues in an economic downturn, this chapter contemplates these arrangements mostly during a strong market.

Reduced-Hour Lawyers Are Profitable

> When asked about reduced hours, the most common concern of employers is profitability. Law firm management says, for example, that a lawyer is more profitable billing 100 percent rather than 75 percent (or another reduced percentage) of his or her hours. However, this calculation relies upon an incorrect assumption. The comparison should be the profitability of a lawyer at 75 percent (or another reduced percentage) versus not at all.[9]

When lawyers seek reduced hours and their employers reject their requests or their workplaces are inhospitable to reduced hours, these lawyers often leave. In strong economic times, high attrition rates reflect a general population of unhappy and overworked lawyers. According to a 2005 report of the NALP Foundation tracking associates in years 2002 to 2004, in a strong market, 78 percent of associates leave their law firms by their fifth year of practice.[10] For women associates of color by their fifth year of practice, the figure is 81 percent.[11]

High attrition disproportionately impacts women lawyers with children who leave the profession. According to the Center for Work-Life Policy, 31 percent of women lawyers take a leave of more than six months at some point in their careers.[12] This attrition does not come cheap. One study found that it costs a law firm $200,000 to $500,000 to replace a second-year associate.[13] Another study found that it costs one and a half to two times a departing employee's annual salary to recruit and train a replacement.[14] By either measure, these numbers are prohibitive.

Additionally, research by *The Lawyer* shows a direct link between usage of reduced-hour programs and female partner retention.[15] In a survey of the largest 50 law firms in the United Kingdom, *The Lawyer* found that the firm with the highest level of female partners, Berrymans Lace Mawer LLP (BLM), also had the highest percentage of partners working reduced hours. At BLM, 14 percent of the firm's partners worked reduced hours, while 35 percent of its combined equity and non-equity partners were women.[16] Among its equity partnership, 28 percent were women.[17] Additionally, some of the firms with the lowest numbers of female partners also had fewer reduced-hours partners. For example, *The Lawyer* reported that at Freshfields Bruckhaus Deringer LLP, Herbert Smith, LLP and Taylor Wessing LLP, 12 percent, 14 percent, and 11 percent, respectively, of all partners were women. The respective percentages for partners working reduced hours at these firms was 2 percent, 4 percent, and 3 percent.[18] Thus, *The Lawyer* findings demonstrate the use of reduced-hour schedules as a retention tool to ultimately increase the representation of women at the top.

Law firm management sometimes dismisses the attrition argument, claiming that the law firm economic model relies on attrition and the "up or out" policy. However, management wants control over who leaves. When the lawyers who leave are the talented ones whom management wants to retain and promote, the law firm suffers. Law firms are increasingly recognizing that attrition is costly and damaging to the talent-management model. As discussed in Chapter 3, future plans at many firms today are to hire fewer attorneys and improve their retention rates for those they hire.

Additionally, client relations are improved when clients face less firm turnover. Continuity of lawyers minimizes client frustration and disruption of service and avoids the cost of training new lawyers.[19] Clients are skeptical when told they are not being charged for a new lawyer's learning curve. "When we have turnover with our outside counsel, it costs us money," said Teri Plummer McClure, senior vice president at United Parcel Service Inc.[20] "You lose that knowledge base and the experience that comes with long-standing relationships."[21] Clients may also lose confidence in firms that are unable to retain their lawyers.[22]

With Overhead Costs, Reduced-Hour Lawyers Are Still Profitable

Another common argument against reduced hours is that a law firm's fixed overhead costs prevent reduced hours from being economically feasible. This argument usually assumes an economic model that divides overhead costs equally among all attorneys. But these costs and resources (e.g., building rental, maintenance, and support staff) are not used equally by all firm lawyers. In other words, the overhead argument is based on an accounting convenience rather than individual lawyers' different use of economic resources.[23] For example, a senior partner with a significant portfolio of business and high billable hours uses more resources than a reduced-hour lawyer who may occasionally telecommute, does not use support staff heavily, and does not have as many associates working under him or her.[24] Additionally, if a significant number of attorneys choose to work reduced hours or telecommute on a regular basis, the firm could look at shared work spaces and "green" office solutions, as discussed in Chapter 10.

Reduced-Hour Schedules Provide an Economic Cushion

A reduced-hours schedule also can provide an economic cushion for employers as it anticipates the unpredictable demands of life and the market. When the inevitable crises arise—illnesses or emergencies—

lawyers working reduced hours can often make up the lost work by working other times not regularly scheduled for work.[25] In a law firm setting, the lawyer generates the same revenue working from home as he or she does in the office. So the attorney can make up hours lost at home, recouping the revenue for the firm. Additionally, in a down market, this cushion further buffers an employer from economic hardships. When work slows down, these lawyers, already being paid less to work less, impose less of a burden on the firm.

Reduced-Hour Lawyers Are Efficient and Productive

The potential to increase productivity and efficiency is another reason why employers should support flexible and reduced schedules. As discussed in Chapter 3, the BOLD Initiative study found that by implementing telecommuting, flex-time, and compressed workweeks at ten companies during a pilot project, each company increased productivity by 5 to 10 percent.[26]

While the billable hour still governs most law firms, there is often an inverse relationship between profitability and efficiency. However, as more law firms are being pressed by clients to move to an alternative fee model, efficiency and productivity will become more important to enhance a firm's profitability. For example, in an alternative fee arrangement where the client is being billed a flat fee to file a brief, the firm has the opportunity to enhance its revenue generation through its lawyers' efficiency.

Clients Demand Diversity and Consistency

Increasingly, in-house lawyers are articulating their desire to have the law firms who represent them more accurately represent their diversity—not just at the lower levels, but also at the top. In 2010, there were 94 women top legal officers at the Fortune 500 companies, 82 of whom were white/Caucasian (non-Hispanic), 7 African American, 3 Hispanic, and 2 Asian Pacific American.[27] Additionally, among the Fortune 501 to 1000, there were 81 women general counsel, 73 of whom were white/Caucasian (non-Hispanic), 6 of whom were African American, 1 Hispanic, and 1 Asian Pacific American.[28] With the rising number of women and minorities in corporate legal departments, law firms would financially benefit from improving their retention of diverse lawyers.[29]

Some law firms have expressed concern that clients will not want to work with lawyers working flexible or reduced hours, but the research does not support these concerns. The Project for Attorney Retention found in its Corporate Counsel Project that generally, clients are concerned about two factors involving outside counsel's availability: responsiveness and accessibility.[30] Assuming those requirements are met (from full-time lawyers as well as those working flexible or reduced hours), clients have not expressed concerns about outside counsel's schedule.[31] In fact, clients have remarked that essentially all of their outside lawyers are "part-time."[32] What law firm lawyer works exclusively on one matter for one client?[33] That would be a risky proposition. Also, law firms need to be careful to treat their lawyers working flexible or reduced hours properly. Disgruntled lawyers who go in-house will be less likely to refer matters to their former law firms.[34]

Some clients have taken it a step further and are using flexible and reduced-hour schedules as a criterion for selecting outside counsel. The objective is to increase the number of women attorneys, as the majority of those using these schedules are women. In 2009, I cofounded an initiative called Balanomics™ with Darragh J. Davis, Vice President and General Counsel of PETCO's Law Department; Rupa G. Singh, Federal Appellate Staff Attorney and Liaison to the North American South Asian Bar Association; and Elizabeth B. Daniels, Of Counsel, Juniper Sanderson Wiggins LLP and Immediate Past President, Association of Corporate Counsel, San Diego Chapter. Part of the mission of Balanomics™ is to make work/life balance integral to the diversity discussion. Along these lines, we developed a Balanomics™ reporting form template (that appears in Appendix A) to provide employers with a form to evaluate their representation of diverse lawyers and their availability and usage rates of work/life policies.

I encourage in-house legal departments and law firms to consider the factors enumerated in the Balanomics™ reporting form template to fully incorporate work/life balance into the diversity assessment. The form provides a standardized means to collect data on full-time and reduced-hour schedules, other work/life policies, parental leave, and representation rates of attorneys at all seniority levels. In the queries, the form provides breakdowns by women, men, ethnic minorities, and lesbian, gay, bisexual, or transgender (LGBT) attorneys.

Additionally, Vault and the Minority Corporate Counsel Association have created the Vault/MCCA Law Firm Diversity Database based on an annual diversity survey of more than 250 law firms. The result is an impressive, free diversity database that enables users to evaluate through qualitative and quantitative data, the diversity programs and representation of women, minorities, LGBT, and lawyers with disabilities at the top law firms nationally.[35] I encourage law departments and law firms to also consider the work/life policies, usage rates, and representation factors outlined in the Balanomics™ reporting form template to fully integrate work/life balance into the diversity analysis.

Companies including Accenture Ltd., Allstate Insurance Co., Del Monte Foods Co., DuPont Co., United Parcel Service Inc., and Wal-Mart Stores Inc. have joined an initiative called the Diversity & Flexibility Connection to boost the number of women and minorities in top law firm positions by adding reduced hours and flexible work schedules to the list of criteria they require of outside counsel.[36] In addition to directing business to firms that take reduced-hour opportunities seriously, these legal departments are also discussing opportunities to refer work directly to attorneys on reduced-hour schedules.[37]

Competition to Recruit and Retain the Best Talent Requires Flexibility

Competing for talent and avoiding a "brain drain" is another reason why legal employers need to support flexible and reduced schedules. With women making up the majority of lawyers working flexible and reduced schedules,[38] the legal profession cannot operate without maximizing the potential of half of its brainpower. The return of a strong economic market will create competition to recruit female talent at the law school level and to retain and promote that talent at the lateral level. As discussed in Chapter 1, the war for talent will become more fierce as the Baby Boomers retire and there will not be enough Gen X lawyers to fill the Boomers' shoes.

In strong economic markets, law firms compete on diversity committees, women, and work/life initiatives.[39] They hire former practicing lawyers to play professional development roles to improve their firms' profiles on these issues. Making diversity, work/life balance, and women's issues a basis of competition among law firms, just like salary or pro bono commitment, has been a key element to making change.[40] Providing a forum to educate and share information, as well as an opportunity to make information public among lawyers and legal employers, has also been critical.[41] The similar hierarchy of law firms has lent itself to easy comparison.[42] Whether law firms are competing to recruit candidates, retain their existing lawyers, or solicit clients, firms have felt pressure to change their culture and improve their existing training, programs, and statistics or be left behind.[43] As the increased demand for labor returns, these competition principles will surely take hold again.

Qualitative Benefits for Law Firms to Support Flexibility

Flexible and reduced-hour programs foster commitment, efficiency, and loyalty for lawyers availing themselves of such opportunities.[44] These lawyers become committed because the employers make an investment in them. Employers that have strong work/life programs also benefit in their recruiting efforts. Flexible and reduced-hour programs have become emblematic of employers being progressive on a wide range of issues. "In other words, an effective flexible and reduced hour policy reflects a general tolerance and positive atmosphere that law school candidates gravitate to as an ideal work environment, even if they never intend to work a flexible or reduced schedule."[45] Employers can also benefit from the public relations of being known as a positive place to work.[46]

Flexibility Brings Opportunities

The flexibility in a lawyer's schedule also may bring more business. With greater opportunities to develop business in unconventional ways, and with fewer lines delineating work and home, lawyers who are spending more time with their children and in their communities are also expanding their networking base and business development opportunities.[47] These lawyers have the opportunity to interact with other professionals and potential business prospects who are also spending more time in their communities—on the playground, in PTA meetings, with religious and volunteer organizations, and on boards.

The business case for flexibility is one that goes well beyond the scope of reduced hours and it is not just a woman's issue, as evidenced by mounting research. In 2001, Catalyst reported that 71 percent of male and female law graduates with children reported work/life conflict. For law graduates without children, 62 percent of the women and 56 percent of the men reported work/life conflict.[48] As discussed in Chapter 1, the 2008 A Better Balance survey demonstrated even greater concerns among law students of integrating work and life.[49] With technology that enables lawyers to work anywhere comes the desire to do so, particularly from Gen Y lawyers, both female and male.

Senior and supervisory lawyers often worry about accountability and that important training and work bonds cannot be formed when work is performed in fewer hours or it is done remotely. They fear junior lawyers are losing training and mentoring opportunities and the ability to develop close relationships with colleagues and clients.[50] Many law firms believe that the institutionalization of full-time flex-time, where lawyers work a full week in less conventional hours and locations, is even more troubling than the formalization of reduced time, as it can threaten the established corporate culture, even though the economic model would essentially remain the same. Thus, when we analyze the business case for reduced hours, we also need to look at the psychological case for flexibility and how to build support for a change in how we work while still ensuring collegiality, proper training, and the bottom line. Overcoming these concerns will be addressed in Chapter 8.

Notes

1. Nat'l Ass'n for Law Placement, Most Lawyers Working Part-time Are Women—Overall Number of Lawyers Working Part-time Remains Small (2009), at tbl.4, *available at* http://www.nalp.org/parttimesched2009.

2. *Id.* at tbl.1.

3. *Id.* Usage rates for reduced-hour schedules were the lowest at 5.2 percent at firms with 51 to 100 attorneys. Usage rates for reduced-hour schedules were the highest at 6.1 percent at firms of 251–500 attorneys and firms of 701 attorneys or more. *Id.* at tbl.4.

4. *Id.* at tbl.1.

5. Joan C. Williams & Cynthia Thomas Calvert, Nat'l Ass'n for Law Placement, Solving the Part-Time Puzzle: The Law Firm's Guide to Balanced Hours 137 (2004).

6. Nat'l Ass'n for Law Placement, Part-time Schedules for Lawyers Widely Available, Minimally Utilized (1995).

7. *Id.*

8. *See generally* Deborah Epstein Henry, *The Business Case for Flexibility: Why Flexible and Reduced Hours Are in a Legal Employer's Financial Interest*, Diversity & the Bar, Mar./Apr. 2007, *available at* http://www.flextimelawyers.com/pdf/art4.pdf; Lisa Carney Eldridge & Deborah Epstein Henry, *Cashing In on Part-Time*, Bencher, Mar./Apr. 2003, *available at* http://www.flextimelawyers.com/pdf/art2.pdf.

9. Eldridge & Henry, *supra* note 8, at 14.

10. Paula A. Patton & Cynthia L. Spanhel, Nat'l Ass'n for Law Placement, Toward Effective Management of Associate Mobility: A Status Report on Attrition 21, tbl.6 (2005).

11. *Id.* at 24, tbl.12.

12. Sylvia Ann Hewlett et al., Ctr. for Work-Life Policy, Off-Ramps and On-Ramps Revisited 8 (2010).

13. Joan Williams & Cynthia Thomas Calvert, *Balanced Hours: Effective Part-Time Policies for Washington Law Firms*, *in* The Project for Attorney Retention Final Report 7 (2d ed. 2001), *available at* http://www.pardc.org/Publications/BalancedHours2nd.pdf.

14. Steven K. Berenson, *Creating Workplace Solutions for Women Attorneys: Report of the Lawyers Club of San Diego Balance Campaign*, 28 T. Jefferson L. Rev. 449, 466 (2006).

15. Luke McLeod-Roberts, *Part-Time Schemes Help Firms Keep Female Partners Working*, Lawyer, Feb. 1, 2010, *available at* http://www.thelawyer.com/part-time-schemes-help-firms-keep-female-partners-working/1003280.article.

16. *Id.*

17. *Id.*

18. *Id.*

19. Darragh J. Davis et al., *Increase Profits and Savings Through Work/Life Balance*, ACC Docket, Nov. 2009, Vol. 27 at 98, *available at* http://www.balanomics.net/pdf/acc.pdf; Deborah Epstein Henry, *The Case for Flex-Time and Part-Time Lawyering*, Pa. Law., Jan./Feb. 2001, 45–46, *available at* http://www.flextimelawyers.com/pdf/art1.pdf; *see also* Joan C. Williams et al., Project for Attorney Retention

Corporate Counsel Project, Better On Balance? The Corporate Counsel Work/Life Report 51–52 (2003), *available at* http://www.pardc.org/Publications/BetterOnBalance.pdf.

20. Karen Sloan, *Companies Push for Flexible Schedules to Boost Women Attorneys*, Nat'l L.J., Dec. 3, 2009, *available at* http://www.law.com/jsp/article.jsp?id=1202436003132.

21. *Id.*

22. Karen Sloan, *Can Women Climb the Law Firm Ladder if Work Schedules Are More Flexible*, Nat'l L.J., Nov. 30, 2009; Henry, *supra* note 19, at 46; *see also* Williams et al., *supra* note 19.

23. Eldridge & Henry, *supra* note 8, at 14; *see also* James J. Sandman, Remarks at American Bar Association Litigation Section Summit on Keeping Her in Her Place: New Challenges to the Integration of Women in the Profession, The Business Case for Effective Part-Time Programs (Aug. 11, 2002) (former Arnold & Porter LLP managing partner provides economic analysis relying on 2001 figures, demonstrating that reduced-hour lawyers are profitable, despite the two biggest overhead items of rent and malpractice insurance).

24. Eldridge & Henry, *supra* note 8, at 14–15.

25. *Id.*

26. Leah Carlson, *Flexibility Proves Profitable for Large Firms*, Emp. Benefit News, Sept. 15, 2005, *available at* http://www.allbusiness.com/labor-employment/working-hours-patterns-flextime/8008526-1.html.

27. *MCCA's 2010 Survey of Fortune 500 Women General Counsel*, Diversity & the Bar, 23, Jul./Aug. 2010, *available at* http://www.mcca.com/index.cfm?fuseaction=page.viewPage&pageID=2107.

28. *Id.* at 24 (at one company, two women share the general counsel position so 81 women represent 80 companies).

29. For a further discussion of how diversity is being used as a criterion for selection of counsel, *see* Melanie Lasoff Levs, *Call to Action. Sara Lee's General Counsel: Making Diversity a Priority*, Diversity & the Bar, Jan. 2005, *available at* http://www.mcca.com/index.cfm?fuseaction=page.viewpage&pageid=803; *see also* Nathan Koppel, *Courting Shell*, Am. Law., June 24, 2004.

30. Williams et al., *supra* note 19.

31. *Id.*

32. *Id.*

33. *Id.*

34. Williams & Calvert, *supra* note 5, at 18.

35. http://mcca.vault.com/.

36. Sloan, *supra* note 20.

37. *Id.*

38. Nat'l Ass'n for Law Placement, *supra* note 1, at tbl.1.

39. Although women and work/life initiatives are part of the overall work of diversity committees, they are referenced separately because they are often treated differently by employers. The diversity committee is usually the overarching body and then many firms have separate task forces or committees that address issues specific to people of color, women, or work/life balance.

40. *See generally* Deborah Epstein Henry, *Competition as an Instrument of Change*, The Balance Beam, 2005–2006, *available at* http://www.flextimelawyers.com/pdf/2005_2006newsletter.pdf.

41. *Id.*

42. *Id.* An example of creating competition to improve work/life balance and the status of women in law firms is the survey and list of the Working Mother & Flex-Time Lawyers Best Law Firms for Women.

43. *Id.*

44. Eldridge & Henry, *supra* note 8, at 15.

45. *Id.*

46. *Id.*

47. Deborah Epstein Henry, *Business Development Beyond Rubber Chicken Dinners*, The Balance Beam, 2004–2005, *available at* http://www.flextimelawyer.com/pdf/2004_2005newsletter.pdf; *see also* Eldridge & Henry, *supra* note 8, at 14–15.

48. *See* Catalyst, Women in Law: Making the Case 9 (2001), *available at* http://www.catalyst.org/file/165/women_in_law_making_the_case.pdf.

49. Nancy Rankin et al., *Seeking a Just Balance*, A Better Balance, 3 (June 2008), *available at* http://abetterbalance.org/cms/index.php?option=com_docman&task=cat_view&gid=33&Itemid=99999999.

50. In a session I co-facilitated as a consultant to the New York State Bar Association Special Committee of Balanced Lives in the Law,

partners of large New York law firms expressed this concern. *See generally*, SPECIAL COMM. ON BALANCED LIVES IN THE LAW, N.Y. STATE BAR ASS'N, FINAL REPORT (2008), *available at* http://www.nysba.org/Content/NavigationMenu/LawPracticeManagementResources/ReportonBalancedLivesintheLaw/NYSBABalancedLivesReportDEHrevisions2.08.pdf.

APPENDIX A

BALANOMICS™ REPORTING FORM TEMPLATE

BALANOMIC$™

FIRM NAME: ________________________ **Reporting Form Template**

I. Reduced Hour Work Schedule Statistics

____ (Y/N): The Firm has a policy that allows firm attorneys at all levels to work a Reduced Hour (RH) work schedule, i.e., where attorneys bill a reduced percentage of the target billable hours, typically 60 – 80% of the target billable hours of full-time attorneys. (If "Yes" please complete the following):

Is the policy written ____ or informal ____?

____ (Y/N): Does the Firm allow a RH lawyer to be elevated to equity partner without requiring his or her return to a full-time schedule before being considered?

As of [DATE], please provide in the chart below the number and percentage of attorneys who are currently on a RH work schedule firm-wide and as assigned to [CLIENT].

	Total # of RH Attorneys working for [Client]	Total % of RH Attorneys Firm-Wide	Total # of RH Equity Partners working for [Client]	Total % of RH Equity Partners Firm-Wide	Total # of RH Non-Equity Partners working for [Client]	Total % of RH Non-Equity Partners Firm-Wide	Total # of RH Counsel/Of Counsel or equivalent working for [Client]	Total % of RH Counsel/Of Counsel or equivalent Firm-Wide	Total # of RH Associates working for [Client]	Total % of RH Associates Firm-Wide
All Attorneys										
Women										
Men										
Ethnic Minorities*										
Lesbian, Gay or Bisexual Attorneys										
Non-Minorities										

*"Ethnic Minorities" means: Native Americans; Asian/Pacific Islanders; Black/African Americans; Hispanics; and Multi-Racial individuals.

BALANOMICS™ FOUNDING PARTNERS

PETCO Law Department   Flex-Time Lawyers LLC   North American South Asian Bar Association   Association of Corporate Counsel-San Diego Chapter

BALANOMICS

FIRM NAME: ______________________ **Reporting Form Template**

II. <u>Full-Time Flex-Time Work Schedule Statistics</u>

____ (Y/N): The Firm has a policy that allows firm attorneys at all levels to work a Full-Time Flex-Time (Full-Flex) schedule, i.e., where the attorney bills and is paid full-time but has sought approval and regularly works one or more days out of the office or works compressed days on a regular basis. (If "Yes" please complete the following):

Is the policy written ____ or informal ____?

As of [DATE], please provide in the chart below the number and percentage of attorneys who are currently on a Full-Flex work schedule firm-wide and as assigned to [CLIENT].

	Total # of Full-Flex Attorneys working for [Client]	Total % of Full-Flex Attorneys Firm-Wide	Total # of Full-Flex Equity Partners working for [Client]	Total % of Full-Flex Equity Partners Firm-Wide	Total # of Full-Flex Non-Equity Partners working for [Client]	Total % of Full-Flex Non-Equity Partners Firm-Wide	Total # of Full-Flex Counsel/Of Counsel or equivalent working for [Client]	Total % of Full-Flex Counsel/Of Counsel or equivalent Firm-Wide	Total # of Full-Flex Associates working for [Client]	Total % of Full-Flex Associates Firm-Wide
All Attorneys										
Women										
Men										
Ethnic Minorities*										
Lesbian, Gay, Bisexual or Transgender Attorneys										
Non-Minorities										

*"Ethnic Minorities" means: Native Americans; Asian/Pacific Islanders; Black/African Americans; Hispanics; and Multi-Racial individuals.

BALANOMICS™ FOUNDING PARTNERS

PETCO Law Department   Flex-Time Lawyers LLC   North American South Asian Bar Association   Association of Corporate Counsel-San Diego Chapter

BALANOMIC$™

FIRM NAME: ______________________ **Reporting Form Template**

III. Parental Leave Statistics: Firm-Wide

As of [DATE], please provide in the chart below the number of attorneys firm-wide, regardless of whether they perform work for [CLIENT], who have taken advantage of parental leave. Note that if the length of paid leave varies for different attorneys, please provide the amount for associates.

	Number of attorneys who have given birth, adopted or whose partner has given birth during the previous calendar year.	**Number of attorneys who have used parental leave during the previous calendar year.**
All Attorneys		
Women		
Men		
Ethnic Minorities*		
Lesbian, Gay, Bisexual or Transgender Attorneys		
Non-Minorities		

*"Ethnic Minorities" means: Native Americans; Asian/Pacific Islanders; Black/African Americans; Hispanics; and Multi-Racial.

Types of Paid Leave Offered	**Number of Weeks of Paid Leave in Full**
Maternity or Primary Caregiver	
Paternity or Secondary Caregiver	
Adoption	

BALANOMICS™ FOUNDING PARTNERS

PETCO Law Department Flex-Time Lawyers LLC North American South Asian Bar Association Association of Corporate Counsel-San Diego Chapter

BALANOMICS™

FIRM NAME: ______________________ **Reporting Form Template**

IV. Additional Work/Life Policy Information

1. In the last three years as of [DATE], the following attorneys became equity partners:

   a. ___(#) while working a RH schedule

   b. ___(#) while working a Full-Flex schedule

   c. ___(#) while pregnant

   d. ___(#) after being on maternity leave

   e. ___(#) after being on paternity leave

2. _____ (Y/N): Does the firm have a written or informal policy that allows job shares?

3. _____ (Y/N): Does the firm have a written or informal policy that allows Annualized Hours, i.e., where lawyers work RH by working intensely on a matter or deal and when the matter or deal ends, they take a longer reprieve before being staffed again and their cumulative billable hours at the end of the year are a reduced percentage of the firm's billable hour target?

4. _____ (Y/N): Does the Firm have a written or informal policy that allows attorneys to automatically transition from maternity leave to a RH schedule temporarily for up to one year to ensure a smooth transition?

5. _____ (Y/N): Does the Firm have a written or informal policy to keep in touch with attorneys who leave the profession to become stay-at-home parents and maintain a connection to ideally recruit back the talent when they are ready to re-enter the workplace?

6. _____ (Y/N): Does the Firm provide training programs for attorneys at all levels on how to effectively manage and use the Firm's Work/Life Policies, i.e., policies addressing Full- Flex schedules, RH schedules, parental leave and transitions from/re-entry into the profession.

7. _____ (Y/N): Does the Firm regularly solicit feedback from its attorneys at all levels on ways to improve the usage, promotion rates, and implementation of Work/Life Policies?

BALANOMICS™ FOUNDING PARTNERS

PETCO Law Department   Flex-Time Lawyers LLC   North American South Asian Bar Association   Association of Corporate Counsel-San Diego Chapter

BALANOMIC$™

FIRM NAME: ______________________ **Reporting Form Template**

V. General Firm Information

As of [DATE], please provide in the chart below the number and percentage of attorneys who are currently on a Full-Time conventional work schedule firm-wide and as assigned to [CLIENT].

	Total # of Full-Time Attorneys working for [Client]	Total % of Full-Time Attorneys Firm-Wide	Total # of Full-Time Equity Partners working for [Client]	Total % of Full-Time Equity Partners Firm-Wide	Total # of Full-Time Non-Equity Partners working for [Client]	Total % of Full-Time Non-Equity Partners Firm-Wide	Total # of Full-Time Counsel/Of Counsel or equivalent working for [Client]	Total % of Full-Time Counsel/Of Counsel or equivalent Firm-Wide	Total # of Full-Time Associates working for [Client]	Total % of Full-Time Associates Firm-Wide
All Attorneys										
Women										
Men										
Ethnic Minorities*										
Lesbian, Gay, Bisexual or Transgender Attorneys										
Non-Minorities										

*"Ethnic Minorities" means: Native Americans; Asian/Pacific Islanders; Black/African Americans; Hispanics; and Multi-Racial.

BALANOMICS™ FOUNDING PARTNERS

PETCO Law Department | Flex-Time Lawyers LLC | North American South Asian Bar Association | Association of Corporate Counsel-San Diego Chapter

CHAPTER 7
CREATING A WORK/ LIFE-FRIENDLY EMPLOYER

When our oldest son, Oliver, was six years old, he was in the kitchen one night and asked my husband Gordon if he could play outside after dinner. Gordon said no since it was late and getting close to bath and story time. Once Gordon left the room and I entered, unaware of the conversation that had preceded me, Ollie asked me the same question. I told him he could play outside for a short while. When Gordon reentered the room and saw Ollie outside, he was annoyed. I overheard him ask Ollie what he was doing outside. Ollie responded, "I asked Mommy and she said it was okay." Gordon followed up: "Well, why did you listen to Mommy and not me?" To which Ollie replied, "Because she's the lawyer."

Ollie's response reflected that he saw me as an authority figure not only in the home but outside of it. In that moment, my six-year-old articulated for me what so many lawyers are trying to achieve—finding a way to play an integral role at home while succeeding at work.

In 2008, when the economic downturn unfolded, the discussion about work/life balance changed. Many lawyers began to fear that work/life balance would be viewed as a luxury, that those who were still employed should just feel lucky to have a job.[1] But work/life balance is an issue that is here to stay, regardless of economic cycles. As legal employers contemplate restructure, work/life balance should be a paramount concern. Legal employers need to understand that the needs of the talent pool are changing. To be successful, employers will need to create an environment that maximizes their performance.

In a strong economic climate, work/life balance is directly linked to attrition. A 2007 MIT study, for example, revealed that lack of work/life balance was the number-one reason why women left law firms and among the top three reasons why men left law firms while remaining in the workforce.[2] Similarly, in corporate legal departments, when lawyers do not have the flexibility they need, they leave.[3] Work/life balance has become even more important for future lawyers in Generation Y. As discussed in Chapter 1, in a 2008 survey of New York University School of Law students, work/life balance was the biggest concern for both male and female law students, with eight out of ten students willing to trade money for time.[4]

> There are many components to designing a work/life-friendly employer. A starting point is to make the environment work/life-friendly for all lawyers. Work/life balance is no longer an issue impacting just working mothers. In order for a work/life initiative to be successful, it must focus on men and women at all levels of seniority and address issues in addition to parenting.

The expansion of work/life balance issues to address issues faced by men as well as women, for reasons in addition to parenting, has been evolving for some time. While the work/life issues continue to impact women most acutely, the fact that men are also facing and prioritizing work/life issues will help reduce stigma and expedite change.

To assess the viability of an employer's work/life policies, it is valuable to look at law firm trends on work/life balance against national benchmarks. Many of the work/life statistics from the Working Mother & Flex-Time Lawyers Best Law Firms for Women survey were discussed in Chapter 5, which focused on creating a woman-friendly employer and included a discussion of work/life policies and usage. To avoid repetition, the Best Law Firms for Women statistics will not be repeated here; instead, Chapter 5 will be referenced in the pertinent sections should readers choose to refer back to those benchmarks. This chapter will focus on the components of a successful work/life environment with the exception of the larger topic of flexible and reduced hours, which will be addressed in Chapter 8, and additional flexible work arrangements that will be explored in Chapter 9.

Reasonable Hours for All Lawyers

Setting a reasonable number of hours for a lawyer to work is an important foundation for creating a work/life-friendly culture. In the 2007 MIT study, long hours were an important factor in why lawyers left law firms.[5] Over 60 percent of female and over 40 percent of male lawyers who left firm practice cited difficulty integrating work with family and personal life.[6] This is not surprising. In a strong economic climate, average billable hours at large firms were climbing to 2,000 to 2,200 hours,[7] and billing 2,500 to 3,000 hours was not unusual.[8] Such hours leave little time for a balanced life. In the American Bar Association billable hours report, it recommended that full-time billable hours be 1,900 a year,[9] which is quite demanding, especially after adding the additional and expected non-billable time.

The nature of the practice of law is such that, at times, lawyers' actual hours will exceed their expected hours. But employers with a billable hour infrastructure should still set a reasonable general target. Reasonable hours allow lawyers not only to play a more integral role in their families and communities but also to contribute to the profession. They allow lawyers to assume more leadership roles with bar associations, boards, and other professional organizations; take on pro bono work; and be more engaged in their community.[10] These opportunities will enrich the lives of the lawyers and their personal and professional communities and will also likely lead to networking and business development opportunities.

Protecting Vacation

Another important foundation in creating a work/life-friendly culture is to protect, where possible, lawyers' vacations. Lawyers covet the time they schedule for vacation with family and friends, and when vacations get cancelled or interrupted or if lawyers are required to work during their vacations, it interferes with the need to recharge, relax, and escape.

When assessing the effectiveness of an employer's vacation policy, it is important to go beyond the number of vacation days offered. It is also instructive to look at the usage rates at all levels of seniority. In the 2009 Best Law Firms for Women survey, vacation usage rates at the partnership level declined considerably from the prior year. In the 2008 Best Law Firms for Women survey, among the 50 winning firms the average number of vacation days taken by associates was 14; counsel, 18; non-equity partners, 25; and equity partners, 20.[11] In contrast, in 2009, the average number of vacation days taken by associates was 14; counsel, 16; non-equity partners, 16; and equity partners, 16.[12] These lower usage rates reflect the economic downturn and lawyers' reluctance to leave the office in unstable times.

In addition to vacation days allotted, vacation policies should also indicate:

- expectations, if any, for availability during vacation
- the number of hours billed before a day is no longer considered a vacation day
- implications of cancellation or interruption of a vacation
- carryover and compensation for unused vacation time[13]

Supporting Parental and Other Leaves

It is important that lawyers are offered parental, sick, and other necessary leaves. Employers need to respect leave time so lawyers can tend to their needs outside of work. Every legal employer should have a written parental leave policy that encompasses male and female birth, nonbirth, and adoptive parents at all levels of seniority. The policy should be accessible in the employer's handbook and online through the employer's intranet site. Transparency with a parental leave policy will help encourage usage. When assessing viability of an employer's parental leave policy, it is important that men and women avail themselves of the policy, from the associate through the partnership levels.

With parental leave, it is important that lawyers be paid for a sufficient period of time during the leave so they can take the time off without undue financial hardship.[14] Lawyers should also be entitled to take unpaid leave without fear of losing their jobs. It is important for employers to compare their policies and usage rates to the national benchmarks set by the Best Law Firms for Women initiative as discussed in Chapter 5.

Lawyers should feel comfortable using leave policies without fear of being penalized. Lawyers' concerns typically revolve around whether taking the leave and the amount of leave they take will negatively impact their career advancement. Particularly with lawyers who consider taking a longer leave, there is concern that they will be viewed as uncommitted. Lawyers also worry whether they will be able to effectively maintain client and colleague relationships during their leave.

Lawyers' concerns can be allayed by scheduling a meeting—what I call the "parental leave sit down" before going out on leave to review expectations and parameters. What follows is a list of the components of a parental leave policy. The parental leave sit down should cover the issues enumerated in the Components of a Parental Leave Policy box below as well as the issues discussed in the Parental Leave Punch List in Chapter 12. The success of most leave arrangements hinges on aligning the expectations of the lawyer and employer. Lawyers should have a clear understanding of how to transition their work before they go out on leave. The parental leave sit down should also address, among other issues, the employer's expectation of reasonable availability on pending matters while the lawyer is on leave and what communications and work, if any, will be expected of a lawyer while on leave.[15]

Components of a Parental Leave Policy

A parental leave policy should include the following information:[16]

- Job-guaranteed leave with pay
- Job-guaranteed leave without pay
- Impact, if any, on bonus pay and salary increases
- Impact, if any, on promotion
- Compensation for work during unpaid leave
- Additional leave time, if any, for work during leave
- Availability of short-term disability
- Ability to use vacation, sick, and personal days for paid and unpaid leave time
- Minimum length of service, if any
- Health insurance
- For adoption, cost reimbursement
- Applicability to non–birth parents

- Applicability to all lawyers, including equity partners
- Communication, work expectations, and coverage while on leave
- Transition process of leaving and returning from leave

Instituting Phase-Back from Parental Leave

Parental leave is a particularly vulnerable time to lose lawyers from the profession. As discussed in Chapter 5, a phase-back policy that automatically allows a lawyer returning from parental leave to transition back on flexible or reduced hours is helpful in facilitating a successful return. Phase-back policies typically allow an automatic flexible or reduced-hour return for six to twelve months. A written phase-back policy should outline eligibility and the process by which a lawyer informs the employer of an interest to return to work on flexible or reduced hours. It should also articulate the transition back to full-time hours or the process by which to request a continuation of flexible or reduced hours beyond the automatic period. To assess the success of a phase-back policy, employers should compare prior retention rates before the policy was enacted and also track the comparative retention rates of those lawyers who go out on leave and use the policy and those who do not.

Childcare and Eldercare Offerings and Support

Another vulnerable time when employers lose talented lawyers is when they face childcare or eldercare needs. In speaking to hundreds of women who have left the profession, a significant number say they ultimately left because they could not find the right childcare arrangement. Work/life-friendly employers can help by providing support on a multitude of levels. Employers can provide on-site or near-site daycare for everyday usage. Employers can also provide corporate emergency backup childcare at a site for children who are healthy when regular childcare providers are unavailable.

Employers also can subsidize emergency backup childcare at home where a prescreened childcare provider is sent to a lawyer's home to care for a sick or well child. This option, like the others, helps ensure the bottom line by enabling the lawyer to find suitable care for his or her child and get his or her work done. Some employers go the extra mile and host an on-site facility providing childcare to attorneys and staff.

An on-site facility can often make the difference for lawyers in choosing one employer over another. Such a facility also sends a powerful message that the employer understands the importance of family and childcare. These policies, as outlined in Chapter 5, provide layers of support to help keep parents of young children, and especially women, in the workforce and contributing at a higher level.

Employers should also provide elder/adult backup care at home by affiliating with providers that offer such services. The backup adult care services typically include both companion and personal care services. The employee usually pays an hourly rate for the care that is subsidized by the employer's affiliation. The care helps employees with elderly or sick relatives when the employee has a gap in his or her adult care arrangements and needs to get to work. The benefit usually extends to any adult dependent in an employee's family or extended family for whom the employee has caregiving responsibilities.

Backup independent childcare and adult/elder care programs have proved to be cost-effective for firms. According to Dorene Blythe, Senior Director of Client Services for Bright Horizons Family Solutions LLC, in 2010, the average cost of a Bright Horizons *Back-Up Care Advantage* program for a law firm with 500 employees in a major city was $55,000 a year. This fee covers use of dedicated back-up care centers, access to a network of child care centers nationwide, and in-home coverage for these lawyers and staff. If a firm has a $55,000 contract and if one assumes an associate billing rate of $250 per hour or $2,500 per day, the program more than pays for itself after less than 25 associates use the program. Moreover, a 2008 study of approximately 150 Bright Horizons legal clients (977 respondents) who used the *Back-Up Care Advantage* program, found that employees using back-up child care reported that it allowed them, on average, to work 5.2 days when they would not otherwise have been able to over a six-month period. Employees using back-up adult/elder care reported an average of 6.1 work days saved in a period of six months.[17]

Implementing Successful Reentry Policies

Lawyers—women in particular—are leaving the profession in significant numbers. Indeed, 31 percent of women lawyers take a leave from the law of more than six months at some point in their careers.[18] Although there is not an equivalent statistic for male lawyers, it is instructive to look at the comparative numbers for female and male professionals who leave. According to the 2010 Center for Work-Life Policy's *Off-Ramps and On-Ramps Revisited* study, women professionals are about twice as likely to "off-ramp" than men: 31 percent of women professionals compared to 16 percent of male professionals.[19] Thus, the trend of women professionals leaving their jobs is common across industry, and these women stay out of their professions for an average of 2.7 years.[20]

> Reentry among lawyers typically involves women who have left the profession for one or more years to become full-time caregivers and are looking to get back to work. Legal employers need to address the loss of the female talent pool that constitutes these reentry lawyers. A starting point is to stop considering women's career paths as nontraditional when nearly a third of all women lawyers are pursuing them.

Recruiting back reentry lawyers is beneficial to employers because these lawyers are typically experienced and come from a largely untapped talent pool. Benefits to employers of recruiting back their own former lawyers are numerous. These lawyers are proven talent who have already fit into the employer's culture. Recruiting back former lawyers strengthens the alumni bond and may be a helpful referral source, as former lawyers often worked in-house at clients at some point. Further, recruiting back former lawyers can help with future recruiting efforts by creating a positive impression with students. These efforts also result in improved morale because lawyers feel they are part of an ongoing community. It helps with public relations as well.

Cultivate the Relationship with Lawyers Who Want to Leave

Legal employers can take steps to respond to the reentry issue once a lawyer has indicated an intention to leave. The first is to secure the relationship with talented lawyers who are leaving. When a talented lawyer gives notice or indicates an inclination to leave, the employer should consider cultivating the relationship and offering a flexible, mutually beneficial work arrangement. In the Center for Work-Life Policy *Off-Ramps and On-Ramps Revisited* study, 69 percent of women professionals said they would not have left their companies if one or more flexible work options were available.[21] Thus, a legal employer should ask: Is the lawyer looking for greater flexibility or reduced hours? Are the work/life policies that are offered actually viable? Does the lawyer want to switch practice groups or transition to contract work or discrete assignments from home? Legal employers should answer these questions to pursue the lawyer's continued affiliation with the firm or company before his or her affiliation ceases.

Formalize a Reentry Policy and Maintain a Relationship with Lawyers Who Leave

The second step for legal employers in the reentry process is to effectively maintain a relationship with the lawyers who leave. A formal program and written policy creates a foundation to maintain the relationship. Formalizing reentry policies enables legal employers to develop a decisive plan on how to target, maintain, and cultivate the reentry talent pool. Such policies also create predictability and security for lawyers who want to plan their futures and know the variety of options available to them.

Some law firms have expressed fear of the costs of such programs and the opening of the floodgates. Experience in other sectors illustrates the financial benefit of a formal reentry policy. Through its Personal Pursuits program, for example, professional services firm Deloitte keeps connected to employees who leave to pursue personal goals by providing access to organizational news and internal online learning courses, and by paying for ongoing certification requirements for up to five years, as long as they do not seek employment while enrolled in the program.[22] The cost and usage rates of Deloitte's Personal Pursuits program, piloted in 2004 and rolled out across the organization in 2006, should allay employer fears. Even though Deloitte is a large organization with over 45,000 people, Personal Pursuits has only 88 participants. According to Anne Weisberg, a director in Talent at Deloitte Services LP, in 2010 the program cost less than $500 per person.[23] In contrast, the cost to recruit experienced candidates is high. For example, it costs one-and-a-half to two times a departing employee's annual salary to recruit and train a replacement.[24] Personal Pursuits provides a pool of candidates who not only are current but also know Deloitte's culture and business as well.

For legal employers considering formal programs, here are some reentry guidelines:

1. It is best to target lawyers for up to five years after they leave.
2. Employers should stay connected with the lawyers who leave and should keep their credentials current by paying for their bar dues

and attendance at employer functions, alumni events, employer-sponsored training, continuing legal education, and bar association programs.

3. It is helpful to assign a supervisory mentor to whom the departing lawyer already has a close relationship.
4. Employers should inquire whether departing lawyers want to continue to work on a contract basis on discrete assignments.

Although legal employers may not be able to promise lawyers that their jobs would be there if they wanted to return, if the relationship is an ongoing one, ideally it would facilitate a natural transition to reentry into the same or a comparable job.

Skadden Arps Slate Meagher & Flom LLP was the first law firm to announce a formal law firm reentry program entitled Sidebar, where attorneys in good standing are eligible to leave the firm for up to three years with the expectation that they will return.[25] During that time, attorneys stay connected with the firm through firm functions, alumni events, and continuing legal education. These attorneys also may continue to work on small firm projects, but they are not allowed to pursue other employment while participating in the program.[26] As discussed in Chapter 5, the 2009 Best Law Firms for Women statistics reflect that many other firms have followed suit and adopted written policies to keep in touch with and train women who leave their firms for family reasons whom the firm wants to recruit back.[27]

Actively Recruit Reentry Lawyers Back to Work

The third reentry step that legal employers should take is to actively bring women lawyers back to work. They can do this by targeting résumés from reentry lawyers. One challenge is finding these lawyers, but legal employers can start by looking to their alumni and to their lawyers for help. Some legal employers have sponsored conferences that aim at retraining and recruiting reentry lawyers back into the market. Legal employers can also sponsor reentry-focused initiatives of bar associations, law schools, and other organizations. In the 2009 Best Law Firms for Women survey, 54 percent of the 50 winning firms hosted or sponsored programs to keep in touch with, identify, recruit, and hire reentry lawyer moms.[28]

Some legal employers have expressed concern about how to fit reentry lawyers into a traditional hierarchy. For example, where does a reentry lawyer fit in when she has practiced as a litigator for eight years, left the profession for four years, and now is interested in reentering a law firm as a trusts and estates lawyer? Or should a candidate who has been out of law school for 20 years with virtually no legal experience be considered as a first-year? In each lawyer's individual case, the employer would need to assess the candidate's strengths and weaknesses and determine what prior substantive and practical experiences would be transferable. At times, employers considering reentry hires may be more comfortable hiring such candidates if it could be done with an initial trial period. Three-month internships are a helpful way for employers to determine candidates' suitability for a position.

Ensure a Successful Return

The last critical step for employers in the reentry process is to ensure a returning lawyer's success. Once a reentry lawyer is hired, the legal employer needs to lay the groundwork for a smooth transition. The future of reentry initiatives will depend on success stories of those lawyers who have returned and thrived, rather than being placed on a new "mommy track." Assigning a mentor to guide the lawyer through challenges and to provide a network of support is important to ensure a successful transition.

Phased Retirement Program

A well-rounded work/life environment must also address the needs of Baby Boomers who are challenging traditional trends of when and how to retire.[29] As discussed in Chapter 1, legal employers should provide the flexibility to allow Baby Boomers to retire over five to ten years rather than retiring outright. By giving senior lawyers the ability to work flexible or reduced hours over a period of years as they approach retirement, employers will benefit and so will the lawyers. If done right, a phased retirement enables law firms to gradually and effectively transition clients to junior partners while retaining the counsel and experience of senior lawyers. In turn, Boomers will be able to take more time for family, travel, and other interests.

WORK/LIFE INFRASTRUCTURE

Chapter 5, which discusses designing a woman-friendly employer, this chapter, Chapter 8, which addresses how to make flexible and reduced-hours work, and Chapter 9, which addresses additional flexible and reduced-hour arrangements, complete the picture of how to create a work/life-friendly employer.

In addition to implementing the policies and programs covered in these chapters, it is critical to set up an infrastructure to reinforce models of success. The infrastructure—discussed in ten principles in Chapter 8—provides the guideline for these policies and programs to thrive.

Many think that designing a work/life-friendly employer merely means having an effective "part-time" program in place. However, a work/life-friendly employer addresses issues that are much broader. It focuses on all lawyers working in a more hospitable environment, whether or not they work flexible hours or have children. Designing a work/life-friendly environment supports men and women at all levels of seniority in all of their pursuits for a more balanced life, regardless of reason.

NOTES

1. *See, e.g.*, Karen Sloan, *The New Associate Mantra: Keep Quiet*, NAT'L L.J., Apr. 27, 2009, *available at* http://www.law.com/jsp/nlj/PubArticleNLJ.jsp?id=1202430128598&hbxlogin=1; Gina Passarella, *Work-Life Balance Scale Tipping in Work's Favor*, LEGAL INTELLIGENCER, Nov. 3, 2008, *available at* http://www.law.com/jsp/law/careercenter/lawArticleCareerCenter.jsp?id=1202425737910.

2. Mona Harrington & Helen Hsi, *Women Lawyers and Obstacles to Leadership*, *in* A REPORT OF MIT WORKPLACE CENTER SURVEYS ON COMPARATIVE CAREER DECISIONS AND ATTRITION RATES OF WOMEN AND MEN IN MASSACHUSETTS LAW FIRMS 12–13 (2007), *available at* http://web.mit.edu/workplacecenter/docs/law-report_4-07.pdf.

3. WOMEN'S BAR ASSOCIATION OF THE DISTRICT OF COLUMBIA INITIATIVE ON ADVANCEMENT AND RETENTION OF WOMEN, NAVIGATING THE CORPORATE MATRIX, 27–28 (2010), *available at* http://www.wbadc.org/files/Advocacy%20&%20Endorsements%20Files/Initiative%20Reports/WBA_Navigating_the_Corporate_Matrix_May_2010.pdf.

4. Nancy Rankin et al., *Seeking a Just Balance*, A BETTER BALANCE, 3–4, 6 (June 2008), *available at* http://abetterbalance.org/cms/index.php?option=com_docman&task=cat_view&gid=33&Itemid=99999999.

5. Harrington & Hsi, *supra* note 2, at 14–15 & tbl.2(c).

6. *Id.* at 13, chart 2(a) & (b).

7. Scott Turow, *The Billable Hour Must Die*, A.B.A.J., Aug. 2007, *available at* http://www.abajournal.com/magazine/article/the_billable_hour_must_die/; Adam Liptak, "*Stop the Clock? Critics Call the Billable Hour a Legal Fiction*," N.Y. TIMES, Oct. 29, 2002, *available at* http://www.nytimes.com/2002/10/29/business/businessspecial/29LIPT.html.

8. Liptak, *supra* note 7.

9. AM. BAR ASS'N, ABA COMMISSION ON BILLABLE HOURS REPORT 2001–2002, at 49–50 (2002), *available at* http://www.abanet.org/careercounsel/billable/toolkit/bhcomplete.pdf.

10. *See generally* SPECIAL COMM. ON BALANCED LIVES IN THE LAW, N.Y. STATE BAR ASS'N, FINAL REPORT (2008), *available at* http://www.nysba.org/Content/NavigationMenu/LawPracticeManagementResources/ReportonBalancedLivesintheLaw/NYSBABalancedLivesReportDEHrevisions2.08.pdf [hereinafter N.Y. STATE BAR ASS'N, FINAL REPORT].

11. WORKING MOTHER MEDIA & FLEX-TIME LAWYERS LLC, EXECUTIVE SUMMARY, HIGHLIGHTS OF WORK/LIFE AND WOMEN TRENDS FROM THE 2009 BEST LAW FIRMS FOR WOMEN SURVEY, *available at* http://www.flextimelawyers.com/best/press20.pdf [hereinafter EXECUTIVE SUMMARY].

12. *Id.*

13. N.Y. STATE BAR ASS'N, FINAL REPORT, *supra* note 10, at app. E.

14. COMM. ON WOMEN IN THE PROFESSION, N.Y. CITY BAR, PARENTAL LEAVE POLICIES AND PRACTICE FOR ATTORNEYS 14 (2007), *available at* http://www.nycbar.org/pdf/report/Parental_Leave_Report.pdf.

15. *Id.* at 23–24.

16. *Id.* at 11–13, 26.

17. E-mails from Dorene Blythe to Deborah Epstein Henry (July 20 and 22, 2010) (citing Bright Horizons, *The Lasting Impact of Employer-Sponsored Back-Up Care* (2008)) (on file with author).

18. SYLVIA ANN HEWLETT ET AL., CTR. FOR WORK-LIFE POLICY, OFF-RAMPS AND ON-RAMPS REVISITED at 8, Fig. 1.2 (2010).

19. *Id.* at 10, Fig. 1.7.

20. *Id.* at 21.

21. *Id.* at 32.

22. Deborah Epstein Henry, *Comeback Lawyers: A Look at Why Re-Entry Is a Hot Work/Life Balance Topic*, Diversity & the Bar, Jan./Feb. 2007, *available at* http://www.flextimelawyers.com/pdf/art11.pdf.

23. E-mail from Anne Weisberg to Deborah Epstein Henry (July 7, 2010) (on file with author).

24. Steven K. Berenson, *Creating Workplace Solutions for Women Attorneys: Report of the Lawyers Club of San Diego Balance Campaign*, 28 T. Jefferson L. Rev. 449, 466 (2006).

25. Henry, *supra* note 22.

26. *Id.*

27. Working Mother Media & Flex-Time Lawyers LLC, 2009 Best Law Firms for Women Survey, unpublished aggregate statistics of the 50 winning firms.

28. Executive Summary, *supra* note 11.

29. Elizabeth Goldberg, *Law Firms Face Gray Area as Boomers Age*, Am. Law., Dec. 10, 2007, *available at* http://www.law.com/jsp/article.jsp?id=1197021878240.

CHAPTER 8

MAKING FLEXIBLE AND REDUCED-HOUR SCHEDULES WORK

When our oldest son, Oliver, turned eight, he got in the habit of picking up the newspaper and reading the sports section in the car while I drove our youngest, Theodore, to preschool. One morning, while Ollie was reading the paper with Theo and Spencer in the car, he casually asked, "Mom, what's great sex?" I'm thankful at these moments that I live in the suburbs, as I find that these types of questions most frequently come up while I'm driving the kids so my back is facing them and they cannot see my reaction.

While thinking up an answer, I delayed by asking, "Where did you hear that?" Ollie replied that there was an ad for "great sex" next to the article he was reading about Sunday's football game. So I told him that I couldn't get into it because this question required a long answer. Ollie then said, "But, Mom, I have all the time in the world," parroting a phrase I often use. I was working hard to hold back the laughs but I said to Ollie, "Unfortunately, I can't explain it right now because after taking you to school, I need to get to work." Ollie assured me that this was not a problem: "If you can't answer me, I can just call this number here where it says 'Please call (999) . . . .'"

Why does this story remind me of flexible and reduced-hour programs? Because, like kids hearing about sex, lawyers interested in flexible and reduced-hour programs should not be left to interpret them on their own. Employers should provide guidelines to make flexible and reduced-hour arrangements work, where appropriate.

Common Complaints and Concerns about Flexible and Reduced Hours

Certain repeated complaints arise from lawyers working flexible and reduced hours.[1] One is stigma. Lawyers working flexible and reduced hours often report feeling isolated, marginalized, and resented by colleagues. They do not have support at the leadership or supervisory level. They worry about being viewed by colleagues as uncommitted. They feel out of the loop as a result of missing impromptu meetings. Often assigned work that is less high profile or rewarding, these lawyers lose opportunities and confront detours to advancement.

Additionally, many lawyers working flexible and reduced hours face unpredictability and lack of control in their hours and schedule. They feel they are always "on call" and they are often not paid commensurate with their contribution. These lawyers find themselves struggling with longer hours than they negotiated and overpaying in childcare to ensure coverage. They face the challenges of delineating lines between work and home, especially because of technological advances. Some worry they will lose benefits because of their status. They also worry more generally about their job security.

In-house lawyers working reduced hours face the issues raised above and often additional challenges as well. As reported in *Better On Balance? The Corporate Counsel Work/Life Report*, some in-house lawyers feel the need to be present because their employers have a "culture of meetings."[2] In contrast, the law firm environment often affords more flexibility. A related issue that further challenges in-house lawyers from working reduced hours is that in-house lawyers are a cost. At law firms, reduced-hour lawyers are revenue generators and the billable hour enables them to demonstrate their value. In contrast, in-house lawyers have to prove their value other than in hours billed, and some lawyers have found that value is harder to demonstrate when they are not there.

In turn, many employers fear flexible and reduced-hour schedules. They fear the floodgates will open—that if they support flexible and reduced schedules, everyone will want to work alternative hours. Employers are concerned that full-time lawyers will resent lawyers working flexibly, or that partners or managers will disagree about whether to support flexible and reduced-hour arrangements. They also worry that reduced-hour lawyers are unprofitable, uncommitted, unresponsive to colleagues and clients, unable to work added hours in crises, unwilling to work as a team. . . . The list goes on.

Five Ground Rules to Lay the Foundation

There are five ground rules that lay the foundation to make a flexible and reduced-hour program work.[3] It is important to recognize that these ground rules and the ten principles that follow pertain to highly talented lawyers seeking advancement while working flexible or reduced hours. These guidelines do not concern the flexible and reduced-hour lawyers who may be seeking predictable hours in exchange for less challenging work and are discussed in Chapters 3, 4 and 9.

1. **The success of flexible and reduced-hour policies should be limited by only two factors: the business case and the creativity of the parties designing the arrangement.** The first question should be whether the person seeking flexible or reduced hours is someone the employer wants to retain and promote and it is in the employer's economic interest to do so. If the answer is "yes," the next question is whether a creative arrangement can be designed that enables the lawyer to gain the balance he or she needs while delivering top-notch work and meeting the business needs of the employer and the demands of clients and colleagues.
2. **The word "accommodation" must be eliminated.** Flexible and reduced-hour schedules must be a win-win economic solution for both the employer and the lawyer.[4] This means that the basis for a lawyer's request to work flexible or reduced hours should be irrelevant, and usage should not be limited to childcare.
3. **Flexible and reduced-hour work arrangements are not an entitlement.** Those who avail themselves of such policies must be talented lawyers whom the firm hopes to retain and promote (though the arrangement should not be restricted to "superstars"[5]).
4. **When managing reduced-hour arrangements, the overriding rule is to treat reduced-hour lawyers the same as their full-**

time colleagues, except when it is appropriate to make pro rata adjustments.[6] This means, for example, that reduced-hour lawyers should be evaluated using the same criteria for partnership and be eligible for bonuses, pro rata, if their full-time counterparts are eligible. Thus, equal treatment, rather than preferential treatment, is sought.

5. **The ten principles that follow must be executed as a whole to maximize the success of flexible and reduced-hour work arrangements.**

Ten Principles for Successful Flexible and Reduced-Hour Policies

1. Laying the Foundation

Written Policies

For flexible and reduced-hour policies to be successful, it is important to put an infrastructure in place. Employers should put their flexible and reduced-hour policies in writing.[7] The exercise of drafting a policy forces colleagues to reach agreement on the issues of implementing flexible and reduced-hour policies. In addition to creating consensus, a written policy can keep managers with extreme tendencies in check and create predictability, especially in tumultuous times with changes in management.[8] The written policy also brings uniformity to the process and minimizes favoritism and ad hoc treatment.[9] Another benefit is that it allows junior lawyers to plan their future and see that a viable path is potentially available to them. Often junior lawyers leave their jobs in anticipation of a belief that the environment will not be manageable in the future—for example, when they have children.

When drafting flexible and reduced-hour policies, the tone is critical. The language should be positive and open rather than suspect and suggesting accommodation. It is important that the policies be written broadly and with creativity, discretion, and individuality in mind, because lawyers seeking flexible and reduced-hour schedules do so for varying reasons and at different points in their lives. The notion of drafting broad policies is also important because different lawyer strengths, skills, and practice areas will thrive under different types of arrangements. According to the 2009 National Association for Law Placement, Inc. (NALP) survey, 98 percent of law firms nationally allowed reduced-hour schedules either by an affirmative written policy or on a case-by-case basis.[10] In the 2009 Best Law Firms for Women survey, 96 percent of the 50 winning firms offered written reduced-hour policies and 42 percent offered written full-time flex-time policies.[11]

> The range of flexible and reduced-hour policies (defined in Chapter 5) that employers should offer include:
>
> 1. Full-time flex-time
> 2. Core hours
> 3. Reduced hours
> 4. Job shares
> 5. Annualized hours
> 6. Telecommuting
> 7. Fixed hours
> 8. Contracting/consulting

There are repeated questions that arise when drafting these policies. Here are some important suggestions to address the nagging issues that come up in many drafting sessions with employers.[12]

- **A flexible and reduced-hour policy should be open and accessible.** Assuming an employer's business needs are met, flexibility should be open to everyone. The policy should be readily accessible in the employer's handbook and intranet, fostering openness and support and allowing lawyers to plan their futures. The policy should not reference parenting as a basis for the request. Nor should the policy place a limit on the number of lawyers who can work flexible and reduced hours or the amount of time lawyers are to work alternative schedules. These limits suggest a negative connotation and discourage usage.
- **A declining number of policies require a certain level of experience before lawyers are eligible for reduced hours.** In the 2009 Best Law Firms for Women survey, 26 percent of the 50 winning firms required one or more years of experience for lawyers seeking reduced hours.[13] Rather than make experience an eligibility requirement, I suggest removing it and building discretion into the policy so that if an individual is not suited for reduced hours at the outset, the request can be denied.
- **A minimum number of days and hours in the office should not be required.** In the 2009 Best Law Firms for Women survey, only

8 percent of the 50 winning firms required a minimum number of days in the office for lawyers working reduced hours, and these firms, on average, required three days.[14] Some firms require reduced-hour lawyers to work a minimum billable hour percentage. The most common minimum percentage is 60 percent, and it is often dictated by insurance company eligibility for employee health care coverage.

- **Firms typically provide full access to benefits and pro-rata vacation for reduced-hour lawyers.** Most large firms contribute the same amount for health care coverage for full-time and reduced-hour lawyers and reduced-hour lawyers are entitled to the same benefits as their full-time counterparts.[15] Vacation for reduced-hour lawyers is typically accrued pro rata.

At the end of this chapter, you will find a checklist that enumerates what a written flexible and reduced-hour policy should entail. The remaining discussion in this chapter explains other key features to make flexible and reduced-hours work.

Proposal

Employers should offer a form for lawyers to use when requesting a flexible or reduced-hour schedule. On the form, the lawyer should state which work/life policy he or she is interested in accessing and include a proposed schedule. The schedule should specify the requested number of days and/or percentage of hours to work and the suggested days and/or hours in the office. The form should also provide a means for the lawyer to propose a transition from a traditional schedule. The proposal should be reviewed by the department or practice group chair as well as a work/life supervisor, if one has been designated.

> As indicated earlier, here are the two questions for an employer to consider in evaluating any proposal for flexible or reduced hours:
>
> 1. Is the person seeking flexible or reduced hours someone the employer wants to retain and promote and is it in the employer's economic interest to support the proposal?
> 2. If the answer to 1. is "yes," can a creative arrangement be designed that enables the lawyer to gain the balance he or she needs while delivering top-notch work and meeting the business needs of the employer and the demands of clients and colleagues?

> Assuming the answer to both of these questions is "yes," the department or practice group chair should then schedule what I call the "flexibility sit down"—a meeting between the department or practice group chair, the work/life supervisor (if one has been designated), and the lawyer seeking flexible or reduced hours.

The "Flexibility Sit-Down"

> Effectively navigating flexible and reduced-hour schedules is about managing expectations. An important part of the process is the flexibility sit-down, where the department or practice group chair, the work/life supervisor and the lawyer seeking flexible or reduced hours meet to discuss how to make the new schedule work.

Specifically, the flexibility sit-down should be a strategy session to ensure that colleagues and clients are not negatively impacted by the lawyer's schedule and that the lawyer has established a schedule that meets his or her needs. The lawyer working flexible or reduced hours needs to be in touch to ensure that work flows when he or she is not in the office. If the lawyer is working flexible or reduced hours because of childcare or eldercare, the lawyer would need backup coverage. This is necessary in case the lawyer needs to work from home or be in the office during non-scheduled work time. If the employer subsidizes full-time emergency backup or at-home care, the flexibility sit-down is the time to outline the process for accessing employer-sponsored care in case such needs arise.

At the flexibility sit-down, the parties should discuss the lawyer's ability and willingness to travel. Travel topics include whether the lawyer needs a certain amount of advance notice before being available to travel, or whether there are any limits on the amount of time he or she can be out of town. At times, senior lawyers have made assumptions about a mother with young children's willingness to travel. As a result, women have lost out on career development opportunities when senior lawyers assumed they would be unwilling to travel. This example reveals the importance of the flexibility sit-down to discuss mutual expectations.

Another topic for discussion is how the flexible or reduced hours will be depicted to colleagues and the outside world. It is important that colleagues know when one of their team members is working flexible or reduced hours for scheduling purposes. For example, a weekly team meeting should not be held on a Friday if one of the team members typically does not work Fridays. Concerning clients, it is important to "know your audience" in deciding what to share. Ideally, if a flexible or reduced-hour arrangement works properly, it is seamless. The clients with whom the lawyer works do not know that he or she is working a flexible or reduced schedule. An out-of-office e-mail message and voice mail recording would simply state that the lawyer is out of the office. It would also indicate the lawyer's availability, return date, and the different means by which the recipient could contact the lawyer or someone else. Similarly, the lawyer's assistant would indicate that the lawyer is outside the office and provide the different means to contact the lawyer or a colleague.

For closer client relationships or to manage certain scheduling issues that arise, it may be appropriate to share the lawyer's flexible or reduced-hour schedule. Additionally, as discussed in Chapter 7, some clients have begun to ask about schedule flexibility as part of their diversity assessment and criteria for evaluating firms to hire.[16] In these circumstances, it would also be fitting to share a lawyer's schedule.

During the flexibility sit-down, the department or practice group chair should discuss the need for the lawyer to switch around his or her schedule for client meetings, court appearances, closings, pressing matters, and emergencies. In turn, the department or practice group chair should also communicate that when matters are not pressing, the lawyer will be able to switch around his or her schedule for personal conflicts that may arise.

The department or practice group chair should counsel the lawyer to maximize his or her visibility when in the office. For example, the lawyer should ensure that one of his or her days in the office is the day when departmental or other well-attended internal meetings are held. At the flexibility sit-down, there should also be discussion about how the lawyer seeking flexible and reduced hours can effectively keep in touch, when necessary, through voice mail and e-mail when outside the office.

A point of emphasis during the flexibility sit-down should be the process of transitioning from a traditional schedule to a flexible or reduced one. The best way to make the transition work smoothly and minimize colleague resentment is to time the transition with a natural break in the workload. For example, it is much better for a lawyer seeking reduced hours to wait until a deal closes, a case settles, or a trial ends instead of passing along a file to a colleague. Also, I suggest transitioning work at the time when a lawyer is preparing for parental leave. If these opportunities do not arise, then care should be taken to minimize colleague resentment and transition the work at a time when it does not unfairly burden a colleague.

In addition to the issues raised above, at the end of this chapter there is a checklist that enumerates all of the topics for an employer to raise at a flexibility sit-down. In Chapter 13, I provide a summary for lawyers of what they should include in a proposal for flexible and reduced hours. It is important that all of these suggestions are read together to assess the range of issues that employers face when managing these schedules and lawyers face when seeking them.

2. Leadership and Openness

The success of work/life policies is contingent upon support from the top.[17] Management—e.g., a managing partner, chairperson, general counsel, or executive director—should publicly endorse (both internally and externally) an employer's policies and be transparent about the range of options available. This facilitates openness about the policies, setting the tone for ease of accessibility and usage. Ideally, management should be well-versed in articulating the employer's business case in supporting such policies.[18] If management articulates its support for flexible and reduced hours inside and outside of the workplace to clients and the press, it strengthens the internal belief that flexible and reduced-hour schedules are valued and supported.

In addition to management, leadership support should be reinforced by the supervising lawyers who work with lawyers availing themselves of such policies on a daily basis. In order for flexible and reduced-hour arrangements to be successful, supervisory lawyers must understand the financial incentive of endorsing work/life policies and the reasons to become ambassadors of the cause. So many employers think that if management is in support, then they have secured buy-in. But that is only half the battle. Supervisory lawyers impact the daily lives of lawyers, and if the supervisory lawyers are not educated and trained in effectively managing these lawyers, all of the management support will be for naught. Additionally, if supervisory lawyers demonstrate, by example, the use of flexible or reduced-hour schedules, the support for these arrangements will be that much greater.

3. *Mutual Flexibility and Ongoing Communication*

Mutual flexibility on the part of the lawyer and the employer is critical to ensure the success of work/life policies.[19] Under a billable-hour model, law firm lawyers working reduced hours (unless these lawyers are working fixed, contract, or staff attorney hours) are staffed on proportionately fewer matters, but they are still responsible for their matters 100 percent of the time. This arrangement means that these lawyers are expected to be professionals and responsive to deadlines and crises, even if they are not scheduled to be working or in the office.

In turn, employers need to be flexible to ensure that lawyers' schedules are not compromised and to allow for changes in lawyers' schedules when matters are not pressing and personal needs arise. When expectations are realistic and the focus is on mutual flexibility rather than predictability, lawyers and employers are more satisfied by the arrangements and there is less frustration. Flexibility also entails allowing for weekly, monthly, seasonal, and annual scheduling adjustments as the demands of work and home shift and change.

Along with mutual flexibility, ongoing communication is essential between lawyers availing themselves of work/life policies and those who work with them.[20] Following the flexibility sit-down, ongoing communication is necessary. With effective communication, colleagues and clients will not be inconvenienced by alternative schedules. The flexible or reduced-hour lawyer needs to inform supervisory lawyers of changes in schedules. Both parties must provide regular feedback about how the arrangement is working.

Effective communication is necessary with every member of a work team. When the flexible or reduced-hour lawyer is outside the office, the colleagues with whom he or she works should be confident of the lawyer's accessibility and responsiveness should the need arise. The flexible or reduced-hour lawyer's assistant should always know how the lawyer can be reached when outside the office. The assistant should be provided with explicit instructions about what clients should be told when the lawyer is outside the office. The onus is on the lawyer working flexible or reduced hours to make his or her availability and schedule clear. Additionally, every time a flexible or reduced-hour lawyer is staffed on a matter with new colleagues, that lawyer should discuss scheduling.

4. Support and Monitoring

Historically, lawyers who availed themselves of work/life policies (especially reduced hours) kept it a secret, because the arrangement was so tenuous that they did not want to jeopardize it. As a result, lawyers who used work/life policies had to keep reinventing the wheel and did not benefit from each other's wisdom. Lawyers who use work/life policies need the support of a community that nurtures and encourages them to thrive.[21]

A successful work/life community starts with a designee at each place of employment who serves as the supervisor[22] in charge of issues relating to flexible and reduced hours. This work/life supervisor may be a professional development administrator or partner, as long as at least part of the person's job description is to oversee lawyers working flexible and reduced hours. At smaller workplaces, there may not be the resources to dedicate a person to this role, but at a minimum someone should be accountable to oversee these lawyers.

A work/life supervisor's responsibilities include reviewing hours on a monthly basis to verify that the agreed-upon schedule is being honored. The work/life supervisor is also responsible for ensuring that the flexible and reduced-hour lawyers are getting the right type of professional development exposure, experience, and quality of work. This includes keeping track of the flexible and reduced-hour lawyers' developmental milestones and ensuring that these lawyers are engaged in high-level and challenging work with influential colleagues and clients. For example, if a reduced-hour mid-level associate is a litigator, the work/life supervisor should be identifying opportunities for that lawyer to take depositions, argue motions, or second chair a trial.

The work/life supervisor should be part of the proposal process, flexibility sit-down, annual review, and ongoing assessment of whether the arrangement is succeeding. If a flexible or reduced-hour lawyer is regularly billing in excess of his or her agreed-upon hours or if the lawyer's quality of work or exposure declines,[23] these are times when the work/life supervisor would intervene. The supervisor should also be available to follow up, redirect, or facilitate resolution of issues that may arise. For example, the work/life supervisor should ensure that partners do not have documents regularly sitting on their desks that could be acted upon. Or the supervisor should run interference when there are conflicts facing reduced-hour lawyers to repeatedly get excessive amounts of work done simultaneously for different partners. The work/

life supervisor should also intervene when the flexible or reduced-hour lawyer is consistently staffed on too many matters.

Beyond the work/life supervisor, it is helpful to build in other layers of support. Some law firms find it helpful to designate one partner to serve as the point person on work/life issues for each department or office. Other firms assign partner mentors for each lawyer working flexible or reduced hours. A partner mentor becomes another "go to" person to ensure that the arrangement runs smoothly and to facilitate resolution of issues that may arise. If partner mentors are assigned, it is preferable to assign a mentor who does not otherwise supervise the flexible or reduced-hour lawyer's work to avoid the mentor potentially both playing a supportive role and creating challenges for the lawyer.

Flexible and reduced-hour lawyers can also derive support from employers who create a community of lawyers accessing work/life policies who can advise each other, share successes and challenges, and serve as role models. The goal is to create a resource for support and information and enhance camaraderie, retention, and promotion among lawyers availing themselves of work/life policies. Creating a community may involve an employer generating an internal list of lawyers accessing work/life policies and creating affinity or informal mentoring groups. An employer may want to encourage these groups to meet monthly or quarterly or create an online community to discuss strategies to successfully manage their work and outside demands. Once a community is formed, use the forum to celebrate role models and publicize successes to create inspiration and resources. In the 2009 Best Law Firms for Women survey, 86 percent of the 50 winning firms had a support or affinity network for lawyers working reduced hours.[24] These networks can help minimize feelings of isolation and can enhance a lawyer's connectedness and loyalty to his or her employer.

5. *Assignments and Advancement*

Lawyers using work/life policies need to be assigned challenging work to give them the necessary experience and exposure to develop and advance. They also need to be mentored by influential colleagues and staffed on important client matters. In turn, lawyers working reduced hours should be eligible for non-equity (where applicable) and equity partnership and evaluated by the same criteria as their full-time colleagues.[25]

If partnership promotion decisions are determined by billable hours, among other factors, it may be appropriate for lawyers working reduced hours to be eligible for partnership after they have met the same requisite number of billable hours as their full-time colleagues. The delay in consideration (often a year or two) helps minimize colleague resentment and may improve the likelihood of promotion because the lawyer has more time to gain experience and exposure. In the 2009 Best Law Firms for Women survey, about one-third of the winning firms promoted their reduced-hour lawyers at a delayed pro rata rate, based on their percentage of full-time hours.[26] At firms where partnership promotion decisions are determined by experience gained, competencies achieved, or business produced, it may not be necessary to delay advancement for lawyers who work reduced hours. In the 2009 Best Law Firms for Women survey, reduced-hour lawyers were eligible for promotion at about two-thirds of the winning firms at the same rate as their full-time colleagues.[27]

Some colleagues of flexible and reduced-hour lawyers do not believe they should be partner eligible. These colleagues may resent that flexible and reduced-hour lawyers are not called upon as frequently for the emergency work on Friday afternoons or other inconvenient times, and therefore they believe they should not get the exciting work or be eligible for promotion. This issue can be partially remedied by putting flexible and reduced-hour lawyers on a rotation schedule for emergency work on new matters. Under this system, different attorneys each week are notified in advance that they are "on weekend call" from Friday afternoon through the weekend, and if a new matter or deal comes in during that time frame, they should expect the call. Those working reduced hours and paid a proportionate reduction would be included less frequently and proportionately in the rotation schedule.[28]

6. *Compensation*

Fair compensation is a critical area of focus when designing a flexible and reduced-hour program. When lawyers working flexible and reduced hours are not paid commensurate with their contribution, it results in stigma, resentment, and second-class status. Lawyers working full-time flex-time should be paid the same as those lawyers working a full-time conventional schedule. Lawyers working reduced hours should be paid on the same scale as their full-time colleagues, with a proportionate reduction in pay if based on a billable hour model.[29] In the 2009 Best Law Firms for Women survey, 90 percent of the 50 winning firms paid the reduced-hour lawyers the same percentage as their reduced percentage target.[30]

Under a lockstep compensation system, lawyers working flexible and reduced hours should be eligible for pro rata bonuses based on the same consideration, factors, and scale as their colleagues working a full-time conventional schedule.[31] In the 2009 Best Law Firms for Women survey, at 92 percent of the 50 winning firms, reduced-hour lawyers were eligible for bonuses for working in excess of their agreed-upon hours.[32] All lawyers' schedules fluctuate, but for reduced-hour lawyers, the risk of working a disproportionate number of hours is greater; therefore, their hours must be closely tracked by the work/life supervisor.[33] When reduced-hour lawyers work significantly in excess of their hours, they should be compensated accordingly and possibly should increase their billable-hour target temporarily.[34] Pay that is commensurate with work performed will minimize stigma and second-class status. However, this arrangement is only a partial remedy—the lawyer negotiated reduced hours to gain more time outside the office, so a compensation increase is only a short-term solution. Careful monitoring and restaffing, where appropriate, is the better long-term remedy.

Under a core competency system, lawyers working reduced hours may stay within a level for a longer period of time than their full-time counterparts who are working more hours. As discussed in Chapter 4, it is important that reduced-hour lawyers' compensation in a level system be evaluated by the same process as compensation for full-time colleagues.

Most reduced-hour lawyers who are associates, counsel, or non-equity partners are salaried. In contrast, for equity partner compensation, firms use various methods, and in most cases, reduced-hour partners' pay is proportional. In *Reduced Hours, Full Success: Part-Time Partners in U.S. Law Firms,* The Project for Attorney Retention provides a helpful analysis of equity partner compensation for reduced-hour lawyers that is summarized here. When firms use a system where equity partners are awarded shares, units, or points, a dollar amount is assigned once profits are determined.[35] In such firms, reduced-hour equity partners are typically awarded shares as if they were full-time, and then when profits are distributed they earn the reduced percentage of a full-time partner that matches the reduced percentage they worked.[36] At other firms, shares or points are awarded to partners and then partners with similar contributions are grouped into tiers or levels and receive the same compensation.[37] Under this system, once again, most firms assess a reduced-hour partner's level as if he or she were full-time and then award a proportional percentage received by full-time partners at their level, based on hours worked.[38] At firms with lockstep pay, partner compensation is determined by seniority and usually increases each year.[39] Reduced-hour partners at lockstep firms are typically paid proportionate to the number of hours they bill.[40] As with associates, it is critical that equity partners are paid proportionate to their contribution and are bonus eligible, like their full-time colleagues.

7. Nonbillable Contribution

Lawyers who work flexible and reduced schedules need to do non-client work and be part of the overall team.[41] This contribution is important to give back to the organization, enrich a lawyer's professional development, and minimize colleague resentment. At law firms, this means contributing nonbillable hours to the operation of the firm, whether it be through committee work or otherwise.[42] In law departments, it similarly involves assuming responsibilities and roles beyond the workload for the legal department. For example, flexible and reduced-hour lawyers should still serve on committees or mentor junior lawyers, but if they are working reduced hours, their contributions should be at a proportionately reduced rate.

A flexible or reduced-hour lawyer's contributions benefit not only the employer but also the individual lawyer.[43] If the flexible or reduced hour lawyer chooses visible ways to get involved, for example, it will help his or her access to influential lawyers who may then request that lawyer for future staffing. Additionally, these contributions may help the flexible or reduced-hour lawyer improve or develop a helpful set of skills, such as writing, public speaking, or networking.

8. Technology

It is essential for lawyers working alternative schedules to receive effective technological support.[44] With the advent of technology such as e-mail, faxes, scanners, cell phones, and Internet-enabled smartphones, it is easier than ever for lawyers to work remotely and for legal employers to provide efficient technological support. At the larger law firms and companies, appropriate technological support often means that employers will provide computers, scanners, Internet access, Black-

Berrys, or the equivalent and provide the technical assistance when there is the need for troubleshooting.

While technology is a means to enable lawyers to gain the flexibility they need, it is important that employers establish parameters in how to use technology responsibly. Lawyers are suffering from greater work/life conflict and difficulty delineating lines between work and home because of technology.[45] Employers should help their lawyers use technology wisely by being clear about reasonable expectations for responsiveness and accessibility to clients and colleagues. For example, lawyers on parental leave should know what their e-mail out-of-office message should say or what level of responsiveness, if any, is expected while on leave.

Technology usage is often about expectations. For that reason, when a lawyer is outside the office or unavailable for a day or more, employers should tell the lawyer to put an out-of-office message on his or her e-mail so that recipients are aware that the lawyer is unavailable. I even encourage employers to create a standardized greeting for remote workers to give employers greater comfort and give lawyers guidance. Time-sensitive requests from clients and colleagues should be responded to as soon as possible. If a lawyer is unable to check e-mail for any extended period of time, it is important that the lawyer's out-of-office message indicates whom to contact in an emergency.

When less pressing matters arise with clients or colleagues, lawyers often do not follow an established protocol. When a request is made, usually the colleague or client initially just wants a confirmation that the request has been received and will be addressed. Instead, many lawyers wait to respond until they have the answer. This often leads to frustration. Employers should train their lawyers that it usually improves communication to have the lawyer send a brief e-mail, stating that the lawyer received the request and is working on a response and will be back in touch when the issue has been addressed.

Also, employers should impress upon lawyers that a lawyer's method of using technology establishes a pattern of expectations. For example, if a client e-mails a lawyer a non-pressing question on a Saturday night and the lawyer responds within five minutes, that establishes an expectation with the client that the lawyer is always available instantly on his or her BlackBerry. In a competitive legal market, this might be just the expectation that an employer wants its lawyers to create. However, some lawyers will resist the temptation of immediately responding to off-hour, non-pressing requests because they do not want to convey that they are available 24/7. If employers are silent on technology issues, then their lawyers may handle such scenarios differently than their employers might like. Instead, employers that give guidelines to this effect will help lawyers exercise proper judgment and more effectively manage the challenges of delineating lines between work and home while meeting the expectations of clients and colleagues.

9. Training

Repeated firmwide training is necessary to educate lawyers about the firm's economic interest in supporting work/life policies.[46] Additionally, supervisors and lawyers availing themselves of work/life policies need to be trained in what I call the "nitty-gritty" of effectively managing and implementing work/life policies, respectively. The nitty-gritty training for the lawyers contemplating or using work/life policies should focus on organization and time management that will be explored in Chapters 11, 13 and 14[47] as well as the issues listed in the checklist at the end of this chapter.

Training for supervisory lawyers is often neglected by employers, and it is the necessary complement to the training of lawyers who use work/life policies. Supervisory lawyers are the ones who have the real impact on lawyers' daily lives, and they need to understand the obligations and expectations of the lawyers they supervise. The "nitty-gritty" training for the supervisory lawyers of those using work/life policies should focus on the issues enumerated in the checklist at the end of this chapter. It is also important that the supervisory lawyers learn to effectively delegate and supervise flexible and reduced-hour lawyers so assigning and mentoring do not become unnecessarily burdensome or complicated.

Education of the general population of lawyers is also critical. It helps to: dispel misconceptions; explain the general expectations of a flexible or reduced-hour lawyer in working with clients and colleagues; demonstrate why it is in the employer's economic interest to support flexible and reduced-hour schedules; and create a forum for support, openness, discussion, and improvement.

10. Track, Benchmark, Review, and Reassess

In order to ensure the success of flexible and reduced-hour arrangements, it is critical to track, benchmark, review, and reassess them annually. By tracking challenges and successes, policies can be improved upon and changes can be made to more closely align objectives with results. Tracking involves looking closely at an employers' availability of work/life policies and usage rates. Employers should benchmark themselves against any national and local usage rates that are available. They should also benchmark themselves against any other recognized sources that are available. For example, a New York City law firm should compare its reduced-hour usage rates to the latest NALP numbers that show that as of 2009, 5.9 percent of lawyers were working reduced hours nationally and 4.2 percent of lawyers were working reduced hours in New York City.[48] Additionally, the New York City firm should compare its numbers to the 2009 Best Law Firms for Women survey finding that 8 percent of lawyers worked reduced hours at the 50 winning firms.[49] Employers should break down the usage rates in terms of gender, seniority, and reasons for use. Employers should also track comparative promotion, attrition, and layoff rates.

It is not enough for employers to compare their usage rates to other benchmarks. Employers must also evaluate who is using their work/life policies and why. Therefore, employers should assess:

1. Whether men as well as women are availing themselves of the policies;
2. Whether lawyers are availing themselves of the policies for reasons in addition to parenting;
3. Whether lawyers accessing the policies are at the management, leadership, and partnership level, not just at the associate, junior lawyer, staff attorney, or counsel level;
4. Whether junior lawyers availing themselves of work/life policies are still being promoted to non-equity partner, equity partner, and management positions;
5. Whether junior lawyers availing themselves of work/life policies are being promoted at a slower rate; and
6. Whether lawyers working flexible and reduced-hour schedules have higher attrition and layoff rates.

Lawyers working flexible and reduced hours should be reviewed at least annually and on the same cycle as lawyers working a full-time conventional schedule. In addition to covering the regular content during the review, employers should evaluate whether the flexible or reduced-hour lawyers and the lawyers with whom they work are satisfied with the arrangement. Employers should use the annual review to determine whether the flexible or reduced-hour lawyer is on track for advancement. The reviewer should assess whether the lawyer is getting exposure to influential lawyers as well as high-level assignments, and professional development opportunities.

The annual review is also an important time to reassess hourly commitments and workload. The employer should evaluate and communicate its needs in terms of staffing and the lawyer should communicate his or her interest in increasing, decreasing, or maintaining the current workload and schedule. The lawyer and employer should then come to a mutually beneficial agreement on hours and scheduling to meet the lawyer's and employer's needs.

The Flexible and Reduced Hour Checklist

The Flexible and Reduced Hours Checklist governs:

1. What information should be contained in a written flexible and reduced hour policy;
2. What topics should be covered at a "flexible sit-down" meeting; and
3. What issues should be addressed in training lawyers working flexible or reduced hours and those who supervise them.[50]

The Flexible and Reduced Hours Checklist:

- Eligibility criteria
- Description of the range of flexible and reduced hour options
- Proposal process and what it entails
- Determination of billable hours, percentage, and/or workload
- Schedule and location for working
- Timing and transition to and from flexible and reduced hours
- Mutual flexibility expectations
- Communication expectations
- Nonbillable contribution expectations
- Work/life supervisor, affinity group, and support
- Assignment process
- Promotion eligibility and process
- Compensation, including bonuses
- Training
- Travel restrictions, if any

- Childcare or eldercare coverage, if applicable
- Strategies to ensure work flow does not negatively impact colleagues and clients
- Strategies to increase visibility
- Information provided about schedule to clients
- Technology expectations of responsiveness and accessibility
- Emergency contact information
- Applicability to non-equity and equity partners
- Benefits
- Vacation
- Annual review of workload, schedules, and feedback

To make flexible and reduced-hour schedules work, there must be a meeting in the middle between employers and lawyers. This is evident when looking at the ten prevailing principles that make flexible and reduced hours work. The quid pro quo between flexible and reduced-hour lawyers and their employers is the key to a successful work/life arrangement.

Notes

1. *See generally* Deborah Epstein Henry, *Prevailing Principles to Make Reduced Hour Schedules Succeed*, Diversity & the Bar, Sept./Oct. 2007, at 16, *available at* http://www.flextimelawyers.com/pdf/art9.pdf; Deborah Epstein Henry, *The Nitty-Gritty of How and Why to Make Part-Time Work*, The Balance Beam, 2003–2004, *available at* http://www.flextimelawyers.com/pdf/2003_2004newsletter.pdf.

2. WorkLife Law, Better On Balance? The Corporate Counsel Work/Life Report 4, 35 (2003), *available at* http://www.pardc.org/Publications/BetterOnBalance.pdf.

3. *See generally* Henry, *Prevailing Principles*, *supra* note 1.

4. Deborah Epstein Henry, *The Business Case for Flexibility: Why Flexible and Reduced Hours Are in a Legal Employer's Financial Interest*, Diversity & the Bar, Mar./Apr. 2007, *available at* www.flextimelawyers.com/pdf/art4.pdf.

5. Joan C. Williams & Cynthia Thomas Calvert, Nat'l Ass'n for Law Placement, Solving the Part-Time Puzzle: The Law Firm's Guide to Balanced Hours 32 (2004).

6. Joan Williams & Cynthia Thomas Calvert, *Balanced Hours: Effective Part-Time Policies for Washington Law Firms*, *in* The Project for Attorney Retention Final Report 21–26 (2nd. ed. 2001), *available at* www.pardc.org/Publications/BalancedHours2nd.pdf ("principle of proportionality" applies to pay, benefits, bonus, assignments, billable hour ratio, and advancement).

7. Henry, *Prevailing Principles*, *supra* note 1, at 17.

8. *Id.*

9. Williams & Calvert, *supra* note 6, at 27–29.

10. Nat'l Ass'n for Law Placement, Most Lawyers Working Part-time Are Women—Overall Number of Lawyers Working Part-time Remains Small (2009), *available at* http://www.nalp.org/parttimesched2009 [hereinafter Nat'l Ass'n for Law Placement].

11. Working Mother Media & Flex-Time Lawyers LLC, Executive Summary: Highlights of Work/Life and Women Trends from the 2009 Best Law Firms for Women Survey, *available at* http://www.flextimelawyers.com/best/press20.pdf [hereinafter Executive Summary].

12. *See generally* Deborah Epstein Henry, *Tips on Drafting a Flex-Time and Reduced-Time Policy—and Negotiating the Right Arrangement for You*, The Balance Beam, 2002–2003, *available at* http://www.flextimelawyers.com/pdf/2002_2003newsletter.pdf.

13. Working Mother Media & Flex-Time Lawyers LLC, 2009 Best Law Firms for Women Survey, unpublished aggregate statistics of the 50 winning firms [hereinafter Unpublished aggregate statistics].

14. *Id.*

15. *Id.*

16. Sheri Qualters, *Flextime Among the New Criteria for Clients' Evaluation of Law Firms*, Nat'l L.J., Oct. 27, 2009, *available at* http://www.law.com/jsp/article.jsp?id=1202434954310.

17. Henry, *Prevailing Principles*, *supra* note 1, at 17.

18. Henry, *supra* note 4.

19. Lisa Carney Eldridge & Deborah Epstein Henry, *Cashing In on Part-Time*, BENCHER, Mar./Apr. 2003, at 13, *available at* www.flextime lawyers.com/pdf/art2.pdf.

20. *Id.*

21. Henry, *Prevailing Principles*, *supra* note 1, at 17.

22. Williams & Calvert, *supra* note 6, at 36–37.

23. Henry, *The Nitty-Gritty*, *supra* note 1, at 2–6.

24. Unpublished aggregate statistics, *supra* note 13.

25. Eldridge & Henry, *supra* note 19, at 14.

26. Unpublished aggregate statistics, *supra* note 13.

27. *Id.*

28. *See* Deborah Epstein Henry, *Facing the FACTS: Introducing Work/Life Choices for All Firm Lawyers Within the Billable Hour Model*, DIVERSITY & THE BAR, Nov./Dec. 2007, *available at* http://www .flextimelawyers.com/pdf/art10.pdf.

29. Henry, *Prevailing Principles*, *supra* note 1.

30. Unpublished aggregate statistics, *supra* note 13.

31. Williams & Calvert, *supra* note 6, at 21–23.

32. Unpublished aggregate statistics, *supra* note 13.

33. Deborah Epstein Henry, *The Case for Flex-Time and Part-Time Lawyering*, PA. LAW., Jan./Feb. 2001, at 45, *available at* http://www .flextimelawyers.com/pdf/art1.pdf.

34. Williams & Calvert, *supra* note 6, at 35.

35. Cynthia Thomas Calvert et al., *Reduced Hours, Full Success: Part-Time Partners in U.S. Law Firms*, *in* THE PROJECT FOR ATTORNEY RETENTION 19 (2009), *available at* http://www.pardc.org/Publications/ Part-TimePartner.pdf.

36. *Id.*

37. *Id.*

38. *Id.*

39. *Id.* at 20.

40. For a further discussion of reduced hour partner compensation, *see id.*

41. Henry, *supra* note 28.

42. Eldridge & Henry, *supra* note 19, at 14.

43. Henry, *The Nitty-Gritty*, *supra* note 1, at 4–6.

44. Henry, *Prevailing Principles*, *supra* note 1.

45. *See, e.g.*, LAUREN STILLER RIKLEEN, ENDING THE GAUNTLET: REMOVING BARRIERS TO WOMEN'S SUCCESS IN THE LAW 248–49 (2006); *see also* MAGGIE JACKSON, WHAT'S HAPPENING TO HOME? 21–38 (2002).

46. Henry, *Prevailing Principles*, *supra* note 1, at 20.

47. Henry, *The Nitty-Gritty*, *supra* note 1, at 2–6.

48. NAT'L ASS'N FOR LAW PLACEMENT, *supra* note 10.

49. EXECUTIVE SUMMARY, *supra* note 11.

50. *See* Henry, *supra* note 28, at 22.

CHAPTER 9

FACING FACTS: RECONSTRUCTING THE BILLABLE HOUR

When my middle son, Spencer, was four years old, he came home from preschool one day and told my husband Gordon and me that he and his friends were talking about God. He recounted some of the things they shared and then added, "But Mommy, all I really wanted to know is: What's she really like?" To which Gordon turned to me and asked, "Did you put him up to this?"

I like to think that Spence's perception of a female God reflects both my influence on him and how he is willing to see the world. This innocent question also reveals the opportunity to take an age-old concept and look at it with a fresh set of eyes.

Why Face the FACTS?

Nobody knows for sure whether law firms of the future will abandon billable hours wholesale or redesign them. If the billable hour is to remain fully or partially intact in law firms of the future, it is critical that two perceptions change. First, billable hour expectations need to shift so there is no longer one standard for "full-time" and one for "part-time." Second, the billable hour needs to be reconstructed to give lawyers the work/life benefits that it can afford.

If the billable hour prevails, I recommend that all firms consider using FACTS—a methodology I developed in 2007[1] that offers employers and lawyers more choices in the way work gets done while maximizing the profitability of the billable hour. FACTS stands for Fixed, Annualized, Core, Target, and Shared hours. Under FACTS, all firm lawyers fit into at least one category.

Target Hours—The "T" in FACTS

While the word FACTS begins with "F," the concept of FACTS discussed here hinges on "T"—replacing the terms "full-time" and "part-time" with Target hours (the "T" in FACTS). Thus, I begin this section with a discussion of the concept of Target hours and why Target hours are critical to rethinking the billable hour.

"Full-time" and "part-time" are misnomers that have resulted in stigmatization (because they are not uniformly defined or applied) and inequity (because salary and treatment do not match contribution). "Part-time" law firm lawyers typically work a 40-hour week, when billable and nonbillable hours are combined, while "full-time" lawyer hours vary widely. For example, for associates at the same large firm in the same year, a "full-time" litigator may bill 2,300 hours and a "full-time" trusts and estates lawyer may bill 1,800 hours, while a "part-time" corporate lawyer may bill 1,800 hours and a "part-time" real estate lawyer may bill 1,500 hours. Just as areas of specialization may affect billable hour demands, billing also varies depending on an individual lawyer's work habits, the stage of a lawyer's career, the lawyer's outside demands, and the firm at which a lawyer works. A "full-time" lawyer on the cusp of partnership consideration might bill 500 more hours that year than a more seasoned "full-time" partner in the same firm who is spending more time on business development or firm management. Similarly, a small firm "full-time" lawyer might work hundreds of hours less than a large firm "full-time" lawyer.

Under FACTS, the terms "full-time" and "part-time" are eliminated and, instead, a firm creates four to six Target billable hour tracks that reflect the reality of current attorney billing patterns. These different Target tracks are determined by a firm—typically by office, department, and level of experience—and they are based on the four to six most popular Target hours that attorneys bill.[2] For example, one firm may establish six Target hour tracks of 1,200, 1,500, 1,650, 1,800, 2,000, and 2,200, after identifying that most attorneys' hours at the firm cluster around these six Targets. Under FACTS, firms would not separately categorize lawyers billing fewer hours—these lawyers would simply be on the lower end of a firm's Target hour tracks.

Those working fewer Target hours would remain eligible for partnership, assuming they meet the criteria for advancement, with a potential delay in consideration for some. For example, if a firm generally considers an associate for partnership after billing an average of 2,000 Target hours per year for eight years and an attorney billed 1,500 Target hours for four years, that attorney might be considered for partnership a year later than his or her class. High-billing attorneys could elect to continue to bill hours exceeding firm averages.

Multiple Target Hours

FACTS is what I call a "Multiple Target Hours" approach, and it requires firms to estimate their billable hour needs by department and across the firm annually. Hourly needs and expectations would then be communicated at attorney annual reviews to ensure that business and individual needs are met. Attorney Targets would vary yearly and more accurately reflect the natural fluctuations in business and individual needs. For attorneys who do not meet their year-end Target, it would be discussed at their annual review whether to adjust their hours for the following year. If it is anticipated that an attorney's hours would be down again for the following year, a new lower Target would be set for the following year and the attorney's pay would be adjusted downward accordingly.

Compensation under FACTS would be determined in one of two ways, depending on whether a firm has a lockstep or core competency system in place. Firms with lockstep compensation would set salaries at the highest Target for each associate class, and then adjust salaries downward for attorneys in the lower Target tracks. For example, if 2,000 hours is a law firm's highest Target and third-year associates billing 2,000 are paid $200,000, a third-year associate with a 1,500 Target would be paid $150,000. Individual compensation may be further adjusted to reflect work quality, additional hours worked, nonbillable contribution, and business generation, where appropriate.[3] One of the significant benefits to employers of adopting FACTS under a lockstep system is that compensation would be adjusted to reflect the natural clustering of Target hours that is already in place at firms. In other words, firms would no longer pay all third-year associates as if they were billing 2,000 hours, even if they had never met that Target. Instead, pro rata adjustments in pay would be made based on the closest Target range that attorneys bill and these Targets would be reviewed annually to keep pay and contribution aligned.

For firms that have switched to merit-based compensation, there are typically compensation bands for each of the three to four associate levels that have been created. In a merit-based system, decisions regarding compensation should be based on the achievement of defined competencies rather than hours. Lawyers working lower Target hours would be evaluated using the same criteria as lawyers at their level who worked higher Target hours. Lower Target-hour lawyers would then be compensated based on their achievement of the designated competencies within their level. For those lawyers working lower Target hours, it may take them longer to achieve the designated competencies and be compensated at the next level. For a further discussion of compensation, see Chapters 4 and 8.

A number of firms have adopted at least two different hour and compensation tracks. In 2007, Chicago-based Chapman and Cutler LLP allowed associates to choose between two different tracks.[4] They could opt to work 1,850 billable hours at less pay or 2,000 hours with higher pay.[5] Both tracks were partner eligible but the lawyers on the 1,850 track were partner eligible at a slower advancement pace.[6] Given the choice, more than half of the associates took the lower target track.[7] As of 2007, other firms with comparable programs included Hogan & Hartson LLP (now Hogan Lovells), Wiley Rein LLP, and Fenwick & West LLP.[8]

The benefits to a Multiple Target Hours system are significant. It is a way for firms to compete with certain firms with higher salaries and also minimize associate attrition as a result of long hours.[9] The two tracks can provide an economic cushion for firms with the natural ebbs and flows of work while also meeting different lifestyle needs of attorneys. There is a risk that the lower-hour track will become a "mommy track." However, by following the Ten Principles for Successful Flexible and Reduced-Hour Policies outlined in Chapter 8, that risk can be minimized.

While Target hours provide a framework for FACTS, they do not reflect where, what, how, and when work gets done. This is the focus of the four other prongs in FACTS. These four other prongs address the gaps and weaknesses in the current reduced-hour arrangements at law firms that were discussed in Chapter 8. Thus, after setting Target hours, lawyers who want to further delineate type of work, hours, and scheduling would discuss at their annual review whether to work Fixed, Annualized, Core, and/or Shared hours. These flexible work arrangements are discussed here in the context of billable hours but these arrangements also work under an alternative fee system or other non-billable model. For these Fixed, Annualized, Core, and Shared hour work arrangements, the ten prevailing principles explained in Chapter 8 would apply, as well as the additional considerations outlined below. Lawyers not seeking additional flexibility in the way they work would simply rely on their determined Target hours.

> The unrealized benefit of the billable hour is its flexibility—a firm generates the same revenue from a lawyer billing from home in pajamas as from one in the office. Yet this benefit has never been fully capitalized upon, largely due to law firms' face-time culture. FACTS provides an opportunity to manipulate the billable hour to capitalize on its flexibility, maximize profitability, and create new ways to get work done.

Fixed Hours—The "F" in FACTS

Certain high-caliber lawyers are interested in taking on less challenging work in exchange for more control over their schedules. Firms, in turn, often have certain work that is more predictable, but less high-profile or exciting or demanding, resulting in Fixed hours (the "F" in FACTS). This is the type of work, such as document review, for which clients are often unwilling to pay high rates. Fixed-hour work is not always available, and therefore may be offered on a temporary basis. As discussed in Chapter 3, highly talented lawyers may choose to work Fixed hours only temporarily or during a certain life stage, and later resume more challenging work, often with irregular hours. Fixed-hour lawyers do not necessarily work lower Target hours. Given the nature of the work, Fixed-hour lawyers are not partner eligible. They are also paid less given that the work is less challenging and more predictable and that clients are billed less for the end product.

Fixed-hour work gives high-caliber lawyers the control that many are seeking, in exchange for less demanding work. In my experience, lack of predictability and control is the number one source of law firm lawyer dissatisfaction. In a comparison of the 2003 Quality of Life Survey and *The American Lawyer*'s annual report, *Corporate Counsel* found that even though in-house lawyers were working nearly the same hours as law firm lawyers, in-house counsel reported greater work/life satisfaction. The increased satisfaction was attributable to in-house lawyers' greater control over their schedules.[10]

The benefits of separately labeling Fixed-hour work are twofold. First, it is to avoid confusing Fixed-hour lawyers with those lawyers who work lower Target hours but who engage in highly challenging work to advance. As discussed in Chapter 4, some law firm management have made the mistake of assuming that all lawyers interested in lower Target hours are interested in Fixed-hour work. A second benefit of separately labeling Fixed-hour work is to avoid confusing it from the expanding staff attorney role at law firms. There are two types of attorneys who seek out less challenging, predictable work. The first are Fixed-hour lawyers who are highly credentialed and talented but who seek more control in their lives and are willing to forgo challenging work and higher compensation so they can gain the lifestyle they need. The second are lawyers who cannot get hired for the higher-paid work and cannot manage the more challenging work, so they seek a permanent staff attorney role. Neither group of lawyers should be partner eligible and both should be paid less while doing the predictable and less challenging work. However, the Fixed-hour group should be able to return to the partnership track, assuming they are willing to resume the more challenging work and the often more erratic hours that accompany that work. For a further discussion of these issues and minimizing the "mommy track" associated risks, see Chapters 3 and 4.

Employers that have a written Fixed-hour policy should define Fixed-hour work. The policy should include the process for transitioning to and from Fixed-hour work. The policy should address the compensation and bonus eligibility differences. It should also specify that Fixed-hour lawyers are not partner eligible due to the less demanding nature of the work but if the business needs exist, they can resume the partnership track.

Annualized Hours—The "A" in FACTS

Some lawyers want to work lower Target hours but do not want to sacrifice the challenging nature of their work. They are willing to accept erratic hours and the expectation of 24/7 availability, but prefer more frequent or longer reprieves between high-intensity deals or matters. These lawyers should opt for Annualized hours (the "A" in FACTS), where they are staffed on high-profile deals or matters, followed by breaks before being staffed again. Annualized hours are more popular in corporate departments or other practice groups involving staffing on all-encompassing deals.

Annualized hours are essentially the opposite of Fixed hours. People who thrive working Annualized hours are those who are comfortable with inconsistency and significant changes in schedules or are willing to put up with an erratic schedule to ensure that they will continue to be staffed on the challenging and high-profile deals. For example, a large New York City law firm client had lawyers working Annualized hours in the corporate department. These lawyers could be staffed on high-level deals and not compromise the quality of their experiences and exposure. Yet when a deal closed, they would often take off a month or more before being staffed on a matter again.

It is preferable to track Annualized hours quarterly, rather than monthly, so that as the year progresses, the attorney and firm can make necessary adjustments to ensure that they are mutually on pace with the Target hours. Lawyers working Annualized hours who have young children will need backup full-time childcare in place to step in on short notice. Lawyers seeking Annualized hours should be aware that this type of work is difficult to plan and therefore they may be more likely to work more or less than their agreed-upon hours. A written Annualized-hour policy should anticipate these issues. It should also address the process for seeking Annualized-hour work and the staffing and tracking of hours.

Core Hours—The "C" in FACTS

Some lawyers want quality, high-level work while working less conventional hours. Core hours (the "C" in FACTS) would apply to these lawyers. Core hours are the blocks of key hours in some or all workdays when a firm would expect the lawyer to be working and/or available. Core hours would apply to those who telecommute (from home or another location)[11] and those who work unconventional hours in the office, whether they are higher, average, or lower Target hours. Full-time flex-time is the same as Core hours, although it only pertains to lawyers working a full caseload (not lower Target hours). Core hours "can be a compressed work week: Longer hours Monday through Thursday, to earn Fridays off. Or, it might mean modified start and end times organized around core or peak work times. . . . Or, perhaps an employee wants to incorporate training into the middle of the day and will work later to make up the time. In other words, the possibilities . . . are limitless."[12]

To determine Core hours for an individual lawyer, a department chair should consult with supervisors and meet with the lawyer to determine the lawyer's requested workweek schedule and location preferences and match them with departmental and client demands. For example, a working parent may request to work what I call "bus-stop hours" from 9:00 to 3:30 two days per week from home, with two longer days in the office. Another lawyer who has a long commute during rush hour may prefer to work in the office from noon to 9:00 p.m. daily.

Lawyers working Core hours, and especially those working fewer Target hours, must maintain excellent communication. Law firms and Core hour lawyers need to establish a protocol for communication during non-Core hours so that Core hour lawyers are flexible and available for crises, unexpected deadlines, and client and colleague needs during non-Core hours.[13] In turn, the firm needs to be flexible and allow for changes in an individual lawyer's scheduling when matters are not pressing.[14]

Given the ability to work anywhere thanks to technology and the expectation of 24/7 availability, flexibility in the way lawyers work has become a business reality. Professionals generally expect and appreciate the ability to work flexibly, and, in turn, they have a greater sense of loyalty and want to stay with the employers that provide it.[15] An example of this is Ross & Associates, an environmental consulting firm that executed formal flex-time and telework plans for its consultants. Bill Ross, the president of the firm, found that "telework and flex-time put more fuel in the engine of our business by allowing people to take care of personal issues."[16] At Ross & Associates, the Remote Work Plan was created to formalize and create standard guidelines and expectations for employees seeking to work regularly or occasionally from home.[17] As a result of the plan's implementation, more than 50 percent of employees adopted a flexible start and stop time and 14 percent of employees teleworked at least occasionally. The firm credits the plan for increased employee retention and productivity and improved work/life balance.[18]

To implement a Core-hour or full-time flex-time policy, an employer must put into place communication protocols that provide a framework for employees to be responsive and accessible when outside the office.[19] At Ross & Associates, a committee drafted guidelines that were reviewed to ensure "convenience for remote workers without creating a burden on their co-workers; providing seamless service to clients; maintaining management comfort with people spontaneously working from home; and determining how to allow remote workers to have productive access to the company's systems without posing a security threat."[20] Interested consultants worked with their mentors to complete a form that articulated expectations for remote working.[21]

The notion of formalizing flexibility for lawyers working a full caseload in the legal profession is gaining traction. In the Working Mother & Flex-Time Lawyers 2008 Best Law Firms for Women findings, 36 percent of the 50 winning firms had written full-time flex-time policies and in 2009, the number jumped to 42 percent.[22] "Even in a bad economy, the concept of work flexibility has staying power. For starters, it doesn't cost anything. Unlike reduced time or job sharing, lawyers on flexible schedules aren't typically looking to cut down their workload or billable hours. Many are happy to work like maniacs—provided they do it their way, at home or on schedules that deviate from normal office hours."[23]

But firms have never fully capitalized on formalizing flexibility, largely because of the face-time culture. This is a significant missed opportunity. Firms' ability to give their lawyers more flexibility and work/life satisfaction through full-time flex-time while not impacting the revenue model creates a win-win situation. Back in 1990, Davis Wright Tremaine LLP invested $4 to 5 million in telework because the firm recognized the business benefits. From his own experience and observations, then managing partner Brad Diggs said "[T]elework results in more work being accomplished. It can raise productivity levels by allowing staff more control over interruptions, eliminating or decreasing commute time, increasing job satisfaction, and providing the opportunity to focus on in-depth reading, writing and analysis."[24]

Many firm lawyers are working flexible hours unofficially and some question the value of formalizing Core-hour or full-time flex-time arrangements. The argument goes that lawyers are professionals and they are given the freedom to come and go; formalizing flexibility may diminish the freedoms they already have. However, there are many benefits to a written policy, as enumerated in Chapter 8. The key is that the policies are written broadly with creativity, discretion, and individuality in mind, because of the varying needs of different practice areas and lawyers. One particular benefit of formalization is that a written Core-hour or full-time flex-time policy anticipates the otherwise inevitable crises that result from not being able to reach someone who has not disclosed a planned absence from the office.

Some firms are fearful that formalizing flexibility will result in loss of control over the workforce and the way work gets done. One firm addressed this concern by putting parameters around the access to flexibility. Cleary Gottlieb Steen & Hamilton LLP instituted a telecommuting policy in 2008 under which all associates who have been at the firm up to one year can work one day per month from home or another location. Associates at the Firm more than one year can work from home or another location two days per month.[25] Cleary's policy minimizes stigma because it is open to all lawyers and there is no association with childcare.

Another employer fear is that by providing more flexibility to all lawyers, there will be a loss of community and culture within the law firm. In 2007, as a consultant to the New York State Bar Association Special Committee for Balanced Lives in the Law, I co-facilitated a session of New York partners in charge of associate issues, and this was raised as a significant concern. These partners relayed that they built bonds with their colleagues by having late-night dinners and working weekends at the office in jeans. They were puzzled at how to manage Gen Y lawyers who said they wanted more mentoring and feedback but who did not want to be in the office to receive it. These concerns, while real, are not insurmountable.

Creating a policy that formalizes access and usage of flexibility can actually create a greater sense of community because there will be guidelines for being in the office. For example, departments could create certain Core hours where lawyers are in the office or working. Or practice groups could set a weekly meeting on a certain day, asking all lawyers to be in the office, when possible. Some firms may grant more flexibility to more experienced lawyers and provide flexibility to junior lawyers at a gradually expanding rate. Some employers fear that by formalizing flexibility and endorsing telecommuting, they will inadvertently hurt the intellectual exchange in the office. True, impromptu in-person debate and discussion drops when team members are outside the office. But this is already a business reality as a result of global teams, varying time zones, and individuals more routinely working from multiple offices. For smaller offices where there is more of a premium on presence, these same opportunities for engaging discussion can be realized with proper planning. For example, if a Core-hour lawyer is regularly in the office three days a week, schedule a team meeting on one of those days to provide a forum for brainstorming.

Another reason to formalize flexibility is that it standardizes a process and reduces stigma. Women more often seek permission for the flexibility they seek. Men are more comfortable coming and going without publicly declaring it.[26] The problem arises when different assumptions are made about men's and women's absence from the office. For example, the majority of lawyers who work reduced hours are women and when a woman who works reduced hours has a dark office, the assumption is more likely that she is with her kids rather than at a client meeting, closing, or deposition.[27] Gender bias training and monitoring is effective in raising awareness and reducing the impact of the unconscious stereotypes that lawyers bring to the workplace.[28] Formalizing flexibility is another means to standardize the playing field and reduce the associated stigma that more often attaches to women.

> A Core-hour policy should include the components outlined in the Chapter 8 Checklist. Additionally, it should articulate a firm's expectation of responsiveness and accessibility during non-Core hours and specify the need for emergency contact information for such circumstances.

Shared Hours—The "S" in FACTS

Some lawyers seek challenging work but also want the ability to be "off call" and have more control over their schedules. They crave the traditional medical practice model in which one doctor in the practice figuratively steps into the other's shoes and handles the patients while the other doctor is "off call." Although the doctor is sometimes pulled away from his or her personal life at odd hours, those are times when he or she is "on call" and has been forewarned that work might intervene. The doctor is also able to plan and avoid many conflicts by arranging for coverage and switching "call" hours when personal conflicts arise.

> If stepping into a doctor's shoes has become an accepted practice to handle patients' critical health issues and very lives, it certainly is long overdue that this model be adopted as a means to manage clients' legal problems. In other words, if patients can accept that doctors can be interchangeable in managing life and death matters, it is time for clients to accept that lawyers can be interchangeable in managing client's legal matters.

For lawyers who seek fewer hours and more predictability and control in their lives, but not at the expense of losing challenging work, Shared hours (the "S" in FACTS) is the right fit. The job share enables two attorneys to share the same position and functions, with each stepping into the other's shoes on a preset rotating basis to share the workload of one lawyer.[29] Shared hours minimizes the largest source of work/life dissatisfaction—lack of predictability and control. It minimizes many of the other reduced-hour pitfalls too, such as needing to always be available, working more hours than negotiated, not getting paid for excess hours, difficulty separating work from home life, and overpaying for child care.[30] With the job-share team covering the office all week, management concerns about responsiveness and accessibility, and lawyer concerns about their schedules not being honored, or not getting the plum assignments or necessary experience, are minimized.[31] The job-share model has worked for in-house legal department, not-for-profit, and government lawyers, but remains rare in the law firm context.

The Best Venues for Law Firm Job Shares

Effective communication is the key to successful job shares. Lawyers need to communicate so that each member of the team knows what the other is doing and colleagues and clients are not negatively affected by the arrangement. The biggest challenge to law firm job shares is that neither the client nor the firm wants to pay more to keep two lawyers apprised of the same information. Thus, the best venue to implement law firm job shares is on matters staffed with a team of lawyers who already have to keep each other informed. For example, when I was a mid-level litigation associate, I was staffed on a large matter with a partner, another mid-level associate, and a junior associate. As a team, we were required to communicate with each other on a regular basis. The other mid-level associate and I had to read all of the same cases in writing the briefs and preparing the partner for oral argument. If the other mid-level associate and I had been working a job share, we would have communicated to each other just as we otherwise would have done with our other colleagues. This would have been an ideal opportunity for a job share because the other mid-level associate and I were already required to know all of the same information for motion practice and oral argument.

The governing principles concerning whether the client should pay for the communication costs in a billable hour system would be the same as with a lawyer with a full workload. One job-share team member's time would be billed whenever the client would otherwise be billed for team updates and meetings (an increasingly infrequent occurrence). However, the client should not be billed for any time it takes to update a job-share team member. That time, which should be minimized, should be absorbed by the job-share lawyers. It can be minimized by having both team members parse out their work and complete their own projects to avoid relearning or redoing any projects or taking them over mid-stream. If the job-share team has complementary strengths, their own projects may be divided up accordingly. The client billing manager needs to be vigilant when reviewing bills to ensure that the client is not being billed for duplication of work or job-share team updates.

Another ripe venue to start law firm job shares is in small departments where lawyers are frequently and informally covering for each other. For example, in family law, real estate, and trusts and estates departments, colleagues often step in for each other on small matters. In these departments, colleagues also are more inclined to keep each other informed about their matters. Lawyers working reduced hours in these departments are already often asked to work complementary days so that coverage throughout the week is available.

Two new trends in the industry should further encourage the use of job shares in law firms. In an alternative fee system, there is even greater ease in implementing job shares. With alternative fees, where clients are paying for efficiency and results rather than time, the tension over time spent on communication between job-share team members will be minimized. Also, with the growing trend to disaggregate work, it will be easier for job-share arrangements to work. Indeed, all lawyers will increasingly be parsing out their work and working on discrete tasks of a larger project.

Proposing a Job Share

Lawyers seeking a job share should find each other first and then prepare a proposal. Job-share teams usually work best when the participants know each other and have worked together successfully in the past. It is critical for the members of the team to have organizational skills, compatible work styles, and similar ways of resolving legal dilemmas. The job-share proposal may be even stronger if the team members have related but complementary skills, demonstrating that the team could bring more to the job than just one person.

The proposal should explain how the team plans to do the work without negatively impacting colleagues and clients. It should also explain why the arrangement is in the employer's economic interest.[32] A full explanation of how lawyers should make a flexible work schedule proposal will be explored in Chapter 13. Once the job share is granted, the evaluation process will be ongoing. In the law firm context, the job share is a novelty so the team will be under scrutiny to see how they will make it work.

Employers of job-share teams benefit from the double coverage. If a personal conflict, sick day, vacation, or emergency arises, often the two attorneys will be able to switch their schedules around to cover for each other. If a work emergency requires weekend coverage, the team could either split the weekend or alternate handling such crises. Legal employers and clients will also benefit from having two heads working on a case or deal rather than one.[33]

Making a Job Share Work

When a law firm job-share team is assigned to a new matter, both team members may attend the first client meeting; after that, there is seldom a reason to meet jointly with clients. Clients do not necessarily need to be informed of the job-share arrangement. Usually it is enough to tell the client that either team member is available to discuss the matter and that they will keep each other informed of developments. The client should never be asked about what transpired at a meeting or during a call. The objective is that anyone can contact either team member and receive the same information and end product.

Job-share lawyers often work best at a 60 percent schedule and proportionate pay,[34] with each team member in the office three days per week and one overlap day. One lawyer usually works Monday through Wednesday and the other Wednesday through Friday. Wednesday is an important overlap day in the office to transition, brainstorm, and take part in meetings or conference calls. The job-share team needs to communicate effectively through regular transition e-mails, notes, and phone calls. They should communicate what work has been done and what conversations and events have transpired while the other team member has been out of the office. Technology can help make the transition seamless.

To maximize each team member's opportunity to be "off call" when not in the office, they can share e-mail and voice mail accounts. This way, the team member outside the office does not need to be disturbed, other than if a pressing matter arises, but that team member can remain "up to speed" while out of the office. Also, no time is lost waiting for the team member outside the office to check in, forward e-mails, or report on new information. If accounts are shared, job-share team members should also be given private e-mail and voice mail accounts, if requested.[35] The respective reviews of job-share team members should be performed together. The individuals are typically advanced as a team. If one member has a specific performance issue, it should be handled separately by a practice group or department chair, who should notify the other team member.

While the three-day-a-week schedule may be the most typical job-share arrangement, as with all flexible and reduced-hour arrangements, the only limits should be the business case, (i.e., that it is economically in an employer's interest to support the job-share) and the creativity of the employer and lawyer designing the arrangement to meet the needs of the lawyer, client, and employer. As one in-house attorney wrote to me several years back, he envisions a type of job share where two senior lawyers, in their years before retirement, share a job by each working six months every year—dividing the year, for example, into two halves or four quarters. I call this a "seasonal job share" and it is consistent with the phased retirement trends that appeal to many Baby Boomers rather than retiring outright. A seasonal job share would offer employers the expertise and experience they need from their senior lawyers. In turn, the senior lawyers would enjoy more extended periods of time off for family, travel, or hobbies while remaining engaged in meaningful work. Seasonal job shares minimize many of the weekly transitional requirements and challenges of a traditional job share.

Another type of job share is one where two lawyers share one position but they work separately and do not work on the same matters.[36] This variation is more for employer headcount and overhead purposes. For example, these job-share teams may share an office or support staff to minimize expenses. However, this job-share variation does not otherwise create the work/life benefits for lawyers and the additional gains for employers.

Envisioning the Future Impact of Job Shares

Implementing more job shares in the in-house, government, and not-for-profit worlds as well as in law firms will improve the quality of life for all lawyers. Creating an infrastructure for lawyers to step into one another's shoes will enable lawyers to better plan for and take vacations and arrange for coverage while they are away. Lawyers taking parental leave also will benefit from the job-share model to arrange for extended coverage in the office.

The notion of shared roles can also have a reverberating impact in other contexts, outside of work/life balance. For example, women lawyers sometimes shy away from leadership roles because of time pressures; they may be more inclined to assume leadership positions if these roles could be shared. Some firms, for example, have co-managing partners or co-department or co-committee chairs.

In law firms, if salaries and billable hour expectations remain high, more law firm lawyers may entertain the job share as a viable alternative to gain predictability, control, and more time for life outside of work. However, the challenges of ensuring that the arrangement is successful and the reduced salaries associated with job shares should minimize law firm management's concern that everyone will soon be seeking to work a job share.

Just the FACTS

In sum, the goals of FACTS are straightforward: eliminate the misnomers of "full-time" and "part-time" and create a way to manipulate the billable hour to maximize profitability and new ways to get work done. The FACTS model recognizes and adapts to the reality that firms' and lawyers' needs change over time. The benefit of recognizing the shift in both business and individual needs is that FACTS can save employers money by adjusting pay to reflect the varying work output in different practice areas and simultaneously meet the range of lawyers' work/life needs at different stages of their career trajectory.[37]

Firms will benefit from the transparency of the varying needs of individual lawyers because they will be better able to plan, for example, a Millennial's anticipated commitment or a Baby Boomer's use of lower Target hours to phase into retirement. By creating a methodology where everyone is in the same system,[38] firms can better utilize and understand lawyers' contributions and more accurately reflect their billable and nonbillable hours. In this way, firms can help minimize the stigma attached to lawyers working flexible or reduced hours and create equity and flexibility among all lawyers. Firms will maximize their opportunities to attract and retain high-quality and satisfied lawyers, with greater continuity for clients and productivity for law firms.

Notes

1. Deborah Epstein Henry, *Facing the FACTS: Introducing Work/Life Choices for All Firm Lawyers Within the Billable Hour Model*, Diversity & the Bar, Nov./Dec. 2007, *available at* http://www.flextimelawyers.com/pdf/art10.pdf.

2. The FACTS methodology is intended for all lawyers, including partners, and law firms can tailor the recommendations herein to the varying ways that partners differ. *See generally id.*

3. Methods of compensating partners vary widely, but the FACTS framework can be generally adapted to partners. *Id.*

4. Leigh Jones, *Midsize Law Firms Go for Big Changes*, Nat'l L.J., Oct. 23, 2007, *available at* http://www.law.com/jsp/article.jsp?id=1193043814292.

5. Lisa Belkin, *Who's Cuddly Now? Law Firms*, N.Y. Times, Jan. 24, 2008, *available at* http://www.nytimes.com/2008/01/24/fashion/24 WORK.html.

6. *Id.*

7. *Id.*

8. David Lat, *Chapman and Cutler Blazes The Trail of Tiers*, Above the Law, Oct.18, 2007, *available at* http://abovethelaw.com/2007/10/ chapman-and-cutler-blazes-the-trail-of-tiers/.

9. *Id.*

10. Eriq Gardner, *Picking Up the Pace*, Corporate Counsel, Nov. 20, 2003.

11. Depending on firm culture and other circumstances, some firms may require that lawyers working Core hours be in the office a minimum number of days a week while other firms may allow lawyers to telecommute all week.

12. Mary Teresa Bitti, *What Are the Pros and Cons of Flex Time?*, Financial Post, July 14, 2008, *available at* http://www.financialpost .com/small_business/businesssolutions/story.html?id=645783.

13. *See* Deborah Epstein Henry, *Prevailing Principles to Make Reduced Hour Schedules Succeed*, Diversity & the Bar, Sept./Oct. 2007, *available at* http://www.flextimelawyers.com/pdf/art9.pdf.

14. *See id.*

15. Bitti, *supra* note 12.

16. *Case Study: Ross & Associates. Environmental Consulting, Ltd., Commuter Challenge*, Commuter Challenge, Oct. 2005, *available at* http:// www.commuterchallenge.org/cc/casestudies/cs_rossassociates.html.

17. *Id.*

18. *Id.*

19. Bitti, *supra* note 12.

20. *Case Study*, *supra* note 16.

21. *Id.*

22. Working Mother Media & Flex-Time Lawyers LLC, Executive Summary: Highlights of Work/Life and Women Trends from the 2009 Best Law Firms for Women Survey, *available at* http://www.flextimelawyers.com/best/press20.pdf (comparing 2008 and 2009 findings).

23. Vivia Chen, *Law Firm Perk of the Moment: Flextime*, AM. LAW., Nov. 12, 2008, *available at* http://www.flextimelawyers.com/news/news56.pdf.

24. *Case Study: Davis Wright Tremaine LLP*, WASH. STATE UNIV. COOP. EXTENSION ENERGY PROGRAM AND COMMUTER CHALLENGE, COMMUTER CHALLENGE (1999), *available at* http://www.commuterchallenge.org/cc/csdwt.html.

25. *Biglaw Perk Watch: One Two Three Four, Cleary Declares Perk War!*, ABOVE THE LAW, Feb. 13, 2008, *available at* http://abovethelaw.com/2008/02/biglaw-perk-watch-one-two-three-four-cleary-declares-perk-war/. Additionally, lawyers who have been at the firm for two years can seek greater flexibility, including reduced hours by taking off a day or more a week (lower Target hours) or taking certain months off yearly or breaks at the end of deals (Annualized hours) or assuming a full workload but telecommuting more (full-time flex-time). *Id.*

26. Chen, *supra* note 23.

27. JOAN C. WILLIAMS & CONSUELA A. PINTO, AM. BAR ASS'N COMM'N ON WOMEN IN THE PROFESSION, FAIR MEASURE: TOWARD EFFECTIVE ATTORNEY EVALUATIONS, 19 (2008).

28. *Id.* at 29–31.

29. *See* Deborah Epstein Henry, *Stepping into Your Shoes: It's Time for Job-Shares in Law Firms*, DIVERSITY & THE BAR, July/Aug. 2007, *available at* http://www.flextimelawyers.com/pdf/art7.pdf.

30. *Id.*

31. *Id.*

32. *See* Deborah Epstein Henry, *The Business Case for Flexibility: Why Flexible and Reduced Hours Are in a Legal Employer's Financial Interest*, DIVERSITY & THE BAR, Mar./Apr. 2007, *available at* http://www.flextimelawyers.com/pdf/art4.pdf.

33. *See generally*, Henry, *supra* note 29.

34. *Id.* Law firms should handle benefits payments for job-share lawyers as they do for their other reduced-hour lawyers. In most cases, firms treat reduced-hour lawyers the same as full-time lawyers for purposes of benefits.

35. *Id.*

36. WorkLife Law, Better On Balance? The Corporate Counsel Work/Life Report 32 (2003), *available at* http://www.pardc.org/Publications/BetterOnBalance.pdf.

37. This notion of work/life demands changing over the course of a professional's career has gained traction in the accounting profession. *See, e.g.*, Cathleen Benko & Anne Weisberg, Mass Career Customization (2007).

38. Deloitte's Mass Career Customization model is founded on transparency and accessibility for all employees. *Id.*

CHAPTER 10

REDUCED HOURS AND OTHER ALTERNATIVE COST SAVING MEASURES IN A RECESSION

When I was 9, my sister Susie was turning 13 and was due to have her bat mitzvah, a Jewish ceremony marking the beginning of adulthood and responsibility for her actions. Our temple gave her a Friday night bat mitzvah date. This was customary at the time among temples in the conservative movement of Judaism; the girls' bat mitzvahs were on Friday nights, the boys' equivalent ceremonies—bar mitzvahs—were on Saturdays. Susie wanted to be able to read from the Torah. However, Torah reading is usually not allowed on Fridays, according to Jewish Law. So Susie—who could only have her bat mitzvah on a Friday night—could not read from the Torah. After Susie's Friday night bat mitzvah, my dad and my sister spent the next three years appearing before the Temple Board, petitioning the Temple to change its policy and allow girls to perform their bat mitzvahs on Saturdays. When I was 13, I was one of the first girls at our temple to have a Saturday morning bat mitzvah.

The process of making change is not easy. When Susie and my dad argued before the Temple Board, they said it was unfair not to allow girls to have the same opportunities as boys. There was no basis to keep the policy other than that was the way it had always been done. Other conservative temples were making this change and our temple was at risk of losing members by retaining its policy. The fact that other conservative temples were changing was a compelling factor in reversing the Board's decision. Ultimately, the Board relented, finding that just because something had always been done a certain way was not an adequate basis to continue doing something that way when it no longer could stand up to changing times.

As we focus in this chapter on how to use reduced hours and other alternatives as an economic solution in a recession, an important step is to look at existing mechanisms and see if we can view them differently than we did in the past. It may bring about surprising results.

Reduced Hours and Alternatives to Avoid Layoffs

Employers can use work/life programs in both strong and weak economic climates to improve profitability, but this opportunity has yet to be capitalized upon fully. In particular, firms have resisted the economic benefits of reduced hours in an economic downturn, when the benefits are even more apparent. Under the billable-hour model, firms can increase their profits, create client savings, and improve lawyer morale by using reduced hours in a recession.

For many law firms, the response to the recession that began in 2008 was to clamp down on costs by cutting heads. Instead, firms should have been thinking of creative ways to maximize productivity and avoid non-performance-based layoffs.[1] This notion has gained acceptance among some in the legal profession[2] and beyond. A December 2008 *New York Times* front page feature reported that "[a] growing number of employers, hoping to avoid or limit layoffs, are introducing four-day workweeks, unpaid vacations and voluntary or enforced furloughs, along with wage freezes, pension cuts and flexible work schedules. These employers are still cutting labor costs, but hanging onto the labor."[3]

Firms should avoid or minimize layoffs and find a better way to manage during an economic slowdown. Law firms that have laid off lawyers in the past have endured negative consequences for years. When lawyers leave, employers lose institutional knowledge and suffer severance, outplacement, and long-term recruiting and replacement costs.[4] The departures also disrupt continuity of service, delay resolution of pending matters, and alienate clients and potential future hires.[5] For remaining employees, morale and productivity decline.

> In response to an economic downturn, firms have the opportunity to offer a range of cost saving options that include:
>
> - Encouraging reduced hours with commensurate reductions in pay
> - Promoting telecommuting (to save on energy costs)
> - Proposing unpaid sabbaticals
> - Offering unpaid vacations
> - Issuing wage and hiring freezes
> - Delaying raises and eliminating bonuses
> - Making pension cuts
> - Offering early retirement packages
> - Cutting temporary staff
> - Reducing spending on marketing and travel
> - Redeploying remaining lawyers to busier departments[6]

If firms applied some or all of these steps, the savings would be considerable. However, many firms are unwilling or unable to impose these changes on a large-scale basis when economic challenges face them. For example, some firms argue that the stigma surrounding reduced hours has kept usage rates low, resulting in fewer savings than if a large number of lawyers volunteered to work less and get paid less.[7] Particularly in a weak economic climate, lawyers are less inclined to volunteer for reduced hours, for fear of drawing attention to themselves and placing themselves at greater risk of being laid off.[8] Also, most of these options are seen as negative ones involving the removal of former privileges. Negative solutions are unlikely to produce the positive atmosphere and results that employers would aim for, particularly in challenging times.

Introducing Balanomics™—Linking Reduced Hours and Employer Profitability

To assess alternatives to layoffs and attrition and to more generally determine profitability in the legal profession, I collaborated with three other lawyers to perform an economic analysis of the assumptions underlying the billable-hour model, and the impact of those assumptions on the bottom line.[9] This analysis was part of an initiative called Balanomics™ that I cofounded along with Darragh J. Davis, Vice President and General Counsel of PETCO's Law Department; Rupa G. Singh, Federal Appellate Staff Attorney and Liaison to the North American South Asian Bar Association; and Elizabeth B. Daniels, Of Counsel, Juniper Sanderson Wiggins LLP and Immediate Past President, Association of Corporate Counsel, San Diego Chapter. Launched in January 2009, Balanomics™ demonstrates a direct economic link between productivity, profitability, and work/life balance in the legal profession. Also, as discussed in Chapter 7, it aims to make work/life balance integral to the diversity discussion.[10]

Using the computer-based law firm model developed by the economic consulting firm NERA (National Economic Research Associates) for the Association of Corporate Counsel (ACC) Value Challenge,[11] Balanomics™ has demonstrated that firms can increase their firm profits and profits per partner by decreasing hours and salaries and reducing layoffs or attrition. In turn, those increased earnings for firms can translate into increased savings for law departments.

The pages beginning on page 200 below through page 203 are reprinted with permission of the authors and the Association of Corporate Counsel as it originally appeared: Darragh J. Davis, Deborah Epstein Henry, Rupa G. Singh and Elizabeth B. Daniels, "Increase Profits and Savings Through Work/Life Balance," ACC Docket 27, *no. 9, Nov. 2009, at 92–104.* *If you are interested in joining ACC, please go to* www.acc.com, *call (202) 293-4103 x360, or e-mail membership@acc.com.*

Balanomics™ Use of the NERA Economic Model Shows Increased Firm Profitability

The NERA economic model allows firms to input data about seven variables to calculate how each impacts profits over a five-year period:

(1) law firms' size and expected growth (including associate layoffs/attrition);

(2) annual billable hours;
(3) billing rates;
(4) salaries;
(5) rate of recovery;
(6) recruiting costs; and
(7) overhead costs.

In using the model, [Balanomics™] adopted some of NERA's original figures and modified others based on more recent, publicly available data, as the ACC Value Challenge encourages users to do. . . . (All the figures and assumptions used are included in the [A]ppendix [B] to this [chapter].) In applying the model, we ran three "profitability reports" over a five-year period to evaluate the impact of associate layoffs/attrition on the one hand and reduced hours/reduced salaries on the other. By comparing a change in *only* the factors related to associate layoffs/attrition, billable hours, and salaries, we found that long-term law firm profitability improves by instituting reduced hours and reduced salaries instead of decreasing associate headcount through either layoffs or attrition.

In the first report, we calculated profitability for a large law firm with the standard number of 1,364 timekeepers in the base year and 1,886 in year five. Here, associates are expected to bill 2,000 hours a year. Management relies on a ten percent associate layoff or attrition rate to cut costs (see Layoff/Attrition Models). This resulted in an overall firm profit range of $491,198,232 in the base year to $755,502,987 in year five and a profit per partner range of $1,158,486 in the base year to $1,519,312 in year five. (Note that the NERA model does not have a separate step for implementing layoffs versus attrition. Thus, we reasoned that attrition in a down market would remain low at five percent, and include unavoidable departures such as performance-based terminations or retirements instead of the voluntary departures that are more common during robust economic times. We then estimated a conservative five percent layoff rate based on reports of layoffs ranging from five to ten percent at large law firms. Adding the five percent attrition rate and the conservative five percent layoff rate, we reached a ten percent overall layoff/attrition rate.)

In the second report, we calculated profitability for the same size large law firm where management instead uses reduced-hour options to cut costs (1,900 Reduced Hours/Reduced Salaries Model) with a marginal *five percent* associate layoff or attrition rate. We decreased associate billed hours to 1,900 per year and commensurately decreased associates' lockstep salaries by five percent (since the 100 hour reduction constitutes a five percent change). This resulted in a better long-term overall firm profit range of $483,016,707 in the base year to $800,676,115 in year five and a profit per partner range of $1,139,190 in the base year to $1,582,401 in year five. (Again, because the NERA model does not have a separate step for implementing layoffs versus attrition, we reasoned that attrition in a down market would remain low at five percent and include the types of departures noted above. Instead of then increasing this rate to reflect layoffs, we kept it at five percent to test what would happen if a firm used reduced-hour options as an alternative.)

In the third report, we calculated profitability for the same size large law firm where management now uses an even greater reduction in hours and salaries to cut costs (see 1,800 Reduced Hours/Reduced Salaries Model), again with a marginal *five percent* associate layoff or attrition rate. We decreased associate billable hours to 1,800 per year and commensurately decreased associates' lockstep salaries by ten percent (since the 200 hour reduction constitutes a 10 percent change). This resulted in an overall firm profit range of $474,835,182 in the base year to $782,361,678 in year five and a profit per partner range of $1,119,894 in the base year to $1,546,206 in year five. (Again, we reasoned that attrition in a down market would remain low at five percent and the firm would use even greater reduced-hour options as an alternative to conducting layoffs.)

Thus, the three reports demonstrate that the most profitable approach for a law firm is under the 1,900 Reduced Hours/Reduced Salaries Model, with increased profitability over the Layoff/Attrition Model beginning in year two. The 1,800 Reduced Hours/Reduced Salaries Model is also more profitable than the Layoff/Attrition Model, with the improved profitability numbers beginning in year three. . . .

The graphs on the next page visually demonstrate the above findings—that profits, whether measured overall in the first graph or per partner in the second graph—increase over five years for firms that reduce associate billable hours and commensurately lower compensation instead of decreasing headcount through layoffs or attrition.

Graph 1: Overall Firm Profits for Layoff/Attrition vs. Reduced Hours/Salary Models

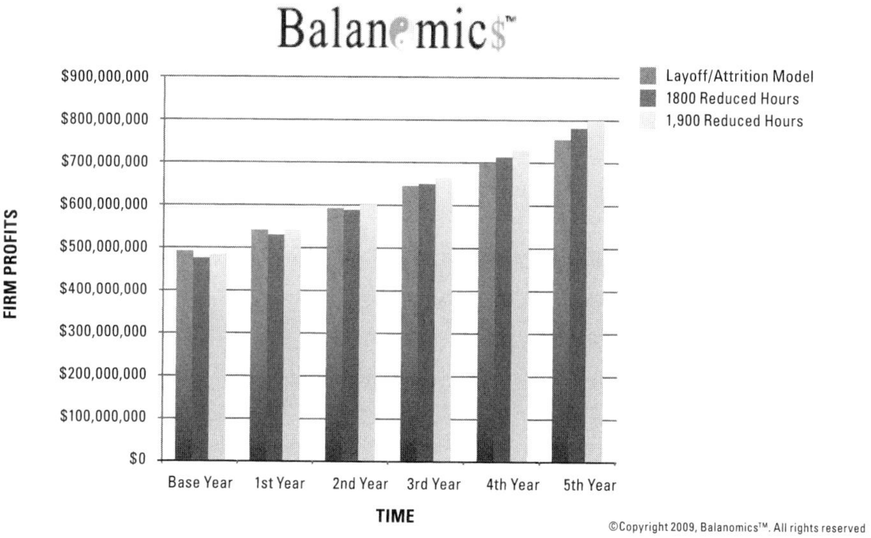

Graph 2: Profits Per Partner for Layoff/Attrition vs. Reduced Hours/Salary Models

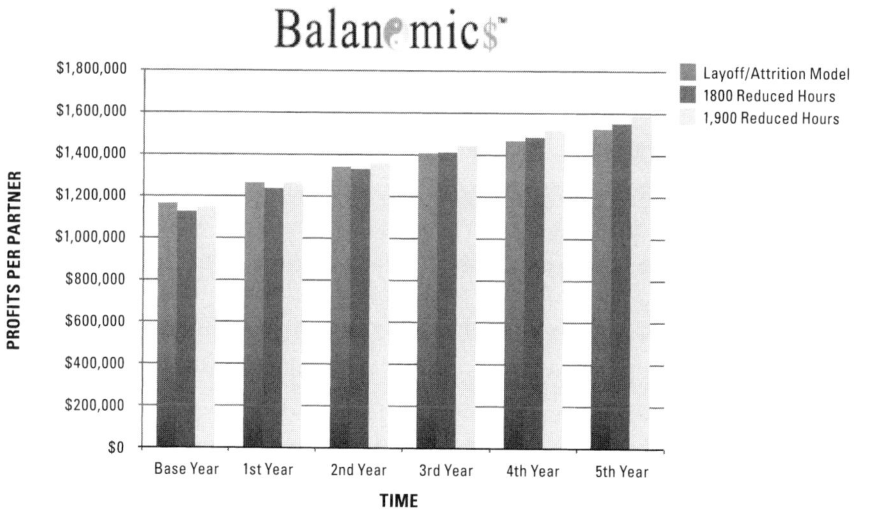

This is the end of the material reprinted with permission.

The Balanomics™ Findings Tie into FACTS

The Balanomics™ findings demonstrate a means to avoid layoffs and reduce salaries and hours to increase profitability. In the two Balanomics™ Reduced Hours/Reduced Salaries Models, all associate hours were reduced from 2,000 to 1,900 or 1,800, as that was the only way to change hours in the NERA Model's parameters. But the above benefits would also accrue if individual associates billed different hours—ranging from, say, 1,200 to 2,000 a year depending on practice area, market demands, client needs, personal needs, or other factors—as long as when all of the total associate hours were tallied, they averaged 1,800 or 1,900 annual hours per associate[12]

The Balanomics™ findings tie in to the complementary approach that I developed called FACTS Multiple Billable Hours (discussed in Chapter 9), where a firm establishes four to six Target hour tracks after identifying the different tracks where most attorneys' hours cluster.[13] Under the FACTS Multiple Billable Hours approach, there are numerous benefits.[14] It enables a firm to retain its valuable talent while paying them proportionately less so that expenses are reduced. Outplacement and severance costs associated with layoffs are avoided. Reducing attrition or layoffs also assures clients of continuity of service and avoids delays when new attorneys join a client team. Clients often believe they bear the cost of training a new lawyer staffed on their matters, and they resent doing so. They also become alienated and frustrated by the need to develop new relationships and by the loss of institutional knowledge. These client challenges translate into in-house legal department economic losses. By avoiding turnover, having more lawyers work reduced hours provides additional benefits to firms that can be translated into client savings.[15]

If a firm used reduced hours as an alternative to layoffs, when the economy improved, the firm would avoid the additional expenses and risk of recruiting new talent that may not be a good match for the firm. Instead, it could increase certain clusters of attorneys' hours to match the market demand. U.K.-based Norton Rose LLP imposed mandatory reduced hours to avoid layoffs during the economic downturn; when work picked up, it increased the hours of its lawyers again.[16] By doing so, the firm retained its talent and avoided the additional expenses of layoffs and replacement costs. "Flex was central to our cost-cutting programme," said the firm's chief executive, Peter Martyr. "We didn't make anyone redundant and in fact grew lawyer numbers by 40."[17] This approach provides continuity and savings for clients and improved morale for lawyers.

A firm's decision to offer reduced-hour options to avoid layoffs will engender loyalty among lawyers. The decision to retain lawyers at reduced hours and lower pay will not only impact the lawyers who use these options. It will also improve the morale of the whole firm by minimizing the burnout and lack of productivity that ensues among employees who remain after layoffs.

Implementing a FACTS Multiple Billable Hours approach as a cost-saving measure should also help address the intractable problem of stigma that has plagued lawyers accessing reduced-hour programs since their inception. Under the FACTS Multiple Billable Hours approach, all lawyers would work in one system, diminishing the risk of stigmatizing a small group.[18] Additionally, applying a FACTS Multiple Billable Hours approach in a downturn would change the perception of reduced hours to an economic imperative rather than an accommodation. Having lawyers work reduced hours with commensurate reductions in pay provides an economic cushion for firms when there is less work. With the economic benefits of reduced hours more clear than ever, firms can seize the opportunity to introduce reduced hours and improve how lawyers working reduced hours are treated.

If a firm decides to use a Multiple Target Hours approach in response to a recession, it must educate its lawyers about the firm's policy.[19] In doing so, the firm should hold a meeting where management presents the opportunity for lawyers to work different Target hours in exchange for less pay and circulate and explain the firm's policy. It is important to tell lawyers that this option may be offered only on a temporary basis, depending on the demands of the market, but that it is a solution to manage the reduced amount of work. Management should announce an ideal Target hours and the percentage of lawyers needed at each Target and whether the needs vary by department. Management should then invite lawyers to submit proposals indicating the proposed Target billable hours that the lawyer would like to bill and how the lawyer plans to achieve those hours without negatively impacting colleagues and clients. As discussed in Chapters 8 and 9, once lawyers' Targets are determined, they should receive training on how to make lower Target hours work to ensure the success of the new arrangement.[20]

Telecommuting and Rethinking Office Space

Firms that are able to redesign new office space could significantly reduce their overhead and thereby increase profits. As Darragh Davis, Vice President and General Counsel of PETCO Law Department, put it, "re-thinking office space is just the logical extension of business casual."[21] Cesar Alvarez, Executive Chairman of Greenberg Traurig, LLP, shared valuable insights in this regard when he was chief executive officer of the firm.[22] He opined that law firm offices were built for Baby Boomers, with large corner offices and nice artwork to impress clients. But those clients seldom visit their lawyers, except during closings and large meetings, which are held in conference centers at the office. When clients see expensive attorney offices, they often assume they are paying for those offices in their fees. Also, Gen Y is not generally interested in big corner offices—in fact, it may deter rather than impress them. With this in mind, Greenberg's new Miami office, scheduled to be completed in late 2010, was designed differently than prior offices.[23] The office was built smaller—about 150,000 square feet[24]—but it was designed for more lawyers. Less space is needed for several reasons. Younger lawyers are interested in more communal work spaces, not big corner offices. Also, telecommuting is on the rise and more lawyers will be out of the office regularly. Creating alternative ways to work would also help a firm like Greenberg in an emergency—its capacity for preparedness and business continuity in a crisis would surpass most of its competitors.

Additionally, Greenberg is attuned to the importance of "going green."[25] It had noticed that its lawyers were enjoying shorter commutes and going to their clients' offices and not to the main office every day. Indeed, usage of offices like its one in Westchester, New York, near major and expensive metropolitan centers, increased beginning in 2008, as lawyers prioritized saving time and money and reducing their carbon footprint by not commuting to Manhattan every day.[26] Additionally, several large law firms have invested in a growing number of cutting-edge videoconferencing systems, like Telepresence, designed to replicate the feeling of in-person meetings that are being used to save on costs and minimize travel.[27]

The legal profession can also learn from ingenuity in other industries. Blue Work, an innovative program developed at American Express Co., takes the notion of office redesign a step further. It is maximizing real estate savings and better aligning employees' and employers' office space needs. The project, being driven by American Express's human resources, global real estate, and global technology teams, is lowering costs while improving productivity and innovation.[28] Their motto: "Let's get rid of space, not people."[29]

Under Blue Work, there are four types of work spaces—Hub, Club, Roam, and Home—and they work as follows:[30]

- **Hub** employees have jobs that require work and face time in one of the company's office locations.
- **Club** employees go into a hub office no more than three times a week, either because they work reduced hours or work some days from another location. When they work in the hub office, Club employees are given space to use that day.
- **Roam** employees are "road warriors," typically salespeople or employees with client management responsibilities, who have no office. As American Express's Chief Diversity Officer Kerrie Peraino put it: "These are employees we are paying to not be in the office. They are out closing deals and meeting new customers, so why should we be paying for office space?"[31]
- **Home** employees are given a stipend to work from home.

The benefits to the Blue Work program are overwhelming. Blue Work is very new, but the future real estate savings for American Express from its implementation should be considerable. Additionally, for Club employees, who work in communal spaces, American Express is seeing increased collaboration and innovation among team members. While some company leaders were initially worried about losing control of employees without offices, these leaders have been transformed by the increased productivity, engagement, and idea generation. As Peraino explained:

> [This program] helps us meet people where they want to be met, in terms of preferred work type, and we marry that with what the job requires. Not every job requires you to be sitting in a corporate

> office or for the company to bear the expense of company space. Plus, you have people across generations who want a different [working] arrangement.[32]

In short, the increased desire and ability to work offsite and in communal work spaces, combined with the interest in saving time and costs and "going green," mandate law firms to reconsider large, traditional offices when they renew their leases and redesign new office spaces. American Express's Hub, Club, Roam, Home model is one that could easily be adapted to law firms. The additional benefit is that when firms become more cost-efficient in their delivery of services and real estate savings, they will be able to pass along some of these savings to their clients.

Reengineering Talent and Filling Gaps

With talented lawyers, it is better to invest in training them to develop new areas of expertise than to let them go.[33] These lawyers can be asked to develop new practice areas or help with spillover work in the busier departments. If some layoffs have already been implemented at an employer, the remaining lawyers who are not as busy should start developing the expertise to fill the talent gaps that the departing attorneys have left behind. It is important that management effectively supervise remaining lawyers to minimize burnout, anxiety, and low morale.

Another source for filling expertise gaps are reentry lawyers—typically lawyers who have left the profession for one or more years, primarily for child-rearing purposes, and are seeking to return. There has been growing awareness of the value of recruiting back reentry talent for several years.[34] When layoffs have taken place, reentry lawyers can take deliberate steps and become a valuable resource to fill in for niche practice areas that are lost.[35] Employers can minimize their risk in hiring reentry lawyers by hiring their own former lawyers. However, if these lawyers are not available, employers can also minimize risk by hiring first on a temporary and hourly basis.

The advantages of hiring reentry attorneys are numerous. These lawyers are not coming from a prior job, so there are fewer issues about matching salaries and hours. Instead, reentry lawyers can be tapped to perform spillover work, fill in expertise gaps, and minimize burnout for lawyers who have remained. For employers who are uncertain of their staffing needs, if reentry lawyers start on a temporary basis and are paid hourly, there are no additional costs if the work disappears. At the same time, they can be groomed to be future employees when the economy improves. If existing talent is redistributed to new departments or reentry lawyers are recruited back as employees, it is critical that these lawyers are properly trained to ensure a smooth transition into a fragmented workforce.[36]

In sum, there are numerous ways that employers can increase profitability, save on costs, and avoid layoffs in a recession. By instituting reduced hours with commensurate reductions in pay and minimizing layoffs and attrition, firms can increase profitability and avoid incurring the costs that ensue from laying off talent. By reengineering office space and reengaging talent, firms can maximize their profitability and pass on their savings to clients.

Notes

1. *See generally* Deborah Epstein Henry, *Creative Ways for Law Firms to Survive the Economic Downturn*, The Balance Beam (2007–2008), *available at* http://www.flextimelawyers.com/pdf/newsletter_08.pdf.

2. Gina Passarella, *Work-Life Balance Scale Tipping in Work's Favor*, Legal Intelligencer, Nov. 3, 2008, *available at* http://www.law.com/jsp/law/careercenter/lawArticleCareerCenter.jsp?id=1202425737910.

3. Matt Richtel, *More Companies Cut Labor Costs Without Layoffs*, N.Y. Times, Dec. 21, 2008, *available at* http://www.nytimes.com/2008/12/22/business/22layoffs.html.

4. Henry, *supra* note 1, at 1–2.

5. Deborah Epstein Henry, *Face the FACTS: Implement a Multiple Target Billable Hours Approach to Address the Economic Downturn*, Yale Law Women Blog, Mar. 24, 2009, *available at* http://www.flextimelawyers.com/pdf/art15.pdf.

6. Henry, *supra* note 1, at 2 (citing Cari Tuna, *Some Firms Cut Costs Without Resorting to Layoffs*, Wall St. J., Dec. 15, 2008, *available at* http://online.wsj.com/article/SB122929306421405071.html).

7. Henry, *supra* note 5.

8. Tara Weiss, *Will Flextime Set You Up to Be Laid Off*, *Forbes.com*, July 15, 2009, *available at* http://www.forbes.com/2009/07/15/flextime-layoff-danger-leadership-careers-advice.html; Karen Sloan, *The New Associate Mantra: Keep Quiet*, NAT'L L.J., Apr. 27 2009, *available at* http://www.law.com/jsp/nlj/PubArticleNLJ.jsp?id=1202430128598&hbxlogin=1; Debra Cassens Weiss, *Fearful Associates Opt for Partner Face Time Over Work-at-Home Time*, A.B.A.J., Apr. 23, 2009, *available at* http://www.abajournal.com/news/article/fearful_associates_opt_for_partner_face_time_over_work-at-home_time.

9. *See generally* Darragh J. Davis et al., *Increase Profits and Savings Through Work/Life Balance*, ACC DOCKET, Nov. 2009, at 92–104, *available at* http://www.balanomics.net/pdf/acc.pdf.

10. For more information, please visit www.balanomics.net.

11. The model is available on ACC's website: http://www.acc.com/valuechallenge/resources/upload/Calibrated-Law-Firm-Profitability-Growth-Model.xls.

12. Davis et al., *supra* note 9, at 103–04 n.5.

13. *See generally* Henry, *supra* note 5; Deborah Epstein Henry, *Facing the FACTS: Introducing Work/Life Choices for All Firm Lawyers Within the Billable Hour Model*, DIVERSITY & THE BAR, Nov./Dec. 2007, *available at* http://www.flextimelawyers.com/pdf/art10.pdf.

14. *See generally* Henry, *supra* note 5; Henry, *supra* note 1, at 1–3.

15. Davis et al., *supra* note 9, at 98.

16. Zach Lowe, *A Reduced Work Week: One Way to Avoid Layoffs*, AMLAW DAILY, Mar. 13 2009, *available at* http://amlawdaily.typepad.com/amlawdaily/2009/03/norton-rose.html; Emma Sadowski, *Norton Rose Moves Staff Back to Full Hours as Work Levels Rise*, LEGALWEEK.COM, Nov. 5, 2009, *available at* http://www.legalweek.com/legal-week/news/1561057/norton-rose-moves-staff-hours-levels-rise.

17. Matt Byrne, *Costs in Translation*, THE LAWYER, July 5, 2010, *available at* http://www.thelawyer.com/costs-in-translation/1004932.article.

18. *See generally* Henry, *supra* note 5; Henry, *supra* note 1, at 2.; Henry, *supra* note 13, at 22.

19. Henry, *supra* note 1, at 2–3.

20. *See generally* Deborah Epstein Henry, *The Nitty-Gritty of How and Why to Make Part-Time Work*, THE BALANCE BEAM (2003–2004),

available at http://www.flextimelawyers.com/pdf/2003_2004newsletter.pdf.

21. Henry, *supra* note 1, at 4.

22. *Id.*

23. *Greenberg Traurig's New Miami Office Focuses on the Future*, *City Core*, July 9, 2008, *available at* http://www.gtlaw.com/NewsEvents/Newsroom/PressReleases?find=107664.

24. *Id.*

25. Henry, *supra* note 1, at 4.

26. *Id.*

27. Karen Sloan, *Will Meetings of the Future Be Televised?*, Nat'l L.J., Nov. 10, 2009, *available at* http://www.legalweek.com/legal-week/analysis/1562428/will-meetings-future-televised.

28. *American Express Marries Work Styles with Work Spaces*, Network of Executive Women, Jan. 20, 2010, *available at* http://www.newonline.org/general/print.asp?PrintView=1&OpenDialog=1&s=aHR0cDovL3d3dy5uZXdvbmxpbmUub3Jn&p=L25ld3MvbmV3cy5hc3A=&d=aWQ9MzUzODc=.

29. *Id.* (quoting Chief Diversity Officer Kerrie Peraino).

30. *American Express*, *supra* note 28.

31. *Id.*

32. *Id.*

33. *See generally* Henry, *supra* note 1.

34. Leigh Jones, *A Promising Talent Pool: Alumni*, Nat'l L.J., Oct. 16, 2006.

35. Deborah Epstein Henry, *Getting Back: The Path for Lawyers to Return to Practice*, Nat'l Ass'n Women Law. J., Spring 2007, *available at* http://www.flextimelawyers.com/pdf/art8.pdf.

36. Deborah Epstein Henry, *Comeback Lawyers: A Look at Why Re-Entry Is a Hot Work/Life Balance Topic*, Diversity & the Bar, Jan./Feb. 2007, *available at* http://www.flextimelawyers.com/pdf/art11.pdf.

APPENDIX B

PROFITABILITY MODEL: HERE'S THE BOTTOM LINE

Profitability Model: Here's the Bottom Line

Applying the NERA Economic Model, Balanomics™ Demonstrates that increasing reduced hours schedules is more profitable than conducting layoffs (or suffering significant attrition).

Below is Balanomics'™ step-by-step approach in using the NERA Economic Model, as well as a summary of the three profitability reports we ran. At each of the Model's seven steps (available at *www.acc.com/valuechallenge/resources/upload/calibrated-law-firm-profitability-growth-model.xls*), Balanomics™ either adopted the default assumptions in place for a large law firm or replaced them with more recent data. The three profitability reports we ran were for the following three models: (1) first, a model for a firm that maintains its 2,000 hour associate annual billable expectations but increases layoffs or attrition from five percent to ten percent to cut costs (Layoff/Attrition Model); (2) second, a model that maintains its layoff or attrition at the default rate of five percent and instead uses a five percent reduction in associate hours and salary to cut costs (1,900 Reduced Hours/Reduced Salaries Model); and (3) finally, a model that again maintains its layoff or attrition at the default rate of five percent and instead uses an even greater, ten percent reduction in associate hours and salary to cut costs (1,800 Reduced Hours/Reduced Salaries Model).

STEP 1 (Headcount and Layoffs/Attrition): The NERA proposed assumptions were used for total headcount of timekeepers—including paralegals, contract lawyers, of counsel, associates, and partners—over five years based on a large law firm model. Specifically, we started with the number of timekeepers ranging from 1,364 in the baseline year to 1,886 in year five. For the Layoff/Attrition Model, we increased the NERA assumption in associate layoff/attrition from five percent to ten percent (which resulted in timekeepers ranging from 1,364 in the baseline year to 1,719 in year five). Note that the NERA model does not have a separate step for implementing layoffs versus attrition. Thus, we reasoned that while attrition in a down market remains low at five percent, it is conservative to add an additional five percent layoff rate to reach a ten percent overall layoff/attrition rate. For the two Reduced Hours/Reduced Salaries Models, associate layoff/attrition was kept at the NERA assumption of five percent (because minimal attrition or performance-based terminations is unavoidable and possibly desirable).

STEP 2 (Billing Rates): Some NERA assumptions were adopted and others modified:

2A: Adopted 1st-year to 8th-year associate rates, from $220 to $450 per hour.

2B: Adopted 5th-tier to 1st-tier partner rates, from $600 to $980 per hour.

2C: Increased paralegal billing rates from $100 to $200 per hour.

2D: Increased of counsel billing rates from $150 to $400 per hour.[25]

2E: Increased contract lawyer billing rates from $170 to $200 per hour.

2F: Decreased anticipated annual increase in billing rates from seven percent to three percent.[26]

STEP 3 (Total Annual Hours Billed): For the Layoff/Attrition Model, all the NERA assumptions were adopted—that associates bill 2,000 hours; partners 1,800 hours; and of counsel, contract lawyers and paralegals 1,500 hours per year. For the 1,900 Reduced Hours/Reduced Salaries Model, only the assumption regarding associate annual billable hours was changed to 1,900 hours. For the 1,800 Reduced Hours/Reduced Salaries Model, only the assumption regarding associate annual billable hours was changed to 1,800 hours.

STEP 4 (Annual Recovery): Adopted assumption of 95 percent recovery rate of hours billed.

25. "2008 Law Firm Compensation, Billing Rate, and Benefits Survey," Conducted by RBZ, CPAs (demonstrating need for increase in contract lawyer paralegal and of counsel billing rates).

26. Karen Sloan, "Law business index reports ugly first quarter results," *National Law Journal* (May 11, 2009). www.law.northwestern.edu/career/markettrends/2009/pr8urousri7s.pdf.

STEP 5 (Salaries): Some NERA assumptions were adopted and others were modified:

5A: Adopted 1st-year to 8th-year associate salaries from $160K to $255K per year.

5B: Increased paralegal salaries from $50K to $75K per year.

5C: Increased of counsel salaries from $75K to $230K per year.[27]

5D: Increased contract lawyer salaries from $95K to $200K per year.

5E: Adopted five percent annual salary increase for paralegals, contract lawyers, and of counsel only, and not associates given raises implicit in lockstep compensation.

STEP 6 (Recruiting Costs): Adopted assumption of $400K 1st year associate recruiting costs.

STEP 7 (Overhead): Adopted assumption that other overhead costs (including rent, employee benefits, malpractice insurance, etc.) equal 33 percent of total law firm revenue.

Balanomics™ then ran the following three "profitability reports:"

Profitability Report – Layoff/Attrition Model: To calculate profitability for the Layoff/Attrition Model, the only change was to increase associate layoffs/attrition from five percent to ten percent. This resulted in an overall firm profit range of $491,198,232M in the base year to $755,502,987M profits in year five and a profit per partner range of $1,158,486 in the base year to $1,519,312 in year five.

Profitability Report – 1,900 Reduced Hours/Reduced Salaries Model: To calculate profitability for the 1,900 Reduced Hours/Reduced Salaries Model, the only factors changed were to decrease the associate billable hours from 2,000 per year to 1,900 per year and commensurately decrease associates' lockstep salaries by five percent (since the 100 hour reduction constitutes a five percent change). This resulted in an overall firm profit range of $483,016,707M in the base year to $800,676,115M in year five and a profit per partner range of $1,139,190 in the base year to $1,582,401 in year five.

Profitability Report – 1,800 Reduced Hours/Reduced Salaries Model: Finally, to calculate profitability for the 1,800 Reduced Hours/Reduced Salaries Model, the only factors changed were to decrease the associate billable hours from 2,000 per year to 1,800 per year and commensurately decrease associates' lockstep salaries by ten percent (since the 200 hour reduction constitutes a ten percent change). This resulted in a profit range of $474,835,182M in the base year to $782,361,678M in year five and a profit per partner range of $1,119,894 in the base year to $1,546,206 in year five.

Comparing these reports establishes that profitability *increases* over five years if law firms reduce associate hours and compensation rather than conduct layoffs or endure significant attrition. There are more significant gains after a five percent reduction in hours (from 2,000 hours to 1,900) and commensurate salary decreases, and slightly less dramatic gains after a ten percent reduction in hours (from 2,000 hours to 1,800) and commensurate salary decreases. Notably, either of the reduced hours/reduced salary options is better for *long term* law firm profitability (and therefore law department savings) than the layoff/attrition option. The 1,900 Reduced Hours/Reduced Salaries Model begins to be more profitable than the Layoff/Attrition Model in year two while the 1,800 Reduced Hours/Reduced Salaries Model begins to be more profitable than the Layoff/Attrition Model in year three.

27. "2008 Law Firm Compensation, Billing Rate, and Benefits Survey." Conducted by RBZ, CPAs (demonstrating need for increase in contract lawyer, paralegal and of counsel salaries).

PART II

ADVICE FOR LAWYERS AND LAW STUDENTS

CHAPTER 11

CONNECT FOUR: MAXIMIZING YOUR PRODUCTIVITY AND SATISFACTION

It was 1993. I was 25, newly married and in my third year of law school. One day, while working at my law school's journal, I started seeing flashing opaque spots, like the spots you see when a photograph is taken of you using a flashbulb. I laid down for a while and the spots seemed to disappear.

A month later, shortly after my 26th birthday, Gordon and I were at our favorite New York City diner and the same sensation came over me. We rushed back to our apartment. The spots intensified. So did a feeling that my mind was racing and I couldn't keep track of my thoughts. Next came what I later learned was a grand mal seizure. I remember hearing Gordon on the phone as I regained consciousness, asking my parents to meet us at the hospital emergency room. Then he asked me if I knew the President's name.

The emergency room diagnosis was a brain tumor. But soon after, we found a specialist and what he discovered was quite heartening. In layman's terms, he said, I had a lesion in the back of my brain. He thought it was from a rare parasite, Cysticercosis, typically found in Latin American countries. Apparently I had contracted it years earlier in a trip abroad and it had an incubation period of years. The parasite usually multiplies so that when a brain scan is done post seizure, the brain looks like Swiss cheese. In my case, there was only one lesion. To be sure it was the parasite and not a brain tumor, he would need to operate.

Five days after the seizure, I underwent successful brain surgery to remove the parasite. My vision was blurry for about a month and I had to take steroids and antiseizure medication for a few months more, but I was told I would soon be as good as new.

Brain surgery as a 26-year-old newly married law student changed my life. The emotional swing from thinking I was going to die to a bright prognosis five days later was overwhelming. But the seizure, the conflicting diagnoses, the brain surgery, and the experience of having family and friends rally around me gave me an unusual perspective. I felt inspired to figure out what was important in my life and what would give me greater satisfaction. The experience gave me confidence not to defer important choices and not to be as concerned with keeping all my options open.

Had I not had this experience, I doubt I would have had my first child at 27. I probably would have waited two years to see if I could secure a partner title before starting my consulting practice. Or maybe I wouldn't have had the guts to start Flex-Time Lawyers LLC and leave practice in the first place. But when faced with the prospect that life may end abruptly, time and choices never looked quite the same.

Four Personal/Environmental Factors Impacting Your Productivity and Satisfaction

To become more productive and satisfied in managing your work and life, the first step is to identify the key personal and environmental factors that impact you. Through the thousands of "Dear Debbie" e-mails I've received over the years, I've identified four key personal/environmental factors that impact a lawyer's daily productivity and satisfaction with work and life.[1] While the context in which I discuss these personal/environmental factors is for lawyers, this analysis and the discussion of daily personal/environmental factors and work/life goals that follow apply to any person in any industry.

Nature of the Work

The first personal/environmental factor is the nature of the work itself. Does the nature of your work lend itself to more erratic workloads that are crisis-oriented or is the work consistent, with a steady flow? Is the work subject to external factors that impact the pace and amount of your work—e.g., outside counsel, business demands, or demands of the court? For example, in the corporate deal context, the work can involve around-the-clock hours, especially prior to a closing. Similarly, litigation can require very inconsistent and long hours due to the demands of the court and opposing counsel, particularly, in the buildup to a trial.

Venue

The second personal/environmental factor is venue—where you work and for whom—and the way in which your employer supports your needs. Are you in a law firm, in-house, government, not-for-profit, or solo practitioner setting? Do colleagues distribute work timely and effectively to avoid crises? Does your employer pay consideration to enhancing work/life satisfaction and are colleagues considerate of your priorities outside of work? Is there flexibility in where and how you work? Are you self employed and therefore responsible for setting your own boundaries?

As discussed in Chapters 7, 8, and 9, there are many steps that employers can take to make their environments more hospitable. These steps involve employers implementing written policies and creating a supportive infrastructure for their lawyers to get work done. It also requires training supervisory lawyers about how to assign and supervise work and training lawyers about how to manage their work.

Home

The third personal/environmental factor is your home and how much support you get from your family, friends, and community. The scope of the home sphere includes your age, health, marital status, caregiving responsibilities, and financial demands. A big part of your home life and demands include whether you have children or elderly or sick family members and, if so, their degree of dependency. Home involves not only the support you derive from your family, extended family, friends, and community but also the extent of your family and community commitments.

You

The fourth personal/environmental factor is you and your ability to effectively manage your work/life challenges, stresses, and needs and the circumstances upon which you thrive. How effective are you at managing your time and multiple responsibilities? Do you thrive on last-minute deadlines and feel you cannot perform unless the pressure is on? Or are you a planner who needs to be organized? Do you get stressed by erratic schedules that you believe are not conducive to your lifestyle?

Of the four personal/environmental factors, the first one—the nature of your work—is the hardest to change. If the nature of your work is erratic and dictated by outside factors, it is more difficult to control. You can influence the perspectives of judges, employers, and clients by educating them, but this process is slow and difficult.

You have more control over the remaining personal/environmental factors—venue, home, and you. For example, with venue, you can choose an employer whose programs, policies, and environment suit you. On the home front, you can construct a support system consisting of family, friends, nannies, etc. Or, you can focus more on yourself and how to become more effective at delegating or relinquishing nonessential roles that you play. You can also become more effective in managing your time, as will be discussed in Chapter 14.

It is important to regularly and individually assess each of these key personal/environmental factors in order to determine their positive or negative impact upon your productivity and satisfaction. You can then evaluate what steps to take to minimize the negative circumstances. If you are a job seeker, you should assess each opportunity within these four personal/environmental factors as further outlined below. In going through this process, you will also need to identify your work/life goals.

Four Work/Life Goals

Over the past eleven years, the "Dear Debbie" e-mails I've received can be narrowed into four key work/life goals that lawyers seek:

1. Flexibility
2. Predictability
3. Reduced hours
4. Proximity

Not all lawyers seek all four work/life goals, but they typically articulate at least one of them when they express the need to improve their satisfaction both at work and at home.

Flexibility

Most lawyers want and need flexibility. They view themselves as professionals and want the freedom to work on their own terms. Many believe that if their work product is top-notch and clients and colleagues are unaffected by their comings and goings, they should be able to work flexibly. The billable hour affords law firms flexibility because it enables firms to generate the same revenue from someone billing at home or at work. However, that flexibility has never been fully capitalized upon. As discussed in Chapters 6 and 9, with proper training, lawyers working with flexibility can actually increase their productivity.

Predictability

The most common source of dissatisfaction among firm lawyers is lack of predictability and control. These lawyers do not necessarily mind the long hours, but they need the ability to plan ahead. They want to be able to tell their eight-year-old "I'll be at your play" or tell their blind date "I can have dinner with you tonight." In a comparison of the 2003 Quality of Life Survey and *The American Lawyer*'s annual report, *Corporate Counsel* found that even though in-house lawyers were increasingly working close to law firm hours, in-house lawyers reported greater work/life satisfaction. The increased satisfaction was attributable to in-house lawyers' greater control over their schedules.[2] This desire for more predictability and control exists for lawyers working a traditional full-time schedule as well as those working reduced hours.

Once these lawyers leave the office, they want to be "off call." Technology has changed legal practice, and many lawyers, especially in the law firm context, can never escape. Technology—especially BlackBerrys and ubiquitous broadband Internet for the personal computer—has created the expectation of immediate responsiveness and accessibility, which has interfered with lawyers' ability to delineate lines between work and home.

Reduced Hours

Some lawyers want to work fewer hours. With the expectation that some law firm lawyers bill 2,000 to 2,200 hours or more,[3] many lawyers are overwhelmed by the sheer number of hours they are expected to work. Not surprisingly, long hours are a major reason for lawyers' attrition. In a 2007 MIT study, for example, long hours were an important factor in why lawyers left their firms.[4]

Proximity

Some lawyers accept the long hours or lack of predictability and instead, they are focused on proximity in where they work. These lawyers either need to work at an office in a certain location (typically near their home, their child's school, or a dependent family member's home or long-term care facility) or they seek to telecommute on a partial or regular basis. For some lawyers, the need for proximity in where they work is sporadic. For example, certain lawyers may need flexibility to work from home when their children are sick or their childcare or eldercare provider cancels, or when there's a snow day or house projects are being done. While these incidents are often isolated, they can add up and make the difference for a lawyer choosing an employer that can be generally flexible in this regard.

Managing Personal/Environmental Factors and Work/Life Goals

How these four personal/environmental factors—nature of your work, venue, home, and you—interplay with your work/life goals—flexibility, predictability, reduced hours, and proximity—drive a lawyer's productivity and satisfaction. In fact, I am frequently asked by law students and others whether they should choose certain practice areas or certain types of employers for a more satisfying career. This is when I typically joke that a practice area like trusts and estates, where your client is dead, makes for a more reasonable life. My attempt at humor reflects my struggle with the question and my difficulty in answering it.

For the legal profession, the real answer is not to steer lawyers into certain practice areas or to certain types of employers. The result is the creation of "pink ghettos" as well as lawyers winding up practicing without a genuine interest in or commitment to their work. Instead, the objective is to raise awareness, implement better work/life policies and training, facilitate higher work/life policy usage rates, and make the demands of the profession more reasonable for all attorneys.[5]

But progress is slow and difficult for any one person to achieve. In the meantime, you can improve your own existing and future circumstances by engaging in a thorough evaluation of the personal/environmental factors in your life and the work/life balance goals you seek.

Using the Productivity/Satisfaction Index

In Appendix C, you will find Connect Four: The Productivity/Satisfaction Index that you can use to analyze your own set of circumstances. Across the top of the Index, you will see four personal/environmental factors (nature of your work, venue, home, and you). Along the side of the Index, you will find four work/life goals (flexibility, predictability, reduced hours, and proximity).

> To use the Index as an effective self-assessment, you should consider completing the boxes by focusing on three guiding principles:
>
> - Positives
> - Negatives
> - Action steps
>
> You will not put all of the guiding principles in each box or complete all of the boxes—only those that pertain to your circumstances and the needs and demands you face.

On the next page is a completed sample of the Connect Four: Productivity/Satisfaction Index of a corporate lawyer seeking flexibility and reduced hours that will demonstrate how to complete an Index with your own set of circumstances. While you add in your Positives, Negatives, and Action Steps, you also should feel free to add to the Index general likes and dislikes about your job and life circumstances. For example, are there promotional opportunities? Is the compensation good? Do you like your colleagues? Are you overwhelmed with too many commitments in your community? Examples of these comments are included in the sample to give you an idea. Each person's Index will vary. For example, if you are a full-time lawyer not seeking reduced hours, you would leave the reduced hours column blank.

CONNECT FOUR: THE PRODUCTIVITY/SATISFACTION SAMPLE INDEX

	PERSONAL/ENVIRONMENTAL FACTORS				
	THREE GUIDING PRINCIPLES: **POSITIVES** **NEGATIVES** **ACTION STEPS**	**NATURE OF YOUR WORK**	**VENUE (WHERE YOU WORK & FOR WHOM)**	**HOME (FAMILY, COMMUNITY)**	**YOU (TIME MANAGEMENT & PERSONAL FACTORS)**
WORK/ LIFE GOALS	**FLEXIBILITY**	**POSITIVES:** Love deal work. Have flex in type of work & how & where it gets done.	**POSITIVES:** Enjoy colleagues. Great opportunities for promotion & good comp here. Have flex to work less before deal heats up. Time sensitive work is delegated promptly. No unnecessary crises or artificial internal deadlines.	**POSITIVES:** Husband & grandparents have flex to help out when work gets busy. **NEGATIVES:** Need to give husband & grandparents advance notice for additional coverage. Work demands prevent me from always being able to give advance notice.	**POSITIVES:** Perform well under pressure. Thrive on being staffed on high profile & high intensity deals. **NEGATIVES:** Feel guilty about not seeing kids & fear I'm missing out. Worry my kids & husband will resent my absence.
	PREDICTABILITY	**NEGATIVES:** Corp deal work is feast or famine. If pursue high level work, won't get the predictability.	**NEGATIVES:** To get good deals in firm, I need to be willing to work around the clock.	**NEGATIVES:** When deals heat up, I don't see the kids for weeks. My absence disrupts their routines & causes anxiety for all of us.	**ACTION STEPS:** Learn more about staffing & pace of deals to anticipate crises better. Prep kids better for erratic disappearances to minimize impact. Carve out special time w/ each of the kids when work is slower.

	REDUCED HOURS	**NEGATIVES:** Can't afford to work reduced hours & take pay cut until another year.	**POSITIVES:** Firm offers Annualized hours—work reduced hours by being on a deal full-time & then taking a longer reprieve before being staffed again. Reduced hours but doesn't compromise quality of work.	**ACTION STEPS:** Need to reduce # of hours spent on civic ass'n. Announce that I will not run for the Board again next yr.	**ACTION STEPS:** Next year, plan to propose that I want to reduce my hours and work Annualized hours.
	PROXIMITY	**POSITIVES:** Some of my work can be done from home with no revenue impact for me or the firm.	**POSITIVES:** Firm allows lawyers to work from home part of the week & retain full-time status & pay.		**ACTION STEPS:** Next month, propose to work 2 days from home but remain full-time. Continue to earn full income but gain more flex & control. Good solution until I can afford to work fewer hours with less pay. Prepare proposal to include why it's in firm's interest & how I will work flex & not negatively impact colleagues & clients.

You should undertake this Productivity/Satisfaction Index assessment at least annually. It provides a means to evaluate your circumstances and determine whether you are maximizing your performance and whether your current work situation is meeting your needs. If you are not maximizing your performance and/or your needs are not being met, the Index provides an exercise for you to parse out what is not working and how you can improve upon your circumstances. If you are seeking a new job, the boxes provide a framework for you to compare the strengths and weaknesses of different scenarios. As your circumstances and needs change, you should continue to assess the interplay between your personal/environmental factors and work/life goals to determine what will enable you to become a more productive and satisfied lawyer.

Notes

1. *See generally* Deborah Epstein Henry, *The Elusive Balance: Tips to Assess and Meet Your Work-Life Needs*, The Woman Advocate, A Newsletter of the American Bar Association, Section of Litigation, Summer 2008, at 11, *available at* http://www.flextimelawyers.com/pdf/art13.pdf.

2. Eriq Gardner, *Picking Up the Pace*, Corporate Counsel, Nov. 20, 2003.

3. Scott Turow, *The Billable Hour Must Die*, A.B.A.J., Aug. 2007, *available at* http://www.abajournal.com/magazine/article/the_billable_hour_must_die./

4. Mona Harrington & Helen Hsi, *Women Lawyers and Obstacles to Leadership*, *in* A Report of MIT Workplace Center Surveys on Comparative Career Decisions and Attrition Rates of Women and Men in Massachusetts Law Firms 14–15 & tbl.2(c) (2007), *available at* http://web.mit.edu/workplacecenter/docs/law-report_4-07.pdf.

5. *See generally* Deborah Epstein Henry, *Facing the FACTS: Introducing Work/Life Choices for All Firm Lawyers Within the Billable Hour Model*, Diversity & the Bar, Nov./Dec. 2007, *available at* http://www.flextimelawyers.com/pdf/art10.pdf.

APPENDIX C

CONNECT FOUR: THE PRODUCTIVITY/ SATISFACTION INDEX

Instructions for Use

Here is a template for Connect Four: The Productivity/Satisfaction Index. Across the top of the Index, you will see four personal/environmental factors (nature of your work, venue, home, and you). Along the side of the Index, you will find four work/life goals (flexibility, predictability, reduced hours, and proximity). To use the Index as an effective self-assessment, you should consider completing the boxes by focusing on three guiding principles: Positives; Negatives; and Action Steps. You will not put all of the guiding principles in each box or complete all of the boxes—only those that pertain to your circumstances and the needs and demands you face.

While you add in your Positives, Negatives, and Action Steps, you also should feel free to add to the Index general likes and dislikes about your job and life circumstances. Each person's Index will vary.

You should undertake this Productivity/Satisfaction Index assessment at least annually. It provides a means to evaluate your circumstances and determine whether you are maximizing your performance and whether your current work situation is meeting your needs.

Connect Four: The Productivity/Satisfaction Index

	PERSONAL/ENVIRONMENTAL FACTORS				
	THREE GUIDING PRINCIPLES: POSITIVES NEGATIVES ACTION STEPS	NATURE OF YOUR WORK	VENUE (WHERE YOU WORK & FOR WHOM)	HOME (FAMILY, COMMUNITY)	YOU (TIME MANAGEMENT & PERSONAL FACTORS)
WORK/ LIFE GOALS	FLEXIBILITY	POSITIVES: NEGATIVES: ACTION STEPS:	POSITIVES: NEGATIVES: ACTION STEPS:	POSITIVES: NEGATIVES: ACTION STEPS:	POSITIVES: NEGATIVES: ACTION STEPS:
	PREDICTABILITY	POSITIVES: NEGATIVES: ACTION STEPS:	POSITIVES: NEGATIVES: ACTION STEPS:	POSITIVES: NEGATIVES: ACTION STEPS:	POSITIVES: NEGATIVES: ACTION STEPS:
	REDUCED HOURS	POSITIVES: NEGATIVES: ACTION STEPS:	POSITIVES: NEGATIVES: ACTION STEPS:	POSITIVES: NEGATIVES: ACTION STEPS:	POSITIVES: NEGATIVES: ACTION STEPS:
	PROXIMITY	POSITIVES: NEGATIVES: ACTION STEPS:	POSITIVES: NEGATIVES: ACTION STEPS:	POSITIVES: NEGATIVES: ACTION STEPS:	POSITIVES: NEGATIVES: ACTION STEPS:

CHAPTER 12
NAVIGATING PARENTAL LEAVE

About two years ago, during our kids' basketball season, I started noticing a minty smell when I would go into our youngest son Theodore's room to kiss him good night. I couldn't place the smell but it was vaguely familiar. One night as I was heading to kiss the other boys good night, I caught a glimpse of Theo in his room. He had taken our oldest son Oliver's Mennen Speed Stick and was lathering it all over his stomach. Apparently Theo had watched from behind as Ollie was putting on deodorant. To Theo, Ollie appeared to be putting deodorant on his stomach, not under his arms. When I asked Theo why he was using Ollie's deodorant, he casually answered that he noticed Ollie was using it and he had been playing well during his basketball games. Theo hoped it would help his game, too. When I explained to Theo why Ollie needed deodorant at age 13 and he at age 7 did not, Theo wouldn't hear of it. "This is my body, mom," he asserted. "And I know what to do with it."

When to Have a Baby

Many people will have opinions about when is the right time for you, your spouse, or your partner to have a baby. But, ultimately, you and your spouse or partner will be the only ones fit to make that choice. The prudent approach is to wait until you have a few years of legal experience before having a baby. This ideally gives you the opportunity to focus on gaining legal experience, impressing your colleagues and clients, and learning how to manage your time as well as navigate a new profession.

That said, the conservative approach of waiting may not work for everyone. I had my first child 14 months out of law school. My husband is six years older than me, and when I was 27 we were ready to have our first child. I was in the second year of my clerkship with the Honorable Jacob Mishler of the Eastern District of New York. When I was a summer associate at a big New York City law firm, I had learned that several junior partners had delayed childbearing until making partner and then were immersed in fertility treatments. I didn't want that to be me.

The truth is that it's never a good time professionally to have kids. While it is easier and makes more sense to have a few years of practice under your belt before becoming a parent, you will need to balance the competing factors and weigh the best personal choice for you.

Disclosing Your Pregnancy

Most women have anxiety about when to disclose their pregnancy to their employer. My recommendation is to do so promptly after you first hear the baby's heartbeat. There is no reason to get your employer involved until you know that you are actually having a baby.

After the baby's viability is confirmed, do not delay in reporting it. You want to extend the courtesy of giving colleagues as much notice as possible so that they can plan accordingly. Also, you want to minimize the risk of rumors and resentment that might ensue if colleagues feel you are not being aboveboard. When I was pregnant with my third child, I remember patiently waiting until I heard the heartbeat. When I announced my pregnancy to my colleagues promptly thereafter, their response was simple. "Of course, Debbie, we knew. Congrats!" Apparently, I was not so good at concealing my swelling stomach the third time around.

When you make your disclosure, tell your boss or supervising attorney first. Then, you can share the news with other colleagues. Be prepared if some of your colleagues are not congratulatory or supportive at first. Recognize the sensitivity of the issue and that some colleagues might react initially to how it will impact them rather than you. While you will have gone through emotions ranging from elation to anxiety, your colleagues will be receiving and digesting the information for the first time and some may need time to absorb it before they can be outwardly supportive.

News of pregnancy strikes a nerve. For some, it is positive. For others, it is not. For example, your boss with whom you first share the news may be in fertility treatment herself. Perhaps another colleague's wife was never able to get pregnant. Your news may, therefore, be challenging for them. Some colleagues' initial reaction may be concern about your workload and how your absence will impact their work. You may be surprised about who is supportive of your pregnancy. It is not always the people you expect. Be aware that colleagues' reactions shift as they become comfortable with the news. So the best approach is to be patient and let your colleagues process the information before having in-depth conversations about your plans.

If you interview for jobs and you are pregnant, you may choose not to disclose your pregnancy.[1] However, once you have an offer in hand, I would encourage you to disclose your pregnancy before accepting. The employer's reaction may be helpful to you in assessing whether this is the type of employer for whom you want to work. In 1997, when I was pregnant with our second son, we moved to Philadelphia and I interviewed for jobs. I disclosed that I was interested in working reduced hours but I did not disclose my pregnancy before securing some offers. It was a hot lateral market and I had my pick of reduced-hour offers. There were two firms that I was deciding between and I remember disclosing my pregnancy to both of them. I was in my fifth month and I suggested I could start right away if the firm needed me but I requested a commitment of a four-month unpaid leave up front. If the firm found that too disruptive, I proposed to instead start work four months following delivery. One of the two firms was instantly chilly to me. The other firm, which I ultimately joined, was receptive and positive. That firm had me start right away and then honored the four-month leave before I returned to practice.

Regardless of whether you have one offer or many, I would still recommend that you disclose your pregnancy before accepting a position. It is important to assess your employer's reaction to your news. In starting a new employment relationship, you want to build it on trust and mutual consideration. Your employer needs to be able to plan to meet its staffing needs. By disclosing your pregnancy, you are doing the right thing to get your relationship off to the right start.

If Your Employer Has No Parental Leave Policy or an Obsolete One

If your employer has no parental leave policy or its policy is obsolete, do your homework to determine what is reasonable to propose. Prepare a written proposal and provide information about what comparable employers offer.[2] *See* Chapter 7 for what a parental leave policy should entail and for a further discussion of parental leave. It will be necessary to demonstrate the business case for parental leave, showing why it is in your employer's financial interest to adopt a parental leave policy to retain its best talent.[3] In light of the recent economic downturn, it is that much more important that any effort to propose or improve a parental leave policy be framed in economic terms. Your focus should be on conveying how your employer is lagging behind the industry standard and why it is in your employer's financial interest to measure up. If your employer's competitors or clients have gotten recognition for their parental leave or other work/life policies, bring this to your employer's attention as well.

If your employer does not have a parental leave policy or you are seeking to revise one, it is better that the associate's committee or work/life task force or affinity group propose the policy. Although women's initiatives at firms are often behind these efforts, I would encourage you to seek broader support and make the requested policy changes gender neutral. Additionally, an effort to initiate or change an employer policy will be more effective if it is made by a group of attorneys rather than by any individual attorney.

How Much Time Should You Take?

Before deciding how much leave you want to take, familiarize yourself with your employer's written statements on parental leave. Review the employee manual, parental leave policy, intranet postings (if any), and any other internal sources on parental leave. Also, be sure to talk to colleagues to see how much leave they took and how their absence was received. Even with all of this information, it is anxiety-producing to decide how much time to take. At certain employers, if you take a long leave you will be viewed as less committed. Also, certain departments or practice groups may be more receptive to a longer leave than others. In a down market, lawyers may be afraid to take a long leave for fear they will be forgotten or the employer may realize it can do without them. Balance this concern with the desire to be home, enjoy the time with your family, rest, and establish reliable childcare to ensure a smooth transition when you return.

In the 2009 Best Law Firms for Women initiative, Working Mother and Flex-Time Lawyers LLC tracked parental leave for male and female lawyers. The 50 winning firms offered, on average, 14 weeks paid maternity leave, 6 weeks paid paternity leave, and 11 weeks paid adoptive leave.[4] Additionally, at most large law firms lawyers are entitled to four weeks of paid vacation each year, and many attorneys tack these weeks on to extend their parental leave. Some attorneys also add on unpaid leave time. Among the 50 winning firms, on average, associate mothers took 18 weeks of leave, counsel and non-equity partner mothers took 11 weeks, and equity partners took 9 weeks.[5] Meanwhile, on average, lawyer fathers took three and a half weeks of leave.[6] For a further discussion of how much leave time to take, see Chapters 5 and 7.

Whether to Reduce Your Work or Hours Before Your Leave

If you are planning to work reduced hours after your leave, you may be wondering whether you should reduce your workload or hours before your leave. If you are currently working a conventional schedule and you are able to continue doing so, I would suggest not making a change until your leave time. Otherwise, your pay will likely be negatively impacted while you are on leave. Additionally, when you go on leave, it will require your work to be disseminated. It will be smoother to transition all of your matters at the same time than to do it piecemeal during your pregnancy.

For existing matters on which you are staffed, you should continue to handle the relationships and the work as you have. For new matters, you and your employer should be mindful of the timeframe and immediate and long-term travel and other demands, to be sure the staffing makes sense. You should also be careful that you do not receive lower-quality assignments once you announce your pregnancy. Your pregnancy should remain a productive time and serve as an opportunity to make a good, lasting impression before your leave from the office.

Establishing the Right Childcare

If you have a spouse or partner who is authorized to take leave, I encourage you to consider staggering your leaves. This can give each of you the opportunity to bond with the baby and minimize your childcare expenses. With a first child, you will likely be using part of your leave time to interview nannies or select a daycare facility. I encourage you to start the childcare investigation process before you go out on leave, because sometimes it takes longer than expected. If you have another child or children and your childcare is already in place, your leave can be a nice time to spend with your older child or children, in addition to the baby.

The decision you will make about childcare is not only critical for your child or children's success. It will also be instrumental to your own success at work. You will need to be confident that your child or children are safe and that your childcare provider is nurturing and exercises good judgment. Other key childcare issues that will impact your success at work are coverage and flexibility. Is your childcare provider reliable, enabling you to regularly get to work on time? If you work from home sometimes, will you have a quiet place to work uninterrupted? Is your childcare arrangement flexible for the times when you need to work late, go in early, or work additional hours? If you work reduced hours and you get a business call on a day you're at home, will you be able to take the call without a client or colleague hearing kids in the background? If you work reduced hours and you need to switch your schedule around and come into the office at the last minute, will you have coverage to do so? Have you built in layers of support from your spouse or partner, relatives, friends, or other babysitters that will give you the coverage when your regular childcare provider has a problem? These challenges are real. Many lawyers who have left the profession say the event that triggered their departure was a childcare challenge. Ultimately, those challenges drove them to stay home. If you are committed to working, take the steps you can to ensure reliable, high-quality care.

If you work at a law firm or another environment where the hours are erratic and the schedule is unpredictable, often the best coverage is a nanny who is able to work flexible hours. If you live outside a city, it is more helpful if your nanny drives. If you work reduced hours and you can afford full-time coverage, a full-time reliable nanny who can work flexible hours will usually give you the best coverage. This will give you the freedom to adjust your schedule for court appearances, depositions, closings, or client visits. It will also relieve you of household duties and give you the ability to work if you have to when your child is sick, which you would not be able to do if your child were in day care or school. If your employer affiliates with a backup corporate childcare center and your nanny calls in sick, then you would be able to bring your child or children to a center in a pinch. Also, if your employer affiliates with a backup at-home childcare agency, then you would be able to have a childcare provider come to your home at the last minute.

If you prefer a day care or preschool or you cannot afford a full-time nanny, build in the support necessary to ensure that you can get to work or work from home when your child is sick or the day care or preschool is closed. This means having backup coverage from a part-time babysitter, local relatives, neighbors, or friends. If your spouse or partner has flexibility to juggle schedules at the last minute, that will help as well.

You do not want to leave this situation to chance. Many lawyers have recounted to me how they had a child who woke up sick one morning and in a moment of crisis, the husband and wife debated whose job was more important or who made more money in order to decide whose appearance at work that day was more important. These conversations are not pleasant or productive, and it is better to have the coverage and backup thought out and planned for in advance.

Plan Your Role While on Leave

You should consider, in advance, what role you plan to play—and what your work requires that you play—while on leave. Some law firm partners report that while on leave, they do not want to transfer their client relationships or they are too worried to do so. They want to remain the point of contact while on leave. Other lawyers may want to maintain regular contact, while still others may want to completely disengage. It is important to try to anticipate how you will feel and plan accordingly. If you plan to disengage, you should ensure that you effectively transition the matters on which you are working.

Don't be surprised if you feel anxious and ambivalent as you approach your leave—particularly the first time. I was pregnant with our first son during the second year of my clerkship. I remember how strange it was towards the end of my pregnancy to leave my desk each day thinking that if I went into labor, I wouldn't be back the next day. I shared the

Judge's caseload with my co-clerk—I had the even-numbered cases and he had the odd. I remember being anxious about giving over my cases. It felt like a loss. So many of the women preparing to go out on leave relay this anxiety. They want to effectively transition their matters and position their colleagues to take over seamlessly. Yet it is hard to give up the control, particularly when facing the parenting unknown.

You should be prepared for how you will respond if work opportunities arise while you are on leave. During my second maternity leave, a judge scheduled an oral argument and a partner invited me to argue the motion, since I had written the brief. It was a generous opportunity from the partner and I wanted the experience. But it was a difficult choice. I accepted the offer and prepared for and argued the motion during my leave. I would have liked to ask for the oral argument to be rescheduled but I didn't feel I could do so, since that would have delayed the matter for the client. If I declined the opportunity, I was concerned I would not have been viewed as a go-getter. That said, taking on the matter required working during my leave and not enjoying the type of respite I would have liked. I share this story so that you can prepare for these eventualities. Often the process of taking leave is not neat and tidy.

Preparing for Parental Leave

Several months before going out on leave, you should suggest what I call the "parental leave sit down"—a meeting with your employer to discuss how to ensure a smooth transition to and from parental leave. Even if your employer does not hold these sorts of meetings as a matter of course, you should initiate one and hopefully help implement a new process. At the parental leave sit down, you want to be sure to address the Parental Leave Punch List topics outlined below.

Parental Leave Punch List

- Who will "babysit" your matters while you are on leave?
- How will the client be informed of your leave?
- What does an effective transition memo entail?
- Does your employer offer subsidized childcare?
- What will your availability be while on leave?
- Should you return to work on a reduced-hours schedule?

Who will "babysit" your matters while you are on leave? Typically, someone will be assigned to, what I call, "babysit" your matters while you are on leave. Ideally, this colleague should be someone with a similar expertise who is not otherwise overloaded with work. Be sensitive to issues of colleague resentment when transferring matters. I recommend, where possible, that you request that your matters be assigned to an attorney who has taken or likely will take parental leave or an attorney for whom you have or can later provide reciprocal support.

How will the client be informed of your leave? If you work at a law firm, discuss with your firm how best to inform clients of your leave. If you are the key client contact and you want to remain as such while on leave, communicate that to your firm. If you do not want to remain the client contact while on leave, request that one of the other lawyers staffed on your matters assume the client contact role. In either case, after conferring with your firm, it is important that if you have client relationships, you communicate your plans to each client directly. Explain how your client's matter will be transitioned and how the client's needs will continue to be served. You should also welcome suggestions from clients themselves to ensure a smooth transition.

What does an effective transition memo entail? You should prepare a transition memo for each of your matters. Each memo should include: case/deal status; contact information for the primary parties and people involved; anticipated activity while you are on leave; deadlines; and any other outstanding issues or special circumstances about which you should apprise your colleagues.

Does your employer offer subsidized childcare? Find out if your employer offers full-time care, corporate backup, or at-home childcare. If so, determine the fee and eligibility requirements, as well as any timelines, waiting lists, age limits, or other restrictions.

What will your availability be while on leave? You should emphasize that you will be available and responsive for questions as they arise during your leave. As discussed above, if you are interested in remaining more actively engaged on your matters while you are on leave, you should communicate that. Be specific. For example, if you want to be copied on all e-mails and correspondence, communicate that. If you plan to do significant amounts of work while on leave, consider discussing an extended leave with your employer or additional compensation to recoup the time if you work during unpaid leave.[7]

Should you return on a reduced-hours schedule? If you wish to work reduced hours upon returning to work, communicate that as early as possible so your employer can plan accordingly. Some lawyers automatically work reduced hours for up to one year as they transition back from parental leave. Some lawyers return to work before their leave time expires and then extend the length of time that they work a reduced-hour schedule. There are many ways to rearrange your schedule, as explored in Chapters 8, 9, and 13, that may help you to facilitate a smoother transition back to work.

Staying Current While on Leave

For those of you who plan to take six months or more of leave, you should keep current with the substantive law and remain in touch with your colleagues. Continue to read legal newspapers and periodicals to remain informed about substantive law and news about your professional contacts. Keep apprised of internal newsletters or articles authored by colleagues or issued by your employer. You should also remain generally informed about the former matters on which you were staffed. In addition to remaining current on legal happenings, you should initiate regular contact with your colleagues. This may involve e-mails, phone calls, and occasional office visits. If you are planning a longer leave, for a year or more, refer to Chapter 15 for advice on how to stay engaged while out of the office and how to navigate the transition.

How to Transition Back Effectively

The transition back from parental leave is not always smooth. Many find it very emotional to leave their babies at home after a leave. For some, the transition is made easier by working reduced hours for 6 to 12 months upon their return. This option is increasingly being offered by law firms. Among the 2009 Best Law Firms for Women, 58 percent of the 50 winning firms had a written policy that gives women lawyers the option to automatically work reduced hours for up to one year after maternity leave.[8] If this option is available to you, it may be something you want to consider.

A key to returning to work successfully is to delegate effectively and give up some control both at work and home. If you can build a support network with a spouse or partner as well as babysitters, relatives, neighbors, and friends, it will help you find your way. Also, you may want to seek out parents at work who can serve as role models or peer mentors. If your employer has an affinity group for parents or one focused on work/life balance, it may be helpful to join in or start a new one if none exist.

In sum, the transition to and from parental leave is an exciting but anxiety-producing one. With proper planning and effective communication, you can smooth the transition. To maximize your success, remember to be flexible and balance your needs with those of your employer.

Notes

1. The author's advice throughout this book, and otherwise, is being provided as an expert on work/life balance, the retention and promotion of women, and new models of legal practice. As the disclosure in the beginning of this book indicates, the author does not provide legal or employment law advice, and no recommendations provided herein shall be construed as such.
2. *See* Comm. on Women in the Profession, N.Y. City Bar, Parental Leave Policies and Practice for Attorneys 26–28 (2007), *available at* http://www.nycbar.org/pdf/report/Parental_Leave_Report.pdf [hereinafter Parental Leave Report].
3. *See id.* at 28.
4. Working Mother Media & Flex-Time Lawyers LLC, Executive Summary: Highlights of Work/Life and Women Trends from the 2009 Best Law Firms for Women Survey, *available at* http://www.flextimelawyers.com/best/press20.pdf [hereinafter Executive Summary].
5. Working Mother Media & Flex-Time Lawyers LLC, 2009 Best Law Firms for Women Survey, unpublished aggregate statistics of the 50 winning firms.
6. *Id.*
7. *See* Parental Leave Report, *supra* note 2, at 27.
8. Executive Summary, supra note 4.

CHAPTER 13:
FLEXIBLE AND REDUCED HOURS: READY; SET; GO!

When I returned to work after my third maternity leave, I was extremely busy but no longer enjoying the work. Our middle son, Spencer, had a friend who was having a birthday party, and usually I would pick up the gift. But I was pressed for time and I asked Gordon to get it. I was specific about the type of blue Power Rangers I wanted him to buy. When he arrived home with the wrong ones, I flew off the handle. I remember being immensely frustrated. Why couldn't I delegate a simple task? Why couldn't he just follow directions? In the midst of my tirade, Gordon looked at me calmly and said: "When you're yelling at me over Power Rangers, I think it's time for you to make a change."

In my years of working with lawyers who have transitioned to flexible or reduced hours, I find that almost all of them have a similar story to recount—what I call "the triggering event." In fact, when I ask what led to their decision, they typically relay a precise moment in time—"It was June 14, 2007, I was standing in my kitchen . . . ." These lawyers had been thinking of making a lifestyle change for years but some incident became symbolic of the urgency to do so.

For those of you not working flexible or reduced hours but seriously contemplating it, one of the goals of this chapter is to encourage you not to wait until you reach this breaking point. My mother always says: "Don't make important decisions at a time of weakness. Do so from a position of strength." I want to impart that same wisdom here. Transitioning from full-time to flexible or reduced hours is an important decision that can impact your compensation and your opportunity for promotion, among other aspects of your career. This chapter will show you how to take thoughtful and deliberate steps to ensure a successful transition to flexible or reduced hours if it is appropriate for you to do so. If you are already working a flexible or reduced-hour schedule, it will show you how to do it better.

Chapter 6 of this book discusses the business case for becoming a work/life-friendly employer and Chapter 8 discusses making flexible and reduced hours work from the employer perspective. To successfully negotiate and work flexible and reduced hours, it is critical that you understand the issues facing employers that are discussed in these chapters, as well as the issues that you face personally.

Ready?

Figuring Out Your Priorities

Before determining what is the best work arrangement for you, outline your Personal/Environmental Factors and Work/Life Goals, as discussed in Chapter 11. When you do this, you need to remember that these Factors and Goals change as your life circumstances change.

The question you need to ask yourself is: Why are you hoping to transition to a flexible or reduced schedule? Is it to be with your kids more? To manage your family life better? To pursue your lifelong dream of becoming a concert pianist or competitive athlete? Your reasons for wanting to work flexible or reduced hours are likely some combination of factors.

You must weigh the factors influencing your decision to seek flexible or reduced hours against your reasons for working: Is it because you need to make money? Because you enjoy the intellectual stimulation? Or because you seek professional achievement? Are you striving to advance or trying to keep your foot in the door to maintain future opportunities? Once again, your reasons for working are likely a combination of factors.

The decision whether to transition to flexible or reduced hours can only be made by you, and in the end, it is often a gut instinct. When I was working full-time and I only had Oliver, I remember being plagued by guilt. I talked to my mom about it and she assured me I had nothing to worry about. "He's thriving," she said. But I realized for me, that was not the only question to consider. The other question was: Am I missing out? I felt like I was, which is ultimately why I pursued reduced hours when Oliver was a year and a half.

Challenges and Benefits of Working Reduced Hours

As discussed in Chapter 8, there are certain repeated complaints that arise from lawyers working flexible and reduced hours.[1] One is stigma. Many lawyers working flexible and reduced hours feel isolated, marginalized, and resented by colleagues. They often lack support or leadership at the supervisory level. They worry about being viewed by colleagues as uncommitted. They feel out of the loop as a result of missing impromptu meetings or discussions. They are often assigned work that is less exciting, not as high-profile, or less rewarding. These lawyers lose experiences and opportunities and confront detours to advancement and partnership.

Additionally, many lawyers working flexible and reduced hours face unpredictability and lack of control in their hours and schedule. They feel that they are always "on call" and that they are often not paid commensurate with their contribution. They struggle with continued long hours and overpaying in childcare to ensure proper coverage. They feel the line blurring between work and home, with BlackBerrys permanently attached to their hips. Some worry they will lose benefits due to their status and they worry more generally about their job security.

It is important to evaluate these concerns when you assess whether flexible or reduced hours are right for you.[2] You must compare the challenges against the benefits of working flexible or reduced hours, which include maximizing flexibility and the ability to switch around schedules to meet outside demands; earning an income; gaining more involvement in the lives of those who need your attention; keeping your foot in the door professionally; challenging yourself intellectually; continuing your professional development; feeling independent and accomplished; pursuing opportunities and outside interests; becoming a better lawyer by having more time to focus on fewer matters; reaping more business development rewards by having more time to devote to it; enjoying work by having a more humane schedule; and effecting change by redefining the model of a lawyer.

If you are working flexible or reduced hours or considering doing so, you will likely face both the pros and cons—the challenges as well as the rewards. Depending on your own set of circumstances, the balance may be struck where the rewards outweigh the challenges or vice versa. It is only once you analyze your own circumstances that you will be able to determine the right arrangement for you.

Set?

Proposing a Flexible or Reduced-Hour Schedule

1. When Is It Too Early to Ask?

If you are fresh out of law school, try to work for an employer for at least one or two years before requesting a flexible or reduced schedule. This way, your colleagues are comfortable with you and your employer is confident that you have some experience in managing your time and work. It is also helpful to build good will with your colleagues by being a team player and working a conventional schedule.

But sometimes the need to work flexible or reduced hours arises before that one- or two-year mark. If this happens to you, take the same steps to secure the change but be sensitive to the fact that sometimes such a schedule is not looked upon favorably with a more junior lawyer. While employers are increasingly allowing entry-level lawyers to work reduced-hour schedules, few entry-level lawyers are availing themselves of such policies. Low usage rates are typically an indicator that lawyers are not comfortable accessing a policy or that the policy is not fully supported. In the National Association for Law Placement, Inc. (NALP) 2009 study, 98 percent of the 1,475 law firms surveyed allowed lawyers to work reduced hours, either as an affirmative policy or on a case-by-case basis.[3] However, 53 percent of the offices that offered a reduced-hour option precluded entry-level associates from working reduced hours, and less than 12 percent had an affirmative reduced-hour policy that made the option available to all lawyers.[4] In the 2009 Best Law Firms for Women initiative, 26 percent of the 50 winning firms required lawyers to have one or more years of experience before becoming eligible for reduced hours.[5]

While NALP does not separately track usage for entry-level lawyers, the usage rates for all lawyers working reduced hours is very low. In 2009, just 5.9 percent of lawyers worked reduced hours, and of those

72.5 percent were women.[6] Among the lawyers working reduced hours, 5.0 percent were associates, 3.5 percent were partners and 20.7 percent were "other lawyers," such as of counsel and staff attorneys.[7] For lateral hires, employers typically still prefer a full-time schedule before offering a flexible arrangement. This may gradually change due to the economic downturn and employers being less certain of their future hiring needs. For example, I'm seeing some employers hire lawyers on a flexible or reduced-hours schedule with the understanding that these lawyers will expand and contract their hours as the employers' work demands ebb and flow.

If you are able to secure a lateral job opportunity on reduced hours, the issues you face will be different. You will not have to face the challenge of changed standards or expectations ("She used to bill X and now she's only billing Y" or "He used to always stay late on Wednesdays and now he's running out the door"). You will also face less colleague resentment because you are working the arrangement that the employer specifically hired you to do. The challenge instead is that in starting a new job, you want to impress your colleagues and be a team player. When you are working flexible or reduced hours, though, you also need to erect boundaries to protect your schedule. Balancing these two priorities when starting a new job can be challenging. However, the tips below can help you manage these competing demands.

2. What Is the Right Schedule or Percentage of Hours to Work?

The decision of what schedule or percentage of hours to work is different for everyone. It also evolves over time. I often joke that whatever schedule you settle on is one day more than your ideal. When my kids were young, I worked a 75 percent schedule at a law firm and went into the office three days per week. This worked well for me because my kids attended a preschool the same three days I went into the office. Also, I had a part-time babysitter/housekeeper, who was home with me the two days I was home. She did not have another job so she was often flexible to come in when need be on an unscheduled day. But generally, she was there to be an extra set of hands and be a backup if one of the kids was sick or if the kids' school was closed or if I needed to take a work call or switch around my schedule and go into the office. With three young kids and a demanding litigation practice, these were frequent occurrences. Now that I run a consulting practice and my kids are school age, I prefer working five compressed days per week. I work early in the morning before the kids get up. For the rest of the day, I try to work what I call "bus stop hours." In other words, I try to have my work schedule mirror the kids' school schedule when I'm not traveling. The Blackberry affords me the ability to be with the kids in the late afternoon and I fit in extra work while the kids do homework or after their bedtime, if need be.

When selecting a schedule, identify the important days in the office for your department, colleagues, and clients and try to arrange your regular work days to match up. For example, if you are in the corporate department and they have a regular Thursday departmental meeting, plan to be in the office on Thursdays. When deciding which days to be in the office, select a schedule that will not inconvenience colleagues and clients while not creating additional work for you at home. Some lawyers who work three days per week select Tuesday, Wednesday, and Thursday as the days to be in the office. Although it is nice to have your Mondays and Fridays out of the office, it may not be an ideal schedule for clients and colleagues—or even for you, because inevitably you will be working more from home if you are out of the office two consecutive work days.

Unconventional hours or altering your schedule may also help to minimize the work interruptions at home. For example, when I worked three days per week as a law firm litigator, I worked Monday, Tuesday, and Thursday. As an early riser, I liked getting work done before most people got to the office. On Mondays and Tuesdays, my schedule was 7 a.m. to 5 p.m. When necessary, I worked from home at night, after putting our kids to bed. If I had an important filing or I was preparing for trial, I was able to make other arrangements to stay later. On Wednesdays, I stayed home and I called Thursday my "late night." I worked from 7 a.m. until very late, sometimes as late as midnight. It was helpful to have one day a week when I didn't have to run out the door. Also, Thursday night gave me the opportunity to clear my desk and, when possible, avoid work on Friday or the weekend. If I needed to take an extended business lunch or even a dinner, I would try to do it on Thursdays, too.

When you choose a percentage or schedule for the office, I encourage you to assess what is realistic and balance the reality against your preferences. So, if you want to work a 60 percent schedule but you know the work demands in your department for the next year will be more like 80 percent, then request to work the 80 percent schedule so that your compensation and contribution are in line. But express the desire to reduce your hours further once the work permits. If you are a law firm lawyer, I suggest giving yourself a buffer to allow for spillover work in selecting your percentage. For example, when I worked three days in the office at a law firm, I selected a 75 percent schedule because I anticipated the inevitable spillover work that I performed from home and I wanted to be compensated for it.

Law firm lawyers frequently ask what the minimum percentage is that they should work if they want to remain partner eligible. This varies widely at firms, but to generalize, I would suggest a 75 to 80 percent schedule or higher. Lawyers working fewer hours are more often overlooked for partner promotions. At law firms, 60 percent of the required billable hours is often a minimum number of hours that lawyers are required to bill.

Some lawyers wonder whether it is better to meet or exceed target billable hours as a reduced-hour lawyer or whether to remain full-time and not necessarily meet your hours. Those who remain full-time contend that it is better to be well-compensated and avoid the stigma of reduced hours. Also, they argue that many lawyers do not meet a firm's billable-hour targets—why should they feel the need to take less pay when others are not. Ultimately, I think this is a matter of personal comfort. Some women, in particular, feel uncomfortable if they are not meeting or exceeding expectations such that it would cause more anxiety to work full-time hours and run the risk of not meeting the target. Others are more at ease aiming to reach the target and not fretting if they don't quite get there. Ultimately, this is a personal choice based on your judgment and comfort level.

> Keep in mind that both your needs and the demands of your employer will continue to evolve. One key to a successful flexible or reduced-hour schedule is to adjust it when demands at work or home require it.

3. What Should a Proposal to Work Flexible or Reduced Hours Entail?

Whether or not your employer requires it, if you are interested in working flexible or reduced hours, submit a proposal outlining your aspirations and how you plan to make it work for your employer. The logistics of how to make this work will be addressed later in this chapter.

What follows is a summary of what you should consider including in a flexible or reduced-hour proposal. As discussed in Chapter 8, I recommend that an employer have a standard form that lawyers can use to propose their flexible or reduced-hour schedule. I also recommend that employers schedule a "flexible sit-down" meeting to discuss the issues outlined below. As the lawyer, you will have less control over the process. In any event, you should be prepared to address the issues outlined below, and if your employer does not initiate the process, you should. Depending on your employer's protocol, some of the outlined issues may be addressed orally rather than in a written proposal.

a. **The schedule.** State which type of flexible arrangement you are interested in working and include a proposed schedule. Specify the requested number of days and/or percentage of hours to work and the suggested days and/or hours in the office. If you propose telecommuting for part or all of the week, specify that, too.
b. **The business case.** At the outset, the key is to emphasize that your proposed flexible or reduced-hours schedule is a win-win situation and not an accommodation. Using the reasoning articulated in Chapter 6, explain why it is in your employer's financial interest to agree to your proposal. Additionally, as discussed in Chapter 15, flexibility can be proposed as an asset in a down market.
c. **Impact on colleagues and clients.** A significant concern for employers that you will want to address directly is how you will work flexible and reduced hours seamlessly so as not to negatively impact colleagues and clients.
d. **Responsiveness and accessibility.** Address how you will be responsive and accessible when matters arise when you are outside the office and how you will ensure that work will get done even when you are not there. Emphasize that you understand that flexibility and communication are the key to making flexible and reduced-hour arrangements successful and that work or client demands may require switching around your schedule or working additional hours.
e. **Assignments and promotion.** If you want to remain engaged in challenging work, articulate that despite changing your sched-

ule, you plan to continue to receive challenging assignments and deliver top notch work. If you want to remain on a promotion track, express that interest. Ask whether a potential promotion will be impacted by your changed schedule. If you are seeking less-challenging work and you want to be removed from a promotion track, you should communicate that but assure your employer that the quality of your work product will not be impacted.

f. **Nonbillable work.** If you are at a law firm, emphasize that you plan to continue contributing to the firm by doing nonbillable work. In a non-law-firm venue, communicate your interest in continuing your contribution to your employer, in addition to your regular workload. However, if you are transitioning to reduced hours, you can propose making a pro rata adjustment to your committee work. If you are seeking less-challenging work and to be removed from a promotion track, the obligation to do nonbillable work should diminish.

g. **Travel.** If you are amenable to travel under a flexible or reduced hour schedule, communicate your interest. If there are any parameters such as a limit on the number of days you could be away or the amount of advance notice you would require, indicate that as well.

h. **Compensation, benefits, and vacation.** Your employer should have a policy that articulates how compensation, benefits, and vacation are handled for lawyers working flexible or reduced hours. If not, propose a pro rata adjustment to your compensation based on the reduction in hours or days you propose to work. Propose that pro rata adjustments also be made to any bonus pay and vacation time. Be clear that you are not looking for preferential treatment, but rather the same pay and vacation time as your full-time colleagues, pro rata. Most large firms do contribute the same amount for health care coverage for full-time and reduced-hour lawyers, and reduced-hour lawyers are typically entitled to the same benefits as their full-time counterparts.[8] If you are proposing to work flexible hours but still carry a full workload, propose that your compensation, benefits, and vacation status remain the same as full-time lawyers working a conventional schedule.

i. **Proposed transition.** Propose how to make the transition from a full-time traditional schedule to a flexible one. To minimize colleague resentment, consider waiting until you have a natural break in your schedule to have the transition take effect. For example, good times to reduce your workload are when you are going out on parental leave or if a case settles, a trial ends, or a deal closes. If you are able to avoid transitioning a file of yours to a colleague, you will minimize the tension that often results when colleagues feel they have to pick up the slack for someone else's work.

4. What If Your Request Is Denied or Your Employer Is Skeptical?
If your request for flexible or reduced hours is denied, you may be able to have your employer reconsider. You first want to evaluate the basis for the denial. If you proposed working three days a week and the employer was concerned that the department was too busy to support that reduction of hours, propose four days a week or perhaps three days in the office and one from home. Or, if your employer believes the department is too busy and cannot support any reduction of hours, propose continuing your full-time schedule but working one or two days from home.

If your employer is new to or skeptical about flexible or reduced hours, offer a three- or six-month trial period. After the trial period, propose that the employer evaluate whether your schedule negatively impacted the quality of your work or your colleagues or clients. If the answer is no, then you have a strong argument to continue with the new schedule. During a trial period, track your own perceptions and any positive feedback or successes to make your case anew at the end of the trial period.

GO!

The Nitty-Gritty of Working Flexible and Reduced Hours Successfully[9]

Here are some general parameters for working a flexible or reduced-hour arrangement effectively and what I call the "nitty-gritty" guidelines that will maximize your day-to-day success.

1. Educate.

- Regularly educate and broadcast the business case for flexible and reduced-hour arrangements and the positive impact that such arrangements have on the retention and promotion of women, in particular. This means circulating reports or news articles or highlighting recognition that clients and competitors are getting in this regard. It also means celebrating internal success stories when lawyers working flexible and reduced hours at your place of employment are thriving, gaining recognition, or being promoted.

2. **Be indispensable.**
   - As James Sandman, former managing partner of Arnold & Porter LLP, said as a guest speaker at a Flex-Time Lawyers LLC event in 2005, maintain the same level of professionalism, responsiveness, and accessibility with your colleagues as you do with your clients.
   - Demonstrate your value by delivering top-notch work, meeting deadlines, and being responsive to clients and colleagues. The better your work product and contribution to colleagues and clients, the greater your negotiating power and your employer's interest in retaining and promoting you.

3. **Be flexible and communicative.**
   - Approach your flexible or reduced-hour arrangement as one of mutual flexibility. If your work expectation is flexibility rather than predictability, you will have more realistic expectations and will likely experience more job satisfaction.
   - Be clear and communicative with colleagues about your schedule in and out of the office as well as your accessibility and responsiveness (based on your employer's reasonable expectation of you). Your colleagues need to have a clear understanding of how to work best with you. Convey an understanding that you are working in a service profession and anticipate being flexible.
   - One way to make it easier for your colleagues to keep current on your schedule is to share an online calendar that indicates your availability and days in the office. An online calendar is also an easy way to allow you to switch around your schedule when necessary and have your colleagues remain informed.
   - Discuss with your employer how your schedule should be communicated to clients. At many employers, colleagues are informed of the flexible and reduced-hour lawyers' schedules, but for clients, it will depend on the particular client and the nature of the relationship.
   - Discuss with your employer what your voice mail and out-of-office message on your e-mail should say when you are outside the office.

Also, discuss with your employer what your assistant should say when you are outside the office. In most cases, the e-mail, voice mail, and assistant relay that the lawyer is outside the office and do not provide an explanation of where.

- Communicate with your assistant and be clear about how you can be reached when you are outside the office.

4. **Gain favorable assignments.**
   - Make your work interests known. Be outspoken about the types of matters or types of experiences you are seeking. This active approach will improve your likelihood of being staffed on matters that are in line with your desired professional development.
   - If there are particular attorneys or clients with whom you want to work, specify that, too. You may seek to work with certain lawyers because of their practice area, expertise, or influence.

5. **Develop meaningful relationships.**
   - Develop relationships with senior management and lawyers in your department who can support you and advocate on your behalf.
   - Nurture relationships and build alliances with colleagues and clients, while accepting that you will not win everyone over.
   - Develop relationships and work with colleagues in different practice areas or departments. This may enhance your job security by helping you draw support from a broader network. It will also enable you to learn and benefit from lawyers with different knowledge and work styles.

6. **Be a team player.**
   - Show colleagues through your conduct that you are committed and a team player. This means developing a reputation for helping colleagues out in a pinch. This willingness is important for overcoming negative biases and also for developing reciprocal support. When you need to call on someone for help, they will be happy to oblige.
   - When you need coverage in the office, arrange for coverage by other flexible and reduced-hour lawyers, where possible, or lawyers for whom you would provide reciprocal support. Be sensitive to minimizing colleague resentment.

7. **Delegate.**
   - Consider ways to improve your efficiency—for example, by delegating more to your assistant and to junior lawyers.
   - As Sandman also suggested at the 2005 Flex-Time Lawyers LLC event, if you are senior enough, delegate to a multitude of people. It is better to rely on different people for varying tasks so that you are not vulnerable if the one person you rely on happens to leave your place of employment.

8. **Contribute.**
   - Be deliberate in choosing visible, nonbillable ways to contribute to your firm in areas that you enjoy. For example, if you like or want to work on business development or recruiting, volunteer to focus on those areas that are important to the firm. If you are not at a law firm, you should still contribute to your employer's operations, outside of your regular workload.
   - Be systematic. Plan ahead for the contributions you make to your employer. For example, if you participate in recruiting for a law firm summer program, schedule one recruiting lunch per week with two summer associates and another colleague. It is a way to meet summer associates and catch up with colleagues. The cumulative contribution is significant.

9. **Be visible.**
   - Maximize your visibility by attendance at, for example, departmental meetings and well-attended internal events. You can also maximize your "presence" by keeping in regular touch through voice mail and e-mail.

10. **Have good coverage.**
    - If you can afford it, secure full-time childcare coverage. This will alleviate the stress when you are required to switch your days around or work on days when you are scheduled to be outside the office. It also is important to maintain a level of professionalism so you do not have children or distractions in the background while you are trying to provide legal advice.
    - If you are working reduced hours to care for young children, build in layers of support for coverage for when the eventual need arises.

This coverage may mean support from a spouse or partner, family member, neighbor, friend, or babysitter who can be a backup.

11. Make it seamless.

- Pay attention to how work is flowing when you are outside the office. By ensuring that work continues to circulate when you are outside the office, you are making sure that there are no delays due to your schedule. It also shows your colleagues that you are "present" even when not physically there.
- Get back to colleagues and clients promptly, even if you do not have the answer yet. Often, when a request is made, the sender merely wants acknowledgment that the request has been received. A two-line message, thanking the person for the e-mail and letting him or her know that the issue is being looked into, is usually all the person needs to feel that his or her needs are being met.

12. Adjust expectations

- Many lawyers are their own worst enemies. They are perfectionists and self critical. This often results in women lawyers, in particular, leaving the profession because they feel they can't manage their work and home lives at the impossibly high standards they set for themselves. Instead, they should consider adjusting their expectations. Here's an example: I ran a Flex-Time Lawyers LLC event in 2002 with the Honorable Norma L. Shapiro of the Eastern District of Pennsylvania as my guest. Judge Shapiro is a revered judge, role model, and mentor to countless women in the Philadelphia legal community and around the country. She was also the first reduced-hour partner in Philadelphia. When I asked Judge Shapiro how she managed a successful career with motherhood when her children were young, she explained that she adjusted her expectations. As an example, she relayed that, much to her mother's dismay, she decided she no longer had the time to line her drawers every Spring and Fall. After Judge Shapiro shared this example to a room full of women lawyers in their 30s, there was silence—until one lawyer blurted out with laughter: "I didn't even know we were supposed to." This story is symbolic to me that we each have our own personal standards. To transition successfully to flexible or reduced hours, you need to re-evaluate those expectations and adjust them so that you can feel more satisfied in how you meet the demands of work and home.

13. Be a leader.

- Assume a leadership role in your place of employment in an area about which you are knowledgeable and passionate. Become the point person on the subject so that you can be a resource and authority for your colleagues.

14. Seek promotion.

- For those seeking promotion, be vigilant about the types of matters on which you are staffed and your exposure to influential clients and colleagues. In the law firm context, vigilance means working with influential partners and clients and, where possible, being selective about how you are staffed on matters. For example, get staffed on at least one high-profile matter at a time to maintain contact with the influential internal lawyers and clients working on such matters and to gain the experience necessary to advance.
- If you are at a law firm that has switched to a core competency evaluation system, be systematic about mastering the core competencies articulated for the next promotion level. If the competencies are not defined at your firm, seek the advice of partners and others who are knowledgeable to understand what experience is necessary to be promoted. Then make your work interests known about seeking the next level of experience.
- In the law firm setting, choose business development as your key nonbillable contribution. This means seeking out the marketing department (if your firm has one) and learning how to be considered for new client pitches. It also means getting advice from partners about what steps you should take to enhance your networking and visibility. Success in developing business will maximize your flexibility and power at your firm and your ability to switch firms if you are inclined to do so.
- In the law firm context, become informed about how credit is awarded from new and existing clients. For example, does the firm facilitate shared credit or award credit to a lawyer who does not originate the business but services the client and expands the business?

- If you have achieved partnership status at a firm as a reduced-hour lawyer, become knowledgeable about how a reduced-hour schedule impacts current and future compensation.[10]

15. Self advocate.

- Advocate for yourself. As lawyers, we advocate zealously for our clients. We seldom remember to advocate for ourselves.
- Keep track of your results and successes. If you receive accolades from clients or colleagues or if you are otherwise recognized for your work, share those acknowledgments as you receive them.
- At your annual review or the equivalent, prepare and distribute a "brag memo" to those reviewing you. The memo should highlight your successes and contributions and the value you brought to your employer that year. It should also include any acknowledgments or recognition that you have received from colleagues, clients, or others.
- At your annual review or equivalent, give feedback on the challenges and successes of the flexible or reduced-hour schedule and offer thoughts on how it can be improved. Solicit feedback from those for whom you worked on how the arrangement has worked for them and what can be done to make it work better.

16. Reevaluate and adapt.

- The onus is on you to continue to develop creative solutions and proposals to make the flexible and reduced-hour arrangement mutually beneficial. This may mean changing your days, percentage, or hours in the office to continue to meet your work and home demands.
- As you work with different colleagues, continue to manage perceived expectations about your work/life choices. This means educating new colleagues about your schedule and availability so they know how to work with you effectively. It also means continuing to educate colleagues and demonstrate, through your conduct, why it is in your employer's financial interest to retain and promote you.

Ultimately, the "nitty-gritty" ways to make flexible and reduced-hour schedules work are tools for lawyers to gain control over their lives while remaining effective and talented contributors. Lawyers working flexible and reduced schedules will achieve greater success and satisfaction both at work and at home if they establish their priorities and maximize the benefits of their schedules.

Notes

1. *See generally* Deborah Epstein Henry, *Prevailing Principles to Make Reduced Hour Schedules Succeed*, Diversity & the Bar, Sept./Oct. 2007, at 16, *available at* http://www.flextimelawyers.com/pdf/art9.pdf; Deborah Epstein Henry, *The Nitty-Gritty of How and Why to Make Part-Time Work*, The Balance Beam (2003–2004), *available at* http://www.flextimelawyers.com/pdf/2003_2004newsletter.pdf.

2. *See generally* Henry, *The Nitty-Gritty*, *supra* note 1.

3. Nat'l Ass'n for Law Placement, Most Lawyers Working Part-time Are Women—Overall Number of Lawyers Working Part-time Remains Small, tbl. 4 (2009), *available at* http://www.nalp.org/parttimesched2009.

4. *Id.*

5. Working Mother Media & Flex-Time Lawyers LLC, 2009 Best Law Firms for Women Survey, unpublished aggregate statistics of the 50 winning firms.

6. Nat'l Ass'n for Law Placement, *supra* note 3.

7. *Id.* at tbl. 1.

8. Working Mother Media & Flex-Time Lawyers LLC, 2008 Best Law Firms for Women Survey, unpublished aggregate statistics of the 50 winning firms.

9. *See generally* Henry, *The Nitty-Gritty*, *supra* note 1.

10. Cynthia Thomas Calvert et al., *Reduced Hours, Full Success: Part-Time Partners in U.S. Law Firms*, *in* The Project for Attorney Retention 39 (2009), *available at* http://www.pardc.org/Publications/Part-TimePartner.pdf.

CHAPTER 14
THE ABCs OF TIME MANAGEMENT

Before our sons played travel soccer, I coached them at the intramural level. They started in the Pee Wee division, where children need to be four years old to participate. When our youngest son, Theodore, started, he was familiar with the sport, having watched many of his brothers' games. At Theo's first game, the boys were clustered around the ball, which was hardly moving. Finally, someone took a big kick and the ball went flying off the field. Theo called out, "The ball. It's out of balance." Adam, the eighth-grade referee, responded, "Theo, I think you mean it's 'out of bounds.'" To which Theo replied, "No, ask my mom. She says it's out of balance!"

As we explore ways to manage our time in this chapter, we need to be mindful that our day-to-day time management not only impacts our schedules and lives. It also has a significant influence on those around us—whether we think they're paying attention or not.

Time Management Tips to Tailor to Your Life

In advising lawyers on time management over the years, I find that more often than not, lawyers want detailed tips and advice, rather than a broad discussion of concepts. So, in this chapter, I share my favorite time management tips that I have seen work. I have organized the ideas around the ABCs as a metaphor for how fundamental time management is to our everyday success. Time management, like the ABCs, provides the foundation you need to manage, contribute, and engage in your work and home life in the most fulfilling way. You will see that the tips below include advice about prioritizing and allocating your time beyond your daily tasks. This is deliberate, because being effective at time management is about maximizing your visibility, relationships, impact, and success beyond your daily workload.

Lawyers have very different work styles so the tips below that work for some may not work for others. As you read along, select the ideas that are most suitable to your work style to help you seek more control, productivity, satisfaction, and success in your work and life.

The ABCs of Time Management

ACCESSIBILITY—Be Responsive
BACKUP—Don't Leave Home Without It
CLUTTER—Get Rid of It
DELINEATE Lines Between Work and Home
EXTRACURRICULARS—Maximize and Manage Them
FLEXIBILITY—Bend, Don't Break
GROUP Your Activities
HABITS—Routinize to Maximize
INDISPENSABILITY—Deliver Top-Notch Work
JUDGE—Judiciously
KEEP Your Eye on the Prize
LINK Short Term to Long Term
MULTITASK Meticulously
NETWORK Incessantly
ORGANIZE and Reorganize
PRIORITIZE and Prepare
QUALITY Relationships Are Critical
REFLECT, Reassess, and Redefine
SUPPORT—Delegate Effectively
TECHNOLOGY—Tune In
UNDERSTAND Others
VALUE over Volume
WRITE and Reach Out
XEROX and Recycle
YOU—An Investment Worth Making
ZEAL—A Zest for Life

ACCESSIBILITY—Be Responsive. Some employers worry that lawyers seeking control over their lives will no longer meet the demands of practice. However, if you are responsive and accessible to clients and colleagues, then the way in which you work should be irrelevant. Let's say you get a client request to research a legal question on Wednesday, a day you're at home with your kids. If the research assignment is something you would delegate, forward it immediately to the person responsible for the research so that no time is lost. This way, no one is inconvenienced by your schedule and work flows while you are outside the office. If the work is not the sort you would delegate, assess whether the request is time sensitive. If so, you will need to tend to it. If not, you will tend to it when you return to the office. In all three scenarios, you should e-mail the client saying the question will be or is being researched and you will be back in touch with a response when you have it. The client is now assured that his or her needs are being addressed. If you are not available to check e-mail regularly for any extended period of time during a work day, you should either have your assistant do so or have an out-of-office message indicate who to contact for a pressing matter and when you will next be available.

BACKUP—Don't Leave Home Without It. Ideally, you should have backup systems in place (and extra childcare, if you can afford it) for the inevitable changes in plans and crises. Your support system at home should be broad—a spouse, partner, nanny, backup babysitters, family members, and friends. It is important to plan ahead and be proactive. Avoid waiting for an emergency to force you to handle a situation. For example, anticipate and plan for the problems that arise when the kids are sick, the nanny is unreliable, the eldercare provider has an emergency, or the kids' school closes.

CLUTTER—Get Rid of It. To rid yourself of the clutter in your physical space, set aside time on a weekly (or at least monthly) basis to clear your desk and get rid of anything nonessential or obsolete. The cleansing of your workspace will help clear your mind and give you a fresh start.

DELINEATE Lines Between Work and Home. Success in delineating lines starts with how you work. Do you regularly work from home so that your work and home lives are integrated? Or do you try to separate your two identities (something that is increasingly hard to do)? Committing to outside interests helps take you away from work and helps prevent your home life from being consumed by work. Think twice about giving out your cell or home numbers to work contacts and have your assistant (if you have one) serve as a buffer for non-pressing matters. When you are not able to do something, it is usually not necessary to disclose the reason. Also, try to have at least one time of day, in addition to meal times, where you prioritize something not work-related, e.g., taking the kids to school, exercising, taking a class, going to a board meeting, or attending a cultural event.

EXTRACURRICULARS—Maximize and Manage Them. At least annually, make a list of your professional and personal commitments. Determine which responsibilities you no longer want and where your roles are nonessential. Keep these guidelines in mind as new opportunities arise. Make time for your personal outlets—dance, music, culture, sports, or socializing—and prioritize the community and professional organizations that you enjoy.

FLEXIBILITY—Bend, Don't Break. To be successful in managing your time, be flexible when circumstances are beyond your control. Being flexible means that you realize that the demands of work and home often conflict and are in constant flux and require regular adjustments. If you are interested in working reduced hours, the need for you to be flexible is that much more important to ensure that the needs of colleagues and clients are met. That being said, you should covet the time where you can separate from your work. You want to avoid being so flexible and accommodating all the time that it is at a personal cost resulting in a breaking point.

GROUP Your Activities. In managing your daily work, it often helps to group similar activities where the tasks are the same, such as responding to e-mails, returning phone calls, or drafting letters. Or it may be better for you to work matter by matter and complete assorted tasks for the same matter or project before moving on to the next. Others organize their work based on commitments to different people. If they are working with a few key people, they will focus on those projects needed for one person and then move on to the next.

HABITS—Routinize to Maximize. Each of us has different times of the day when we are most productive. To be more efficient, it is important to tap into your natural rhythms, plan around the outside distractions, and develop routines. For example, if you are a morning person or a late-night person or you have lower energy after lunch, concentrate your work during peak performance times and leave the less demanding tasks for those times when you are not at your best or when you know you will more often be interrupted. Once you have identified your most productive work time, protect it. Do not spend that time responding to routine e-mails. By having a routine, you will also minimize the inefficiency of rethinking how to organize your time on a daily basis.

INDISPENSABILITY—Deliver Top-Notch Work. The more talented you are, the more negotiating power you will have. The key to gaining more control over your work and life is to make yourself indispensable. You need to deliver top-notch work and demonstrate that you are a team player who steps up to handle crises when necessary.

JUDGE—Judiciously. To be effective at managing your time, you cannot say "yes" to everything. You need to be judicious in what work you seek out, volunteer for, and decline. In deciding what work to decline, you need to consider both the import of the work and the potential influence of the people with whom you would work. If you have enough work to keep you busy, you should decline further work to avoid the risk of delivering shoddy work. If you decline work, be diplomatic and careful in explaining the circumstances so that your reasoning is understood.

KEEP Your Eye on the Prize. Each year, you should establish your goals and objectives. You should enumerate the contributions you plan to make both at work and at home. When you develop long-term goals, you should consider your skills, interests, strengths, weaknesses, and aspirations. Your annual goals should then be broken out into concrete milestones you plan to achieve.

LINK Short Term to Long Term. To reach your long-term goals, break them down into tasks and set deadlines to achieve them. Ideally, link some of your daily to-dos to your long-term goals so that your daily work advances the direction in which you want to take your career. In this process, invoke the support of people who will be instrumental in helping you attain your goals.

MULTITASK Meticulously. Multitasking at work and home can save you time when you do it right. For example, if you have to go to a continuing legal education seminar, you should go with a friend, colleague, or prospective client. Or if you want to exercise and you do it with a friend, it can be that much more enjoyable. Multitasking also means making use of your down time when you are waiting or going somewhere. For example, use the blocks of time commuting, waiting in court, or waiting at doctor's offices to catch up on reading or to return phone calls or e-mails. Be mindful that multitasking can backfire when you focus on too many things and it prevents you from doing any of them well.

NETWORK Incessantly. Networking outside the office is important for marketability, client development, and future job opportunities. Networking inside the office is critical to build alliances and support for quality work, mentorship, and advancement. When you are short on time, it is important that you are deliberate, plan ahead, and maximize each opportunity to network. Go to key meetings or events with large attendance at your office so you can mingle and interact with many people at once. When you select committees to participate in, ideally choose those that interest you that will also give you high visibility. Play an integral role in one or two committees or organizations that are meaningful to you rather than participating superficially in many.

ORGANIZE and Reorganize. Using a scheduling system of some sort—day planner, calendar, PDA—is critical to keeping your commitments straight. Whether you keep your calendar or have an assistant manage it, you should share your calendar with the team with whom you work, where appropriate. You also want to develop systems for managing files, information, articles, e-mails, phone calls, and correspondence that are intuitive to the way you think. For example, color-coded files may help you look for certain documents. Or, if you are trying to rid yourself of paper, create e-mail and document folders and subfolders on your computer and organize your work through key words that will trigger your memory.

PRIORITIZE and Prepare. Many find it helpful to take a few minutes at the beginning or end of each day to make a to-do list for that day or the next. The exercise of creating to-do lists and deadlines and otherwise prioritizing your work forces you to differentiate between what I call "to do" and "to respond." Often, people fill their days just responding to others' requests. When the day ends, they feel as if they have gotten nothing accomplished. Keeping your to-do list will help you stay on task. In addition to daily lists, you want to look at the week and the month to plan your longer-term projects and deadlines. The to-do lists should be realistic in terms of tasks and time frames. Ideally, you want to leave a cushion in your schedule for the unanticipated work that arises or spillover projects. Creating to-do lists for your family and community commitments (as well as for your family members themselves) is also helpful.

QUALITY Relationships Are Critical. To enrich your work experience, you should seek to develop quality relationships. It is important to seek out mentors both inside and outside of your place of employment to help guide your career path. Developing camaraderie with your professional peers will also help you become more invested at work. At home, you want to cultivate close friendships to enrich your life and commitment to your community.

REFLECT, Reassess, and Redefine. After you conclude a case, matter, or deal, consider the lessons learned, including what you should have done or prioritized differently. Seek input from colleagues with whom you work about what could have been done better. Also, consider the crises that you regularly face and whether they can be managed better or whether they result from the nature of your work or home life. When you feel frustrated that your schedule is not working, remind yourself of your priorities and try a realignment. Also, think about what you do and whether you love it and what defines success for you. This may be a different model of success than your employer uses or different from what you initially conceived of when you graduated law school. Your redefinition of success should be based on your priorities today that enable you to achieve greater productivity and satisfaction in work and life.

SUPPORT—Delegate Effectively. Build support and delegate at both work and home. Accepting support requires you to give up some control. When you delegate at work, you want to be clear about deadlines and deliverables. Keep track of what you delegate and pay attention to how work is flowing once it leaves your hands. If you are able to delegate to a multitude of people, it will help you build a larger base of support. On the home front, when I speak to law students, I always get a laugh when I emphasize the importance of choosing your spouse or partner wisely. But, this choice cannot be underestimated. As I once read in an insightful *New York Times* letter to the editor: "We will never have equity in the workplace until we have equity at home." It also helps at home if you create predetermined roles and responsibilities so that each time a crisis occurs, there is not a discussion about who is responsible for handling it.

TECHNOLOGY—Tune In. Use technology to your advantage. Understand your employer's expectation of responsiveness and accessibility and then place self-imposed limits on checking into the office based on what is expected. For example, choose not to be on the phone or BlackBerry when dropping or picking up your kids, seeing your kids for the first time of the day, and during mealtimes. Also, consider creating sacred spaces at home where technology does not enter, e.g., your bedroom (or at least your bed). Technology will be integral to your time management success. You want to be sure that e-mails do not become your daily to-do list. Either designate a few times during the day when you will respond to e-mails en masse or decide to respond to e-mails on a project-by-project (or person-by-person) basis. But the default of just responding to e-mails as they come in will divert your day and diminish your productivity.

UNDERSTAND Others. While the nature of legal practice makes it hard to manage, you can be proactive in managing your work environment, deadlines, and expectations from colleagues and adversaries. For example, if you initiate conversations with supervisors about their work expectations, preferences, habits, and deadlines, you will be better able to plan accordingly. Also, if you assume responsibility for scheduling when you work on a team, you can set internal deadlines and be more deliberate in coordinating convenient meetings or time frames with colleagues, clients, and outside counsel.

VALUE over Volume. Your focus should be on delivering value and quality work rather than quantity. This principle should prevail whether you are participating in a discussion or producing a written work product. In other words, focus on contributing where you can deliver value rather than just to contribute.

WRITE and Reach Out. You should aspire to be visible for your work and contributions beyond the parameters of your employer. This goal requires having articles published and/or doing public speaking to enhance the exposure of your work and the profile of your employer. Writing and speaking opportunities will overlap with other time-management goals of networking, multitasking, and recycling.

XEROX and Recycle. Much of the work you do can be copied or recycled. You can often use your old documents as drafts or templates to write or create new ones. If you give a talk internally for your employer, it can often be converted into an external talk and article and may result in subsequent press. The key to recycling is seeing each project as an opportunity to build on something and expand its reach. The focus is on translating the old and developing the new rather than repeating or redoing what already has been done.

YOU—An Investment Worth Making. It is important that you assume responsibility for your own professional development. This responsibility may mean investing in the training that you need at various points to upgrade your skills. This will also mean not losing sight of your long-term goals when you are buried in your daily to-do lists. You will need to advocate for yourself, self-promote, track and report your contributions, and not be shy about taking credit where credit is due. Investing in yourself also means allowing for relaxation and leisure time. You will need to find a way to channel your stress to do things that can help you rejuvenate.

ZEAL—A Zest for Life. If you approach your work with zeal and have a zest for life inside and outside the office, you will be more motivated to exercise all of the recommendations herein. There is no replacement for having a passion for what you do.

The ABCs of time management are tips that you can integrate into your daily life. When your work or home life is particularly busy, you won't be able to do everything you want to do. But if you keep these tips top of mind, you will become more efficient and productive with your time and in turn, bring greater satisfaction and fulfillment at work and home.

CHAPTER 15

ADVICE FOR REENTRY LAWYERS AND LAWYERS IN TRANSITION

After returning from my third maternity leave, I became increasingly disenchanted with practicing law. For some time, I had recognized that litigation was not for me. Although I enjoyed the satisfaction of completing projects and working with colleagues, I did not enjoy the work itself. Yet, I was on partnership track at a law firm with two years to go and the idea of stepping off track was scary. But I had a pull to do something different. Since 1999, I had run Flex-Time Lawyers LLC pro bono while practicing, and it was clear that focusing on work/life balance and women's issues was my passion. After three years, I felt I had the knowledge and enough of a following to develop a consulting practice.

In early 2002, after much obsessing and rehearsing, I went to the Chair of the Litigation Department and gave notice. The response was straightforward: "Notice denied." The Chair's reaction caught me off guard. He told me that I was a valued associate and that the firm wanted to maintain a relationship with me. He suggested that I prepare a memo describing how I would like to remain affiliated with the firm, and it would be considered. So I prepared a one-page memo of my dream scenario: that my title would change to Of Counsel; that I would continue to receive a percentage of the paid bills on clients I was bringing and would bring into the firm, but I would no longer have a billable-hour requirement or draw a salary; and that I could choose to work on matters that I originated or refer them to my colleagues.

To my surprise the firm approved the proposal, and for the next five years I remained Of Counsel under those terms. The experience taught me a valuable lesson. When you are ready to walk out the door, you have the best negotiating power you will ever have as an employee. Don't waste it. If you are ready to quit and there is an ideal arrangement to propose that would enable you to stay affiliated, propose it. If worse comes to worst and your proposal is denied, you are in the same position you otherwise would have been.

Defining Reentry Lawyers and Lawyers in Transition

This chapter addresses issues facing lawyers who are considering leaving the profession as well as those who have left and who are seeking to return.

These lawyers can be grouped into two categories.

- "Reentry lawyers"—most often women lawyers who have voluntarily left the profession or felt they had no choice but to leave and they became full-time caregivers and are seeking to return.
- "Lawyers in transition"—a much broader group of lawyers who are not currently employed and who have either been laid off or voluntarily left the profession to reinvent themselves.

While some of the discussion below is focused on reentry lawyers, most of the advice applies equally to the broader audience of lawyers in transition.

One distinction between these groups may be the biases each needs to overcome. For lawyers in transition, there is often a competency bias. For example, if you were laid off in 2009 among thousands of others, you still may face the stigma of why you were the one let go. For reentry lawyers, there may be a competency bias but also a bias concerning the lawyer's relevance and commitment. Some wonder whether reentry lawyers can regain their skills and knowledge to be effective contributors again and whether they are truly committed lawyers.

The similarities between these two groups far outweigh any potential differences. These similarities were most evident in the recent economic downturn when reentry lawyers felt they were competing with lawyers in transition. Opportunities were harder to come by because of an abundance of available talent. Whether you would categorize yourself as a reentry lawyer or lawyer in transition, apply the reasoning below to your individual set of circumstances to maximize your successful return to practice.

Wait! Before You Go!

If you are a lawyer considering leaving the practice, you should reflect and reassess before giving notice. The Center for Work–Life Policy reports that women who left their professions earn, on average, 16 percent less of their earning potential than their counterparts who never took time out.[1] Before deciding whether to leave, do your research. It is helpful to speak with and observe the daily routines of lawyers who have left the profession. You should talk not only to lawyers who have been out of the profession for a year or two but also to lawyers who have been out for five or more years. It is useful to seek out colleagues who have faced similar challenges at work and learn how they reached a resolution to stay. Speak to lawyers or other professionals who left their professions and went back to work years later, too. If you ultimately decide to give notice, you should do so from a position of strength and knowledge, rather than weakness.

When women lawyers who are considering leaving practice approach me, they often will say that a significant reason for leaving is that their salary, after taxes, is barely enough to cover the nanny or day care. This reasoning always frustrates me. Why is it that the woman's salary is the only one compared to the nanny or day care cost? Why isn't childcare just considered another family expense, weighed against both the husband and wife's joint earnings? Income is not static and that woman's earnings will presumably increase as she continues to practice. In contrast, if she leaves the profession, she will negatively impact her earnings for a lifetime,[2] as well as her career prospects. Additionally, money, of course, is not the only reason why lawyers continue to work. Work fulfills many individual needs and opportunities for professional and personal growth beyond the paycheck.[3]

If you are seriously considering leaving the profession, think about whether there are terms that you would consider that would entice you to remain in practice. If so, submit a proposal outlining the terms under which you would work, how you would continue to satisfy the needs of clients and colleagues, and why it is in your employer's economic interest to agree to the new arrangement. If you are at the point where you are willing to leave the profession, try to negotiate ways to work differently. You have nothing to lose if the employer declines the proposal.

While You Are on Leave

According to the Center for Work-Life Policy, 31 percent of women lawyers take a leave from practice of more than six months at some point in their careers.[4] This means that nearly one-third of women lawyers have a nonlinear career trajectory. If you are one of these lawyers, you want to develop ways to distinguish yourself by remaining engaged while you are out of the conventional workforce.

Many of the women I speak to who have taken a leave say they do "nothing" to keep connected or maintain ties to the workforce while they are at home. I recommend that if you are on leave from practice, you should remain involved in the working world. It will ensure an easier transition back to paid work and help you assess what is the right venue for you upon your return. Additionally, it will enrich your experiences and confidence to maintain a connection to life outside your home and family.

In counseling reentry attorneys over the years, I have compiled a to-do list of things they *wished* they had done while they were on leave. If you are already on leave and have not taken these steps, do not despair. Instead, start now and begin to reengage.

Reentry and Lawyer in Transition At-Home To-Do List

1. **Keep your bar membership current.** You should maintain at least one active bar membership. In many states, if you let your license lapse, the process of renewing your license is slow, cumbersome, and expensive. Keep your license active.
2. **Stay current on substantive law.** If your state requires continuing legal education courses, use your annual credits to keep current with your existing practice area or develop knowledge in a

new area of interest. Continue to read legal newspapers and periodicals of interest to keep current on substantive law and news about your professional contacts.

3. **Seek and maintain professional affiliations.** If you have been active on boards, in local or state bar associations, or in other professional associations, remain engaged in your role. While on leave, you may have more time to participate or seek out leadership roles in professional associations that you otherwise did not have time to pursue.
4. **Volunteer.** Consider doing pro bono work through your local bar association or a not-for-profit as a way to contribute and to keep your legal skills and contacts current. This work may stimulate a new interest, refocus your career pursuits, and enrich your networking connections.
5. **Network.** Keep in touch with professional contacts. Whether they are former colleagues, law school friends, or people you know through professional associations, these people know your work and may be instrumental in helping you find paid work again. Become informed about your at-home network and what the people in your community do. These may be people you know through your kids' schools, civic associations, religious organizations, or volunteer or community organizations. If most of your current time is spent at home and in your community, this is a rich network of people about whom you should be knowledgeable.
6. **Update your technology skills.** Whether it is computer, Internet, legal research, or social networking, you want to remain or become literate and at ease with using ever-changing technology.

Fears of Reentry Lawyers and Lawyers in Transition

The concerns of lawyers reentering or transitioning are numerous, including:

- Confidence about your value and ability to perform in a traditional work setting
- Access to sources and employers who would consider hiring you

- Concern about competency and commitment biases
- Anxiety about networking with personal contacts and tapping into the right professional networks
- Confusion about whether to return to your previous practice area, learn a new one, or leave legal practice entirely
- Economic implications of changing fields or practice areas
- Concern in an economic downturn about whether opportunities exist
- Stress about accounting for the gap in your résumé since leaving the paid workforce
- Intimidation about the interview process
- Confusion about how to provide a compelling résumé
- Age bias and concerns about whether you, as a mature worker, will be perceived as fitting into the work culture
- Technology and concerns about becoming proficient
- Apprehension about brushing up on both substantive and practical skills
- Family dynamics and concerns about how your new role will be supported

When I work with unemployed lawyers, I want to hear their concerns, but before walking them through strategies to handle the obstacles, I ask them to see the issues from the other side. In other words, to be effective in a job search, you need to anticipate and resolve the challenges that prospective *employers* face in hiring you. Once you identify the issues that impede employers, you will be more successful in demonstrating your value. Here, we will walk through the most common employer concerns and how to combat them.

Addressing Employer Hiring Concerns

Believe it or not, employers find it challenging to identify talented candidates. While employers may be flooded with lawyers seeking positions, it is cumbersome for them to sift through the talent and find the best candidate. Thus, reentry lawyers and lawyers in transition need to research and seek out the employers who are hiring candidates in their demographic or who are receptive to doing so. This process requires candidates to network with former employers, within their professional and personal networks, and within the bar association. By talking to others about potential opportunities, going on informational interviews, and applying for jobs, a returning lawyer eliminates possibilities, narrows options, and identifies the most suitable positions.

Employers often find the résumés of reentry lawyers and lawyers in transition to be mysterious. They cannot make sense of them. For this reason, you must fill the unexplained gaps, account for your time away from paid work, and prioritize the most relevant job experience for the job you are seeking. Lehman Brothers ran a successful reentry program targeting financial services professionals. One of the sessions included a professional storyteller who demonstrated how to convey a story of interest about a nonlinear career path.[5] The storyteller image is helpful to keep in mind as you develop your résumé to ensure that it effectively tells your story and creates a picture of who you are and where you want to be. It is helpful to have someone experienced in résumé review give you feedback. I also encourage you to have two laypersons take a look, at least one being a non-lawyer. Make sure your résumé makes intuitive sense and conveys not just a chronology but a clear message as well.

Despite your having been out of the workforce, it is important that your résumé still feels current. If you have taken a concentrated number of continuing legal education courses in a substantive area, list them on your résumé. This reassures prospective employers that your knowledge is current and there will be less of a learning curve in transitioning you back to work. For reentry lawyers, it also shows a commitment to going back to work. If you have done pro bono work for bar associations while on leave, add that to your résumé under your legal experience. List your volunteer experience and any skills that are applicable and transferable to the desired job. For example, titles that demonstrate skills such as research, leadership, management, and fundraising may be particularly relevant to prospective employers.

Even less-transferable experience should be listed on your résumé. Once again, it tells the story of who you are and accounts for your time, interests, and contributions. Have several versions of your résumé, with each one emphasizing the experience and skills that are more suited to the different venues and practice areas where you seek to apply. If your path has not been linear, I recommend a two- to three-sentence Objective statement at the top of your résumé that articulates your experience and direction. If you have several versions of your résumé, look closely at the Objective statement, as it may need to be reworked to better align your experience and direction with the different prospective employers you are targeting.

> Here is an example of an Objective statement for a reentry attorney résumé:
>
> Seasoned litigator with eight years of large and small firm experience handling products liability and employment law disputes. Took temporary leave from practice and honed leadership, management, and development skills. Seeking in-house position managing litigation and outside counsel relationships in a pharmaceutical company.

Law firms are hierarchical and often dismiss reentry lawyer or lawyer in transition candidates because they cannot easily ascertain where the candidate would fit into a traditional organizational structure. Thus, the onus is on you to help the potential employer understand where you would fit into their culture. Be clear about what you have been doing while outside of the paid workforce, what department you hope to join, and at what level you think you should return. It also may be appropriate to indicate your expectations for salary and schedule.

In my experience counseling reentry lawyers and lawyers in transition, about half are seeking flexible or reduced hours upon their return. *Many employers are fearful of lawyers' flexibility needs.* Thus, if you are seeking flexibility, you need to convey that hiring a reentry lawyer or lawyer in transition is not about making an accommodation. It is about making a financially beneficial decision for the employer that also meets a lawyer's needs. Articulate how you will get the work done flexibly and how the needs of colleagues and clients will not be negatively impacted. Emphasize your ability to deliver high-quality work and to be flexible, communicative, responsive, and accessible. Also, determine whether you can use flexibility as an asset in getting back to work, as discussed below. Keep in mind that even with these efforts, you may have to start your job with less flexibility than you desire. For a further discussion of negotiating flexible and reduced hours, see Chapter 13.

Employers are concerned about placement failure. They worry that they are taking a risk on reentry candidates because their skills may be rusty or they may not fit in with the corporate culture. With lawyers in transition, there may be a concern that their work is not of the same caliber. You can overcome this by offering to intern without compensation for a limited term (typically three months) so that both parties can assess each other on a trial basis. The internship allows the employer to ensure that the candidate is the right fit. But the internship is also a great way for you to regain confidence, demonstrate talent, obtain experience, freshen up your skills, build your résumé, network, and develop potential references, all while ensuring that the new venue is the right one for you.

Choosing the Right Work Venue

In maximizing your job search, you need to assess your experience, interests, and skills and match them with market demands. When evaluating the market, you should identify growing practice areas. If your experience lies in bankruptcy and corporate deal work but deal work has slowed while opportunities remain in bankruptcy, perhaps bankruptcy is where you should focus your search. Pay attention to which types of employers are hiring. Are there more opportunities in regional, midsize, and smaller firms rather than large firms? Identify whether certain roles at certain jobs are expanding. If law firms are expanding the staff attorney role (where attorneys often have more predictable work that is not as demanding), is that a nice entrée back to work for you or are you concerned that will put you on a "mommy track"?

Economics will be a significant driving force for many of you returning to work. Are you willing to take lower pay to move into a new area of interest, as opposed to your former practice area? How much of your prior work and volunteer skills are transferable? As you consider different work opportunities, think broadly about the types of legal employers: small, medium, and large law firms; new-model law firms; in-house; government; not-for-profit; solo practice; and academia. You may also consider non-legal positions in a legal environment, such as legal recruiting, professional development, or marketing roles at a law firm or administrative or career advisory roles at a law school. Of course, you may also consider non-legal jobs in a non-legal setting as well. Whatever course you pursue, you will want to weigh the impact on your earning potential. If you pursue reduced hours, you also will want to evaluate how and to what extent that will reduce your earnings.

As you conduct your job search, you should try to identify the right culture and work environment. Assess where you want to work and what will be important to you upon your return. If being in a women-friendly environment is important to you, this may involve evaluating women's representation at all levels of the organization and, specifically, the presence of women in leadership positions. It may also involve assessing programs and policies on flexibility, mentoring, training, business development, and advancement. Whether you have children, your children's ages, your own age, your marital status, your eldercare responsibilities, and your financial demands will all impact how you integrate yourself into the workforce. For a further discussion of identifying a women- and work/life-friendly employer, see Chapters 5, 7, 8, and 16.[6]

Using Flexibility as an Asset to Get Back to Work

As you contemplate your transition back to work, you should assess how important lifestyle concerns will be, if at all, in choosing your prospective employer. As discussed in Chapter 11, the four most common work/life goals I hear from lawyers are the need for flexibility, predictability, reduced hours, and/or proximity. Some lawyers prioritize most or all of these factors in their job search while others may just focus on one or two, or none at all.

If you are prioritizing lifestyle in the positions you are seeking, determine whether you can use flexibility as an asset in selling yourself to prospective employers. For example, in an unpredictable market, employers are less certain of their staffing needs and may be reluctant to hire a full-time permanent lawyer. Here you could propose working reduced hours on a project basis to meet your prospective employer's financial concerns. Additionally, you could offer to work temporarily and transition into a permanent position if your work meets your employer's expectations and the work expands. Another example is an employer that is a start-up where employees work virtually or the company does not have enough office space to have all employees work on site. You could offer to telecommute and save the additional office expense for the company while you enjoy working from home. Or, if you don't need benefits, an employer may be willing to hire you more readily without having to incur this expense. You should try to make yourself as flexible as possible but do not devalue yourself or undersell your ability to contribute.

I have repeatedly seen how flexible and reduced hours can be an asset in getting your foot in the door. I have placed lawyers into flexible and reduced-hour positions where employers were specifically seeking a reentry lawyer or lawyer in transition. In one case, a start-up did not want the pressure of plucking a talented full-time lawyer from a high-paying law firm job when it was unsure if it had enough work to justify that level of expense. Instead, it liked the idea of hiring an unemployed lawyer because the lawyer could start right away on a reduced-hour basis and grow with the needs of the position. I have seen many successful hires of reentry lawyers and lawyers in transition with employers who were uncertain of their staffing needs. These employers liked the flexibility they had with lawyers willing to work a range of hours depending on workload. To maximize your marketability, be flexible, since the needs of your employer may fluctuate. But also be patient and recognize that you may need to compromise or prove yourself and establish a reputation before earning greater flexibility.

Investing in the Process

Once you decide to go back to work, use your time at home wisely. If you have not done so already, follow the steps outlined above in "While You Are on Leave." Recognize that the process of going back to work requires investment. This investment includes fees associated with bar memberships, continuing legal education courses, computer courses, career counseling sessions, getting-back-to-work programs, networking events, meals, childcare expenses, and even new clothes. It can be hard for lawyers to invest in the process, particularly if they are not financially contributing to the household. Some fear that the investment will not be worthwhile. But you need to be willing to invest in your future and have the confidence that you will see the return.

Many reentry lawyers with young kids do not want to invest in childcare for fear that it may take a year or more to find a job. While you may not need regular full-time childcare while you are job seeking, you need enough coverage so you can network and attend interviews and informational meetings. Additionally, you need to start tapping into your childcare network so that when you get a job, you can promptly secure the childcare coverage you need upon your return.

NETWORKING YOUR WAY BACK TO WORK

Networking is a key aspect to getting back to work that will be covered more extensively in Chapter 17. Confidence can be a significant impediment to reentry and lawyers in transition as they seek to network and find employment. For lawyers in transition, it is often embarrassing and painful to explain the circumstances of a layoff. For reentry lawyers, there can be a sense of diminished value resulting from being out of the paid workforce. For both groups, it is important to overcome these insecurities by becoming immersed in the process and gaining needed support from family and friends. I often say that the biggest networking luxury for an unemployed lawyer is the ability to tell everyone you know that you are looking for a job. Unlike traditional job seekers, you don't have to worry about jeopardizing your relationship with an existing employer. But maximizing this advantage requires that you overcome your fear of exposure and that you recognize that networking will be the key to your next job. The more comfortable you can get with honestly explaining your situation (without apologizing for it or being defensive), the more successful your search will be.

Another significant challenge (discussed more extensively in Chapter 17), for women lawyers in particular, is an awkwardness in translating or expanding personal relationships into professional ones.[7] Many women worry that they will jeopardize their personal relationships if they leverage their personal contacts for job opportunities. This obstacle is problematic for lawyers who have been at home because their personal network is their most developed one. By not being willing to tap into your home network, you are cutting yourself off from countless opportunities.

Women lawyers have told me that even if they overcome their awkwardness in translating personal relationships into professional ones, they do not believe that these relationships will prove fruitful in their job search. They worry that their personal contacts know them in a different context—at the bake sale, driving carpool—and these images do not conjure up professionalism. I disagree. There are certain qualities that people carry with them whether they are at the office, on the soccer field, or at a PTA meeting. If you are a leader in any of these venues, you should be able to demonstrate that you would be a strong asset to a future employer. In fact, many of you may initially be more comfortable in your community venues, whether it be at your children's school, doing not-for-profit work, at your religious organizations, on boards, or elsewhere. Indeed, your best qualities may be even more evident when you volunteer in your community.

> If you are a reentry lawyer, one way to face your fear of contacting your personal network is to prepare a short form e-mail that says something like:
>
> Dear ______:
>
> I'm writing with exciting news to let you know that I'm planning to return to work. My prior legal experience has involved ________. I'm seeking a position doing _____ at a _________. If you can recommend anyone whom I can contact or if you know of any opportunities and you can pass along my attached résumé, I would greatly appreciate it. Thank you.
>
> Best regards,
>
> _______
>
> (insert full name, preferred e-mail address, home office and/or cell number)

If you are a lawyer in transition the same type of e-mail would work, but you could alter the first sentence to say: "I'm writing to let you know that I'm planning a career transition." You may want to tailor the language to suit your style, but be sure to keep the e-mail short.

People are busy and if the request is not quick and easy, it will be less likely to be read or addressed. Even those who do not forward your résumé will, if they read a brief description of your background and what you are seeking, have it in their minds if they hear of fitting opportunities. Do not write in the text of the e-mail that you expect a response. Remember that you want to minimize the obligation and maximize the chance of someone forwarding your résumé or otherwise recommending you.

Remember the first thing in an e-mail that people read is the subject line. This should convey your message like a news headline, and it should contain your objective. For example, it could read "Elizabeth Smith Seeking New Job," or if you're sending the e-mail to a former colleague named Jennifer Jones, it could say, "Jennifer Jones—seeking help with job search." By putting a recipient's name in the subject line, he or she is more likely to open it because the e-mail is personal and not, presumably, a mass e-mail. The subject line should not read "Hi!" or "What's Up?" because it is not businesslike and may create a negative impression if your e-mail is forwarded to someone who is unfamiliar with you. Additionally, "Hi!" or "What's Up?" is an ineffective subject line because it loses the opportunity for the reader to get a quick assessment of your needs by scanning his or her inbox. Finally, some spam filters deposit "Hi!"-type headlines in the junk mail box since they are often used by spammers.

Although these are form e-mails that you prepare, I suggest that you personalize them by inserting the name of each contact and including a personal detail or two rather than send one version as a mass e-mail. This approach will maximize accountability and the likelihood of follow-up. If you are asking for a favor, you will get better results if you take the time to write to the recipient directly. I suggest that you send this e-mail to at least 50 (but preferably 100) people you know, including your personal contacts. I know this may be a terrifying idea to some of you. I recently made this suggestion to a group of reentry hopefuls at Pace University School of Law's New Directions program. A participant came up to me afterwards and said she could not heed my suggestion because she was too embarrassed to send such an e-mail and didn't want to impose on her contacts. She had been unsuccessfully job searching for three years. I responded that I thought her inhibition was a significant factor impeding her success. Until she is willing to tap into her personal network and reach out to the people in her community who know her best, she is limiting her ability to achieve her job-search potential.

As explored in Chapter 17, women in particular also limit their networking success when they are reluctant to self promote, or even to take credit where credit is due.[8] A large part of the job-seeking process is to be able to sell yourself effectively. If you are interviewing with a prospective employer and you are not able to sell yourself, the employer may have an equal concern that you will not be effective representing the employer, were you to be hired. So it is critical to focus on highlighting your strengths and contributions in order to convey your value.

In addition to networking with personal contacts, reconnect with former colleagues and clients. Expand your professional network through bar associations or other professional organizations. Pro bono work for bar associations or other organizations is an ideal way to update your professional skills while expanding your network. Committee work at bar associations is a wonderful way to get reengaged with the legal community by planning programs, writing reports, or working with others in a subject area of interest. You should also get involved in other professional associations. As you become reengaged, though, be wise in your choice of organizations with which to affiliate. It is better to be active or seek a leadership role in a few organizations that you believe in and can genuinely contribute to than belong to many networks but be invisible.

Your law school and undergraduate institutions, particularly if they are nationally recognized schools or close to where you seek to practice, are invaluable networks. It is in your law school's financial interest to have you gainfully employed so that you can contribute to the school and help with opportunities for their students and alumni. If your law school has an alumni directory that you can access or a database of opportunities that you can tap into, these should be an integral part of your job search. Your law school should also have current information on which types of employers are hiring, what practice areas are thriving, and where alumni are practicing who may be able to help. You should also research where your law school and college classmates are through LinkedIn, Facebook, and other social networks to see if these classmates work in positions, companies, law firms, government agencies, not-for-profits, or organizations that interest you.

While these steps may not bring you job interviews immediately, they may lead to fruitful connections and informational interviews that will lead you to eventual job opportunities. As you tap into your networks, be mindful and considerate. If you ask people for telephone informational interviews, do so according to their schedule and be prepared with questions at hand. If you propose meeting with people, do so at their convenience, in terms of both time and location. Propose coffee rather than lunch to be considerate of a person's time. Pick up the tab for your meeting. Handwritten thank-you notes are a nice and unusual touch that people appreciate when they go out of their way for you. A personal note is also an opportunity to demonstrate the type of person that you are—a high-quality person whom an employer would want as a representative.

The Interview

An important way to become more comfortable in the interview process is to be prepared. Learn everything you can about the prospective employer before the interview. Do your homework. Spend time on the employer's website and do Internet searches to get up to speed on recent happenings, newsworthy items, programs, and initiatives. If you are able to find out in advance with whom you will be interviewing, research these individuals. Review their biographical backgrounds, know their practice areas, professional milestones, and affiliations, and try to determine if you have interests or people in common.

Another way to get more comfortable with interviews is to practice. There are career coaches you can work with to help you develop interview skills with greater confidence. There are seminars you can attend that will provide guidelines and include role-playing so that you can become more at ease. Role-play and practice with friends and in front of the mirror. Bottom line: be prepared. Preparation includes knowing everything on your résumé and being able to articulate your experiences. For reentry attorneys, it means being able to summarize your time on leave and highlight the activities in which you were engaged. In most cases, you should address the time gap head-on to eliminate the mystery. Without being defensive, you should provide assurances that you are committed to going back to work and explain why. For lawyers in transition who have been laid off, in most cases I would encourage you to raise and address the circumstances at your former job directly. Without appearing defensive or resentful, it is important to invite the topic into the conversation and resolve any concerns the prospective employer might have about your competency.

Once You Have Landed the Job

Transitioning back to work will be an adjustment for everyone involved. You need to anticipate the pushback, as well as the support, you will receive. For some, your transition back may be threatening. If you have family or friends who have stayed home with you, it may be hard for them to watch you transition as they remain in the same routine. If you have children and a spouse or partner, they may miss some of the things you did for them that you no longer will be able to do. There may be an unrealistic expectation that you will continue to do all that you did previously—plus your job. This expectation will prevent you from thriving in either venue. To ensure a successful return, it is important to delegate some of your prior tasks. For everyone involved, be open about how you plan to transition into your new role and invite support and feedback. Communicate the excitement about starting a new chapter of your life and invite them to be a part of your next journey.

The biggest transition adjustment will likely be for you. To help in the process, I would recommend that you focus on how to redefine success for yourself. It is unlikely to be how you defined success when you graduated from law school. The notion of redefining success reminds me of the controversial 2003 article authored by Lisa Belkin in *The New York Times Magazine* entitled "The Opt-Out Revolution." In the piece, Belkin profiled eight privileged Princeton women who had left their prestigious jobs and degrees to stay home with their children. One conclusion of the article in response to the query "Why don't women run the world?" was that "Maybe it's because they don't want to."[9] In the article, Belkin relays how when she started her career, she had grand plans to be editor of the *New York Times* or at least editor of its magazine. But after her second child was born, she left the full-time newsroom job for a more flexible freelance life, writing from home about work/life issues.[10] Belkin's article stimulated vigorous debate and generated more letters to the editor than any other article in the paper at that time. In my unpublished letter to the editor, I wrote that Belkin's piece demonstrated an important subtlety that was lost. Rather than be disappointed that Belkin was not holding the top job at the *Times*, I think we should have celebrated that she started a national debate from her home office. The point is simple: As you venture back into the paid workforce, dismiss the "should have been" and "could have been" voices in your head. Instead, be proud of where you are and what you will achieve on your new path to success.

Notes

1. Sylvia Ann Hewlett et al., Ctr. for Work-Life Policy, Off-Ramps and On-Ramps Revisited at 22 (2010).
2. *Id.*
3. *See, e.g.*, Chapter 13 discussing the benefits of flexible and reduced hours work.

4. Hewlett et al., *supra* note 1, at 8, Fig. 1.2.

5. Deborah Epstein Henry, *Comeback Lawyers: A Look at Why Re-Entry Is a Hot Work/Life Balance Topic*, Diversity & the Bar, Jan./Feb. 2007, at 2, *available at* http://www.flextimelawyers.com/pdf/art11.pdf.

6. To identify questions that will help you answer what makes a work/life- and women-friendly employer, *see* Flex-Time Lawyers LLC & The Ass'n of the Bar of the City of New York, Committee on Women in the Profession, The Cheat Sheet, Sept. 2006, *available at* http://www.flextimelawyers.com/pdf/art3.pdf.

7. *See* Deborah Epstein Henry, *Business Development in a 24/7 World*, Diversity & the Bar, May/June 2007, *available at* http://www.flextimelawyers.com/pdf/art6.pdf; Deborah Epstein Henry, *Business Development Beyond Rubber Chicken Dinners*, The Balance Beam, 2004–2005, *available at* http://www.flextimelawyers.com/pdf/2004_2005 newsletter.pdf.

8. Henry, *Business Development in a 24/7 World*, *supra* note 7; Henry, *Business Development Beyond Rubber Chicken Dinners*, *supra* note 7.

9. Lisa Belkin, *The Opt-Out Revolution*, N.Y. Times Mag., Oct. 26, 2003, *available at* http://www.nytimes.com/2003/10/26/magazine/the-opt-out-revolution.html?pagewanted=1.

10. *Id.*

CHAPTER 16

"BLUEPRINTING" WOMEN LAW STUDENTS AND LAWYERS FOR SUCCESS

In 2006, I attended a law school graduation at Lincoln Center in New York. I was a guest and sat on stage to give a graduate his diploma. The room was filled to capacity, with about 2,500 guests. The Dean announced the five names of the summa cum laude graduates. These five gathered at the foot of the stage. The valedictorian was a woman and the other four summa graduates were men. One of the men was standing closest to the stairs of the stage and he turned to the valedictorian and gestured that she go first. She gestured back at him to go ahead. So, he shrugged, walked on stage and was announced first.

When the valedictorian walked on stage and was announced second, I used all the restraint I could muster not to run across the stage and wring her neck.

Watching the scene unfold reminded me of one of the many mistakes I see women make. Not only do they fail to self promote but, as in this case, they fail to even take credit where credit is due.

So many women just think they need to be smart and talented and the "worker bee." But they miss the importance of all of the other intangibles that differentiate between those who succeed in the workforce and those who do not. I left the graduation, inspired to articulate those intangibles so that women could begin to identify the key factors to success.

Selecting, Creating, and Ensuring a Woman-Friendly Employer

In the spring of 2006, I approached the New York City Bar Committee on Women in the Profession with a proposal to partner on developing a guide for women law students called *The Cheat Sheet*.[1] To view *The Cheat Sheet* in its entirety, *see* Appendix D to this chapter. *The Cheat Sheet* was meant to help train women law students about how to select women-friendly employers. My goal was simple: help women law students chart their success and avoid the traditional stumbling blocks of their female predecessors *before* those same patterns repeated themselves.

There were a number of motivations behind working with women law students.

1. As a consultant, I advise employers and lawyers on, among other things, overcoming the challenges that women often face in legal practice. I realized women lawyers and the profession would be better served if women were given the tools to avoid these challenges before they begin or at the beginning of practice.
2. One of the prevailing principles of my work has been competition as an instrument of change.[2] Women have made up about half of law school graduating classes for 25 years[3] and it was time to create more of an impetus for the profession to compete over this talent. The objective was to create an incentive for legal employers to compete for women law students based on whether they provided a woman-friendly working environment.
3. All New York area law schools were invited to participate in a forum in September 2006 where *The Cheat Sheet* was released. The goal was to capitalize on women law students' power in numbers. These numbers are a means to shape how legal employers focus their women-friendly efforts and programs.
4. Large law firms, corporations, and other legal employer representatives were invited to participate in the forum to create a venue for information sharing and to have all interested parties play a role.

5. The goal was also to extend the impact beyond New York by initiating similar law school and bar association programs across the country. These national programs followed and these ideas carried beyond the women law student population.

The Cheat Sheet

The Cheat Sheet is organized around six sections with questions under each topic area that identify an employer's commitment to women's retention and advancement. The first section, Statistical and Background Information, lays the foundation. The next five sections each reflect an area where women need to focus. These include Partnership & Advancement, Leadership & Accountability, Business Development & Networking, Workplace Flexibility, and Mentoring.

The Cheat Sheet is intended to be used by women law students during the process of deciding where to work—when they are contemplating where to apply, when they are evaluating callbacks, and when they are weighing offers. While *The Cheat Sheet* is an invaluable tool, students must be careful about how, when, and to whom they pose its questions. As *The Cheat Sheet* admonishes, "*The Cheat Sheet* is not intended as a 'script' to use when speaking with employers. Rather, the questions in *The Cheat Sheet* should be used to identify key issues on each topic. Law students and attorneys should use their discretion and recognize that some topics are better raised informally with individual attorneys or personal contacts rather than with the human resources department or a hiring or supervising partner."[4] Timing of these sorts of questions is also important. It is often safer to make sensitive inquiries once the offer is in hand. Care still should be taken in choosing whom you ask sensitive questions. You do not want to create an awkward situation if you ultimately end up working there.

Many employers have their recruiting committees review *The Cheat Sheet* to be prepared to answer its questions. *The Cheat Sheet* questions provide law students with an effective outline to evaluate an employer. Here is how *The Cheat Sheet* is typically used by law students. If a law student wants to learn about a firm's commitment to reduced hours, rather than simply ask whether the firm allows reduced hours, the student would try to find answers to these questions from the Flexibility subsection of *The Cheat Sheet*:

Flexible Work Arrangement Utilization

- What percentage of the firm's associates work flexible or reduced hours? Of these associates, what percentage is female?
- What percentage of the firm's partners work flexible or reduced hours? Of these partners, what percentage is female?
- What percentage of the firm's lawyers work flexible or reduced hours for reasons other than parenting?
- How many partners have been elevated to partner after working reduced hours? Of these partners, what percentage were women?
- How many reduced-hour associates have been elevated to partnership without requiring their return to full-time status before consideration? Of these partners, what percentage were women?[5]

If the student had only asked whether the firm allowed reduced hours, the answer would not have provided helpful information to assess an employer's commitment. In 2009, according to the National Association for Law Placement, Inc. (NALP), 98 percent of law firms nationally allowed reduced-hours schedules and 5.9 percent of lawyers worked reduced hours.[6] Instead, *The Cheat Sheet* questions delve into usage and representation rates that reveal the success of an employer's commitment to reduced hours.

Another example is leadership. If a student is interested in leadership, rather than simply asking whether women play leadership roles at a firm, the student may seek to determine: "What are the percentages of women on the more powerful firm committees, including the executive or management committee and compensation committee?"[7]

This question identifies the two most powerful committees of a firm. As such, the inquiry is more relevant to assessing women's leadership than a more general question about committees that are not as influential at a firm.

Additionally, in the Mentoring section of *The Cheat Sheet*, it includes these three questions, among others:

- Does the firm have mentoring circles where women associates are grouped with senior women and meet regularly?
- Does the firm have targeted mentoring for women senior associates to help with their professional development and advancement?
- Does the firm have a mentoring program for newly admitted partners to aid in the transition from associate to partner and help with business development efforts?[8]

Many interviewees would simply ask whether an employer has a mentoring program. Instead, these mentoring questions drill down to determine what specific efforts an employer is making to improve mentoring for women.

Although *The Cheat Sheet* was initially conceived as a guide for law students selecting an employer, its use has become broader. It has become a guide for practicing lawyers to assist them when contemplating lateral moves. For legal employers, the same questions have been used as a checklist to determine their strengths, weaknesses, and gaps to improve the role of women. Additionally, *The Cheat Sheet* provides tips for legal employers and law schools. There is also a resources section at the end that lists key online sources providing information on work/life balance, women's issues, and diversity in the law.

"Blueprinting"—Training Women Law Students and Junior Lawyers for Success

Since the release of *The Cheat Sheet in 2006*, in my talks at law schools I initially focused on educating women law students about how to identify women-friendly employers. From my work, it became clear that the next step is in training women law students and junior women lawyers to plan for success.[9] Women have the capacity to become talented lawyers. The question is whether women lawyers can overcome the intangibles that have traditionally caused many women to stall. Thus, the goal is to enable women law students and junior women lawyers to design what I call "blueprints"—plans for success—by training them at the law school and junior associate level before they face the traditional obstacles.[10]

"Blueprinting" programs are the flip side of the popular reentry programs designed to retool women professionals who have left the profession and who are positioning themselves to return. By focusing on blueprinting at the entry level, ideally it will ensure that more women will not need to leave their careers midstream.

Law schools, legal employers, and bar associations need to incorporate blueprinting programs into their curriculum and train students and junior lawyers. In a blueprinting workshop that I developed at Yale Law School in March 2008, for example, Yale Law alumnae shared their experiences and strategies to be successful lawyers. They gave tangible advice about how to succeed professionally, beyond producing top-notch work. Blueprints will empower women to navigate the hidden obstacles to success, to plan for the challenges they will face, and to gain the awareness and skills they need to succeed.

Here are the five Blueprinting areas of focus from *The Cheat Sheet*:

- Partnership and Advancement
- Leadership and Accountability
- Business Development and Networking
- Workplace Flexibility
- Mentoring

Why Is Blueprinting Necessary?

Why is it important to teach these blueprinting subjects to women law students and junior women lawyers? Because many women are not aware that these skills are necessary for success. For example, when we were writing *The Cheat Sheet*, we convened a focus group and invited the presidents of the New York women's law school associations. We wanted to be sure that while we were writing the guide, we were on the pulse of the issues on law students' minds. The reaction by some was "Why are you creating a guide for us? There's no problem here—we're equal to our male counterparts and by creating a women-specific guide, aren't you creating a self-fulfilling prophecy?"

While I found it heartening that some of the women law student leaders felt equal to their male counterparts, I was concerned that these feelings of equality would result in women continuing to neglect the skill-building necessary for success.

The "there's no problem" reaction also does not acknowledge the diminished representation of female talent at the top. Like the valedictorian described at the opening story of this chapter, women would continue to believe that they just needed to be smart and hard-working. Based on the key areas identified in *The Cheat Sheet*, here is why the Blueprint is important to train women law students and junior women lawyers for success:

- *Partnership and Advancement.* Women have made up 40 to 50 percent of law school graduating classes for 25 years.[11] Yet they are still only 16 percent of law firm equity partners.[12] The representation of women in other legal venues is at an equivalent low level. Until women reach a critical mass of at least 30 percent of equity partners, 30 percent of chief legal officers, and 30 percent of tenured law faculties,[13] women will not have the power to influence the direction of the profession. Women will also not be compensated commensurate to their male counterparts and to their contribution.
- *Leadership and Accountability.* Women's representation as leaders in law firms and other legal venues is similarly low. According to the National Association of Women Lawyers (NAWL), the average firm's highest governing committee has women as 15 percent of its members.[14] About 14 percent of the nation's largest law firms have no women on their governing committees.[15] The lowest representation of women is at the most visible and prominent position at a firm. The national average of female managing partners is only about 6 percent.[16] Until women represent a critical mass on the governing committees of law firms and other legal venues, they will not be able to influence governance, compensation, and promotion, and women's progress will continue to stall.
- *Business Development and Networking.* According to NAWL, in 2009, 46 percent of the 200 largest U.S. law firms surveyed had no women among their top ten rainmakers.[17] Another 32 percent of these firms had one woman rainmaker; 15 percent had two women rainmakers; and the remaining 6 percent had three or four women rainmakers among their top ten.[18] In a law firm, the ability to orig-

inate business carries with it power and money. Women's historically lower representation in this area will perpetuate their status as second-class citizens in terms of influence, decision making, and remuneration at law firms. Being effective at networking and business development maximizes not only women's power internally but also their marketability externally.

- *Workplace Flexibility.* About 40 percent of women law firm lawyers with children work reduced hours for family care in any year.[19] According to NALP, in 2009 only 5.9 percent of law firm lawyers worked reduced hours, 72.5 percent of whom were women.[20] Additionally, 31 percent of women lawyers take a leave from practice of more than six months at some point in their careers.[21] When women leave law firms, long hours are an important factor in why they leave.[22] Work/life balance has been an impediment to women's promotion and a significant contributing factor to their attrition.
- *Mentoring.* Women face barriers to advancement, in part, because of lack of career planning and strategizing. Mentors can provide this type of guidance.[23] Unfortunately for women, people tend to mentor those who are like themselves. Women are therefore less likely to be informally mentored than men.[24] This challenge is even more acute for women of color. Yet mentoring for women, and specifically women of color, is that much more important. As mentoring and professional development expert Ida Abbott explained, "Mentors can bring these lawyers into informal social and professional networks that conquer feelings of alienation and build a sense of connectedness to the firm. Mentors provide access to 'inside' information, plum assignments, and influential partners and clients. They inform associates about the politics and unwritten rules of practice and offer guidance about how to present and position themselves in the organization. As sponsors, mentors can broadcast and promote the associate's abilities and contributions, and help build the associate's reputation."[25]

Designing Your Blueprint

What follows is your Blueprint of skills to develop as you chart your success. The Blueprint is organized around the categories identified in *The Cheat Sheet*. In their "Dear Debbie" e-mails, lawyers tell me that they wished they had known what they were supposed to be doing—in addition to their substantive work—when they started out. The Blueprint tells you just that.

Blueprinting for Success

The Blueprint is your checklist of things to do—or to seek advice or training on—to ensure your success as a lawyer. Rather than being a "how to," the Blueprint is a "what to do." Depending on your place of employment, not all of the suggestions may apply to your set of circumstances. To be successful, you need to take charge of your career with an entrepreneurial spirit rather than wait for someone to show you the way. The Blueprint outlines the intangibles to success that you need to develop, beyond merely delivering high-quality work.

Partnership and Advancement

- Identify the partnership or promotion criteria for each level of seniority.
- Set goals of skills to develop to get to the next promotion level or competency.
- Determine the criteria for bonus eligibility and set that as part of your goals.
- Seek substantive training in skills that are needed in your practice area.
- Identify the type of work that you need to seek to get to the next level.
- Identify the colleagues and clients with whom you will need to work to be considered for promotion.
- Learn the variety of ways compensation is awarded and develop the associated skills to have your efforts rewarded.
- Track and report your contributions and any recognition you receive and summarize them yearly in a memo to present at your annual review.
- Learn to take credit and self promote.

Leadership and Accountability

- Seek out leaders you admire and interview them on their strategies for success.
- Take steps to become a leader in areas of interest to you.

- Seek leadership roles in committee work in professional venues.
- Assume leadership roles in your community and outside organizations.
- Seek training in leadership skills and opportunities.
- Embrace your ambition rather than fear or stifle it.

Business Development and Networking

- Perfect your "elevator pitch."
- Plan to attend events and programs of interest.
- Prioritize organizations and networks to become involved in and selectively assume a leadership role in one, two, or a few.
- Get comfortable interacting with new people and telling them what you do.
- Keep in touch with classmates and contacts.
- Network internally with the assigning partner or supervisor.
- Network internally with the marketing department to be considered for pitches.
- Network internally with influential colleagues.
- Seek out affinity groups (of similarly situated individuals) with which to affiliate.
- Attend and participate in women's initiative events.
- Seek business development and networking training.
- Learn the internal rules of awarding business development credit as a result of originating clients, inheriting clients, and expanding existing business.

Workplace Flexibility

- Identify your work/life needs and priorities.
- Decide if and when to seek flexible or reduced hours.
- Establish reliable and flexible childcare or eldercare, if applicable.
- Consider the impact on promotion if working flexible or reduced hours.
- Consider the impact on compensation if working flexible or reduced hours.
- If you seek flexible or reduced hours, understand the business case for why it is in your employer's interest and convey it.

- If you work flexible or reduced hours, learn the skills to be responsive and accessible, in addition to delivering top-notch work.
- Develop time-management skills.

Mentoring

- Be prepared as a mentee to help your mentors in return for their help.
- Develop skills to update and keep in touch with your mentors.
- Seek out different mentors from different aspects of your life and for different needs:
    - o mentors who are role models or whom you relate to in terms of identity;
    - o mentors whose practice area or expertise is one you are trying to develop;
    - o mentors who can share wisdom and contacts;
    - o mentors who convey internal politics and unwritten rules;
    - o mentors who can endorse, advocate for, and vouch for you; and
    - o mentor peers who can give you advice, support, and camaraderie.
- Participate in mentoring circles (a group of mentors and mentees).
- Participate in formal mentoring programs.

In sum, there are two critical steps that women can take to increase their likelihood of success. First, women need to identify women-friendly employers. Women should use *The Cheat Sheet* as a tool to show them what makes a women-friendly employer; using it, they can garner the information to make an educated decision of where to work. Second, once a woman decides where to practice, she needs to Blueprint her plan for success. This means identifying the skills to develop in these areas—Partnership & Advancement, Leadership & Accountability, Business Development & Networking, Workplace Flexibility, and Mentoring. In doing so, women will no longer be blindsided by opportunities they lost or feel they have no other choice but to leave. Instead, they will be empowered with the tools to become successful.

Notes

1. Flex-Time Lawyers LLC & The Ass'n of the Bar of the City of New York, Committee on Women in the Profession, The Cheat Sheet, Sept. 2006, *available at* http://www.flextimelawyers.com/pdf/art3.pdf.

2. Deborah Epstein Henry, *Competition as an Instrument of Change*, The Balance Beam, 2005–2006, *available at* http://www.flextimelawyers.com/pdf/2005_2006newsletter.pdf.

3. Am. Bar Ass'n, First Year and Total J.D. Enrollment by Gender for 1947–2008, *available at* www.abanet.org/legaled/statistics/charts/stats%20-%206.pdf.

4. The Cheat Sheet, *supra* note 1, at 1.

5. *Id.* at 4.

6. Nat'l Ass'n for Law Placement, Inc., Most Lawyers Working Part-time Are Women—Overall Number of Lawyers Working Part-time Remains Small at tbl. 4 (2009), *available at* http://www.nalp.org/parttimesched2009.

7. The Cheat Sheet, *supra* note 1, at 3.

8. *Id.* at 5–6.

9. Deborah Epstein Henry, *"Blueprint" for Success: A Career-Changing Tool for Women Lawyers*, The Young Lawyer, A Newsletter of the American Bar Association Young Lawyers Division, Feb./Mar. 2009, *available at* http://www.flextimelawyers.com/pdf/art14.pdf.

10. *See generally id.*

11. Am. Bar Ass'n, *supra* note 3.

12. Stephanie A. Scharf et al., Nat'l Ass'n of Women Lawyers, Report of the Fourth Annual National Survey on Retention and Promotion of Women in Law Firms 2 (2009), *available at* http://www.nawl.org/Assets/Documents/2009+Survey.pdf.

13. Nat'l Ass'n of Women Lawyers, NAWL News, Jul./Aug. 2006, *available at* http://www.nawl.org/Assets/Documents/NAWL_News_July-August_2006.pdf.

14. Scharf et al., supra note 12.

15. *Id.*

16. *Id.* at 9.

17. *Id.*

18. *Id.*

19. Mona Harrington & Helen Hsi, *Women Lawyers and Obstacles to Leadership*, *in* A Report of MIT Workplace Center Surveys on Comparative Career Decisions and Attrition Rates of Women and Men in Massachusetts Law Firms 26, 32 (2007), *available at* http://web.mit.edu/workplacecenter/docs/law-report_4-07.pdf.

20. Nat'l Ass'n for Law Placement, *supra* note 6, at tbl. 1.

21. Sylvia Ann Hewlett et al., Ctr. for Work-Life Policy, Off-Ramps and On-Ramps Revisited at 8, Fig. 1.2 (2010).

22. Harrington & Hsi, *supra* note 19, at 14.

23. Ida O. Abbott, Nat'l Ass'n for Law Placement, The Lawyer's Guide to Mentoring 51 (2000) (citing M.N. Ruderman et al., *How Managers View Success: Perspectives of High Achieving Women*, Leadership in Action, Center for Creative Leadership and Jossey-Bass Publishers, Vol. 18, No. 6, (1999)).

24. *Id.* at 51.

25. *Id.* at 52.

APPENDIX D

THE CHEAT SHEET

THE CHEAT SHEET

INTRODUCTION

Improving hiring, training, retention, and advancement of women attorneys requires multiple strategies by all sectors of the legal profession. Although the experience of practicing women attorneys has been the subject of much research and comment, not as much information is available to guide women law students and newly-admitted attorneys. Women law students graduate in numbers roughly equal to men, but they do not advance at the same rate as their male peers. Accordingly, where a woman chooses to launch her legal career has long term consequences for her success and is a decision best made with full information.

The Cheat Sheet, which follows below, is a must-have tool for every woman law student and attorney as well as a reference guide for law schools, law firms, and other legal employers seeking to assure the success of women law students and lawyers.[1] The Cheat Sheet is organized around six key indicia of an employer's commitment to women's retention and advancement: (a) statistical and background information; (b) partnership and advancement; (c) leadership and accountability; (d) business development and networking; (e) workplace flexibility (including time management and work/life balance); and (f) mentoring.

The questions in The Cheat Sheet provide a guide for law students selecting an employer as well as a tool for practicing lawyers to improve their employers' existing policies and to assist them when contemplating lateral moves. The Cheat Sheet is not intended as a "script" to use when speaking with employers. Rather, the questions in The Cheat Sheet should be used to identify key issues on each topic. Law students and attorneys should use their discretion and recognize that some topics are better raised informally with individual attorneys or personal contacts rather than with the human resources department or a hiring or supervising partner. In addition, although many questions are framed in terms of law firms, they equally are applicable to in-house, government, not-for-profit, and academic jobs.

While many legal employers currently are not tracking all of the issues identified in The Cheat Sheet, such monitoring is essential to women's progress in the profession. Additionally, efforts to advance and retain women result in programs and policies that inure to the benefit of all lawyers. For more information on these issues and suggestions on programs and policies, please consult the "Best Practices for the Hiring, Training, Retention, and Advancement of Women Attorneys," released by the New York City Bar's Committee on Women in the Profession in February 2006 (the "Best Practices Report").

[1] While The Cheat Sheet is focused on gender-related issues, many of the questions in it are applicable to overall diversity concerns in the profession.

I. Questions to Consider as Indicia of Success

(a) Statistical & Background Information

Representation of Women

What are the percentages of women associates in the department, office, and firm?

What is the breakdown of percentages of women associates in the office in 1 - 3 years of practice, 4 - 6 years of practice, and 7 plus years of practice?

What percentage of the firm's non-associate and non-partner attorney positions are held by women, e.g., staff attorney, senior attorney, counsel, of counsel, senior counsel, and special counsel?

Committee Representation

If the firm has a women's committee, what percentage is comprised of men?

If the firm has a diversity committee, what percentage is comprised of non-minority men?

Retention

What are the comparative retention rates of women without children and men in the past 5 years?

What are the comparative retention rates of women with children and men in the past 5 years?

What are the comparative retention rates of women with and without children in the past 5 years?

What are the comparative retention rates of men with and without children in the past 5 years?

What are the comparative retention rates of minority women and non-minority women in the past 5 years?

Programs & Initiatives

What women-specific programs does the firm have in place and for how long have they been in place, e.g., mentoring, affinity groups, women's initiatives, a women's network, events with women clients, and networking and business development training?

What is the participation rate for women associates and partners in the firm's women-specific programs?

What are some examples of the firm's women-specific programs from the past two years?

If the firm's efforts with respect to women have been more recent, what initiatives has the firm taken that may not be reflected in its retention and promotion rates or other statistics?

Is the firm aware of the Best Practices Report? If so, what steps has the firm taken to implement its action items?

Is the firm a signatory to the New York City Bar's Statement of Diversity?

(b) Partnership & Advancement

Women Partners

What are the percentages of women partners in the department, office, and firm?

What departments have the highest percentage of women partners?

What departments have the lowest percentage of women partners?

If the firm has non-equity partners, what percentage of the non-equity partners are women and what percentage of the equity partners are women?

Among the top 10% of the most highly compensated partners in the firm, what percentage of those partners are women?

Promotion to Partner

What are the comparative promotion rates to partner of women without children and men in the past 5 years?

What are the comparative promotion rates to partner of women with children and men in the past 5 years?

What are the comparative promotion rates to partner of women with and without children in the past 5 years?

What are the comparative promotion rates to partner of men with and without children in the past 5 years?

What are the comparative promotion rates to partner of minority and non-minority women in the past 5 years?

Partnership Criteria

Does the firm have any objective evaluation criteria to ensure that women associates are being evaluated fairly and without gender bias? Are the criteria transparent?

What kinds of "check-ins" occur so that an associate knows how she is doing and whether she is developing the necessary expertise and training to be elevated to partnership?

Is partnership compensation tied to efforts or successes by partners with respect to diversity? If so, how?

(c) Leadership & Accountability

What are the firm's committees and what percentage of women participate on each committee?

What are the percentages of women on the more powerful firm committees, including the executive or management committee and compensation committee?

What are the departments or practice groups in the firm and what are the numbers of women who chair or co-chair each department or practice group?

Are senior leaders actively involved in diversity/women's efforts? If so, how? Are firm leaders vocal about the business case for retaining and advancing women?

Has the firm or any lawyers at the firm received any nominations, awards, or recognition for diversity efforts?

Is billing credit awarded for diversity activities? If not, is there a separate billing code for diversity activities?

(d) Business Development & Networking

Does the firm have a women's network or affinity group?

Does the firm have networking and business development training targeted to women?

Does the firm host events with the firm's women clients and the firm's women lawyers?

Does the firm designate a budget for women-focused business development activities?

What outside activities are recognized as business development and are they subject to a separate billing code?

(e) Workplace Flexibility

<u>Flexible Work Arrangement Utilization</u>

What percentage of the firm's associates work flexible or reduced hours? Of these associates, what percentage is female?

What percentage of the firm's partners work flexible or reduced hours? Of these partners, what percentage is female?

What percentage of the firm's lawyers work flexible or reduced hours for reasons other than parenting?

How many partners have been elevated to partner after working reduced hours? Of these partners, what percentage were women?

How many reduced-hour associates have been elevated to partnership without requiring their return to full-time status before consideration? Of these partners, what percentage were women?

<u>Parental Status</u>

What are the percentages of associates who are mothers in the department, office, and firm?

What are the percentages of associates who are fathers in the department, office, and firm?

What are the percentages of partners who are mothers in the department, office, and firm?

What are the percentages of partners who are fathers in the department, office, and firm?

Flexibility Policy

Does the firm have a written policy for flexible or reduced hours? If so, does the policy allow lawyers working reduced hours to be elevated to partnership? If so, does the policy require reduced hours lawyers to return to full-time status before being elevated to partnership?

What are the eligibility requirements for working flexible or reduced hours, if any?

Childcare

Does the firm have an emergency back-up child care program?

Does the firm affiliate with an outside company that provides emergency back-up child care at home?

Does the firm have any programs helping parents of newborns transition back to work?

Does the firm run an on-site child care facility for everyday usage?

Does the firm affiliate with an outside company offering child care for everyday usage?

Re-Entry

Does the firm make any formal efforts to keep in touch with and provide training to women lawyers who leave the firm to become full-time mothers, e.g., assign a mentor, provide CLE classes, provide ongoing skills training, host alumni receptions, and hire for contract assignments?

Does the firm host or sponsor any recruiting events or programs targeting women interested in re-entering the profession after time away from practice?

Family/Medical Leave & Benefits

Does the firm provide paid family/medical leave? If so, how much time is provided?

Does the firm provide paid maternity leave in addition to medical leave? If so, how much time is provided and what percentage of mothers utilize this benefit?

Does the firm provide paid paternity or non-birth parent leave? If so, how much time is provided and what percentage of fathers or non-birth parents utilize this benefit?

Does the firm provide paid adoptive leave? If so, how much time is provided and what percentage of parents utilize this benefit?

Does the firm provide same-sex health care benefits?

(f) Mentoring

Does the firm have a mentoring program and if so, how is it structured?

Does the firm monitor its mentoring program and if so, how?

Does the firm have women's mentoring circles where women associates are grouped with senior women and meet regularly?

Does the firm have targeted mentoring for women senior associates to help with their professional development and advancement?

Does the firm have a mentoring program for newly-admitted partners to aid in the transition from associate to partner and help with business development efforts?

Does the firm have a budget for mentoring activities?

II. Additional Steps to Consider After Obtaining an Offer

Ask to talk or meet with a representative of the women's initiative or network.

If there is a women's initiative that runs regular events, ask to attend a meeting or internal event.

Ask to talk or meet with women associates, partners and/or mothers in the practice group or department you plan to join.

Ask to talk or meet with women or men who work flexible or reduced hours.

If you meet with attorneys who took parental leave, ask them about their experience on leave and upon their return.

Speak with friends, law school alumni, and other contacts to find out about the general lifestyle and culture of the firm. For example, does the firm have a face-time culture? How is vacation time and time outside of the office treated?

III. Recommendations for Law Firms for Recruiting

Include a testimonial link on the firm's website representing diverse lawyers who are willing to talk to prospective candidates about issues impacting women.

Run women-focused recruiting events.

Provide a realistic assessment of what it is like to work at the firm, what challenges face the firm regarding diversity, and how the firm is meeting those challenges.

Communicate the firm's commitment to advancing women and diversity in meaningful ways. The managing partner, as well as practice area heads, should be able to articulate why advancing women is important and what the firm is concretely doing to remedy the gender gap. Firm leaders should meet with summer associates to discuss big picture firm issues, advancement strategies, as well as hear what summer associates are grappling with and their suggestions for improvement.

Host meaningful summer associate events that address key issues about retention and advancement, e.g., how to be a successful summer, junior, mid-level, senior associate, and how to start building business development networks early.

Analyze the firm's yield rate at its top ten feeder schools and compare that to the representation of women at those schools.

IV. Recommendations for Law Schools

Run training programs for women students with experts, practitioners, and alumni focused on the key skills for success: (a) career advancement; (b) leadership; (c) business development and networking; (d) flexibility (including time management and work/life balance); and (e) mentoring.

Run panel presentations with practitioners focused on what it is like to practice law as a woman in a variety of settings.

Provide a directory of women alumni from the past 5 years who are willing to be contacted by students about women's issues.

Address the re-entry issue by providing a resource and expertise for women alumni returning to the workplace after a period of not practicing. For example, run events and panels and designate a career professional to be responsive to that demographic. Also, look to the model of a few business and law schools to see how the law school can develop training programs to support women as they transition from time at home back to the practice of law.

Convene women graduates to discuss concrete ways they can mentor junior women and ensure the success of other women graduates.

V. List of Resources & Statistics on Women Attorneys & Diversity in the Legal Profession

A Better Balance, www.abetterbalance.org

American Bar Association (national statistics of lawyers and law students), www.abanet.org/marketresearch/lawyer_demographics_2006.pdf

American Bar Association Commission on Women in the Profession, www.abanet.org/women/home.html

Boston Bar Association, "Facing the Grail: Confronting the Cost of Work-Family Imbalance" (1999), www.bostonbar.org/prs/workfamilychallenges.htm & Implementation Plan (2005), www.bostonbar.org/prs/wfcplan.htm

Catalyst, www.catalyst.org

Flex-Time Lawyers LLC, www.flextimelawyers.com

Georgia Association of Women Lawyers, Atlanta Bar Association Women in the Profession Committee, Georgia Commission on Women, "It's About Time: Part-Time Policies and Practices in Atlanta Law Firms" (Feb. 2004), www.gawl.org/gawl/docs/Its%20About%20TimeFinal.pdf

Ida Abbott Consulting (articles on mentoring and professional development), www.idaabbott.com/articles.html

Lawyers Life Coach, www.LawyersLifeCoach.com

Legal Momentum, www.legalmomentum.org

Minnesota Women Lawyers' Life Balance Taskforce, "Life Balance Resource Guide: Policies, Ideas and Strategies for Parental Leave and Alternative Work Arrangements" (2000), www.mwlawyers.org/MWLInitiatives/LifeBalance/LifeBalanceInitiative.htm

Minority Corporate Counsel Association, www.mcca.com

Multicultural Women Attorney Network, www.abanet.org/minorities/mwan/burdens.html

National Association of Law Placement (statistics on law firm demographics, alphabetized by law firm name, calculation of percentages of women & minority associates & partners & lawyers working reduced hours, among other demographic information), www.nalpdirectory.com/dledir_search_quick.asp

National Association of Law Placement (statistics on law firm lawyers working part-time nationally and broken down by city), www.nalp.org/press/details.php?id=5

National Association of Law Placement (statistics on women and minority law firm lawyers nationally and broken down by city), www.nalp.org/content/index.php?pid=387

National Association of Law Placement (statistics about women, part-time, minority, disabled, gay, lesbian, bisexual and transgender lawyers), www.nalp.org/content/index.php?pid=143

National Association of Law Placement/Catalyst, "Guide for Women Law Students" (2001), www.nalp.org/content/index.php?pid=325

National Association of Women Judges, www.nawj.org

National Association of Women Lawyers, www.abanet.org/nawl

National Conference of Women's Bar Associations, www.ncwba.org

New York City Bar, Committee on Women in the Profession, "Best Practices for the Hiring, Training, Retention, and Advancement of Women Attorneys" (2006), www.nycbar.org/Diversity/WomenLawyers.htm

New York City Bar, "Annual Diversity Benchmarking Study of Signatory Law Firms and Law Departments" (2005), www.nycbar.org/pdf/report/Public_benchmarking_report.pdf

Project for Attorney Retention, www.pardc.org

Nancy Reichman & Joyce S. Sterling, University of Denver, "Gender Penalties Revisited" (2004), www.cwba.org

The Bar Association of San Francisco, "No Glass Ceiling Initiative," www.sfbar.org/diversity/no_glass_ceiling.aspx

Women in the Legal Profession (collection of reports and policies), womenlaw.stanford.edu/model.policies.html

Women's Bar Association of the District of Columbia, "Creating Pathways to Success" (2006), http://www.wbadc.org/associations/1556/files/Creating%20Pathways%20Report%20PDF.pdf

Women's Bar Association of the State of New York, www.wbasny.bluestep.net

Work/Life Law, www.uchastings.edu/?pid=3624

Workplace Flexibility 2010, www.workplaceflexibility2010.org

ACKNOWLEDGMENTS

The Forum on Preparing Tomorrow's Leaders and The Cheat Sheet are a joint project of the New York City Bar and Flex-Time Lawyers LLC. Deborah Epstein Henry of Flex-Time Lawyers LLC developed the idea of conducting the Forum and providing attendees with The Cheat Sheet, with the goal of creating a model for lawyers to improve the status of women in legal markets across the country. In addition, the Forum and The Cheat Sheet both advance the New York City Bar's Best Practices Report, released by the Committee on Women in the Profession.

Flex-Time Lawyers LLC
Deborah Epstein Henry (Founder & President)*

Committee on Women in the Profession
Carrie H. Cohen (Chair)**
Valérie Demont (Chair of Subcommittee on Best Practices)**

C. Elaine Arabatzis
Celia Goldwag Barenholtz
Christina L. Brandt-Young
Sherrie E. Brown
Karen Cacace
Nina Cangiano**
Maureen A. Cronin**
Ayala Deutsch
G. Roxanne Elings
Ann Bailen Fisher
Constance A. Fratianni
Maureen Godfrey
Keisha Ann Grey
Kristina Han
Katherine B. Harrison
Lois Friedman Herzeca
Sarah Hewitt
Robin E. Keller
Caren K. Khoo
Kandis M. Koustenis
Lauren G. Krasnow
Lynne A. Lacoursière
Kathleen A. Leo
Jamie A. Levitt
Amy B. Littman
Lisa S. Pearson
Lori L. Pines
Sali A. Rakower
Angela T. Rella, Secretary
Wendy H. Schwartz
Karin F. Segall
Judith Shampanier
Deirdre J. Sheridan
Rachel Silverman
Estelle Marie-Terese Sohne
Brande M. Stellings**
Nicole G. Tell**
Gillian L. Thomas**
Kathryn J. Webber
Marissa Celeste Wesely
Lisa P. Whittaker
Cecily C. Williams
Verity E. Winship
G. Elaine Wood

*** Principal Author**
****Primary Drafters**

CHAPTER 17
NETWORKING AND BUSINESS DEVELOPMENT FOR WOMEN BEYOND RUBBER CHICKEN DINNERS

Our youngest son, Theodore, has always been desperate to be a big kid like his two older brothers. From the beginning, he has exercised as much independence as possible. So, at three and a half, he stopped accepting help getting dressed. He put his shoes on himself—often on the wrong feet. When he did, I tried to gently suggest, without taking away his sense of accomplishment, that the shoes needed to be switched. One morning when he had put his shoes on the wrong feet, I told him, "Theo, you did a great job getting dressed. Just one little change—you may want to switch around your shoes." Theo replied, "Not any more mommy, look!" As he said this, he jumped up, crossed his legs in the air and landed with his feet crossed.

This story illustrates to me the enigma surrounding women and networking. Theo was seeing things backward. Women similarly see networking backward. Networking is about building relationships and being connected. Women are often more interested and better than men in developing relationships. So why do women fear networking and business development and lag behind men in this area? It's backward. It also makes no sense that women characterize networking as one of the least favorite parts of their job. In this chapter, we will explore the challenges women face with networking and discuss how to overcome those challenges and incorporate networking and business development into your life.

Networking Challenges for Women

Attorneys are expected to network early in their careers, but most feel they do not have the time or inclination. Yet networking and business development are about relationship building, which most people do naturally almost every day. Networking will benefit you in any future career path. Some lawyers, outside of the law firm context, or junior associates who do not aspire to partnership, think networking need not apply to them. Not so. Networking can help you land your next job, assignment, board placement, or appointment, in addition to a new client. Your future networking success requires you to recognize networking opportunities in the activities in which you are already engaged and those relationships you already have. Then you will need to learn how to build effective networking into your already busy life.[1]

In the "Dear Debbie" e-mails that I have received over the years, here are the five most common challenges I hear from women about networking:

1. The traditional framework for networking or developing business is not one in which you feel comfortable and naturally thrive; therefore, you consider your efforts to be a "waste of time." For example, golf courses and sporting events have been traditionally male venues for business development and many women feel shut out of this "old boy's network."
2. Lawyers with children often feel the most time pressed, and marketing is likely to be the first thing you drop once children come along. Women typically shoulder more responsibility for child-

care than men do, and therefore commitments at home encroach upon your evening marketing opportunities.

3. Although many women have meaningful personal relationships, you feel uncomfortable translating personal relationships into professional dealings. This disconnect is further complicated by women often projecting different images in their communities than in their professional venues. For example, you may be respected as an involved parent when you volunteer in your kids' school, but when it's time to hire a hard-core lawyer, you may not come to mind.
4. For those of you who are junior lawyers, in particular, you feel you do not yet have access to the power brokers that would bring in the right type of business. Some of you feel that you will never have access to the decision makers who dole out the opportunities.
5. Many women lose opportunities to gain business development credit or expand existing business because you fail to self-promote or even take credit where credit is due. As a result, your colleagues and clients do not appreciate or recognize your contributions.

The challenges facing women in networking and business development are real. Along with those challenges indicated above, Lauren Stiller Rikleen raises additional networking impediments facing women lawyers in her book *Ending the Gauntlet: Removing Barriers to Women's Success in the Law.* These include, among others, a: "perception[] that women are confident doing the work but not pursuing it"; "failure of firms to promote teamwork in business development efforts"; frustration among women because "they lack a network of women professionals necessary for business development opportunities"; frustration among women about the client development and client inheritance process; "frustration with the lack of training in business-generation skills"; and concern among women that networking with members of the opposite sex would be misinterpreted.[2]

The statistics are evidence of the networking challenges women face. According to the National Association of Women Lawyers (NAWL), in 2009, 46 percent of the 200 largest U.S. law firms surveyed had no women among their top ten rainmakers.[3] Another 32 percent of these firms had one woman rainmaker; 15 percent had two women rainmakers; and the remaining 6 percent had three or four women rainmakers among their top ten.[4]

The best law firms for women, for this reason, are devoting resources to women-focused business development. For example, among the 2009 Best Law Firms for Women winning firms, 36 percent offered an online network for women lawyers; 64 percent had budgets targeted for women business development training and initiatives; and 90 percent offered networking events for women lawyers and the firms' women clients.[5] These firms devoted 16 percent of their business development budget to women-only training or events.[6] Yet, even with these efforts, the networking successes remain limited.

One reason law firms should address women-focused business development is because of the economic implications. In firms with no women among the top ten rainmakers at a firm, the median female compensation is $81,000 less than men.[7] In contrast, in firms with three or four women rainmakers in the top ten, the median female compensation differential shrinks to $11,000.[8] What follows are networking and business development strategies and skills that I have seen work with the women lawyers I counsel.

Start with a Marketing Plan

You will need to develop a marketing plan that will start with information-gathering and identifying the prospective clients and networks you want to target. Once you assess the target market, you should brainstorm about the types of meetings, conferences, organizations, events, and venues where you should be able to meet the people you want to get to know. You should also assess the writing and speaking you will need to do to get your message across and the social media you will use to get the exposure you need.[9] "Make sure your plan includes Specific, Measurable, Attainable, Realistic and Timely action items with stated target deadlines."[10]

Change the Networking Venue to One Where You Thrive

There is no single magical venue where business or client relationships can be developed. But you are likely to succeed in building relationships in a place where you feel comfortable. Participate in activities, events, or organizations that you enjoy. Through such authentic participation, you are much more likely to meet others to whom you can actually relate. And *be selective*; rather than joining everything that even remotely interests you, engage in a few activities in which you play a leadership or integral role.

If you are at a law firm that provides you with a networking budget, consider going beyond the traditional venues. Go to an art opening, theater premiere, auction, cooking class, golf clinic, self-defense workshop, antiquing excursion, spa outing, book reading, or wine tasting. Many firms are now hosting these types of less conventional networking events and outings as part of their women's initiatives. When choosing a less conventional networking outing, make sure that the environment lends itself to relationship-building and conversation. For example, if you choose a spa outing and you and your contact meet for a massage but then go into separate rooms and have no time to reconvene to talk, that is not the networking opportunity that you should seek.

It is important when choosing a networking venue to choose an environment that suits your prospective client. This will enhance the likelihood the client will agree to join you as well as enjoy the outing. Also, while it is important to find networking venues where you will thrive, do not exclude yourself from more typical business development opportunities. If you are at ease in these venues, you will be broadening your exposure by participating in them too.

Maximize Marketing in the Activities in Which You Are Already Engaged

If you belong to bar associations, trade associations, and/or other professional organizations, use these opportunities to make connections with others who may help you and whom you can help. Associations that meet routinely or hold regular events with introductions or that circulate member directories are often more fruitful because they are based on a shared interest and repeated contact, building familiarity and opportunities for follow-up.

If you are a law firm lawyer, *maximize your visibility* through the nonbillable work you already perform. In your required nonbillable time, choose visible work you enjoy and make an effort to attend departmental meetings, firm retreats, and other firm events that command a large audience. Be deliberate and plan ahead to schedule periodic lunches with prospective candidates, clients, and colleagues.

Recycle your work product. If you are asked to give an internal presentation or write a memo for your department, you can convert it into a client alert or article and use it to solicit speaking engagements. Once the initial nonbillable assignment is completed, the conversion process is easy and does not take significantly more work or time. Use the resources available to you through your assistant and the firm's library and marketing department (if applicable) to help with the work. The library can research the best publications; the marketing department can develop a list of contacts for you and help get the article published. Once your article is written or you give your talk, your marketing department can help you seek press attention and publicize it both internally and externally to maximize the visibility of your work.

Translate Personal Relationships into Professional Dealings

Make a list of every nonprofessional activity in which you already participate. Think of all of the networking opportunities at your children's schools, your civic association, religious organizations, charities, boards, book clubs, cultural institutions, sports teams, gym, and other volunteer activities or community interests. You may already be well-known in these venues; the natural next step is to present yourself as a valuable contributor and lawyer.

Keep in mind that you have an opportunity to start a business relationship every time you introduce yourself to someone you do not know. Remember to use your first and last name when you introduce yourself, so people will be able to identify you later. And make sure your new (and old) acquaintances know what you do.

Expanding personal relationships into professional ones requires effort. If you have discussed a legal issue with a friend or social acquaintance, follow up with an e-mail, including your signature line, addressing the topic you discussed. This enables people with whom you have social relationships to gradually expand their vision of you into a professional context. The e-mail follow-up with your signature line is also important if you use a different name professionally than you do socially. If you are a law firm lawyer and you have a marketing budget and you can envision a friend (or a friend's spouse or partner) becoming a prospective client, offer to take them out at the firm's expense and have them get to know you and your work better. If you and your prospective client find that you know people in common, elaborate on these connections—they often build credibility and broaden the context in which people know you. Offer to visit prospective clients at their workplace to demonstrate your interest and gain better knowledge of their business. Be sure to send your firm's holiday cards to potential clients to remind them of your professional affiliation.

If you are uncomfortable selling yourself to friends for fear of bragging or jeopardizing your friendships, you need to remind yourself that networking is a gradual, mutually beneficial process. When it works, it is about listening and being generous with your time. You also have the option to refer business to colleagues, originating the business while distancing yourself from the actual work and the potential awkwardness that may result. But, ultimately, you need to learn how to transition personal relationships into professional ones to benefit both your friends and yourself.

Gain Access to Decision Makers and Become the Point Person

You should not wait until you are well-established to begin networking. You may not have access to decision makers of today; nevertheless, if you nurture the law school, personal, and professional relationships you have now, some of these individuals will inevitably be the power brokers. In the meantime, you have the opportunity to develop your name and reputation through doing excellent work, giving speeches, writing articles, and establishing relationships with junior lawyers who will rise up through the ranks.

There are various ways to develop important relationships early on in your career. If a company frequently uses a certain firm for its work, develop a relationship with lawyers you know at the company to pursue the conflict work. Invite prospective clients to talks that you give, so they can observe you in a position of authority. If you are too junior to be giving the talk, become the chair or join the planning committee of a conference or bar association event and get to know the influential speakers through the planning and event. Attend conferences where senior lawyers speak, and follow up with a helpful article or client alert or offer to help out in the future.

If you are not ready to bring in business based on your own skill, then an interim step is to *become a resource or "go-to" person* so that you can direct opportunities or business to your colleagues. If you refer a case to a colleague or another lawyer, that person likely will think of you when a later opportunity arises to return the favor.

A good example of both the personal relationship challenge and the "go to" opportunity is an experience I had when I was a fifth-year associate. I was coaching my oldest son's soccer team and after one practice, the father of one of the players approached me for advice. He was having an employment dispute and he needed to hire a "really tough litigator." Standing on the field in sweats with my hair in a ponytail at 6:30 p.m. on a Thursday night, I remember thinking: *Wait, I'm that really tough litigator, why isn't he thinking of me?* But rather than becoming frustrated by my inability to meld my professional and personal images, I used my power as the "go to" person to create an opportunity. I referred the business to a colleague, one of the partners for whom I regularly worked. The client was happy to work with the seasoned litigator and I was credited with originating the business for my firm.

Do Excellent Work, Take Credit, and Network Internally

If you cannot envision ever bringing in the types of clients your firm services, then focus on *developing a stellar reputation*, *expanding the firm's existing business*, and *marketing yourself internally* to colleagues. Internal relationship-building is a critical component to networking success. Initiate mentoring relationships with colleagues—the ones you work with, the ones you would like to work with, and the ones you otherwise admire. Develop a relationship with the assigning partner or administrator who determines the type of work you do and the colleagues with whom you work. Nurture relationships with colleagues in the marketing department, who will then more likely recommend you for pitches and otherwise help promote you internally and externally.

Work with as many colleagues as possible, to gain broad support and to benefit directly from varied work styles. Build strong relationships with senior colleagues. Do quality work for them so they invest in you. When it is time for them to retire, these colleagues will more likely want you to inherit their clients to continue the excellent service you have provided. You also need to *become indispensable to the existing clients* of the firm, so that they remain clients and, in turn, insist on working with you. If possible, expand the breadth of clients for whom you work as well.

Make sure your colleagues are aware of your contributions, and make sure you *take credit* for your successes. Review time is an excellent opportunity to summarize the past year by submitting an annual "brag memo" with a summary of your contributions and successes to be discussed at your review. This list of accomplishments then should be added to your file. If you receive accolades throughout the year from supervisory lawyers or clients, forward them to the people in charge so your contributions are recognized. You should also add and attach copies of any outside recognition that you received throughout the year to your annual review memo.

Additional Networking Skills and Strategies

While you will want to tailor networking to meet your needs where possible, you should also attend traditional networking events. When you attend a conventional networking event, such as a cocktail party, *stage the event in your mind.* Take into consideration how long you will be there, and decide how many people you would like to meet, what types of people you would like to meet, and who in particular you would like to meet. If there is an agenda for the event that you can obtain in advance, study it, identify the people you want to meet, and set as a goal that you will approach the people you have identified during the course of the event. Practice initiating and wrapping up brief conversations and exchanging business cards as explained in the elevator pitch advice that follows below. It may be helpful to attend networking events with work contacts with the goal of catching up with those contacts and benefiting from each other's networks, without limiting your evening's socializing to your existing contacts.

Perfecting Your "Elevator Pitch"

A helpful confidence booster before attending a networking event is to perfect your "elevator pitch." The elevator pitch, as I define it, is a powerful punch describing who you are, what you do, and what you hope to achieve in your introduction. Generally, the pitch should be delivered in three sentences. The image you should keep in mind to ensure your brevity is the elevator doors opening or closing, driving the need to complete your three sentences before the moment is lost.

Here is my three-sentence elevator pitch that I suggest you use:

1a. Hi, my name is _______________ and I'm a _______________ at _______________. (Indicates your full name, title, and place of employment)

1b. (Alternative first sentence for those who are unemployed) Hi, my name is _______________ and I'm looking for an opportunity in _____________. (Indicates your full name and the job you are seeking)

2. My area of focus is _______________ and I'm based in _______________. (Indicates practice area or expertise and location)
3. I am seeking (or I hope to get out of this meeting, event, etc.) _______________. (Indicates "the ask," i.e., the networking objective)

In April 2010, I presented this elevator pitch exercise at the American Bar Association Commission on Women in the Profession, Women in Law Leadership (WILL) Academy networking breakfast. Women attendees told me later what an eye-opener it was—they agreed that women have no problem talking, but often the conversations are not fruitful because they are not deliberately focused. The elevator pitch forces you to do just that—focus your business introductions in several ways:

1. In two sentences, you convey the basic professional facts about yourself to someone so they can know your name, seniority, affiliation, area of focus, and location. You can tweak these sentences so that they suit your style. But keep them concise. If you can make your sentences clever and memorable, so much the better. A great example is a successful Chicago lawyer who participated in a networking panel with me in 2009. Her introduction con-

sists of: "Hi, my name is Lynn Grayson and I'm a partner with the law firm of Jenner & Block. I'm an environmental lawyer in Chicago—I do anything related to dirty water and dirty dirt."
2. Many people will attend an event and not have a goal in mind. The third sentence forces you to think, in advance, about what you are seeking. Additionally, I find that most women are uncomfortable with "the ask" and they never get to it. The third sentence puts in the script your obligation to convey your networking objective. Often, the more specific the objective is, the more helpful listeners can be.
3. The three-sentence limit makes you be concise and learn how to distill who you are, what you do, and what you are seeking in brief concepts that others can easily grasp and remember.
4. What is also helpful about the three sentences is that they serve as a conversation starter and they give the listener(s) enough information to make connections. With this foundation, the listener(s) will be able to determine if they know people in common or if there are opportunities to help. A more natural conversation will likely follow. If the elevator pitch does not generate helpful discussion and opportunities, then you can wrap up the conversation with a polite exchange of business cards.

Relationship-Building Tips

If you are not social and networking causes you anxiety, recognize that many of the skills that enhance networking success are regular steps that you would otherwise use in interacting with others. In addition to the skills and strategies identified above, these skills can help you build relationships:

1. **Be present.** To put it simply, you need to be there. As Woody Allen said, "80 percent of life is showing up."[11] You should also be "present" even if you are not physically in the office every day by sending e-mails and personal notes, sharing insights, circulating relevant articles, and using social media.
2. **Repeat.** As with advertising, it often takes repeated contact over a period of years before a networking contact will think of you for an opportunity or a client will hire you. This requires that

you stay in touch and contact people regularly, letting them know what you do and what you can offer.

3. **Inform.** Keep your contacts informed about your contributions and your successes. This means sending e-mails and articles or otherwise sharing information and updates about your work.
4. **Lead.** Demonstrate leadership skills in the activities where you are engaged so that people see you in that role and recognize you as an authority.
5. **Be Generous.** Be generous with your time, advice, and availability. This is important for people to recognize your willingness to help and the value that you can bring.
6. **Multitask.** Networking can be time consuming so be thoughtful and deliberate in bringing networking to the activities in which you are already engaged.
7. **Follow up.** Write notes to yourself on the business cards you collect so that you remember whom you met, what you discussed, and what, if anything, you promised to do afterward. Ideally, follow up with each new contact within one or two days of a meeting, and do what you said you would do. If no promises were made, simply say you enjoyed meeting the person and you hope to cross paths again soon. Handwritten notes are a nice personal touch and a great way to follow up after making contact with someone. Then remember to keep in touch.
8. **Use social media.** Facebook, LinkedIn, and other social media are effective ways to be visible and stay in touch. The more you invest in social media, the greater your return. For example, on LinkedIn, inviting others to become a professional contact in your network is a low-commitment way of building your network (and theirs) and staying in touch, and it gives you (and your contacts) a network with which to build future business. The more complete your profile is on LinkedIn, the more likely your name is to come up on searches. For Facebook, which is often used in the social context and less in the professional world, be careful to keep your comments, pictures, and affiliations appropriate.
9. **Ask.** Unsuccessful marketing efforts often result from a failure to take the last step and actually ask for the business. You can't be shy here. It requires telling a prospective client that you are inter-

ested in working together and that you and your colleagues have the expertise to do the type of work that is required.

10. **Develop and renew.** Develop a timetable and strategy for following up on interactions and leads, as well as a schedule to evaluate your approach and successes on at least an annual basis and commit to new strategies and goals.

Networking activities develop business and opportunities. But to network effectively, you need to be creative in engaging in those opportunities that fit your personality and those of the clients you hope to attract. Identifying your strengths and interests, establishing a rapport with people who share your interests, and making sure your contacts, colleagues, and community view you as trustworthy and a great lawyer will lay the foundation for a strong and productive network. It will also lead to a more lucrative and fulfilling career trajectory.

Notes

1. *See generally* Deborah Epstein Henry, *Business Development in a 24/7 World*, Diversity & the Bar, May/June 2007, *available at* http://www.flextimelawyers.com/pdf/art6.pdf; Deborah Epstein Henry, *Business Development Beyond Rubber Chicken Dinners*, The Balance Beam, 2004–2005, *available at* http://www.flextimelawyers.com/pdf/2004_2005newsletter.pdf.
2. Lauren Stiller Rikleen, Ending the Gauntlet: Removing Barriers to Women's Success in the Law 75–89 (2006).
3. Stephanie A. Scharf et al., Nat'l Ass'n of Women Lawyers, Report of the Fourth Annual National Survey on Retention and Promotion of Women in Law Firms 9 (2009), *available at* http://www.nawl.org/Assets/Documents/2009+Survey.pdf.
4. *Id.*
5. Working Mother Media & Flex-Time Lawyers LLC, Executive Summary: Highlights of Work/Life and Women Trends from the 2009 Best Law Firms for Women Survey, *available at* http://www.flextimelawyers.com/best/press20.pdf.
6. *Id.*
7. Scharf et al., *supra* note 3, at 10.

8. *Id.*

9. For a full guide to developing a networking plan, *see* SARA HOLTZ, BRINGIN' IN THE RAIN: A WOMAN LAWYER'S GUIDE TO BUSINESS DEVELOPMENT (2008); *see also* SUSAN R. SNEIDER, A LAWYER'S GUIDE TO NETWORKING (2006).

10. Marianne M. Trost, *10 Tips to Maximize Your Business Development Efforts in the New Year*, GREATER PHOENIX ATT'Y AT L. MAG., Feb. 2010, *available at* http://thewomenlawyerscoach.com/files/Attorney_at_Law_February_2010_10_Tips_to_Maximize_Your_Business.pdf.

11. Fred Topel, *Dish Talks to Woody Allen*, DISHMAG.COM, March 2010, *available at* http://dishmag.com/issue84/celebrity/8350/dish-talks-to-woody-allen/.

CHAPTER 18

STICKY GENDER AND GENERATIONAL ISSUES AMONG WOMEN: DEVELOPING ADVOCATES IN WOMEN AND MEN

In 1997, my husband Gordon accepted a job offer in Philadelphia and we decided to relocate from New York. I was pregnant with our second son, Spencer. As I interviewed with Philadelphia law firms, I disclosed my interest in working reduced hours. In one litigation department with whom I interviewed, the three reduced-hour litigators in the department were given my résumé. Their "homework assignment" for the weekend was to review my résumé and make a recommendation to the firm on Monday as to whether or not the firm should make me a lateral reduced-hour offer. About ten years prior, the firm had made such an offer to an attorney with special circumstances.

On that Monday, two of the litigators reported excitement at the prospect of me joining the litigation team and the reduced-hour ranks. The third cautiously recommended against my hiring. She believed the risk was too great. What if I wasn't good? I could tarnish the fragile reduced-hour image and jeopardize the good arrangements these three lawyers had worked hard to negotiate and cultivate. What was most important to her was that their arrangements be preserved. The possible benefit of others joining the ranks and expanding the success of reduced-hour arrangements was not worth the risk. The firm did not heed this third lawyer's recommendation and I joined the firm laterally on a reduced-hour basis.

Challenges for Women Supporting Women

As an advocate for women, it pains me to publicly disclose some of the tensions that exist among us. Yet they are real. It's what executive coach Peggy Klaus calls the "pink elephant" in the room.[1] Prominent women have acknowledged the tensions. As Madeleine Albright aptly put it: "I also think it is important for women to help one another. I have a saying: There is a special place in hell for women who don't."[2] In a Workplace Bullying Institute study examining office behaviors—such as verbal abuse, job sabotage, misuse of authority, and destroying of relationships—female bullies targeted other women more than 70 percent of the time. In contrast, male bullies were "equal-opportunity tormentors when it comes to the gender of their target."[3]

These tensions resonate in the legal setting. In a 2007 American Bar Association (ABA) survey, more than 1,400 respondents answered the question of whether gender matters and 42 percent expressed a preference for working with lawyers of a particular gender.[4] Interestingly, of those female attorneys who indicated a preference, they more often preferred working for male supervisors.[5]

Throughout my professional and personal life, I have derived tremendous support and guidance from women. The lawyer network that I've built over the last 11-plus years has been composed largely of women and it has given me the platform to do what I love. I am regularly inspired by the power and collaborative spirit of women helping women. Through my collaborations with the National Association of Women Lawyers (NAWL), the ABA Commission on Women in the Profession, Ms. JD, and the Consortium of women leaders in law spearheaded by the Center for Women in Law of the University of Texas School of Law as well as the Women in the Profession committees, women's bar associations, and women's initiatives around the country,

I am repeatedly struck by the strength of sisterhood. Yet I do believe that tensions among women are more than anecdotal. And, more importantly, I believe women can improve their status in the profession if they acknowledge the tensions and develop solutions to overcome them.

The most common tensions that I see are between these differing groups of women: full-time lawyers who are mothers; reduced-hour lawyers who are mothers; full-time lawyers who are not mothers; and stay-at-home mothers. There is also often tension among senior women who have taken different career paths and who did not have the same choices as junior women. While recognizing these various groups and tensions, it is important to acknowledge that these challenges do not exist among all women and that just because you fall into one of these categories does not mean that you do not support women in another category. Also, acknowledging tensions among women does not excuse men from their obligation to support women.

Many label the tensions among women to be "Queen Bee" battles or "Mommy Wars." I prefer to more narrowly distill the motivation behind the tensions because I think it helps to resolve them. In this chapter, I give examples of scenarios that I've seen arise among women and I categorize them into the three most common ways I see the issues manifest: The Scarcity Concern; The Generational Divide; and The Work/Life Conundrum. After categorizing the tensions (which tend to overlap), I then talk about why women should support each other and how both women and men can support women more effectively. The goal is to ensure that if you are faced with similar situations in the future, you can identify them, strategize to overcome them, and develop more support to advance women.

1. The Scarcity Concern

a. There's Not Room for All of Us

The opening story I relayed is a classic example of "there's not room for all of us" or the "scarcity" concern.[6] The idea is that a few women have earned a coveted status and feel they could lose that status, or the status could be diminished, if it is shared. In the example above, the fear was that the three lawyers working reduced hours would lose their privileged status or their status would be tarnished because I would not meet the standard they had set.

Once I joined the firm, I became friendly with the other reduced-hour litigators and the one who had advocated against my hiring confessed to her initial concerns. She enjoyed the irony: she had feared that I would not meet the firm's standard and then I became a spokesperson on the issue. That irony reveals the risk in excluding women. It forecloses opportunities and prevents women from reaching a critical mass to make an impact.

The notion that "there's not room for all of us" has come up in other settings too. If there are one or two women who sit on an influential board or committee, some may be reluctant to bring in another woman among the ranks. The fear is that their special status will be diminished or that they will be replaced. However, research supports that three or more women on a board constitutes a critical mass. It is a tipping point that shifts the dynamic on an average size board and improves the board's overall performance.[7] If women resist inviting others to join, they won't be able to reach the critical mass required to make a difference.

2. *The Generational Divide*

a. This Is Not What I Fought For

When a friend of mine graduated from college at age 21, she secured a fellowship at a sought-after women's organization. An ardent feminist, my friend had followed the organization's work through college and was excited to move to Washington, D.C. and begin work. On her first day, she saw a senior leader of the organization in the kitchen. My friend had met this woman during the interview process and revered her. My friend enthusiastically introduced herself again, telling her she was honored to work there and was looking forward to the year ahead. In response, the organization's senior leader said hello and then looked down at my friend's shoes—a pair of red high heels. She remarked, "We feminists fought for thirty years so young women like you wouldn't have to squeeze your feet into shoes like that." Feeling her eyes well up with tears, my friend felt as if she had been slapped across the face. But, with a deep breath and a smile to suggest a response somewhat in jest, she replied "I thought that feminists like you fought for all those years so younger women like me could wear whatever shoes we liked."

This story represents the intergenerational divide between some women and the misunderstanding about what each brings to the table. It also reflects possible resentment and jealousy among some senior women who may be skeptical of junior women who are coming at the issues in different ways than their predecessors. Some who read this story may be shocked by the senior leader's remarks. Others may be deeply offended by my young friend's strong retort. These powerful, and often polarizing, feelings are precisely the reason why I'm addressing these issues. In order for women to be more supportive of each other, they need to understand and address these feelings rather than hope they go away. The nice part of the story is that the two were able later to talk and joke about what had happened, and the organization's senior leader even later conveyed that she was embarrassed about what she said.

b. I Succeeded in Shoulder Pads, Why Can't You?

In one of my "Dear Debbie" e-mails, a mid-level associate wrote about being very troubled about a senior woman partner at her firm. The associate had two young kids and was working reduced hours but remained on partnership track. The senior woman partner, for whom she worked, had married later in life and did not have children. The associate relayed that the partner was extremely unsupportive of her choices and disparaged her to other colleagues. The partner told others that she "made it the hard way" and why should anything be different for the associate and others in her generation? She had made it under the male model, dressing in suits with shoulder pads, looking and acting like a man. Why should an exception be made for her junior women colleagues?

The problem with this reasoning is that times have changed (thankfully) and the work environment is evolving, albeit slowly. A generation ago, before e-mail, faxes, and scanners, lawyers would wait three days until they received an opposing counsel's response. Nobody would wait so long today. Why would they expect a woman lawyer today to act like the woman lawyer of a generation ago? Times change; the way lawyers work does, too.

It is very unfortunate that many of the senior women who succeeded had no choices and had to make painful sacrifices. However, it does not justify or better anyone to prevent junior women from benefitting from today's choices.

c. I'm Struggling Myself So How Can I Support You?

When I was a junior litigation associate, the issue of women supporting women began to trouble me. I drafted an article that outlined what I identified to be the problems and tensions among junior and senior women. Before submitting the article for publication, I shared it with a few senior women I knew. Their reaction was negative. They encouraged me to revamp the article, soften it, and minimize the tensions among women. What was ultimately published was a watered-down version of my assessment of the problem. However, I did learn several important lessons from the interchange.

When junior women are not supported by senior women, they often assume that it is willful and negatively motivated. But often that is not the case. There are other reasons why senior women may not be stepping up. Many senior women believe that women have to work that much harder to succeed. In turn, they do not support junior women working flexible or reduced hours because they believe that working those schedules will not help them advance. Others do not lend support because they struggle with their own power and do not believe they have it to wield. An example of this may be a woman partner who has an impressive title but lacks real influence. Some of these women fear that if they raise a voice in support of another woman, they will lose the ability to raise a voice for themselves. Other senior women report that they were not socialized to mentor and support junior colleagues as the men seem groomed to do. It is not their natural inclination to do so and they don't know how to do so effectively. Still others are concerned about being accused of showing favoritism towards women.

These explanations demonstrate the value in communication. Most junior women would not anticipate what is behind their senior colleagues' actions. If junior women understood what was motivating some of the senior women, they would likely interpret their conduct differently and make more of an effort to bridge the gaps where possible.

d. You're Not the Role Model I'm Seeking

In the consulting work that I do with junior women at law firms, one issue repeatedly arises among them. Many feel they have no female role models. They look at the small representation of senior women and they do not aspire to follow their career paths. They see some senior women who had to sacrifice everything to be professionally successful and they do not aspire to be that person. They see other senior women who had a family, but were not engaged parents or spouses, and they do not want to be that person, either. Or they see senior women who were engaged at both work and home but at such a high personal cost—in terms of sheer energy and stamina expended—that the effort either does not seem worth it or the goal seems unattainable. As a result, many junior women feel bereft of realistic, desirable women role models. This void will often contribute to their decisions to ultimately leave.

When I hear these concerns among junior women, I start by encouraging them to recognize that the issues are not so black and white. It is easy to be judgmental of colleagues whom you see at the office but it's hard to know what their true life outside of work entails. Also, in finding role models, it should not be about seeking out one ideal person whom you can emulate. Instead, it is the ability to identify admirable qualities or career paths in different people and see how you can learn from their lessons to design your own unique path.

3. *The Work/Life Conundrum*

a. It Strikes a Nerve

After speaking on the subject of flexible and reduced hours at a conference, I was approached by a female associate who was visibly upset. The associate had two young kids and relayed that she felt very isolated. She shared with me two stories along these lines.

After her first daughter was born, she could not secure a satisfying reduced-hour offer. So she decided to opt for full-time and then negotiate reduced hours once she had more experience. She said she remembers talking to a stay-at-home mom during her maternity leave and told her of her plan. The stay-at-home mom's response was simple: "It's great if you're comfortable having someone else raise your kids. For me and my husband, that wouldn't work." She said that she remembered being horrified. She struggled to gain her composure and not feel the need to defend herself and her choices.

After her second daughter was born, she transitioned to reduced hours. However, one female associate colleague who had kids of comparable age gave her a hard time for her choice. This other colleague had chosen to work full-time and told the reduced-hour associate that it was unfair for lawyers working reduced hours to have the opportunity for promotion. The concessions of taking less pay and having partnership consideration delayed were not enough. The full-time colleague relayed that because lawyers elected to work reduced hours, it created unfair assumptions about full-time associates who were mothers, including that they were uncommitted. This full-time colleague even asked the firm to convene a committee to reopen the discussion of whether reduced-hour lawyers should be allowed to be elevated to partnership, in the hopes of revoking that policy.

These two stories demonstrate the "it strikes a nerve" scenario. The decision about whether and how to work after having children is a personal one. Yet, when children are born, everyone seems to have an opinion about whether and how women work. Why is it anyone's business? Why do they care? The answer is simple. It strikes a nerve. For certain stay-at-home and full-time professionals, someone's choice to work reduced hours threatens their choices. Their reaction, in turn, makes the reduced-hour lawyer feel isolated.

I suggested to the reduced-hour associate that she participate in her firm's affinity group and to seek outside professional and personal networks focused on work/life issues. To minimize her feelings of isolation, she needed a place to safely talk about what many in her generation are trying to do—effectively manage work and life at the same time.

b. You're Tarnishing My Reputation and I Don't Want to Pick Up Your Slack

Often the night before I give a talk, I have dinner with representatives of the hosting firm or organization. I always treasure these dinners because it is an opportunity to get to know the people with whom I've worked and also gain insights into the issues specific to the lawyers in the place where I'm visiting. At one recent dinner with seven women bar association representatives, one woman shared her frustration in working with a reduced-hour colleague. This dinner companion was an impressive in-house lawyer, smart, likable, and funny. She was in her 40s, never married and without kids. She relayed to us how her reduced-hour colleague had a child who was a competitive athlete and she used the "mom card" to regularly either not show up at work or not deliver the work that was required. The result: my dinner companion was saddled with this reduced-hour lawyer's spillover work. She also had to endure the negative stereotypes being made about women because of this reduced-hour colleague's lack of work ethic. My dinner companion was seething to the point that she started tallying on her office whiteboard the number of missed days of her reduced-hour colleague. She resented that she had to shoulder her colleague's responsibilities—so much so that it prohibited her from getting a life outside of work.

Unfortunately, this was not the first time I had heard a story like this. There are specific strategies that can be used, as discussed in Chapters 8 and 13, to avoid this scenario. Colleague resentment among lawyers working reduced hours is common, and in this case, very justified. My advice to my dinner companion: Stop seething and report the circumstances to your manager. You should not be burdened with someone else's work and have to endure the criticisms about women that result from this circumstance. Another reason why it is important to address the scenario is to avoid the inference that many would then make—that all reduced-hour lawyers (or all mothers) are similarly irresponsible and uncommitted. By remedying the situation and demonstrating that the reduced-hour colleague's behavior is unacceptable and will not be tolerated, it separates her from others who are working reduced-hour arrangements responsibly.

c. That's Not My Issue

In 2006, Nassau County District Attorney Kathleen Rice issued a statement, demanding that reduced-hour lawyers in her office either return to full-time status or leave the office. The DA, 41 and without children, argued: "Simply put, criminals do not work part time; neither should prosecutors involved in investigations, trials or appeals."[8] The DA claimed that her critics, who called her "anti-woman" and "anti-family," were not seeing the whole picture because she had placed more women in senior positions than her predecessor and therefore, she said, she was a proponent of women.

In a letter to the editor, I argued that the DA could not claim to be an advocate for women when she only supported women who made the same work choices as her own. If the DA really cared about advancing women as a whole, she would have used her position and power as a leader to make change in archaic policies that disproportionately impacted women. Rather than take on the twelve reduced-hour women lawyers in her office, she could have initiated a movement to change the county-imposed financing and staffing constraint that equated full-time and reduced-time lawyers, which was the supposed impetus for her action. She could have wielded her power to facilitate job shares, like her fellow Suffolk County DA was doing, and supported reduced-time arrangements like her counterparts in Manhattan, Queens, Suffolk, and Staten Island. These changes would have benefited men and women and helped minimize stigma and gender stereotyping.

The DA story exemplifies a scenario I've seen when women who have made certain life choices do not want to affiliate with other women who have made different choices. For example, senior women at a law firm often do not want to get involved with the women's initiative at the firm. There were no women to affiliate with when they were rising through the ranks, so they do not see the need to do so now. Or they find that the issues the women's initiative addresses are not pertinent to their choices—so they choose not to participate. However, there are already a diminishing number of women at the senior levels. If senior women opt out of engaging in women-related events and only support those junior women who make the same life choices, women will continue to lack the critical mass they need to thrive.

What follows are reasons why women should support each other and strategies for women to overcome their challenges and develop collaborative means to support each other.

Why Women Should Support Each Other

After reading about the various challenges and tensions among women, the question remains: Why should women support each other? The reasons are numerous:

- Women have fought hard to promote diversity in the workforce and should support diversity among themselves.[9]
- If women support each other, there is an opportunity to increase women's presence in the workforce to a critical mass. Women's voices are more likely to be heard when women are more visible and concentrated in numbers.[10]
- By supporting women who have made different career choices, it is an opportunity to retain more productive women in the workforce. This support will enhance and strengthen women's power in the senior ranks.
- Forty percent of women law firm lawyers work reduced hours in any one year.[11] The risk in not providing support for different ways for women to work is that many will leave.
- Many women change their career goals over time. Some work reduced hours or not at all when their children are young. They may then rejoin or reengage in the workforce and become motivated to become leaders. If these women are not supported in their earlier stages or welcomed back after a leave, they may not rejoin or recommit later.

How Women Can More Effectively Support Each Other

To improve relationships among women, employers should develop training to address the tensions and improve communication. Here are steps you and your employer can take along these lines.

- *Mentor, encourage, network, guide, and endorse.*[12] These five steps are integral to leading junior women to the next level.
- *Remove the judgment.* Senior women need to stop negatively judging junior women for not doing things the way they used to do them. Junior women need to stop expecting that senior women will be their role models in every way. A good analogy here is friendship. Just as it is difficult to look to any one friend for all advice and satisfaction, it is important to similarly diversify professional supports. Junior women can select different aspects to emulate in different women.[13] They can also seek out role models in men.
- *Support qualities in other women, even if they are qualities that you struggle to develop in yourself.* For example, many women are uncomfortable with ambition, power and self-promotion and they are critical of it when they see it in other women. Resist the temptation to be critical. Instead, see if you can learn from other women's ambition, power, and self-promotion skills and emulate them rather than be threatened by them.
- *Seek or develop training to de-personalize conflict.*[14] Research shows that women are more empathetic and are more attuned to their own and others' feelings.[15] The risk in these qualities is that if women take things too personally when challenged or criticized, they are prone to overreaction.[16]
- *Lower your expectations.*[17] Women often expect other women to be more understanding and nicer to other women. Even though women are more likely to have qualities of empathy, when women do not show kindness, some women feel betrayed.[18] Rather than expect they will be better treated by women, women should expect to be treated the same by women as by men.[19]
- *Get comfortable competing with each other*; learn to compete with and support each other at the same time.[20]
- *Develop your own style.* Many women struggle with their level of assertiveness. They don't want to be too strong and perceived as overly aggressive. They also don't want to be ineffective and perceived as meek. Trial and error will help you develop the right approach that is consistent with your personality. Also, observe other women and emulate the qualities you like in those women whom you think have struck the right balance.

- *Try reverse mentoring.* Reverse mentoring is different from traditional mentoring where a senior person mentors a junior person. With reverse mentoring, the focus is on educating people about different perspectives or vantage points. So, for example, a junior person may mentor a senior person who has made different work/life choices or has faced different life challenges. One-on-one pairings of women lawyers who have made different work/life choices or come from different generations will likely bring greater understanding and acceptance.
- *Engage in facilitated discussions.* Convene women lawyers in your organization to have one or more facilitated discussions where scenarios like those identified here are discussed. With an effective facilitator, camaraderie can be built among participating women as they gain a better perspective on the motivations and misunderstandings that are often behind the behaviors.
- *Remember your shared identity with other women.* Be mindful that you are members of the same group. To encourage women to help one another, we need to develop a sense of pride in women's accomplishments.[21]
- *Seek or develop executive coaching.* Important issues to address among women relate to frustration, personality traits, perceptions of unfair treatment, and the stresses and strains associated with today's workforce.[22]

Men as Proponents for Women

While it is critical for women to improve their communications with each other, it is also important that women are supported by men. Men have created the traditional professional model for success. And for the most part, men have been more successful in business development, leadership, and promotion. Women need to be able to learn from male role models. Also, men continue to make up the majority of the power base, and therefore women need to be supported by men to be promoted.

Men are more likely to support women when they are personally invested in women's issues. James Sandman, former managing partner of Arnold & Porter LLP, began a 2003 talk with these words: "The title of my talk today is 'What a Difference a Dad Makes.' It could also be called 'How Being a Full-Time Father Turned Me into a Feminist,' . . . ."[23] Sandman became a vocal advocate for family-friendly benefits and women issues as a result of his life-changing experience of taking a six-month sabbatical to be a "full-time father" when his first child was born. Similarly, Michael Nannes, Chairman of Dickstein Shapiro LLP, speaks nationally in support of women and work/life issues, partially as a result of navigating these issues with his wife, also a lawyer.

Another example is retired Shearman & Sterling LLP partner Arthur Field. He watched his lawyer/daughter return to her in-house job after several years staying at home full-time with her children. But he knew that many lawyers who left the workforce were being overlooked.[24] Field urged Linda Hayman, then incoming chairwoman of the ABA business law section, to establish a program to reengage lawyers who had left the workforce.[25] As a result, Hayman spearheaded an ABA initiative, "Back to Business Law," to provide seminars and informal networking opportunities for lawyers who had left active practice and were interested in getting back to corporate law.[26]

The challenge becomes getting men engaged to support women when it is not personal for them. In a 2009 study, Catalyst found that the three biggest barriers undermining men's support for gender initiatives were apathy, fear, and ignorance.[27] Fortunately, there are steps employers can take to increase men's support for women.[28] If you work in an environment where management is not ready to address these challenges or has not done so yet, here are steps you can take or encourage your employer to take to improve the support you derive from men. The Catalyst study cited herein provides more explicit direction in how to effectuate these steps.[29]

- *Help men recognize that gender bias exists.*[30]
- *Make it personal.* If men are personally invested in women's success in their home life, show them how that translates in the workplace.
- *Coach men on mentoring women.* Explain the specific challenges that women face.[31]
- *Invite men to play a leadership role in women's initiatives and programs related to women.*[32]
- *Expose men to male role models who support women.*[33]

- *Educate men about what is in it for them to support women and how their support for women will not result in a loss for men.*[34]
- *Educate men about the business case of why their employer needs women to succeed.*

In sum, to enable women to thrive in the workforce, women need the support of both women and men. Women need to learn to embrace their differences—generational, work/life-related, or otherwise. Men need to understand that by supporting women, they will be bettering the workplace and their own stature. With the support of women and men, women will be able to achieve the critical mass they need at the higher levels to gain greater equity in the workforce.

Notes

1. Peggy Klaus, *A Sisterhood of Workplace Infighting*, N.Y. Times, Jan. 11, 2009, *available at* http://www.nytimes.com/2009/01/11/jobs/11pre.html.
2. *10 Questions for Madeleine Albright*, Time, Jan. 10, 2008, *available at* http://www.time.com/time/magazine/article/0,9171,1702358,00.html.
3. Klaus, *supra* note 1.
4. Stephanie Francis Ward, *What Women Lawyers Really Think of Each Other*, A.B.A.J., Feb. 1, 2008, *available at* http://www.abajournal.com/magazine/article/what_women_lawyers_really_think_of_each_other/.
5. *Id.*
6. Klaus, *supra* note 1.
7. Alison M. Konrad & Vicki W. Kramer, *How Many Women Do Boards Need?*, Harv. Bus. Rev., Dec. 2006.
8. Kathleen M. Rice, *Needs of Working Parents Shouldn't Outweigh the Duty of Nassau County to Protect the Community*, Newsday, Jul. 10, 2006.
9. Deborah Epstein Henry, *Flex-, Reduced-Time Workers Deserve Support from Female Attorneys*, Women in the Profession, A Supplement to The Legal Intelligencer, Feb. 2001, *available at* http://www.flextimelawyers.com/news/news34.pdf.
10. Konrad & Kramer, *supra* note 7; *see also* Henry, *supra* note 9.
11. Mona Harrington & Helen Hsi, *Women Lawyers and Obstacles to Leadership*, *in* A Report of MIT Workplace Center Surveys on Comparative Career Decisions and Attrition Rates of Women

and Men in Massachusetts Law Firms 32 (2007), *available at* http://web.mit.edu/workplacecenter/docs/law-report_4-07.pdf.

12. Henry, *supra* note 9.

13. Ward, *supra* note 4.

14. Vivia Chen, *The End of Sisterhood*, Am. Law., May 1, 2009, *available at* http://www.law.com/jsp/tal/PubArticleTAL.jsp?id=1202430182682&slreturn=1&hbxlogin=1 (quoting Lauren Stiller Rikleen); *see also* Klaus, *supra* note 1. ("If women take things too personally when challenged or criticized, they are prone to overreaction. When that happens, there's trouble.")

15. Klaus, *supra* note 1.

16. *Id.*

17. Chen, *supra* note 14.

18. *Id.*

19. Klaus, *supra* note 1.

20. Chen, *supra* note 14 (citing Wendy Tice Wallner); Klaus, *supra* note 1.

21. Mickey Meece, *Backlash: Women Bullying Women at Work*, N.Y. Times, May 10, 2009, *available at* http://www.nytimes.com/2009/05/10/business/10women.html.

22. *Id.*

23. James J. Sandman, What a Difference a Dad Makes, Remarks for the Working Mother Work/Life Congress 8 (Oct. 1, 2003).

24. Ellen Rosen, *Finding a Way Back to the Law*, N.Y. Times, May 26, 2006, *available at* http://www.nytimes.com/2006/05/26/business/26law.html.

25. *Id.*

26. *Id.*

27. Jeanine Prime & Corinne A. Moss-Racusin, Catalyst, Engaging Men in Gender Initiatives: What Change Agents Need to Know 14 (2009), *available at* http://www.catalyst.org/file/283/mdc-web.pdf.

28. *See id.* at 17–23.

29. As the citations reflect, many of these recommendations come from the 2009 Catalyst study where the analysis and recommendations can be explored more fully. *See* Prime & Moss-Racusin, *supra* note 27, at 17–23.

30. *Id.* at 17–19.

31. Carol Hymowitz, *Coaching Men on Mentoring Women Is Ernst & Young Partner's Mission*, Wall St. J., June 14, 2007, *available at* http://online.wsj.com/article/SB118167178575132768.html.

32. Prime & Moss-Racusin, *supra* note 27, at 22.

33. *Id.*

34. *Id.* at 21–22.

CONCLUSION

A central theme of my work has been *competition as an instrument of change*. In the opening, *Why I Wrote This Book*, I talk about how the concept of using competition to effect change evolved for me. Given the similar structure of law firms, I saw what I call the "copycat competitive model" that firms took when raising salaries or investing in pro bono and I believed that similar competitive instincts would apply for issues relating to work/life balance and the retention and promotion of women. In pushing for change, I have seen that law firms will make policy changes when they recognize that failing to do so means they will lag behind their key competitors.

However, the catalyst for change has shifted. In the recession, firms cared less about keeping up with their competitors on issues such as work/life balance and the retention and promotion of women. Many firms were fighting just to remain afloat. Work/life balance was seen by many as a luxury and issues of retention and promotion seemed irrelevant to employers in the face of layoffs and other dramatic cost cuts. Yet as firms have begun to explore structural changes, they have mostly returned to the copycat competitive model. For example, many firms have gotten swept up in the move to core competencies but they have not invested in the new process of developing talent. Instead, they are just copying their competitors who have abandoned lockstep promotion and compensation. With no genuine effort and investment in change, the results, I'm afraid, will be more of the same.

Another shortcoming in the profession discussed in this book that has prevented real change is the mismatch between employer, client, and talent needs and the failure of each to explore the needs of the other. To be effective in making change, all parties need to understand and be willing to consider each other's needs. Change cannot take hold if only one party changes. Thus, employers can no longer use profitability as their sole driver. They must also consider the needs of clients and the talent pool. And clients should require reasonable and predictable fees, but they should not expect law firms to shoulder all of the risk in their future relationship. And lawyers and law students must understand the economic and management challenges facing legal employers and demonstrate their business value. Indeed, a synchronicity of employer, lawyer, and client interests is required to produce a profitable, productive, and changed profession.

My hope for the future of the legal profession is real change. That legal employers, instead of competing by duplicating each other's moves, will compete by *innovating* and developing different models of legal practice. *The difference is that legal employers' decisions would be dictated by initiative rather than reaction.* The survival of the fittest would then be based on what better models of practice evolve that meet the business needs of employers and clients and the performance and satisfaction needs of lawyers. The result of the evolution will ideally be a variety of legal practice models that lawyers can choose to practice and clients can choose to employ. Clients will be given more choices in how they will have their business needs met and lawyers will have different pathways to achieve success in the private sector, as well as in the public.

Developing a variety of models of legal practice and giving more choices to clients and lawyers will improve profitability, productivity, and satisfaction in the profession. By providing more choice, the profession will be able to better align interests, skills, and business needs. Competition to produce a variety of legal models to create profitable and hospitable workplaces, reasonable and predictable fees, and productive and satisfied lawyers are the goals the profession should seek. The future lies in our collective willingness to welcome a *reorder.*

INDEX